SANCTUARY

Sanctuary

AFRICAN AMERICANS AND EMPIRE

Nicole A. Waligora-Davis

OXFORD
UNIVERSITY PRESS

OXFORD
UNIVERSITY PRESS

Oxford University Press, Inc., publishes works that further
Oxford University's objective of excellence
in research, scholarship, and education.

Oxford   New York
Auckland   Cape Town   Dar es Salaam   Hong Kong   Karachi
Kuala Lumpur   Madrid   Melbourne   Mexico City   Nairobi
New Delhi   Shanghai   Taipei   Toronto

With offices in
Argentina   Austria   Brazil   Chile   Czech Republic   France   Greece
Guatemala   Hungary   Italy   Japan   Poland   Portugal   Singapore
South Korea   Switzerland   Thailand   Turkey   Ukraine   Vietnam

Copyright © 2011 by Oxford University Press, Inc.

Published by Oxford University Press, Inc.
198 Madison Avenue, New York, New York 10016

www.oup.com

Oxford is a registered trademark of Oxford University Press

Library of Congress Cataloging-in-Publication Data
Waligora-Davis, Nicole, 1973–
Sanctuary : African Americans and empire / Nicole A. Waligora-Davis.
    p.   cm.
Includes bibliographical references and index.
ISBN 978-0-19-536991-5 (alk. paper)
1. African Americans. 2. African Americans—History. 3. African Americans—Civil rights.
4. African Americans—Social conditions. 5. African Americans—Legal status, laws, etc.
6. Race discrimination—Law and legislation—United States. 7. Racism—United States.
8. Refugees—United States. 9. Race awareness—United States. 10. Race in literature.
11. African Americans in literature. 12. United States—Race relations. 13. United
States—Social policy. 14. United States—Foreign relations. 15. United States—History. I. Title.
E185.W19   2011
305.896'073—dc22   2010025256

1 3 5 7 9 8 6 4 2

Printed in the United States of America
on acid-free paper

For Ernest, Pansy, Marian, and Gabrielle~
With love and thanks

The right to have rights, or the right of every individual to belong to humanity, should be guaranteed by humanity itself. It is by no means certain whether this is possible.

HANNAH ARENDT, *The Origins of Totalitarianism*

Blacks have never been, and are not now, really considered to be citizens here. Blacks exist, in the American imagination, and in relation to American institutions, in reference to the slave codes: the first legal recognition of our presence remains the most compelling.

JAMES BALDWIN, *Evidence of Things Not Seen*

Contents

The phrase "I'm no-where" expresses the feeling borne in upon many Negroes that they have no stable, recognized place in society. One's identity drifts in a capricious reality in which even the most commonly held assumptions are questionable. One "is" literally, but one is nowhere; one wanders dazed in a ghetto maze, a "displaced person" of American democracy.

RALPH ELLISON, "Harlem is Nowhere"

Preface

SEEKING ASYLUM: AN ESSAY ON FORM AND CONTENT

THE CALL FOR refuge punctuates the slave moan. It is heard in the plaint of Negro spirituals and the slave songs whose "[e]very tone" Frederick Douglass tells us "was a testimony against slavery, and a prayer to God for deliverance from chains."[1] It resonates in the timbres of Billie Holiday's throaty belt in "Strange Fruit," and in the wail of Louis Armstrong's blues-toned horn against the bruised black body in "(What did I do to be so) Black and Blue?" It is the hope expressed, and the promise sought, in the forward march of black migrants across the countryside or through the congested train station terminals that Jacob Lawrence painted in his sixty-panel mural, *The Great Migration Series* (1941). It was toward this promise that blacks fled the South, heading north by the thousands during the early decades of the 1900s, rejecting the indignities and violence of Jim Crow with its peonage, sharecropping, chain gangs, mob tyranny, segregated railways, and kangaroo justice. Reappropriating nineteenth-century abolitionist discourse, black newspapers encouraged flight to "The Land of Hope"[2]—the North—and leveled the distance between slavery and the strangled freedom that emerged postemancipation. Urging his readers to leave the neocolonialism of a segregated Dixieland, *The Chicago Defender's* founder and editor, Robert S. Abbott, launched the "Great Northern Drive," a mass exodus to begin May 1917. They would become the migrants Walter Turpin imagined in *O'Cannan!* (1939), families like Richard Wright's, for whom Chicago in 1927 resembled a place without "racial fear."[3] And it is to such a mythologized space that Ralph Ellison's *Invisible Man* escapes, burying himself underground in response to a racism that had rendered his humanity illegible. Borne out of an attempt to grapple with the persistent calls for safe space that have shaped black letters in the United States, a call that underwrote black emigrationist campaigns during the nineteenth and twentieth centuries, that inspired blueprints for a black empire and utopian and migration fictions, and that launched freedmen's colonies and black townships (both real and imagined)—is the plea for sanctuary.

Part of a tradition of writings engaging the particularities of black social and political life, *Sanctuary: African Americans and Empire* participates in a conversation on the state of black citizenship that includes figures like Frederick Douglass and, in the twentieth century, Carter G. Woodson, who would characterize African American political life as simply a state of "qualified citizenship."[4] This book moves a step beyond Douglass and Woodson to articulate how blacks have not only experienced Woodson's "qualified citizenship," but have also been misrepresented as alien by the state. *Sanctuary: African Americans and Empire* urges a more careful, indeed an attuned, reading of moments when blacks describe themselves as refugees, outcasts, aliens—persons without a home, without a nation. Tuning in to these expressions of spiritual and material unmooring, moments that reflect upon the legal and political vestibule blacks occupy in relation to the nation state, complicates how we read the state's alienation of African Americans, and reveals the shortened social, legal, and political distance among refugees, stateless persons, and black Americans. In the chapters that follow, I explore in detail the relationship this anomalous status has to the state's formulation of citizenship, the state's relationship to other states, and the state's conceptualization of its imperial reach and power.

One of two primary figures shaping this text, "sanctuary" impresses the long history of African Americans' petitions for safety, petitions that are themselves critiques of liberalism and American democracy. These grievances rail against a state whose own ambitions for an ideal society risks blacks' human and civil rights, and, at times, their very lives. Focusing on forms of legal, political and social desubjectivation, dispossession, and violence that collectively transfigure black life and justify the call for safety, this book illustrates how sanctuary remains perpetually deferred, tragically unsustainable, or simply untenable precisely because blacks continue to occupy a state of exception—an anomalous legal zone where law is suspended and a new juridical order is effectively produced. Lasting safety and security (in whatever form it manifests itself) requires at least full (read: meaningful) incorporation within the body politic, for only then does the possibility arise of acquiring unmediated access to civil and human rights. Such a claim in no way discounts the multiple spiritual, cultural, and institutional forms through which solace, comfort, and relief have been historically secured. Farah Jasmine Griffith's brilliant cultural and theoretical analysis on safe spaces in *"Who Set You Flowin?" The African-American Migration Narrative* provides our evidence. But the task here is different. The questions and stakes are differently scaled. What asylum or sanctuary signifies for African Americans' is ultimately determined by the shared features expressed across their experiences as black Americans and refugees.

The second, and perhaps even more crucial, figure in this study is the refugee. The multiple forms of desubjectivation historically experienced by black Americans are consolidated in this figure and compel a reconceptualization of histories of black alienation. According to Title 8 § 1101 of the U.S. Code on Aliens and Nationality, the term "refugee" applies to individuals who are outside of the country of their nationality or those who lack a nationality, and "in such special circumstances as the President after appropriate consultation may specify," persons who while they are residing "within the country of [their] nationality" are being "persecuted, or who [have] a well-founded fear of persecution on account of race, religion, nationality, membership in a particular social group, or political opinion."[5] To read the legal definition for eligible asylum seekers is to comprehend the determinative role evidence plays in the asylum process: evidence is the lynchpin upon which security and the possibility of a (new) civil identity and range of protections teeters. Precisely because both the physical body and personal testimony of an asylum seeker are among the primary affidavits used to corroborate a refugee's claim, the valuative rubrics used when weighing testimony and determining if the claim of injury is valid, prove crucial to determining whether a refugee deserves asylum. My attention to the testimony and protocols influencing the legal legibility of an injury in the cases of Rosa Lee Ingram and her sons, Anthony Burns, Celia the slave, and Herman Melville's Babo, emerge as substantive strands within this examination of sanctuary and the modes of legal depersonification effectively linking blacks to refugees and stateless persons.

Immigration law, specifically that governing political asylum, provides only part of the conceptual grammar and subtext for my interrogation of the raced and gendered conventions for validating testimony, the racialization of injury and its determinative effect on realizing a legal remedy, and the legal and sociopolitical vulnerability of the refugee. "Sanctuary," in contradistinction to "asylum," more ably articulates the conditions of the modern black subject. My privileging of "sanctuary," like my reliance on related architectural metaphors to characterize its structural phenomenology (i.e., "the narthex" and "vestibule"), underscores the corollaries historically drawn between this term and the sacred (re: both a holy place and the inviolate/inviolable). "Sanctuary" wields a "signifying property *plus*," to borrow from Hortense Spillers[6]: Clutching at the complex sociopolitical role that "the church" has performed for African Americans as much as it cues references to "Canaan" and "the North," "sanctuary" places pressure on the forms of racial violence grounding its imperative and on the political blueprints imagining its realization. "Sanctuary" connotes more than a sacred space, but a site in which the sanctity of human life is preserved—the same moral imperatives belying the concept of political asylum and for which the church has historically provided respite. In its attempts to track the relationships between domestic racial violence, intracolonialism, state imperialism, and processes transforming black Americans into refugees, *Sanctuary: African Americans and Empire* places the "precarious life" (to draw from Judith Butler) of African Americans in relief. That blacks remain among the most vulnerable and violable communities in the United States is largely owed to the anomalous legal condition—or legal state of exception—circumscribing their life chances. Thus, although "sanctuary" remains saturated by the many permutations under which "safety" is registered in our world, it is a term that I have intentionally deployed to express the political vestibularity and legal liminality of the modern black subject in the United States. Toni Morrison's *Paradise* is but one among many potential guides disclosing the cultural features of sanctuary. Whether it is a space imagined as a geographically isolated convent housing abused, tormented, and alienated females or its nearest neighbor, the black township of Ruby, Morrison illustrates how sanctuaries sustain the violence that necessitated their creation.

BLACK AMERICAN REFUGEES

Three decades after the brutal assassinations of John F. Kennedy, Malcolm X, Martin Luther King, Jr., and Robert Kennedy; after the antiwar demonstrations and anticolonial uprisings of 1968; after Gloria Steinman's plea for women's rights; and in a moment one might label the post-post Civil Rights Movement, Toni Morrison fashioned an account of black exile within the United States—*Paradise*. Featuring the internal displacement of African Americans within the continental United States in the decades after emancipation, *Paradise* demonstrates the stakes of this book: The conditions warranting asylum—refuge—and transforming black Americans into refugees. Morrison opens the novel in striking fashion detailing how black freedmen and women fashioned the relative paradise of an all-black township that would offer reprieve from the assaults and indignities of racism, with an ambush. In this assault against fugitive women seeking safe haven within a nearby convent, she distends the conditions of possibility for asylum for communities at risk, and fingers the grain of a U.S. nationalism that conveniently reimagines members of its own polity as both exogenous and threatening. With lines such as "From the beginning its people were free and protected. A sleepless woman could always rise from her bed . . . and sit on the steps in the moonlight. . . . No lamp and no fear. . . . Nothing for ninety miles around thought she was prey"; and "Now everything requires their protection. From the beginning when the town was founded they knew isolation did not guarantee safety," used to caption the sensibility of the black townships' residents, Morrison focuses on the historical dissonance and distance between being free and being protected for black Americans that justifies these two conditions (freedom and protection) as black domesticity's ideal.[7] Mapping the degrees of racial violence by tinkering with geographical scale, Morrison turns the relationship between the convent's "throwaway" women and the town's residents into a metaphor for the status of this all-black colony in the larger national polity, in other words, the residents are the exiled and preyed upon. Here psychological pain, loss, dispossession, and alienation is transferred from its initial victims—community residents—onto a new population, the convent's female refugees. The transmission of violence depicted here shows, in microcosm, the nationalist project of, and process for, constructing the normative. We are reminded that the contours and content of a community or nation are shaped through a violence that must exclude, purify, and locate the excised as part of a dangerous, threatening "Out There."[8]

Blackness animates the categorical distinction between citizen and noncitizen, between native and foreigner. In other words, the postemancipation black body occupies the intermediary space between slave and citizen. It is a political interstice perhaps best understood by reappropriating the rationale Chief Justice Edward Douglass White argued in the *Insular Cases* during the opening years of the twentieth century: Blacks are "foreign in a domestic sense."[9] And it is the interstitial quality of blacks' legal and political relationship with the state that most markedly reflects the commonalities among refugees, stateless persons, and black Americans.

Although the distinctions among refugees, stateless persons, and African Americans are real and should not be overlooked, that these distinctions appear immaterial to, and are actively deconstructed by the state is the focus of this book. Parsing the differences among blacks, aliens, refugees, exiles, and stateless persons could exclude the ways in which the state has capitalized on the relationships among these terms. In spite of the historical and political particularity of these identities, state power circulates through these categories and, to an extent, depends upon a series of resonances and relationships established in the period between *Dred Scott* and the *Insular Cases*; it is a system that was reanimated and transformed after this period. By attending to the interplays among these terms, I seek to retain critical pressure on the state, and on the ways in which the state relies on this circuitry to effectively constitute these communities. In *Color and Democracy: Colonies and Peace* (1945), his monograph on poverty and race as the primary crucibles for war, W. E. B. Du Bois illustrates the efficiency with which the state collapsed these distinctions. Speaking of the "extraordinary" methods deployed by the state to discriminate against African Americans, Du Bois pores over the instructions on an Immigration and Naturalization Service form issued by the Department of Justice, writing:

> In the Immigration and Naturalization Service of the United States Department of Justice passengers arriving on aircraft are to be labeled according to "race," and race is determined by the stock from which aliens spring and the language they speak, and to some degree by nationality. But "Negroes" apparently can belong to no nation: "Cuban," for instance, refers to the Cuban people "but not to Cubans who are Negroes": "West Indian" refers to the people of the West Indies "except Cubans or Negroes"; "Spanish American" refers to the people of Central and South America and of Spanish descent; but "Negro" refers to the "black African whether from Cuba, the West Indies, North or South America, Europe or Africa," and moreover "any alien with admixture of blood of the African (black) should be classified under this heading" ["Negro"].[10]

Setting aside the prescriptions of the state, when African Americans self-identify as "refugees" or "stateless persons" they intentionally elicit the aporetic tension belying their contradictory civil status: *the citizen who is not*. Couched in the autobiographical first person, Langston Hughes's "Refugee in America"(1943) sidesteps referencing either "refugee" or "America" directly within the poem. Instead, his title announces a category—"refugee"—for which his poem will provide a definitional content. Within these deftly penned poetic lines, Hughes (and, by proxy, black Americans writ large) reveals himself as America's refugee. His precarious sociolegal status is the casualty of failed U.S. democracy.[11] An earlier poem, "Song of the Refugee Road"(1940), though more acerbic, relies on repetition to produce a rhythm that effectively punctuates the speaker's embittered displacement, frustration, and hopelessness: "Home nowhere!"; "Home nowhere! None to care!? Bitter my past! Tomorrow—what's there?/Refugee road! Refugee road! Where do I go from here?/Walking down the refugee road."[12] Ralph Ellison's unpublished essay, "Harlem is Nowhere,"(1948) echoes Hughes: "The phrase 'I'm nowhere' expresses the feeling borne in upon many Negroes that they have no stable, recognized place in society.... One 'is' literally, but one is nowhere; one wanders dazed in a ghetto maze, a 'displaced person' of American democracy."[13] These moments when blacks label themselves refugees testify to the effectiveness of state attempts to dislocate them.

THE REFUGEE'S TIME

Although these examples cluster historically around (post) World War II, and place African Americans within a burgeoning global community of refugees and an international crisis in human rights, they are linguistic nodal points within a black Atlantic vernacular of exile, statelessness, and displacement that sadly moves not only backward in time to slavery's beginnings in the New World, but forward to the twenty-first century. The temporal arc of these enunciations makes one suspect the progressive teleologies that, as Homi Bhabha forcefully reminds us, underwrite histories of modernity and the nation. Lest the moral and ethical imperative shaping these locutions risk dismissal or underestimation, Bhabha's reading of the alternative temporal orders sizing up "minority discourse" commands our attention. Referencing the disruptive effects of what he calls Frantz Fanon's "cultural moment of 'occult instability'" and Julia Kristeva's "'Women's time'" on "nationalist historicism," Bhabha reasons,

> The cultural moment of Fanon's "occult instability" signifies the people in a fluctuating movement *which they are just giving shape to,* so that postcolonial time questions the teleological traditions of past and present, and the polarized historicist *sensibility* of the archaic and the modern. These are not simply attempts to invert the balance of power within an unchanged order of discourse. Fanon and Kristeva seek to define the symbolic process through which the social imaginary—nation, culture or community—becomes the subject of discourse, and the object of psychic identification. These feminist and postcolonial temporalities force us to rethink the sign of history *within* those languages, political or literary, which designate the people "as one."[14]

This project turns away from the privileged temporality of the state—a temporality that Shelley Wong notes is frequently depicted with a developmental model that suggests history is moving forward in some generally positive way and that the state is engaged in an ethical movement (or progress) toward equality. It is a turn that effectively upsets, in Bhahba's words, the "temporality of modernity within which the figure of the 'human' comes to be *authorized.*"[15] By Wong's measure, the statelessness that I insist reflects the character and shape of black life necessarily suspends state time. In other words, to be stateless (according to Wong) is to be outside a developmental narrative. Although the compass of my argument holds faith with Bhabha and Wong, for me the boundary moves even further: to be a black refugee is to be excluded from modernity's narrative of the human.[16]

Precisely because *Sanctuary* tracks and discloses the conditions of the black American refugee—the suspension of law and time animating a racial state of exception—a chronological or what Ann Stoler names a "unidirectional historical"[17] framing works against the ambitions of this project. The temporal undulations shaping the narrative trajectory of this project—a narrative that begins in 1948, shifts to the turn of the century, moves back to 1855, leaps to the 1920s, 1930s, and 1940s, and finally skips more than sixty years in the epilogue to 2005—intentionally permits the structure of this book to echo and reinforce the arguments being cast regarding the experiential realities of the black American refugee. Placing chapters treating slavery ("Sanctuary") and the Chicago race riot ("Graphic Inscriptions of Power") seriatim makes evident how a "racial state of exception" that began with slavery persisted. Likewise, this book demonstrates that the biopolitical frameworks that made the transformation of black citizens into refugees in the aftermath of Hurricane Katrina possible are part of a continuum of state practices that remark upon the similar response to black Chicago residents as refugees in the early 1920s.

In place of chronology, and in an effort to privilege the central figure of this text—the refugee—*Sanctuary* follows a recursive structure, opening and closing in roughly the same historic moment: the late 1930s and 1940s. By locating chapter 1 in the late 1940s around a discussion of the Ingram family's murder trial (1948) and its connection to postwar crises over human rights, I underscore the centrality of this period to the emergence of critical legal and political discourse on "the refugee" and "human rights." The year 1948 marks the ongoing internationalization of human rights that was the consequence of a world war that led to the formation of the United Nations; and it marks the emergence of the Universal Declaration of Human rights and the continuing debates over the U.N. Genocide Convention. It is a moment when the question of human rights gained traction amidst anticolonial movements further solidified by a war whose outcome revealed the impossibility of sustaining an "empire" under the same terms.

This is my beginning and my end. The postscript treating the immediate aftermath of Hurricane Katrina tragically reconfirms the fraught conditions of black political membership more than five decades after the Civil Rights Movement. Almost sixty years after the signing of the U.N. Declaration of Human Rights and the murder conviction of a widowed sharecropper, Rosa Ingram, who, aided by her sons, defended herself against a neighbor's attack, the insensible loss of human life resulting from state negligence and delayed and inadequate federal response underscores how race and poverty cumulatively affect political membership, and how being recognized as legitimate members of the polis continues to determine the extent of our society's willingness to preserve fundamental human rights and protect life.

Acknowledgments

LIKE ALL WRITERS arriving at the end of a project, the moment of reckoning with and attempting to reconcile the list of debts owed seems, and perhaps is, impossible. Every expression of gratitude that I can offer will buckle beneath the enormity of the gifts I received during my work on this project. In writing this book, I came to understand something deeper about the constitution of intellectual generosity, about mentorship and friendship, and about the profound effects of what many might measure as the simplest acts of kindness, fundamental human decency, and respect. I will carry these lessons for a lifetime.

I have often joked that this book has had, in truth, no fewer than three lives, and in each of its iterations I have benefitted from the conversations, careful readings, and generous advice of interlocutors far smarter than I. A special thanks is owed to my dissertation committee—Karla Holloway, Maurice Wallace, Wahneema Lubiano, and Cathy Davidson—for their critical engagement with my work and for their mentorship. At a critical juncture in my career, a cadre of dear friends and colleagues helped to reaffirm me and this work. Without them these pages could never have come to print. Elizabeth DeLoughrey, Mary Pat Brady, Kate McCullough, Ken McClane, Shelley Wong, Blair L.M. Kelley, Maurice Wallace, Karla Holloway, Nahum Chandler, Hortense Spillers, Barry Maxwell, Timothy Murray, Salah Hassan, Melissa Harris-Lacewell, Helena Viramontes, and Cheryl Finley. Blair L. M. Kelley, Elizabeth DeLoughrey, Mary Pat Brady, Kate McCullough, Ken McClane, and Shelley Wong revise the meaning of friendship, and inspire and invigorate all who have the pleasure of being in their presence. This book has been enriched through my conversations and interactions with each of you. I particularly thank Karla Holloway, Nahum Chandler, Hortense Spillers, and Maurice Wallace for the example they offer, the friendship they share, and the sustaining force they have been throughout my work. Nahum Chandler continues to stretch the boundaries of generosity: "Thank you" is insufficient compensation for the ways in which I have benefitted from the rigor of his engagement with drafts of my work, and from his unyielding faith in an intellectual promise that, in the early stage of this project, even I could not see.

This book took its shape within a community of special colleagues and graduate students who cared about me and my work: Laura Donaldson, Ken McClane, Rayna Kalas, Timothy Murray, Shelley Wong, Dagmawi Woubshet, Shirley Samuels, Hortense Spillers, Natalie Melas, Cheryl Finley, Blair L.M. Kelley, Danielle Heard, Belinda Rincon, Anthony Reed, and Kevin Gaines. Thanks goes to my research assistants Danielle Heard, Gregory Scott Parks, and Amelia Lister. Sheri Englund graciously read and reread drafts of every chapter of this book. I am grateful for her keen critical eye, her honesty, her patience, and her friendship. This book is far better for it. I was the beneficiary of an extraordinary group of readers and editors at Oxford University Press, a literal "dream team," whose careful and considered engagement with my work nuanced and enriched this project in significant ways. I would like to especially acknowledge Shannon McLachlan, my editor at Oxford University Press for her faith in me and in this project, Brendan O'Neill, and Christina Gibson who helped usher it along from the very beginning.

I would like to thank my family who prayed this project to fruition and my friends who patiently stood by my side until it was finished. This book is dedicated to my parents and to my husband. Although the conditions surrounding their immigrations to the United States were as different as the regions in the world from which they came, both of my parents have spent a lifetime teaching me the meaning of courage. I hope one day to live up to a measure of that lesson and that the stories told in these pages honor some part of what they have known to be true.

Ernest, I cannot imagine a better partner or friend. Irrespective of the immeasurable debt owed for all the things left undone and all the time lost together, my greatest debt to you is for believing in me and my work. Thank you.

My thanks goes to Harold Ober and Associates, Inc. for permitting me to reprint lines from Langston Hughes's play, *Troubled Island, Emperor of Haiti,* and Alfred A. Knopf, a division of Random House, Inc. for allowing me to reproduce selections from Langston Hughes's "I Dream A World" and "Song of the Refugee Road." Lines from Claude McKay's "Outcast" and "If We Must Die" are reprinted courtesy of the Schomburg Center for Research in Black Culture. An earlier version of chapter 2 was published in slightly different form in the *New Centennial Review,* "W. E. B. Du Bois and the Fourth Dimension" 6 (3) (2006), 57–90.

SANCTUARY

When democracy fails for one group in the United States it fails for the nation, and when it fails for the United States it fails for the world. A disenfranchised group compels the disenfranchisement of other groups.

W. E. B. DU BOIS, "The Negro Citizen"

1

Exile

ON NOVEMBER 4, 1947, Rosa Lee Ingram, an African American woman, was arrested, along with five of her sons,[1] for the murder of her white neighbor, John Ethron Stratford, in Ellaville, Georgia, during a dispute allegedly over livestock. She stoutly maintained that the armed Stratford had physically assaulted her with his rifle. When recounting Rosa Lee's statement to the jury, however, including Stratford's promised threat—"I am going to kill the negroes this morning"—the appellate record transcript was as truncated as her daylong trial was summarily short.[2] Although the terms of an appeal dictate the content of the record, here the Court Report indicates the ways in which race determined the framing and inclusion of evidence. The single, edited paragraph summarizing Rosa Lee's remarks during the trial, in stark contrast to the preserved pages of circumstantial prosecutorial evidence and trial testimonies offered by eleven witnesses for the state locates the racial and gender coordinates that map the outcome of the trial, as well as the appellate and parole processes. Rosa Lee Ingram's edited testimony is nonetheless sufficient to point up the complexities of this case. A trial seemingly hinging on the definition of murder versus self-defense, the judicial proceedings demonstrate malfeasance effected through race, gender, and their conjunction in the economic and social systems of the South.

A widowed mother of twelve, Rosa Lee Ingram—like the deceased—was a sharecropper.[3] Their properties abutted one another and lacking a fence, her livestock routinely wandered onto Stratford's leased land, the issue that provoked his ire that morning. Having taken seriously her neighbor's admonishment to remove a mule from his corn field, Ingram and several of her sons abandoned their fieldwork to pursue the animal. Seeing that neither the grey mule owned by her landlord (C. M. Dillinger) nor any other livestock were presently grazing on Stratford's land, Ingram returned to her work. The work was cut short, however, by an encounter with the armed and angered Stratford. By Ingram's account, Stratford pointed a rifle at her and threatened to "kill the negroes this morning." While a tearful Ingram pled for her life, Stratford cursed and struck her across the shoulder with his rifle. Although the sheriff claimed that she had accused Stratford of shooting her between the eyes, Mrs. Ingram's injuries and her testimony demonstrated that Stratford's assault was initially with the rifle butt and later, after she managed to wrestle the gun from him and strike him in kind, with the handle of an unopened knife. Having joined his mother's unanswered pleas for mercy, Rosa Lee's sixteen-year-old son, Wallace, finally retrieved the gun and struck a lethal blow to Stratford's head.[4] For black intellectuals and activists like W. E. B. Du Bois, the events that day were as clear as the "outrage" was stark—this was a "case of half-grown sons defending their mother."[5]

In the unabridged version of her statement to the jury included in the Brief of Evidence submitted to the Georgia State Supreme Court, Ingram offered a lengthy account of this threatening-turned-deadly exchange that locates her neighbor's hostility at the intersections of race, class, and gender. Stratford's insulting command ("Mr. Stratford hollered at me like he was hollering at a dog") to remove the mule from his land was only the first skein of racialized power he articulated that morning. With his rifle sites still trained on Rosa Lee, Stratford extended his threat from "the damn negroes" to the Dillinger mule she cared for, and assured the widow that she could expect no earnings from this season's crop. Recalling his words to her that day,

> "I have told Mr. Dillinger not to give you a damn thing out of this crop," says "we are going to see to you not getting a damn thing out of this crop" and I says "well, that will be all right"; he says "you ought to have a gun like this one I have and we would throw the gun on each other at the same time and both go down together"; I says "Mr. Stratford, don't shoot me with that gun. . . ."[6]

She continued,

> Mr. Stratford was trouble to me and my children, causing us to leave home on account of him; I was trying to get my crop gathered, corn and peanuts like that; [. . . .] Mr. Stratford come to me; I did not go to him; when he was there across that field and when he spoke I just could not go; I made two or three steps; that is all I could do; I just had to stand there and take.

To read Ingram's testimony is to note the multiple and multiplying scales of white male privilege exerted against her. It is to see the ways in which Stratford violently responded to her presence as an economic equal—repeatedly interrupting her work and attempting to undermine her earnings. His wish that she were armed and that they might "both go down together" inscribes a racial ungendering made complete in the roadway tussle that ensued.

Rosa Lee Ingram and five of her sons—Jackson (eldest), Charles (17), Wallace (16), Sammie Lee (14), and James Frank (12)—were arrested and jailed in separate towns. James was eventually released, but Rosa Lee, Charles, Wallace, and Sammie were indicted for Stratford's murder and remained incarcerated in separate facilities for the next two months pending their trials. Rosa Lee, Wallace, and Sammie Lee were tried together on January 26, 1948; Charles's hearing was convened the next day.[7] Rosa Lee and her sons were not only denied contact with one another, but also legal counsel. With legal representation appointed the morning of their daylong trial, there was little opportunity to prepare an adequate defense. The behavior of the trial judge, Schley County Superior Court Justice William Harper, whom the Ingram's NAACP-appointed appellate attorney, Austin Walden, later described as "the thirteenth juror," forecasts the character of deliberation against this family: throughout the single day of prosecution and defense arguments and jury deliberation, Harper "chewed and spit tobacco . . . with his feet on the desk."[8] The gulf in the legal interpretations of what transpired during that final encounter between the Ingrams and John Stratford permitted murder convictions and death sentences for Rosa Lee and two of her sons and erased the injuries documented by her bleeding and bruised face and torn shirt. The prosecution argued that two fights ensued that morning, and that the interim reflected a "cooling off period," which enabled the premeditation necessary for a first-degree murder conviction. In the state's version of events, a disarmed Stratford attempted to flee and was prevented by Ingram who, aided by her sons, beat the defenseless senior with his own rifle butt and an arsenal of field implements: specifically, a hammer, a hoe, and a claw hammer. Their final blow, according to the prosecution, was delivered against an already unconscious man. The defense told a dramatically different story: Only one struggle occurred that morning. Stratford's death was an act of self-defense, not premeditated murder.

Sanctuary: African Americans and Empire reveals the law's historic alienation of black bodies, which has dislodged civil and human rights, radically transforming citizens into refugees and stateless persons. These domestic refugees experience profound dislocation in the loss of or inability to procure a home, in an anomalous relation to the law, and in a civil identity that gives way to assaults against humanity and life. By tracing the coordinated relationship of U.S. international and domestic interventions and their shared effect on domestic race relations, *Sanctuary* exposes the ways in which race calibrates both civil and human rights and the geopolitical scale of racism as an instrument of state power. This case occurs in a watershed year in human rights policy. The year 1948 included the adoption of the Universal Declaration of Human rights by the UN General Assembly (1948), the passage of the UN Convention on the Prevention and Punishment of the Crime of Genocide (1948), and the Bogotá-Columbia Declaration of the Rights and Duties of Man (1948). The Ingrams' legal and cultural history shows the ugly results of segregation's suspension of law, its inability to recognize individual injuries, and its indiscriminate criminalization of entire communities. The violence lodged within the event speaks to the character of the assault against black life. It is an example of violence that is almost banal in U.S. culture, and among African Americans it has historically generated pleas for safe spaces and radical alternatives, including antislavery and nationalist emigrationism, and real and imagined blueprints for alternative democracys. It is the historical character of this violence and the convergences it produces among African Americans and other rightless persons that is the crux of this book.

"HE TRIED TO GO WITH ME"

This case garnered international support for the Ingram family; in 1954 a delegation of ministers, labor unionists, and civil rights activist Mary Church Terrell met with officials from the U.S. Department of Justice and the White House, six years into the Ingrams' sentence. The case prompted interracial delegations to speak with members of the Georgia parole and pardon boards. And more than $100,000 in donations was contributed to the legal defense of the convicted and incarcerated Ingrams as well as for the support of Rosa Ingram's remaining children. In short, the Ingrams' arrest, indictment, and conviction highlighted the affect of race and gender in the formation of class and the denial of justice.[9] For this "Dixie-indicting drama"[10] was not simply—or perhaps even primarily, as the record suggests—a property dispute. The muted sexual overtones in Rosa Lee Ingram's interview with *Pittsburgh Courier* reporter Robert Ratcliffe on February 21, 1948—"I wanted to leave because Mr. Stratford kept bothering me"—were even more explicit a month later in an article whose title, "He Tried to Go with Me," was a watershed of sexual meaning. "He tried to go with me," said Ingram. "That's the main thing that caused this trouble. He was mad because I wouldn't go into the cotton house with him. . . . He had tried three times to make me go into the cotton house and have something to do with me." Although she quickly dismissed the possibility of rape—"He never tried to rape me"—the succeeding line reaffirms the sexual harassment and threat of violence stated in the interview's opening lines: "He *just* tried to compel me."[11] Ingram's statement reflects the pattern of sex crimes inflicted on black women, practices carried forward from slavery. Sexual harassment and threatened rape appear banal within her account, confirming the sexual violence routinely experienced by black women, as well as the orthodoxies of race, gender, and class governing these crimes. It was an intimidation that bore a lethal charge (see Figure 1.1).

Stratford's intent during that fateful November encounter was so familiar that Ingram had actually planned to relocate after the fall harvest to avoid further harassment. According to Ingram, it was precisely because she had refused Stratford's persistent advances that he, after hiding in a cotton field to wait for her, intimidated and finally beat the widow with a gun and a knife:

> Me and this man had some words. It was about giving him a date. I told him that I was not that kind of a woman. He told me that I would not live hard any more if I would do like he said, but I did not do what he wanted me to do. . . . He could not make me go his way. I cursed him and then he called me everything because I would not do what he wanted me to do. And that is just what this is about—me not having him. I did not want him and I did not have him.[12]

"HE TRIED TO GO WITH ME!"

STRATFORD INVITING MRS. INGRAM TO COTTON HOUSE . . , THE FIGHT IN THE FIELD ROAD . . . THE SLAYING OF STRATFORD.
These three illustrations, drawn by Courier Staff Artist Samuel Milai, present Mrs. Ingram's version of the slaying of John Stratford.

FIGURE 1.1 "He Tried to Go With Me." Stratford Inviting Mrs. Ingram to Cotton House. . . . The Fight in the Field Road. . . . The Slaying of Stratford. These three illustrations, drawn by Courier Staff Artist Samuel Milai present Mrs. Ingram's version of the slaying of John Stratford. Used with permission from the *Pittsburgh Courier* Archives.

Pittsburgh Courier, March 20, 1948.

Stratford's whiteness overruled the harassment and injuries Ingram endured from this married man. In the cotton field and in the courtroom, race took center stage. The racially gendered asymmetries of power governing segregation did more than sanction the sexual harassment she endured: it permitted her injuries to be dismissed, her act of self-defense to be viewed as murder, and it diminished the weight of her testimony.

Part of the irony in this case rests on the primary role played by the raced and gendered body within the court proceedings. Significantly, Rosa Lee's remarks to the jury as the trial concluded echo with the substantive difference between her remarks and the opening testimony of the prosecution's first witness—the widowed Mrs. Irene Stratford. Following the expected assertion of her relationship with the deceased ("I am Mrs. Irene Stratford; I was the wife of John Ethron Stratford in his lifetime"), Irene Stratford quickly turned to a description of her husband's physical vulnerability rather than simply narrating the events of that day. "On November 4 of last year Mr. John Ethron Stratford weighted about 130 pounds; his age was sixty-six; he was not strong; he was weak."[13] This unprompted rhetorical turn affirmed her (armed) husband's defenselessness—a weakened, undernourished, and aging frame—and began the state's efforts to undercut the Ingrams' claims of self-defense. Rosa Lee's decision to return to Stratford's "size" in her brief remarks during the hearing, ironically underscores the ways in which her own, assailed and endangered body, became negligible here. "Some said that I held Mr. Stratford but how could I hold Mr. Stratford; he was a strong man, not a weak man."[14] Her downplayed injuries and testimony, and thwarted possibility of redress, effectively rendered her a refugee. By casting the events of November 4 as self-defense, the Ingrams' attorneys lost sight—according to the trial judge, William Harper—of "the central issue—the defendants were Negro."[15]

INVISIBLE EMPIRE

The family's conviction raised the ire of the nation, calling attention to inequities of race and gender. According to Civil Rights Congress (CRC) member Maude Katz, the Ingrams' conviction "symbolize[d] a society in which womanhood is degraded."[16] Judge Harper eventually stayed their executions, which had been scheduled for February 27, barely six weeks after the trial. That the court sentenced two teenagers to death did not seem to concern the judge or the prosecution.

Granting her testimony and defense a significance that it was not granted in the courtroom, the *Pittsburgh Courier* published articles and interviews featuring "her side of the story," along with a portrait of the tattered shirt, ripped during the altercation with Stratford, and several pictures of Rosa Lee and her children. Competing against cultural tropes of promiscuous, seductive black women, the CRC and the *Courier* repeatedly reinforced the widow's status as mother. The CRC mounted a campaign heralding Ingram "Mother of the Year" for 1948, which found support among other black presses,[17] whereas the *Courier*'s sensational headlines and special features chronicling her life, marriage, incarceration, deteriorating health while in prison, and the status of her remaining children garnered sympathy not found in the court. Even the mainstream press registered the problems within this case. The *Washington* Post's headline, "Georgia Jury Assailed as 'Hog Wild,'"[18] spoke to the inequities of Rosa Lee Ingram's and her children's arrests, detention, group trial, and death sentences.

The linguistic economy of the headline is more than simply journalistic convention: it registers the fragility of black life. In six words, the *Post* names the all-but-absent legal defense for
this indigent family; the kangaroo-court, the day-long trial and summary verdict by an all-
white jury; the relative absence of juvenile justice during the Jim Crow era; the criminalization of black bodies; and the premature black death hastened by segregation.[19] In the
aftermath of the Scottsboro convictions (1931), A. Philip Randolph and Baynard Rustin's
proposed march on the capital (1941), the riots in Harlem, Detroit, Columbia, Tennessee,
and Los Angeles (1943), *Screws* v. *United States* (1945), the Trenton Six (1948), the Martins-
ville Seven (1949), the continuing defeat of federal anti-lynching legislation, the continued
court battles over racial covenants, and of the failures of extending democracy following
World War II, these biased judicial proceedings evidence, to borrow a phrase from Du Bois,
black semicoloniality—the economic and political commonalities shared among communities of people who "while not colonies in the strict sense, yet so approach the colonial status
as to merit the designation semicolonial." It is a designation applicable to African Americans
who "do not form a separate nation and yet who resemble in their economic and political
condition a distinctly colonial status."[20]

NAACP defense attorneys assisted in a failed appellate process, filing motions for new
trials that were rejected, in spite of their arguments that the evidence supported neither the
charges nor the conviction. Harper, the trial judge, oversaw the first petition filed on February 2, and although he rejected the NAACP's motion for a new trial, he vacated the Ingram's
death sentences and commuted them to life imprisonment. The Georgia Supreme Court
upheld the original convictions against the Ingrams, and the NAACP, having failed to realize
the jurisdictional question opened up by the all-white jury who heard the Ingram's case, did
not pursue the case in federal court.[21] The Ingrams remained imprisoned for more than a
decade, before receiving parole in August 1959. Their case increased public attention to the
problem of sexual harassment, the labor economy in the South, and the inequities of Southern black rural life, and reconfirmed the corrupting influence of race within the U.S. legal
system. The Ingrams' specious trial, convictions for murder rather than self-defense, death
sentence, and imprisonment are citations within a calculus of disenfranchisement compress-
ing, in this context, the distinctions among black Americans, colonial persons, and a rightless
population greatly increased by World War II.

Twenty years after its initial publication in Ernest Gruening's *These United States* (1924),
the *New Masses* reprinted W. E. B. Du Bois's "Georgia: The Invisible Empire." His assessment
of Georgian racial politics, sadly, remained relevant in 1944. According to Du Bois, Georgia
had perfected "the economic utility of race," promoting racism as a means to divide and
exploit laboring classes. That the African American Rosa Ingram and the white John Stratford were both sharecroppers matters to the power differential shaping this case. Within the
sexualized framework she presented, his gun became the phallus she refused, and the weapon
to which he must resort to subdue and to assert a supremacy that Du Bois insisted was essential to the character of this "Invisible Empire." Stratford's freedom to rape and beat Rosa Lee
Ingram with impunity was Jim Crow's compensation for the economic exploitation they
mutually endured. In the absence of material power, with a poverty shown in the flesh, the
130-pound, sixty-six-year-old Stratford sought to wield another power: the "fiction of superiority" and its graphically exercised entailments. As Du Bois observed, "The Southern white
laborer gets low wages . . . but in one respect he gets high pay and that is in the . . . social

superiority over masses of other human beings."[22] In Rosa Ingram's words, "He was a share-cropper just like us, but because he was white he tried to boss us."[23] According to Gerald Horne, although Louisiana had convicted an African American male of rape because a white female complainant stated that the rapist "smelled like a Negro," for more than fifty years (1900–52) "[n]o Louisiana-born white man had ever been executed for rape." Meanwhile, black males were being killed by the courts not for an actual crime, but for the "intent to commit rape." Louisiana executed forty-one black men for this alleged criminal ambition.[24] And although African Americans in Ellaville, Georgia, outnumbered whites three to two, their annual earnings only averaged $200.[25] Crying and suffering from deteriorating health, the forty-year-old widow and mother of twelve confessed her financial challenges, challenges representative of the thousands of black sharecroppers living in the rural South in the first half of the twentieth century:

> I didn't make any money on the farm last year . . . and now this year they have taken everything from me. I was working on halves, but since I've been in jail they've taken everything. I was raising thirty hogs, and I had two milk cows of my own. All of that has been taken from me. The owner of the plantation told me he had a [promissory] note from my husband on the cows. . . . I know that's not true.[26]

Competing trial testimonies and histories of the case transfer or share blame for Stratford's death among Rosa Lee and two of her sons and question the degree of her injuries at Strat-ford's hand, but collectively they indicate in these profound legal and social dislocations the problem of deferred citizenship.

The Ingrams' case led to more than a decade of political protest and civil rights agitation, until the family was eventually released in 1959. Featured as a platform item by the Commu-nist Party (1948), the Ingrams' judicial proceedings after the first trial were first managed by the NAACP and later by the CRC (1951); they inspired the CRC and Communist-based women's group, the Women's Committee for Equal Justice, led by Mary Church Terrell;[27] they found support among two additional CRC women's organizations—the Sojourners for Truth and Justice, and the National Committee to Free the Ingram Family; and they were routinely featured in black presses such as the *Courier,* the *Afro American,* and the *Chicago Defender,* in addition to labor and communist serials like the *Daily Worker.*[28] The case reflected the abrogated civil rights of black Americans and an ongoing—and increasingly internationalized—concern with human rights in the aftermath of World War II, which had destabilized colonial territories around the world. The Ingrams' death sentence occurred within a year of the Universal Declaration of Human Rights. For CRC attorney and chair-man William Patterson, the Ingram incident betrayed "the federal government's attitude toward such documents as the Universal Declaration of Human Rights and the Bogotá-Columbia Declaration of the Rights and Duties of Man of 1948."[29] Indeed, for black leaders and civil rights activists like W. E. B. Du Bois, the case highlighted the fictions of a feigned U.S. democracy and signaled the need for a radically refashioned geopolitics that might bring about a republican government more than two centuries overdue. Although his involvement in the case was limited, it was nonetheless paradigmatically consistent with what, up until this event, had been an almost thirty-year campaign for an alternative democ-racy. In one of two appeals he penned to the United Nations (1947, 1949),[30] Du Bois, in his petition to the Human Rights Commission and General Assembly of United Nations on behalf of Rosa Lee Ingram, argued that the verdict against the family reflected the government's betrayal of its citizens, as well as an abridgement of human and civil rights warranting the attention and intervention of the international community. In his appeal, the Ingrams, like the state of Georgia, became a case study for what democracy in the United States means for "its citizens of Negro descent." Offering a sociological accounting of the county where the Ingrams lived, Du Bois noted that only 22 percent of Schley County's black residents voted in the recent elections, that blacks had been denied the right to sit on juries, and that the state spent just four dollars annually on African American children's education, while legislating six times that amount for their white counterparts. He referred to the more than 500 lynched African Americans in the previous six decades, unequal housing and job opportunities, a sharecropping system whose contracts effectively prohibited children from attending school and reduced blacks to a relative slavery, poll taxes and other legal mechanisms of disenfranchisement, and a gubernatorial election in which the successful candidate, Herman Talmadge, bragged that he would bypass the law in order to ensure that 1 million blacks were disenfranchised, concluding that "the rural Negro family [is] the most depressed in the world."[31] By refusing to decouple the prosecution of the Ingrams from the systemic perils to black life, Du Bois's petition challenged U.S. legal culture and urged the United Nations to fulfill its promise to protect human life—even at the expense of state sovereignty.

Formally locating black suffering in the United States as a global legal concern, Du Bois's appeal grafted local politics onto a burgeoning global agenda of human and civil rights: concerns aggravated by, and reform measures intensified in the interest of, the thousands of refugees, stateless persons, and victims of World War II. Representative of an increasing frustration with racial discrimination and failed U.S. policies on civil rights, Du Bois's petition articulated the ways in which racism vitiates the possibility of peace nationally and internationally. From the vantage point of the NAACP, and the CRC and its suborganizations, the abrogation of legal rights reflected in the Ingram case was yet another incident in an accumulating body of civil and human rights abuses. The legal and social dislocations reflected in their trial and incarceration exposed the misalignment of U.S. political rhetoric and cultural practice, challenging the fitness of U.S. democracy and the integrity of the state. Du Bois's appeal followed on the heels of the NAACP's *An Appeal to the World* (1947), which highlighted the discrimination suffered by black U.S. citizens. Although members of the administration privately admitted that segregation impaired U.S. foreign relations, the United States Information Services (which was then a branch of the State Department) chose to respond with "The Negro in American Life" (1951), a propaganda piece intended to improve the United States's image in the international community by playing down, if not denying, the "alleged" violence, discrimination, and rights infringements perpetrated under Jim Crow.[32] Weeks later Patterson presented the CRC's 250-page petition, *We Charge Genocide* (1951), to the UN General Assembly in Paris, while Paul Robeson shared its content with the UN Secretariat in New York. In essence the CRC document insisted that the impoverished social conditions realized through segregation not only claimed the lives of more than 30,000 African Americans annually, but was also an instrument used by the state to manage this population.[33]

Emerging amid the climate of increasing frustration among black Americans that marked the postwar United States, the Ingrams' case provides a social text in which one can view the crisis in U.S. race relations 1) within a larger, global context; 2) within a world compelled to deal with the problem of human rights raised by the massive numbers of refugees and stateless persons produced by the war; and 3) within a world less able to deflect colonial and segregated peoples' demands for civil rights. Finally, their murder trial tracks a resilient black violence. I use the ambiguous term "black violence" strategically to capture a semantic range inflected not simply in this specific incident, but in the more generalizable conditions of black life during—and arguably following—legal segregation. "Black violence" implies the patterns of injury reflexively attached to black bodies, both those culturally presumed to be caused by blacks and those of which blacks are victims. Here, its pattern encompasses the denial of social equality and legal fairness. On February 21, 1948, the *Courier* used some of the weight of this incident for black civil rights and the integrity of U.S. legal culture, stating, "The sharecropper is dead. Only *the word* of a mother and children claiming self-defense remains."[34] That she, along with two of her sons, was in fact convicted and sentenced to death speaks to the problem of legitimacy underlining so much of the history of African Americans' relationship to the state. And in this sense, their convictions signal the central tenets of this book.

The Ingrams' case highlights the troubled citizenship of African Americans in the United States and attests to the racial contingencies of U.S. civil identity. Rosa Lee and her sons fell outside the precincts of law. That her injuries—documented by her bruised forehead and torn shirt—could be considered negligible confirms the criminalization of black bodies and the suspension of the legal presumption of innocence.[35] To be outlawed in this context is not simply a synonym for the criminality appended to this African American family, the self-defense they employed, and the murder for which they were convicted, but specifies the *suspension of law*. I am referring to the erasure of legal standards and conventions—of the all-but-absent application of due process, the nonrepresentative jury, and the court's refusal to appoint legal counsel until the day of the trial. It is, however, when this event is viewed as a quintessential study in U.S. segregation history that the incident betrays the larger coordinates of civil and human rights taken up in this book, coordinates that both supersede the particularities of the historic moment and remain moored to global shifts in political power. The Ingrams' case had everything to do with the legitimacy of the black body in U.S. political culture—with the ability of the black body to successfully petition the court; to serve as witness, in the sense of giving evidence and of listening to and evaluating evidence as a juror; and to procure legal remedy for injuries sustained. The questioned capacity of African Americans that motivated this litany of abridged civil rights testifies to the ways in which race determines not only civil identity but human rights in the United States. This family was outside the law precisely because they were not seen as citizens. In other words, citizenship in the United States regulates access to social space and the privileges access entails, serving as the primary requisite governing human rights.

Rosa Lee Ingram's plan to relocate in an attempt to avoid Stratford's recurring harassment mirrors the pleas for a safe alternative space featured in the headlines of black newspapers that ushered in the Great Migration. This plea for Canaan has marked African American letters since its earliest inscriptions, shaping the character of African American intellectual thought and underwriting critiques of U.S. democracy, governance practices, legal culture, and imperialism. It echoed in the pre-Revolutionary appeals and petitions of black slaves and free issues; in the radical, early black nationalist writings of David Walker (*The Appeal*,

1829); in the emigrationist movements found in the writings and expeditions of Martin Delany, James Theodore Holly, J. Dennis Harris, T. Thomas Fortune, and Marcus Garvey; in Negro spirituals and blues lyrics; and in black settlements like Blackdom, New Mexico, and imagined in fictions like Sutton Griggs's *Imperium in Imperio* (1899) and Toni Morrison's *Paradise* (1998). This cry for sanctuary bound U.S. race relations to larger international projects.

Sanctuary: African Americans and Empire studies the phenomenology of racial violence, revealing the interconnection between U.S. international interventions and domestic policies. "Sanctuary" serves as the organizing trope of this book, through which the fundamental dislocations in law and social space that mark the rightless and the postemancipation black body may be read. Complicating and contextualizing how we understand the radical democratic visions of Du Bois, the black settlements transforming the national topography before and after emancipation, the petitions for rights waged formally and informally (in both subtle and explosive manners), this book limns the contours of a culturally nuanced definition of "sanctuary." Sanctuary operates on two levels, referencing a utopian political economy manifest in domestic and international expressions of colonialism as well as offering a name for the spaces that are produced in kind. A sanctuary is, to borrow the language of legal theorist Gerald Neuman, an "anomalous zone,"[36] a place where law is suspended and a new legal order produced. "Sanctuary" is a threshold; it demarcates the politically provisional. It is the interstitial, the "between," named in the opening lines of Du Bois's *Souls of Black Folk*— "Between the world and me. . . ."[37]

A history of violence compelled the longing for a safe space—a sanctuary—within the African American imaginary, yet sanctuary has so often proved tragically untenable—even dystopian. If we take church architecture as our guide, sanctuaries within the U.S. and African American literary imaginations resemble narthexes, the vestibules cordoning public and private space, the sacred and the secular. More importantly, to name the narthex a sufficient architectural metaphor for sanctuary is to latch onto the conditional quality of these sites: spaces that remain beyond reach—part of a distant future. As both legal and political interstices, they delimit the boundaries of the law. Sanctuaries are Hannah Arendt's camps. They are Giorgio Agamben's state of exception. They are the subterranean refuges of Ralph Ellison's and Richard Wright's titular characters in *Invisible Man* and "The Man Who Lived Underground"; they are the convent in Toni Morrison's *Paradise*. They are spaces of internment in the fullest sense: places realizing forms of social and—tragically—sometimes literal death. Sanctuaries mirror the violence that produced them, calling into question the presumed safety culturally associated with these sites. The refugees who occupy them enter through violence and are expelled with a similar force. Social and literary histories challenge the possibility of refuge and the meaning of immunity for black persons living in the United States. My use of "sanctuary"—as opposed to asylum—seeks to respect the critical distinctions between sanctuary and political asylum, between blacks and refugees, nonetheless restaging the crucial occasions of intersection and overlap. I place "sanctuary" and "asylum" in an uneasy tension, a tension perhaps more thickly wrought in the condition of the refugee and its most extreme figuration—statelessness—and the black diasporan body.

To speak of sanctuary anticipates a discussion of the people who inhabit these spaces. The rhetoric of exile, the refugee, and the alien filters through so much of African American writing, figuring in Du Bois's descriptions of newly emancipated slaves, in emigrationist campaigns, in the antiwar petitions of blacks in 1917 who claimed they "had no country to whom they owed loyalty or life," and in the writings of Hughes, Ellison, Wright, Baldwin, Robeson, and Morrison. The problem of the refugee, the stateless, the semi-colonial that Du Bois names the black American, is a problem of the refugee's relationship to the law and the state. Collectively, such persons signify a community outside the precincts of laws, they remain marginalized as a result of their lost or withheld citizenship. The serial loss of rights exposed in the Ingrams' case speaks to the problems of segregation, which are grounded in the question of citizenship. Yet the compass of this event extends both forward and backward, engaging a trajectory of black experiences in the United States from the eighteenth century to our contemporary moment. This trajectory reflects the problem of alienation, which is captured in public testimonies and material attempts to deny the humanity of African Americans. This book addresses the sites of overlap across several identities—refugee, stateless person, and African American body. They are conjunctions pointing to the use of race as an instrument influencing both U.S. domestic and international policies. The history of alienation that transformed citizens into refugees and stateless persons is inextricable from the United States's larger imperial ambitions. The following chapters chart the inverse relation of the nation's domestic and international interventions, illustrating how in moments of economic and political crises national borders expand while civil identity contracts.

I CHOOSE EXILE

Five years after World War II, Hannah Arendt concluded that the world wars had produced new legal and social categories—specifically, the refugee and the stateless person, whose presence worried the stability of political cultures and troubled extant bodies of law. According to Arendt, these displaced persons are the rightless: individuals who, bereft of civil identities, are consequently stripped of human rights. World War II demonstrated, perhaps even more emphatically than World War I, that human rights are contingent on national identity—that it is the nation-state that grants, protects, and guarantees human rights, but only to representatives of a polity (not even necessarily one's own). This is because we live, in Arendt's words, in "One World." She reasoned that "[o]nly with a completely organized humanity could the loss of home and political status become identical with expulsion from humanity altogether."[38] The rightless are such precisely because of the fundamental losses they endure in exile, among them what Edward Said and Homi Bhabha describe as a quality of "unhomeliness."[39]

For Arendt, home signifies more than a dwelling place, but a social structure, a set of irrecuperable social relations. This enduring loss is evident in her language: "Suddenly, there was no place on earth where migrants could go without the severest restrictions, no country where they would be assimilated, no territory where they could found a new community of their own. . . . It was a problem not of space but of political organization."[40] Inassimilable in a sense, the rightless are innocent, their suffering is unearned. According to Arendt they are "persecuted not because of what they had done or thought, but because of what they unchangeably were—born into the wrong kind of race or the wrong kind of class or drafted by the wrong kind of government."[41] Arendt's stateless persons signify an extreme social, political, and legal dislocation marked by a rightlessness that extends beyond the denial of civil rights to include the erasure of human rights. Within this framework, her writings on the stateless person and the refugee become instructive for thinking through the historical relationship of black diasporic peoples to nation-states.

I am not asserting that the contemporary black body fully occupies Arendt's categories. The substantial historical, legal, social, and political differences among refugees, stateless persons, and blacks matter, and should not be overlooked.[42] I am, however, suggesting that the black diasporic body has historically experienced conditions characteristic of the refugee or the stateless person, resemblances that significantly dilate how we understand the relationship of the black body to the state, and the subsequent discourses framing African Americans' petitions for rights from the eighteenth century to our own.[43] The strategic sites of overlap among these international and domestic communities expose the aggressive legal and political dislocations confronting black Americans. By considering the relationship between race and space, we might begin to understand the persistence of an ontological discourse of human rights within African American civil rights movements: what Karla Holloway names the "shared sensibility," and Paul Gilory the "diasporic intimacy,"[44] found across the Black Atlantic.

Yet, within Arendt's statelessness, the equivalences between the slave and the stateless person ironically collapse around the issue of humanity. Under the orthodoxy she sets forth, the slave cannot be imagined to be a stateless person because "even slaves still belonged to some sort of human community; their labor was needed, used, and exploited, and this kept them within the pale of humanity."[45] Her accounting of the slave body as part of the human community—and therefore beyond her definitional limits for rightlessness—are troubling at best. Black Atlantic migrants clearly resemble stateless persons, and the slavery these individuals suffered necessarily embedded the absolute rightlessness of the stateless person. Within the contours of U.S. slavery, that the humanity of the slave was rigorously and routinely challenged—and upended by law—is almost too commonsensical to bear repetition. The shifting terms used to nominalize the black body—beasts, savages, and particularly in the years immediately preceding the Civil War, children—were modulated perhaps more by economic imperatives challenging the stability of the peculiar institution than by substantial renovations of the pervasive cultural sense that blacks were subhuman, if not entirely inhuman. The social scientific and medical research of the latter half of the nineteenth century—supported in part by the anthropometric studies conducted during the Civil War on black soldiers and by technological innovations—would stabilize the taxonomies of racial difference used to rationalize colonialism and segregation. The three-fifths clause of the U.S. Constitution (1787, 1853) and *Dred Scott* v. *Sandford* (1857) are but two examples of constitutional amendments and legal precedent discounting black humanity. The demeanor of the law toward the black body is perhaps nowhere more cogently exemplified than in the fractioning of black humanity affected by the three-fifths clause: only three-fifths of the black body was politically material. The particulars of these events are the subject of chapter 3, "Sanctuary," but it is important to note here that slavery required the denial of black subjectivity, the baring of black humanity, in order to succeed.

Emancipation marked a movement in the primary relationship of the slave to the state, which had been as chattel property. The statelessness defining the condition of the slave nevertheless remained intact, becoming the preeminent sign for black life after the Civil War. Although emancipation had wrought a transformation of the slave from chattel to person, it failed to realize fully this transformation within the political and social imaginary.

The challenges to black humanity and black citizenship operate within a shared political economy; they are elements within a closed circuit, and the absence of one defeats the realization of the other. In other words, as long as the humanity of the black body remained challenged, citizenship and civil rights would be deferred. Du Bois is instructive here: "The hurt to the Negro in this era was not only his treatment in slavery; it was the wound dealt to his reputation as a human being. Nothing was left; nothing was sacred."[46] As the numerous pieces of civil rights legislation and countless judicial proceedings and cases from the late nineteenth century through the 1960s demonstrate, citizenship would remain a mobile, perpetually deferred, and graduated category.

NATIVE SON

Richard Wright opened "I Choose Exile" (1950), an essay reflecting on his decision to permanently leave the United States in the autumn of 1947, with two seemingly banal claims of identity: "I am a Negro and I was born in America." In the midst of increasing international criticism of U.S. segregation, Wright's ten words require little explanation in and of themselves, raising a bulwark of cultural meaning about the status of black Americans. Intended as a locative anchoring for what will in fact be a narrative of exile—of displacement—Wright's twinned assertions of racial and national identity announced the politics of mobility underpinning the loss he sought to translate, a loss that compelled and continued to frame what he described as a voluntary exile. Wright defined freedom, in part, as mobility—the right to choose freely where to live, to travel, and to engage in public forms of critique and dissent without fear, without recrimination, without surveillance, and without the threat of mob violence. He fled a United States whose topography was so marred by the violent and intransigent character of U.S. race relations that it denied the possibility of respite and refuge for black Americans.[47] His turn to the war-ravaged Paris of 1947, only two years after armistice, where a colonial power, France, offered a sanctuary unavailable in the United States, conveys only part of the indictment he waged. His insistent articulation of citizenship and loyalty (e.g., "my America," "I am not anti-American," and "exile though I am, I remain unalterably and simply but an American"), curiously placed in an essay about a rejected homeland, shifts the character of black expatriation and the lens we might bring to bear on similar departures. According to Edward Said, the exile has become the signal trope of the modern world, a figure predicated by the unprecedented historical scale of displaced persons and mass immigration set off by two world wars. Exiles are persons whose losses cluster around the absence of home, cultural communities, and the social networks these comprise.[48] Wright's loss is not a loss of home per se, but of dignity and rights: "I live in voluntary exile in France, and I like it. There is nothing in America—its drugstores, skyscrapers, television, movies, baseball, Dick Tracy, Black Belt, Jew Town, Irish Section, Bohunks, Wetbacks, dust storms, floods—that I miss or yearn for."[49] This collocation of the United States into a handful of locales and ethnic stereotypes reaffirms the conjunction of freedom and space that segregation legislated. It is precisely this question of access to social space and its privileges on which his departure rested.

Wright's essay raises the question of what might constitute a voluntary exile. Exile is a state-mandated condition, so Wright's decision to label his departure as "exile" points to a tension that has historically governed the relationship of black Americans to the state. "Culturally the

Negro represents a paradox," Wright suggested in another essay. "Though he is an organic part of the nation, he is excluded by the entire tide and direction of American culture."[50] A former member of the Communist Party, a figure of interest and subject of persistent investigation by the FBI for alleged acts of sedition,[51] Wright understood the pernicious distinction of black Americans from the rest of the U.S. polity as a rupture constitutive of U.S. structures of governance. His carefully constructed articulations of un-Americanism (i.e., a willingness to critique and demand from the state promised constitutional privileges) as opposed to anti-Americanism (i.e., disloyalty to the state) measures what James Baldwin labeled the "gulf between [state] conduct and [state] principles."[52] Using this dyad—"un-" versus "anti-" American—to structure his description of the kinds of losses propelling his voluntary exile recalibrates a history of allegations of black disloyalty and sedition, channeling these accusations back at the government. The passage merits lengthy quotation:

> Well, I'll define my idea of freedom, though I'm certain I run the risk of being branded as Un-American. If I am, then I readily plead guilty; but I insist that I'm *not* Anti-American, which, to me, is the important thing.
>
> My Un-Americanism, then consists of the fact that I want the right to hold, without fear of punitive measures, an opinion with which my neighbor does not agree; the right to travel wherever and whenever I please even though my ideas might not coincide with those of whatever Federal Administration might be in power in Washington; the right to express publicly my distrust of the "collective wisdom" of the people; the right to exercise my conscience and intelligence to the extent of refusing to "inform" and "spy" on my neighbor because he holds political convictions differing from mine; the right to express, without fear of reprisal, my rejection of religion.
>
> These Un-American sentiments add up to a fundamental right which I insist upon: the right to live free of mob violence, whether that violence assumes the guise of an anonymous blacklisting or of pressure exerted through character assassination.[53]

Thus, geographical distance Wright initiated between himself and the United States pales in comparison to the state-supported gulf dividing blacks and the larger U.S. polity. Indeed, little in Wright's exile seems voluntary beyond the purchase of a ticket, a ticket discounted by unfulfilled state promises and unyielding persecution. For Wright it is not even a question of abrogated rights to speech and privacy, for these rights simply do not exist. In a moment of similar reflection on the racial contingencies and costs of patriotism for black Americans during World War II, Baldwin considers the confusion posed by the uniform for African Americans: "My brother, describing his life in uniform, did not seem to be representing the America his uniform was meant to represent—: he had never seen the America his uniform was meant to represent. Had anyone?"[54]

Blacks remained un-American within the economy Wright reported precisely because they remained fundamentally wedded to constitutional U.S. ideology. They remained un-American because they remained alienated. And as the diplomat representing the U.S. embassy in France warned Wright, the newly arrived émigré, blacks become *anti*-American when they publicly narrate their social and political disparities.[55] After offering only a grudging critique of French colonialism, Wright noted that he, an alien in a strange land, felt safe for the first time. The pressure placed on nativism in the diplomat's claim upended what

Wright understood to be the fundamental difference between the United States and France—and perhaps, the world: In his eyes, the United States is "isolated" in her response to her human life.[56] "While living in America," he lamented, "I had the illusion that in time my country would evolve a code of humane values."[57] Wright's "Negro paradox" names the ways in which the black body shadows law: it is the body around which civil protections and human rights are delineated, but for whom they remained unconferred. This paradox is the problem of vision, of misrecognition, gathered in Frantz Fanon's memorable restaging of colonial encounters, "Look, a Negro."[58] It references the clutch of an insidiously crafted blackness that makes Rosa Coldfield instinctively recoil from the touch of Thomas Supten's mulatto bastard, Clytemnestra. It is Hemingway's Wesley in *To Have and Have Not*, for whom the appellation "nigger," Morrison reminds us, acts as "shortcut" for "[a] spatial and conceptual difference . . . with all of its color and caste implications."[59] Wright's rejection of the cabal of U.S. legal culture was a rejection of segregation and its discursive foundations; it was a rejection of the mythologies that would prescribe value to race; it was a rejection of the theories of racial degeneracy that further corroded the character of blackness, at which Homer Plessy in 1893 would balk and flee.

In 1896, the year the Supreme Court upheld Louisiana's public accommodations statute in *Plessy* v. *Ferguson* and provided the legal precedent for the intracolonalism that was segregation, Alphonse Bertillon's *Identification Anthropometrique: Instructions Signaletiques* (Signalectic Instructions: Including the Theory and Practice of Anthropometrical Identification) was translated and published in English. Bertillon, a Frenchman, was the founder of anthropometry, a classification system used to index criminals based on body measurements. His handbook was a primer for law enforcement officers, but when its methods were widely adopted in Europe and the United States, it further institutionalized blackness as a radical alterity. In a gesture validating one spectrum of racialized understandings over another, Bertillon offered as the eighty-third and final point of his chapter on "Descriptive Information," these instructions to police officers for handling "the Negro":

> 83. When the peculiarity of coloration is connected with the ethnic or *race* origin, this latter indication then becomes the primary element of the whole descriptive signalment, and should be placed by itself on the *dotted* line which precedes the heading of the descriptive information (I).
>
> Examples: **pure negro, negro greatly** (or **slightly**) crossed, **Chinese, Japanese, cross of Kanaka and European**, etc.[60]

Cross-referencing this initial set of requisites, Bertillon distilled his instructions further in the succeeding chapter, titled "Morphological Characters." He wrote,

> Supposing that we have to describe a subject whose skin is white, but whose external and internal conformation resembles that of a negro. . . .. If the subject in question were a real negro, with black skin, the indication negro type on the dotted line of the DESCRIPTIVE INFORMATION would replace advantageously all other description."[61]

Although fields like medicine, psychology, anthropology, sociology, and criminology strenuously worked during the last two decades of the nineteenth century to suture racial difference to the microphysics of the flesh, they, like Bertillon, exhausted the meaning of blackness. Within the mythology that these epistemologies worked to support and reproduce, blackness became ubiquitous, simultaneously summoning almost every iconographic and discursive figuration for the pathological while offering little evidence on behalf of black subjectivity. In other words, blackness fell within the province of the unknowable known. The attenuation of black subjectivity that Du Bois attributed to slavery could and did persist.

The routine reference to African Americans as refugees—rather than evacuees—in the media coverage following Hurricane Katrina in September 2005 points to the resilience of this disposition toward the black body.[62] As I will argue in the Epilogue, "Requiem," the distinction between these terms goes beyond the semantic. To be a refugee because of Katrina—one of the largest natural disasters in contemporary U.S. history—became a telling shorthand, signaling the distance of the state and the national polity from poor, black Americans. The term's discursive weight carried forward the indictments simultaneously waged against brown and black refugees seeking asylum on U.S. shores. Refugee in the context of this domestic disaster quickly summoned the discursive arsenal aimed at other refugees, as black Americans, like Haitian refugees, were summarily marked as criminals. The critical lens deployed and judgment levied against black victims of the hurricane, struggling to survive despite federal incompetence and belated, disorderly intervention, ill-conceived and ill-executed evacuation plans, absent housing, foodstuffs, and medical care, transfigured survival into crime. Although white Americans entering unattended shops in search of food and supplies were cast as victims who found food, similarly desperate blacks were cited by the press as looters.[63] To measure these collapsed distinctions—refugee, stateless person, and black exile—demands reading the historical trajectory of such claims. The reportage surrounding Katrina recalls the designed state alienation of the black body manifested in slavery and segregation, whose denaturalizing effects echoed black antislavery emigrationist H. Ford Douglass's dismissive, "I can hate this Government without being disloyal, because it has stricken down my manhood, and treated me as a saleable commodity. . . . I can join a foreign enemy and fight against it, without being a traitor, because it treats me as an ALIEN and a STRANGER."[64]

To see black civil rights movements from the nineteenth through the mid-twentieth centuries as singularly invested in civil liberties, justice, and freedom from oppression and discrimination is to risk missing the larger issue mobilizing these petitions: the humanity of the black body and human rights. Black civil rights campaigns in the United States have historically been underwritten by a compelling need to have the humanity of black body recognized—indeed, left unqualified and unchallenged. What the slave body already exposed, and what became all the more evident in the failures of Reconstruction and the rapidly built institution of segregation, is the fiction of "inalienable human rights." As the chapters that follow disclose, human rights are not only alienable, but contingent and socially constructed. The body of treaties and laws that proliferated after World War II, which sought to outline the parameters of human rights, reflected the ways in which these rights have historically remained ambiguous and have been compromised at every turn. The petitions of black Americans responded to a local and a global legal culture, in which, because human rights remained persistently and conveniently unclear, colonialisms and U.S. segregation could persist.

Turning to fugitive slave law and revolutionary politics, *Sanctuary: African Americans and Empire* charts the black body's shift in relation to the state following emancipation, a movement from chattel property to refugee. Although the historical arc of this book moves from the late eighteenth century through the present day, Haiti provides a geographical anchor. The turn to Haiti is warranted on several fronts. Its revolution, in Du Bois's words, "contrived a Negro problem for the Western Hemisphere,"[65] precipitating a body of slave laws intended to further delimit black life. Haiti casts light on black political ambitions because it, like Liberia and Ethiopia, served as a space across which black diasporan visions of political self-determination otherwise denied might be imagined. Envisioned as a refuge, Haiti offered a revolutionary model, a symbol of hope, and a powerful countermand to racialist ideologies of black inferiority. As Frederick Douglass would say in 1893 while serving as minister to Haiti, "We should not forget that the freedom you and I enjoy today is largely due to the brave stand taken by the black sons of Haiti. . . . Striking for their freedom, they struck for the freedom of every black man in the world."[66] Haiti historically offered hope for black Americans, providing a fecund space through which a new set of race relations might be imagined and wrought, both within and beyond the nation's borders.

The chapters that follow trace the historical relationship between the United States's international interventions and domestic practices. The social histories presented here reflect the ways in which the political unconscious has historically collapsed the distinctions between "foreigners" and "citizens" in their conceptualization and treatment of black Americans. In short, this book charts the ways in which blacks living in the United States have been marked, to borrow the colonial logic of U.S. Supreme Court Justice Edward Douglass White in *Downes* v. *Bidwell* (1901), as "foreign to the United States in a domestic sense." Part of what renders the expressions of racial violence particularly pernicious and often misrecognized is a failure to understand the global dimensions of its nationalist indentures: violence against the black body is situated in a transnational struggle over national identities and spaces, such that although the Chicago of the 1919 race riots is the "Heartland" of the United States and signifies an irreducible interiority, U.S. domestic policy measures mark Haiti as part of its outermost geographical claims. Race is an instrument of state management whose local and international character is mutually constitutive and operates in reciprocal relation.

Chapter 2, "W. E. B. Du Bois and the World Citizen," examines Du Bois's vision for an alternative democracy. Labeled "the fourth dimension," this utopian blueprint addresses a U.S. imperialism whose force is felt internationally and domestically. The cartographic imperative and economic reforms grounding Du Bois's social plan place the politically marginalized and colonized "colored world" at the center of global democracy. Du Bois's "fourth dimension" articulates a space outside the prohibitions legislated by the color line. It is a cosmopolitan design that insists on new forms of civil identity (i.e., global citizenship) that find their ideal expression in children. Staged across a range of texts, including *Darkwater* (1919), *Dark Princess* (1928), children's issues of the *Crisis*, and petitions before the United Nations, Du Bois's vision is part of a tradition of African American calls for sanctuary. Offering solutions to global poverty and challenging new ethical relations among citizens, Du Bois's "colored paradise" rehearses the failures of democracy, and urges a shift from capitalism to socialism. Engaging prevalent theories on racial destiny and African American degeneracy, Du Bois frames the dislocations—political, economic, and spatial—experienced by black Americans in relation to exiles and refugees.

Chapter 3, "Sanctuary," examines the cultural and racial contingencies of sanctuary for the African American body, locating the historical and legal underpinnings for this condition within the trafficking for human flesh that marked the beginnings of modernity. I outline the politics of fugitivity (i.e., of being outside the law) that precipitate and frame the structure of asylum for blacks within the United States. Moreover, I argue that the social, political, and legal dislocation marshaled in the production of the slave body remains intransigent. It is my contention that the political provisionality experienced by blacks not only speaks qualitatively to dimensions of statelessness, but is secured through a displacement of the humanity of the black body, a claim that suffuses the chapters that follow. Although chapter 3 offers a template for sanctuary, summoning the complex of legal, social, and political concerns that weigh and shape this condition (specifically the problem of political recognition and legitimacy mitigating the conferral of citizenship privileges and human rights), chapter 4, "Graphic Inscriptions of Power" extends the engagement with the interconnections between the international and the domestic.

A social history of the Chicago race riot of 1919, chapter 4 charts the larger national and international landscape articulated in Johnson's provocative and rich, summarizing heading, "Red Summer." For the Chicago race riot reflects a moment centered in the globally felt shifts in world power codified by World War I. Focusing on the visual repertoires of war encoded within the photographs, maps, and articles that make up the *Chicago Tribune*'s coverage of the riot, this chapter synthesizes the lingering influence of a war psychology on the events that transpired that late July afternoon. To the extent that a persistent war psychology shaped the twenty-five race riots of that bloody summer, it was a violence localized around the figure of the "Negro solider" and the problem of citizenship that the uniformed black body placed in the foreground. The contraction of domestic space realized by segregation—and resecured through riots like that in Chicago—stand in an inverse relation to the concurrent expansion of geopolitical territory—an expansion that may be seen in the imperial ambitions of the United States toward Haiti that justified nineteen years of U.S. occupation.

In an article for *Crisis* in 1920, Protestant Episcopal Bishop John K. Hurst read in the occupation a transatlantic translation of a domestic problem, because for him the occupation was "but the Negro question in a new form." Examining U.S. relations with Haiti during the first decades of the twentieth century, chapter 5, "'I Dream a World': Occupied Haiti and African Americans," limns the political unconscious of a nation-state whose domestic politics are mirrored in its international interventions. This chapter tracks a transnationalist African American response to the occupation that refuses to disarticulate black Americans from a larger, globally waged assault against black life. As voodoo, cannibalism, and mystery were increasingly used as synedoches for the island and as rationales legitimating the presence of the United States, African Americans produced their own counter archive, wielding revolutionary histories of the island as an instrument for extending African American civil rights within the context of a global crisis over race and colonialism.

In the Epilogue, "Requiem," I engage the political dimensions of our social moment, concluding this book with a study of the transformation of black Gulf Coast residents into refugees following Hurricane Katrina in August 2005. The storm became a barometer for the qualified citizenship that is so much of postemancipation black life. Here I take up the use of definitions as instruments for alienating black Americans from the rest of the polity. Charting the retrenchment of segregationist politics, I demonstrate the political and the psychosocial costs of dispossession for black Americans increasingly divested of political power, who are steadily remanded to the peripheries of political life, and who remain second-class citizens.

As a study of the larger global political underpinnings saturating historical events—race riots, occupation—I contend that we might come to better understand and gauge the significance of our domestic racial politics if we look beyond our geopolitical boundaries. This book challenges a return to thinking through the local with an eye toward the international that characterized black internationalist discourse from the nineteenth century through the end of the Civil Rights movement in the late 1960s. It is a challenge to understand the ways in which the quality and character of black civil life remains intimately connected to the sphere of state ambitions. U.S. imperial pursuits became vehicles for further refining the figure of the American in law, culture, and social space. Understanding the way in which race and space are reciprocally connected enhances our ability to apprehend the significance of a color-line that Du Bois described as belting the world.

Rationalizing an anticipated invasion in May 1994, President Bill Clinton redefined Haiti as the United States's "backyard," enlisting the presence of 1 million Haitian "refugees" living in the United States as supporting evidence. This domestication of Haitian national space persisted in his administration's representations of the scheduled fall military invasion as a "police action"; its imperialistic contours were softened by reports characterizing the venture as a UN rather than a strictly U.S. mission. The reterritorialization imagined in Clinton's assertion of Haiti as the United States's backyard not only restructures the terms of the U.S. invasion, transforming occupation, martial law, and military violence into domestic (read: comparatively mild) police protection, but cues the imperatives grounding *Sanctuary: African Americans and the American Empire*. For refugees worry social and political systems, exposing as much as they chafe against the ideological fictions grounding law and public policies. Their presence presses the limits of law, the very boundaries transfixing them to its interstices. To Hortense Spiller's titular question—"Who cuts the border?"[67]—I answer: the refugee. Yet, as much as these communities have challenged political systems, their presence has compelled much needed innovations in civil and human rights. In its turn to both the historic character of these challenges, and to the dignity asserted in these demands, *Sanctuary: African Americans and Empire* offers its most compelling lessons for the future.

America is teaching the world . . . that ability and capacity for culture is not the hereditary monopoly of a few, but the widespread possibility for the majority of mankind if they have a decent chance in life.

W. E. B. DU BOIS, *Dark Princess*

Democracy is a method of realizing the broadest measure of justice to all human beings.

W. E. B. DU BOIS, *Darkwater*

2

W. E. B. Du Bois and the World Citizen

"WHILE I ACKNOWLEDGE I am a traitor, I also pronounce myself a patriot," laments the condemned executioner Beryl Trout in the opening pages of Sutton E. Griggs's *Imperium in Imperio* (1899).[1] Published two years after the Spanish-American War, Griggs's novel engages a prominent paradox that governed U.S. social and political life: a U.S. black serviceman may fight abroad on behalf of the United States but remain "an unprotected foreigner in his own home."[2] *Imperium in Imperio* indexes the stubborn resiliency of an antebellum U.S. political culture that refused to recognize black freedmen as native sons. "Aliens are we in our native land," railed an indignant Frederick Douglass to a crowd gathered for a meeting of the American and Foreign Anti-Slavery Society in New York of May 1853. Douglass went on to say:

> The fundamental principles of the Republic, to which the humblest white man, whether born here or elsewhere may appeal with confidence, in the hope of awakening a favorable response are held to be inapplicable to us. . . . We are literally scourged beyond the beneficent range of both authorities, human and divine.[3]

Appearing within a year of the bloody Wilmington Race Riot (1898), Griggs's story sketches the emergence of a radical black utopian politics reacting against the perils confronting black Americans in the early decades after emancipation—lynching, mob violence, education and employment inequities, theories of "vanishing negroes,"[4] prohibitions on interracial marriage, involuntary scientific experimentation, proliferating Jim Crow legislation, and diminishing federal and judicial protections. Part of a tradition of black empire narratives, Griggs's text reclaims the ambitions of African Americans two generations removed from slavery who envisioned, in Howard Bell's words, "frontier American communities where they would not be under white suzerainty."[5]

In a gesture prefiguring Richard Wright's embodiment, in Bigger Thomas, of American cultural hostility against black males, Griggs's *Imperium in Imperio* imagines an African American coup d'états. The title of the novel became the name for the black nation within a nation that Douglass remarked upon almost half-a-century earlier, and that Griggs insists captures the sociopolitical experience of black Americans. A clandestine, black governing body mirroring the structure of the federal government, complete with its own elected congressional body, judiciary, and president, the Imperio in Imperium seeks to provide a measure of redress and protection otherwise unavailable to black Americans. Structured as a retrospective, the opening moments of the novel presage its end. No longer willing to remain a surrogate to the state, the Imperium in Imperio plans to conquer Texas and establish a sovereign black nation with the assistance of the United States's foreign enemies. It is Trout's refusal of the extremist violence predicated in this radical black military campaign that provide the anchor for the opening chapter: by anticipating the failure of the plan for black secession, the text refuses black violence, shifting attention back to the question of black citizenship/ "While I acknowledge that I am a traitor, I also pronounce myself a patriot. . . . It is true that I have betrayed the immediate plans of the race to which I belong," confesses Trout, "but I have done this in the interest of the whole human family—of which my race is but a part."[6] Although Griggs brings his audience to a frenzy, suggesting the possibility of a seditious and violent black nationalism if the U.S. racial caste system persists, Trout serves as the saboteur of this ambition. The radical politics permeating the story strikes back at the emigrationist campaigns of the nineteenth century ("The day for the wholesale exodus of nations is past. We must, then, remain here."), and coincidentally locates the seat of a new, sovereign black nation in Texas, the very state Kansas Senator H. Lane proposed for black repatriation in 1864.[7] In addition to the ingenuity of the elaborate schemes Griggs attributes to the Imperium, this critical utopian project has several striking elements: the ironic use of an executioner, Beryl Trout, as his narrator, saboteur, and final voice of moral order; the sustained interest in law as the primary vehicle for social change; and the subtly broached politics of peace. Embedded within this late nineteenth-century narrative's critique of U.S. democracy is an ideology of peace that was both international in scope and domestically urgent.

In Trout's final moments before his execution by the Imperium for treason, the character beseeches:

> If the voice of a poor Negro, who thus gave his life, will be heard, I only ask as a return that all mankind will join hands and help my poor downtrodden people to secure those rights for which they organized the Imperium, which my betrayal has now destroyed. I urge this because love of liberty is such an inventive genius, that if you destroy one device it at once constructs another more powerful.[8]

Trout's death memorializes the slain African American soldier and the countless lynched victims cited in the novel's pages and calls attention to a loyalty that persists despite racial inequalities. I point to this plea for civil rights, significant in its international sweep and sensibility, for the manner in which it highlights the ground of Griggs's imagined radical black state and his own ideology. Griggs deliberately sets his Imperio in the eighteenth century ("the early days of the American Republic"), crediting its founding to "a negro scientist who won an international reputation by his skill and erudition." Though unnamed in Griggs's account, this Negro of learning who "enjoyed the association of the moving sprits of the revolutionary period" suggests the black architect, mathematician, and astronomer Benjamin Banneker. Banneker's critique of Thomas Jefferson's views on slavery and blacks, as well as his work for President George Washington as a surveyor for what would become the District of Columbia, are well known, but his model for international peace is less often remembered. Banneker imagined a new cabinet position, Secretary of Peace, responsible for curtailing global crisis and warfare.[9] "In Banneker's vision," writes Robin D. G. Kelley, "the United States would not police the world from a position of dominance but rather partici-pate in a global system in which the 'West' was on an equal footing with the rest of the world. There was no room for colonies."[10] For the historian Carter G. Woodson, Banneker's vision prefigured Woodrow Wilson's plan for a League of Nations. Yet, Banneker and Griggs were not alone in their visions of an alternative model of governance that privileged universal peace, human equality, and civil rights. Just as revolutionary conflicts and warfare became the backdrop for each of these plans—the American and Haitian Revolutions and Spanish-American War, respectively—world war would engender a similar response from other black intellectuals, among them W. E. B. Du Bois.

Du Bois's blueprint for a new world found its fullest articulation in the aftermath of two world wars. The geopolitical imperative and economic reforms underwriting his political philosophy and social plan insisted upon the centrality of both the politically marginalized and the colonized "colored world" to global democracy. Taking shape over several decades as a part of his continuing critique of U.S. culture and governance, it was this plan that grounded Du Bois's 1949 U.N. petition on behalf of Rosa Lee Ingram and her children. Later labeled by his literary executor, Herbert Aptheker, "the fourth dimension," Du Bois's scheme featured a geopolitics radically refashioned within an idealistic, but pragmatic, vision of democratic possibility. Representative of an increasing frustration with racial discrimination and the failed U.S. policies on civil rights that emerged following the two world wars, his fourth dimension joined a continuum of discourse on black rights that included eighteenth-and nineteenth-century judicial slave petitions. Such petitions should also be understood as part of the expressive cultural tradition of African American calls for sanctuary, a repertoire rang-ing from Negro spirituals telling of Canaan to black emigrationist projects to Liberia and Haiti; and from imagined alternative black spaces partially realized in black settlements and longed for in literature, poetry, and plays.

PARADISE, OR, THE FOURTH DIMENSION

In 1945, four years before his petition on behalf of the Ingrams, Du Bois penned a different kind of essay, which gains a certain legibility by way of the title that Herbert Aptheker most likely affixed to the document: "Flashes from Transcaucasia." Angered by University of North Carolina Press director William Terry Couch's critique of "My Evolving Program for Negro Freedom," an essay drafted for Rayford Logan's *What the Negro Wants* (1944), Du Bois penned "Flashes from Transcaucasia" in response. Logan's anthology, which included essays by A. Philip Randolph, Langston Hughes, Mary McLeod Bethune, Sterling Brown, Frederick Patterson, and George Schuyler, had been commissioned by and produced in close consultation with Couch. Nonetheless, in the eyes of Couch, the final product was an affront to a white Southern sensibility. Rejecting the bids for racial equality and social parity expressed by the volume's contributors, Couch threatened to cancel the publication of the book if its contents were not revised. Logan returned Couch's threat with his own rueful reminder—failure to publish this collection constituted a breach of contract: "In reply to your letter of December 14 I have to say that I am consulting my attorneys."[11] With Logan unbending, Couch went forward with the publication unaltered, but appended his own "Publisher's Introduction" to the book without the consent or prior knowledge of Logan, the collection's editor, or any of the volume's contributors. Du Bois summarized the publisher's remarks by noting that "Couch inserted in the book as a publisher's note an apology to the White South, an attack upon the Myrdal monumental study of the Negro in America, and his own firm conclusion as to the inferiority of the Negro."[12] In Du Bois's estimation, Couch's politics were neither singular nor endemic to the South. Rather, they reflected a national attitude toward blacks: "This man represents a singularly large and dangerous section of American public opinion, not only in the South but throughout the country, which is forced to yield even the dogma of 'race inferiority' but still clings to subordination," accused Du Bois that same year in *Color and Democracy: Colonies and Peace (1945)*[13]

Tracing the history of the dispute, Kenneth Janken tells us that it was Du Bois's essay for the collection that drew the greatest condemnation from Couch. With its explicit critique of Jim Crow as an institution undermining human, political, social, and economic rights, for Couch Du Bois's essay epitomized the problems inherent in the entire anthology. Balking at Du Bois's discussion of interracial marriage, Couch associated black claims for social equality with miscegenation.[14] "Does the white man have no right to attempt to separate cultural from biological integration, and help the Negro achieve the first and deny him the second," queried Couch in his introduction to the book. "Can biological integration be regarded as a right?" he challenged. "What happens to the case for the Negro if it is tied up with things to which he not only has no right, but which if granted, would destroy all rights?"[15] Having already insisted in a correspondence with Langston Hughes (another contributor to the volume) that "a mechanically applied . . . discrimination is essential,"[16] Couch resisted the collective interest in severing the color line expressed by all the African American contributors to Logan's book. To Logan he would write,

> The things Negroes are represented [in *What the Negro Wants*] as wanting seem to me far removed from those they ought to want. Most of the things they are represented as wanting can be summarized in the phrase: complete abolition of segregation. If this is what the Negro wants, nothing could be clearer than what he needs, and needs most urgently, is to revise his wants.[17]

Both a deeply personal response and an essay that sought to transfigure the character of Couch's assault, Du Bois's rebuttal deconstructed the rhetoric of racial inferiority that formed the director's grammar.

Du Bois opened "Flashes from Transcaucasia" by recounting the publication history of Logan's collection.[18] Although the ensuing paragraphs bore little relation to the provocative title Aptheker probably chose, Aptheker's notations on the text nonetheless illuminate the title's contribution in framing the political radicalisms suffusing the essay. In a concluding parenthetical note, Aptheker writes, "Transcaucasia is not on the map; it is in the fourth dimension beyond the color line."[19] Aptheker's title and definition are curious and significant. They most likely refer to Du Bois's first use of the term "trans-caucasia," which occurred in 1921 in his essay, "News from Pan-Africa," written two years after the *Chicago Tribune* accused Du Bois's efforts to convene a Pan-African Congress amidst the 1919 Peace Conference of being "quite Utopian" and assuredly having "less than a Chinaman's chance of getting anywhere in the Peace Conference."[20] Du Bois not only successfully gathered an international assembly of more than fifty delegates representing fifteen countries to consider the state of black and brown peoples throughout the world in Paris in February 1919, but by 1921 he was orchestrating a second Pan-African Congress. In "News from Pan-Africa," Du Bois offered spatial coordinates for the fourth dimension, defining "Pan-Africa" as simply a place-holder for a space and an ideology that, he argued, might more accurately be described as "trans-caucasia." He wrote:

> Etymologically Trans-Caucasia was the term I preferred [over Pan-Africa]. But . . . the name has been more than preempted despite its lying so appropriate on the Black Sea. But the Black Sea of which I write lies much farther away than Russia. It lies even beyond Africa and is in that geographical third dimension of Fixed Ideas which makes it unusually difficult to approach; and despite our stream of travel, the cables of Yap and the swift flying trains and steamers, somehow news and embassies from this land beyond the White World filter in even more slowly than before the War.[21]

The anchoring of space and political ideology signaled in trans-caucasia and Pan-Africa reflects how geographies of race are intimately connected to political designs. By 1944, Du Bois's vision of this inaccessible world with race as its borders had matured even further. Trans-caucasia came to refer to a political philosophy even more dramatically transfixed by domestic U.S. race relations than in its first articulation in 1921.[22]

"My Evolving Program," like many of the essays published in Logan's collection, espoused a postwar reconstructionism—a "Black Reconstruction, Part II," if you will—heightening Couch's supremacist anxieties. Couch opposed desegregation, but perhaps even more emphatically, he opposed racial intermarriage and miscegenation.[23] According to the internal reviewer for the press, O. J. Coffin, the ambitions expressed in the manuscript to end segregation threatened "overnight the re-ordering of His world." Quite simply, the essays were the work of "self-elected leaders," individuals who "talk of intermarriage and world congresses of Negroes as nonchalantly as Walrus and Carpenter might discuss cabbages and kings."[24] Du Bois's demands for racial uplift, albeit frustrating to Couch, perhaps rested less uncomfortably with his critic than his pointed characterizations of Germany and of interracial marriage.[25] Du Bois traveled to Europe in 1892 as part of his graduate studies; his studies in Germany transcended the corridors of the university. Through fundamental human social interaction, he came to recognize race as provincial, as peculiarly ethnocentric and geographical in character.

Du Bois opens his remembrance of Germany with a graphic description of sociocultural vestibularity. He is neither exiled nor unequivocally outside, but literally and materially estranged from the United States: "I found myself on the outside of the American world looking in."[26] His assertion testifies to more than geographical distance, but to an ideological and cultural dislocation, a fracture with American consciousness measured and experienced through his shared sympathies with European strangers. "With me were white folk— students, acquaintances, teachers—who viewed the scene with me. They did not pause to regard me as a curiosity, or something subhuman; I was just a man of the somewhat privileged student rank. . . . "[27] For Du Bois, Germany placed the fragile economy of U.S. race relations in relief: "I found to my gratification that they with me did not regard America as the last word in civilization." Although he would, perhaps for the first time, "[look] at the world as a man and not simply from a narrow racial and provincial outlook," not ocean, continent, or culture could sufficiently bar him from the United States's color line: "When the blue-eyed Dora confessed her readiness to marry me 'gleich!' I told her frankly and gravely that it would be unfair to himself and cruel to her for a colored man to take a white bride to America. She could not understand."[28]

To hazard Couch's lens, even momentarily, is to read Du Bois as advocating miscegenation and to believe that Du Bois, too, participated in the translation of black civil rights into black demands for racial intermarriage. It was this rescripting of the political into the sexual that drained the vigor from the 1875 civil rights act,[29] secured segregation as a colonial project partially wrought through regulated sexual intimacies, and contributed to the refusal until the 1960s to enforce social equality for blacks. Although interracial couplings and miscegenation was certainly how black political demands were read by white supremacists, trans-caucasia signifies more than the right to intermarry. The "fourth dimension beyond the color line," trans-caucasia articulates a social space outside the prohibitions legislated by the color line—the possibility of intermarriage is merely symptomatic of such latitude. This utopian vision is a response to the frustrations and reconstructive possibilities in the aftermath of war; it is a new political cartography for the United States following World War II. The ontology of Du Bois's fourth dimension is perhaps less significant than the actual vision itself: it is a blueprint of black life from the late nineteenth century onward through which the status of black people in relation to state politics may be read and engaged.

"Flashes from Transcaucasia" goes beyond Du Bois's commentary on the Logan volume (*What the Negro Wants*) and his original essay for the collection ("My Evolving Program"). The title might be productively elaborated as a political rubric, gathering under itself a body of writing, a set of discursive blueprints, begun decades earlier. Conceding Frederic Jameson's assumption that utopian novels "posit the end of history" and "aim to resolve all political differences," Du Bois's experimental prose collection, *Darkwater* (1920), and his novel, *Dark Princess* (1928), create fecund spaces for thinking through a vision that is at once critically cosmopolitan and epistemologically subversive.[30] Divided into ten chapters, Du Bois's *Darkwater* gathers poems, short stories, and essays to launch his postwar politics, whereas *Dark Princess* uses romance to animate his critique of competing strategies for racial uplift and to articulate his vision of a colored League of Nations. Mirroring their inscriptional moment, these interwar texts appropriate a geographical rubric and its colonial entailments to critique a postwar reconstruction defined by failed liberalisms and reaffirmed colonialisms.

Neil Smith's history of the U.S. empire examines the intensified geographical imperatives influencing national and cultural politics during the period around World War I. During these years of proliferating cartographic and exploration projects, the furthermost points of the earth—the North (1909) and South (1907) Poles—were added to a global map, on which existing national borders would soon be risked and occasionally moved with troop marches and battles won and lost. The Paris Peace Conference boasted the end of world war, the Versailles Treaty, the League of Nations, and the world remapped. "Geographical knowledge," avers Smith, "is itself a condition of conquest. It transforms immediate practical questions of environment and resources into manageable scientific and technical problems."[31] For the historian and sociologist Du Bois, who decided early in his career to insert the "scientific into the sociologic" (and arguably, the sociological into the scientific), any approach to the "Negro problem" must be organized within the context of a geographical and scientific imperative: the color line.[32] While "Wilson's geographer" Isaiah Bowman charted the topographical dimensions of postwar U.S. liberalism in *The New World* (1921), Du Bois offered a different manual on and protocol for U.S. governance and global relations.[33] *Darkwater* and *Dark Princess,* like the numerous other pieces embodying his outlook for the future, directly engaged with what much of the political leadership of the world continued to ignore: the centrality of colored people to the project of global peace and world democracy.

Du Bois understood all too well what Smith describes: that the "geography of empire" plays out on a "simultaneously national and global" scale.[34] Through his Pan-Africanism and Pan-Asianism, Du Bois positioned intranational race conflicts at the center of international colonialisms and imperialisms. In *Darkwater* he wrote, "High wages in the United States and England might be the skillfully manipulated result of slavery in Africa and of peonage in Asia."[35] He continued:

> Conceive this nation, of all human peoples, engaged in a crusade to make the "World Safe for Democracy"! Can you imagine the United States protesting against Turkish atrocities in Armenia, while the Turks are silent about mobs in Chicago and St. Louis; what is Louvain, compared with Memphis, Waco, Washington, Dyersburg, and Estill Springs? In short, what is the black man but America's Belgium, and how could America condemn in Germany that which she commits, just as brutally, within her own borders?[36]

Du Bois's international perspective reveals the imperialism lubricating the political unconscious of the United States. "The Negro problem in America will never be settled [*sic*]," insisted Du Bois in a letter to the editor of the *New York Age*, "so long as Africa or the West Indies are seats of economic slavery and despotism."[37] Six years later, in a 1925 essay for *Foreign Affairs,* Du Bois asked, "How deep were the roots of [World War II] entwined about the color line? And of the legacy left, what of the darker race problems will the world inherit?"[38] The impoverished conditions effected by colonialism—poverty, ill health, unequal distribution and privatization of resources, racial hatred and race anxieties, unemployment, and fear and cultural unease—disclose failures of democracy.[39] Tying race riots, lynchings, and disenfranchisement to larger imperial ambitions, Du Bois stitched together the "isms" (e.g., racism, sexism, terrorism) and phobias (e.g., xenophobia, homophobia) disrupting national peace and compelling war into the problem of economic tyranny. "Our great ethical question today," Du Bois hazards, "is how we may justly distribute the world's goods to satisfy the necessary wants of the mass of men."[40] Du Bois proposed to end global poverty by eradicating class through democratization and the socialization of industry; to fail in this effort, he cautioned in 1920, was to risk further war.[41]

Du Bois's cosmopolitanism poses the question, To whom do we owe our primary political obligations: nation or humanity? His internationalism is part of the cartographic curriculum of his imagined colored paradise. Du Bois's blueprint in *Darkwater,* which he described elsewhere as his "evolving plan for the future," translates into a critically cosmopolitan revision of democracy as racial uplift—a movement from capitalism to socialism, from industry-targeted school curriculums to nurturing individual talents, and from oligarchies and colonialisms to republicanisms. It is worth restating here that utopianism embeds critique as part of its political design. Du Bois's primer for the fourth dimension rehearses the failures of a governance that bears the name of "democracy," but requires all manner of qualification. Du Bois's geopolitics demands a respect for differences and insists upon individual autonomy. They call for a new political vanguard arising from the masses, and not simply among state elites. They require the reevaluation of knowledge forms and will produce new economically driven solidarities. Most importantly, they must be propelled by racial cooperation and the affirmation of civil disobedience as a form of critique.

> The real Pacifist will seek to organize, not simply the masses in white nations, guarding against exploitation and profiteering, but will remember that no permanent relief can come but by including in this organization the lowest and the most exploited races in the world. . . . World philanthropy, like national philanthropy, must come as uplift and prevention, and not merely as alleviation and religious conversion. Reverence for humanity, as such, must be installed in the world and Africa should be the talisman.[42]

Addressing the willful social ignorance akin to failed intimacy that characterizes social interaction, Du Bois speaks to a dimension of sociality that realizes Hortense Spillers's distinction between the flesh and the body. For it is the flesh, according to Spillers, that precedes the body as the "zero degree of social conceptualization."[43] Of this condition Du Bois writes, "We do not really associate with each other." Rather, "We associate with our ideas of each other, and few people have either the ability or the courage to question their own ideas."[44] A republic can only be realized when the experiences and knowledge of political minorities are integrated in the political system. He contends that it is precisely because "no nation, race, or sex has a monopoly of ability or ideas" and because "no human group is so small as to deserve to be ignored" that new structures of governance must incorporate minorities.[45] Pessimistic about the immediate chances for success but filled with hope for the future, Du Bois shifted the weight of his project to the smallest members of the community: black and brown children.

For a man taught by slavery and world war that every quadrant of human life was imperiled, Du Bois's plea for sanctuary is housed in this blueprint for a radically altered domestic politics and world. Du Bois's fourth dimension expresses a profound alienation, an "unhomeliness" signifying the inability of black Americans to meaningfully exert their political claims. In essence, as a repudiation of what he describes as the "tyranny of the Majority,"[46] the fourth dimension presupposes the marginality endemic of the refugee—Arendt's loss of political voice. Precisely because the historic plea for sanctuary among African Americans emanates from the serial loss of legal rights and social access, Du Bois's fourth dimension outlines a radical politics that not only adheres to the principles of black republicanism, but recognizes and politically legitimates black humanity. For him this transnationally inscribed political refuge must in fact reshape global political agendas, structures of governance, and the composition and meaning of citizenship. It is vision of social paradise that views the United States as the catalyst for a parallel domestic and international decolonization movement stimulating peace and republicanism worldwide. Recognizing the dispossession of black peoples as part of a larger world system, Du Bois's rubric for sanctuary subordinates state sovereignty and civil obligations to the larger project of global peace and "world citizenship."

THE WORLD CITIZEN

Aptheker's description of the fourth dimension as a world beyond the color line may too narrowly describe this political habitus, foreclosing readings that could more fully realize the significance of such a spatial displacement. Du Bois's assertion of the color line as *the* central problem of the twentieth century dismisses the view of the color line as exclusively an issue of national character: race has a local inflection, but a global accent. In Du Bois's familiar formulation, "The problem of the Twentieth Century is the problem of the color line—the relation of the darker to the lighter races of men in Asia and Africa, in America and the islands of the sea."[47] The deliberate absence of national signifiers permits Du Bois to claim the multiple, and geographically variable, sites in which race performs. For Du Bois the "color line belts the world."[48]

Engaging the geographical vicissitudes of race, Du Bois's evolving plan remains sensitive to the microphysics of race. By asking in 1944 "What *are* the fundamental questions before the world at war?" Du Bois set the stage for a discussion that privileged race as the primary catalyst for present and future world conflicts. Race rests at the center of what he perceived as internationally felt, and domestically lived, fears over national security, employment, resources, poverty, and health. "To anyone giving thought to these problems," he advanced, "it must be clear that each of them, with all of its own peculiar difficulties, tends to break asunder along the lesions of race difference and race hate."[49] Serving as his interlocutors, the protagonists of *Dark Princess,* Matthew Towns and India's princess Kautilya, expatiate on the geopolitics of race. They mutually sanction the role of "darker peoples" to lead "manhood to health and happiness and . . . away from the morass of hate, poverty, crime, sickness, monopoly, and the mass-murder called war."[50] However, this scene of transnational cooperation is rendered contingent when Du Bois cautions that difference—historical, political, cultural, geographical, racial, and national—matters.

To read *Darkwater* is to read *Souls of Black Folk* forward. The sequel to his 1903 publication, and a similarly structured text which sold 1,400 copies within the first three weeks of publication,[51] *Darkwater* distills yet complicates the content it shares with the earlier work. *Darkwater* extends the available rubrics for reading *Souls,* providing an alternative lens for essays like "Of the Meaning of Progress" and "Of the Training of Black Men," two chapters in which he expressed particular worry about black futures, and which offer education as an affirmation of the possibilities of black life. For Du Bois, education and parental care are the agents that will realize his "world citizen." Significantly, Du Bois first mentions the "world citizen" in *Darkwater* as a presumption cemented to a larger claim about women's suffrage. Part of a future generation, he imagines this figure reflecting back in horror "that as late as 1918 great and civilized nations were making desperate endeavors to confine the development of ability and individuality to one sex."[52] *Darkwater* and *Dark Princess* present black women as counternarratives to a white supremacist civilizing discourse, in which contests over an expanding field of rights are waged across the terrain of female bodies.

Sensitive to the gains that had recently been made by feminists in the suffrage campaign, Du Bois used women as a means to garner sympathy for, and render analogous, black petitions for civil rights. In *Dark Princess,* he fashions a princess from Bowdpur, India, to be the voice for his vision of a realigned global politics orchestrated by colored people and administered through a centralized body. In each text women are presented as sites of essential knowledge, and in *Dark Princess*, as the representative figure of a new world leadership. (Kautilya heads a collective of colored state leaders that resembles the League of Nations, the Great Council of the Darker People; orchestrates a version of the Pan African Congress; and strategizes about how to develop a decolonization movement and racially inclusive alternative world order.) Just as women's suffrage is marked as essential for refitting democracy, women—along with colored males and females—are fundamental to new social, economic, and political futures, and to a new democracy. This practical and strategic emphasis intervenes in a larger, historical paternalism grounding much of social and political thought regarding women. Indeed, Du Bois rearticulates a well-worn calculus of biology as politics: if women are the site of reproduction, then women equally represent the site of greatest sociopolitical vulnerability, because their unregulated sexuality risks compromising, if not hastening, racial genocide.[53] *Darkwater* and *Dark Princess* place particular emphasis on women's reproductive output—Du Bois's "world citizen[s]," children.

Du Bois's preoccupation with children, and with education as a path to alternative black futures, predates these texts. In an essay published in the *American Monthly Review of Reviews* in November 1900, Du Bois contextualizes the material representations of black life featured in the American Negro exhibit for the 1900 Paris Exposition Universelle. Designed to highlight the "history," "present condition," "education," and "literature" of "a small nation of people," the Negro exhibit sought to picture "their life and development without apology or gloss." The review essay and exhibition both celebrated the accomplishments of blacks despite the failures of reconstruction, accomplishments that included 350 patents granted to black inventers and the enrollment of more than half of the nation's black children in school.[54] Du Bois's own gold medal winning contributions to the exhibit included charts and graphs reflecting his studies on the current state of the black community, and 363 photographs documenting black life, arranged within three albums labeled "Types of American Negroes," "Georgia, U.S.A," and "Negro Life in Georgia, U.S.A."[55] These photographs were, as Du Bois claimed of the entire exhibition, "sociological." In Du Bois words, "There are several volumes of photographs of typical Negro faces, which hardly square with conventional American ideas."[56] They challenged typologies of blackness reified within racial sciences and codified in an array of emerging techniques and documentary styles, not the least of which was the criminal "mug shot."[57] The carefully cropped profiles and full frontal views of African Americans strategically call to mind both conventional portraits and mug shots, but the ambiguity of these uncaptioned images amplify their signifying properties,[58] linking them, I would argue, to at least two additional visual registers—photos of students and the dead. The images disturb theories of racial degeneracy, depicting a "small nation" that included healthy, educated, and hardworking black people. Indeed, some of the thickness of this refutation of colonial representations of

FIGURE 2.1 Portrait of an African American male featured in Du Bois's exhibit on African Americans for the 1900 Paris Exposition Universelle. "African American Male, head shot."
The Daniel Murray Collection, Courtesy of the Library of Congress, Prints and Photographs Division (LC-USZ62-124784).

blackness might arguably have rested in the subjects—both the people and the locations—he compiled. (See Figures 2–1 and 2–2.)

Du Bois's albums disrupt and decouple blackness from the "phantasmagoric aesthetics" that Zahid Chaudhary argues underwrites colonial photography. Such photographs, Chadhury explains, were used to "[manage] the very structure of vision and visibility to re/produce the modern form of alienation."[59] From this perspective we would do well to think critically of the role that children play in Du Bois's collection. Representing approximately 10 percent of the collection, these carefully cropped and posed representations of young people not only suggest family albums and mug shots, but also class portraits. Whether alone or in a group, smiling or with a stilted face, the photographs of children in Du Bois's exhibit produce an accumulating sense of innocence and possibility. It is this innocence, I believe, that contextualizes Du Bois's idealization of the child as world citizen. Du Bois offers his most sustained elaboration on the coming world citizen in *Darkwater*'s "The Immortal Child," in part a manual on education. Hidden within this guide to child rearing is a revolutionary understanding of a possible world—and of whom the citizen of such a world might be.

Children are an essential component of Du Bois's radicalism. In *Darkwater*, Du Bois offers what appears to be simple advice for "colored men and women" on raising children. He insists that parents should resist shielding children from the realities of racial discrimination and racial prohibitions, and instead should offer age-appropriate explanations for racialized social inequities. Parents must seek to "transfigure" a child's soul toward "a great, moving, guiding ideal," toward "dignity and self-respect, to breadth and accomplishment, to human

FIGURE 2.2 Portrait of an African American girl that was included among the more than 300 photographs of African Americans that Du Bois displayed at the 1900 Paris Exposition Universelle. "African American Girl, full-length portrait, standing next to chair, facing front."
The Daniel Murray Collection, Courtesy of the Library of Congress, Prints and Photographs Division (LC-USZ62–124806).

service; to beat back every thought of cringing and surrender."[60] As the vanguard for his new world, a world to be wrought in "the day of our children's children," young people and their talents must be encouraged and developed. Education must shift from conformity with industrial demands toward fully developing individual capacities. He declared, "We must not seek to make men carpenters, but to make carpenters men."[61] Couched in his parental instructions and educational reform package is a political agenda and theory for democracy: "Given as the ideal the utmost possible freedom for every human soul, with slavery for none, and equal honor for all necessary human tasks, then our problem of education is greatly simplified: we aim to develop human souls, to make all intelligent; to discover special talents and genius."[62]

Indicting public education as "the handmaiden of production," he continues, "Without wider, deeper intelligence among the masses Democracy cannot accomplish its greater ends. Without a more careful conservation of human ability and talent the world cannot secure the services which its greater needs call for."[63]

Strikingly, Du Bois opens "The Immortal Child" with a brief biographical sketch of the prematurely dead African American composer and musician Samuel Coleridge-Taylor. It is a history at once personal in tone and instructive in content, and significantly begins with Du

Bois recounting his first encounter with Coleridge-Taylor nineteen years earlier at the Paris Exposition Universelle:

> It is now nineteen years since I first saw Coleridge-Taylor. We were in London in some somber hall where there were many meeting, men and women called chiefly to the beautiful World's Fair at Paris; and then a few slipping over to London to meet Pan-Africa. We were there from Cape Colony and Liberia, from Haiti and the States, and from the Islands of the Sea.[64]

This moment is all the more telling because it represents, according to Rebecka Rutledge Fisher, one of the few occasions in Du Bois's extraordinarily prolific career in which the social activist and political theorist discussed the World's Fair, if even in brief.[65] Here, Du Bois's references to the Paris World's Fair and the Pan-African Conference are precursive and genealogical: they subtly prefigure the cosmopolitan sensibility that underlies Du Bois's child development program while demarcating the historic trajectory (or genealogy) of his critical thinking on children in relation to a thesis on world citizenship that finds, as already demonstrated, some of its earliest articulation at the Exposition.

According to Michele Mitchell, by the turn of the twentieth century the discourse on racial destiny modulating theories on emigration and racial uplift had shifted shape. Reacting against a corpus of writings on Negro degeneracy and racial dissolution, African Americans recalibrated racial destiny in relation to the moral and physical health of the black body and its heirs—black children.[66] "The very concept of 'racial destiny,'" asserts Mitchell, "emphasized later generations: it implied that biological processes of generation should result in an abundance of vigorous offspring that would, in theory, continue to reproduce a hearty people."[67] Six years after the Paris exhibition, Du Bois reissued forty-eight of the photographs included in his display for the Exposition as part of the sixty-six images published in his sociological study, *The Health and Physique of the Negro American* (1906), a project that framed the conditions of black life and black futures in the context of racial intermixture. "A word may be added as to race mixture in general and as regards white and black stocks in the future," Du Bois cautioned, "There is, of course, in general no argument against the intermingling of the world's races. 'All the great peoples of the world are the result of a mixture of races.'"[68] The sixty-six photographic profiles of black men and women in this study document the diversity among black peoples.[69] Du Bois uses an alphabetic and numeric system to cross-reference four identified racial types: "Negro," "Mulatto," "Quadroon," and "White Types with Negro Blood." His classificatory practices appropriate the very anthropological strategies that had been used by white scientists in Europe and the United States to reproduce racial taxonomies. A single element within the collection of anthropological evidence published in Du Bois's study, these photographs operate alongside tables and schematics graphing physical differences: height, weight, chest, cephalic index, and intelligence.

Collectively, this documentary evidence intervenes in racialized discourses on heredity, intelligence, and moral and physical degeneracy, discourses preoccupied with the "fitness" of the black body for civil and social life. The Paris Exhibition and *The Health and the Physique of the Negro American* reflect Du Bois's earlier interest in children, education, and disease, as well as the uses to which the young adult body was deployed within his radical politics.

FIGURE 2.3 Series of portraits drawn from the 1900 American Negro exhibit in Paris. Reprinted by W. E. B. Du Bois in his Atlanta University study, *The Health and Physique of the Negro American* (1906).

Providing the photographic evidence for his 1906 study on black health and physique, these well-dressed young people were indentured to the project of racial uplift and racial ideality. The resemblances of these adolescent portraits, along with those of children and young adults in the Paris albums, to student photographs visually intimate his criteria for global change: education and knowledge (see Figure 2–3). Two additional lenses can inform how we imagine the stakes of Du Bois's educational mandates. These are the genres of the class portrait and the photographic obituary. The class portraits of black university students and black kindergarten pupils, respectively featured in the Paris Exposition and the 1906 book, visually secure his celebration of rising matriculations and literacy rates (see Figures 2–4 and 2–5).

The projects' work was extended by the annual *Crisis* education issue, which Du Bois published for several years beginning in 1911. Alongside the names of hundreds of black college students earning bachelors and graduate degrees, Du Bois would feature photographs of "ranking students," columns on fellowships and academic and athletic awards, and comparative assessments of graduation rates across a range of years. The significance of the students pictured at the Paris Exhibition and in later publications, as well as the copious data recorded in *The Health and the Physique of the Negro American* and annually in *Crisis,* should not be underestimated.[70] By documenting the accomplishments of a community only decades removed from slavery with student matriculation and graduation rates, Du Bois articulated the value of education as an instrument of social change. These representations reinforced

FIGURE 2.4 Portrait of Howard University students displayed as part of the 1900 American Negro exhibit in Paris. "Class picture, Male Students, Howard University."
The Daniel Murray Collection, Courtesy of the Library of Congress, Prints and Photographs Division (LC-USZ62–40470).

FIGURE 2.5 "Group of Children from Model School, Fisk University Nashville, Tennessee."
The Daniel Murray Collection, Courtesy of the Library of Congress, Prints and Photographs Division (LC-USZ62–54757).

classroom and student as the primary instruments of racial elevation and refuted discourses on "Negro capacity" promoted by biology, anthropology, criminology, psychology, and medicine.

Du Bois maintained a career-long interest in black health. He frequently used baby photos in periodicals like *Crisis* that mimicked the fit baby contests supported by state health boards and black club women and that appeared in magazines like the *New York Age*.[71] The "dark water" in the title of Du Bois's work refers to supremacist fears of racial propagation and imminent race war. The title worries the rhetoric of the "rising tide of color" effected through (presumably abnormal) colored fertility and reproductive rates.[72] Du Bois's emphasis on the child as world citizen plays on these fears as much as it betrays the comparatively dismal mortality rates for colored infants and children. Reflecting back on his life at the age of ninety Du Bois confessed, "The passing of my first-born boy was an experience from which I never quite recovered."[73] The death of Du Bois's two-year-old son Burghardt in the spring of 1899 from nasopharyngeal diphtheria underscores how personal this investment in improving child survival rates and black access to medical care was for this grieving father. His Paris albums of living children disturb the circulation of another set of images—postcard portraits announcing the birth and the death of a child—claiming instead a future for black children otherwise denied.[74] The catastrophe in *Darkwater*'s apocalyptic ending, "Comet," resides in the gross loss of human life produced by a crashing celestial body, and in the death of the black male survivor's baby. But what *Darkwater* only intimates in selections like "The Second Coming," Du Bois celebrates as redemptive possibility in 1928: the child savior in *Dark Princess*.

Du Bois's October 1916 children's issue of *Crisis* visually prescribes what *Darkwater* and *Dark Princess* inscribe: "the wonderful resources and healing balm" of the black child.[75] The smiling baby on the cover begins a serial representation: the issue includes more than 100 children's photos[76] (see Figure 2–6). Captioned the "child of hope," the forward gaze of a second infant featured on the editorial page captures the futurity rehearsed in the opening lines of the column that directly follows (see Figure 2–7). The symmetries in Du Bois's texts are evident in repeated titles and common theses. Like the essay on education that appeared four years later in *Darkwater*, Du Bois's editorial is entitled, "The Immortal Children."

> Children give us the real immortality," he writes, "the endless life concerning which there is no doubt or casuistry, no selfishness nor fear. With the children ... our life goes on renewed in its splendid youth, uplifted by ... its ever-glorious dreams, like to all life and yet always different because it grasps new worlds and lives in a universe continually unfolding to new possibilities.

He urges his readers to reckon with, and to support, children's responsibility. He commits adults to supporting their development in order to ensure their new world. In an eschatological tongue, he urged readers to become "the followers of their knowledges; the worshippers of their future."[77]

A book whose first articulation of the color line occurs when African American Matthew Towns is denied entrance to an obstetrical course, *Dark Princess* closes with a world reborn through a newborn. Du Bois deploys courtship and romance in this novel in the service of global decolonization. Although Matthew and Kautilya were briefly involved before his

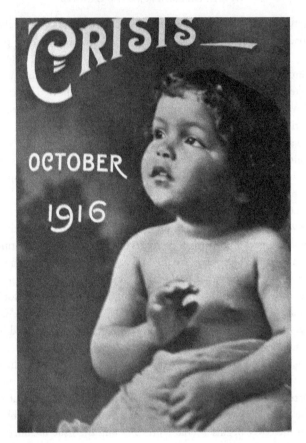

FIGURE 2.6 Cover page.
Crisis, October 1916.

FIGURE 2.7 "Child of Hope."
Editorial Page, *Crisis,* October 1916.

marriage, their eventual affair marks an illicit sexual relationship that signifies upon the illegitimacy attached to colored claims for autonomy, the hyperregulated sexuality of colonialisms, and the political and social intimacy of colonial peoples. The sexual affair has literally been *the affair* of the novel—the plotting of a new world—a plan secured in the eventual birth of their son. The erotica depicted in the novel calls attention to a tradition of discourse on black sexuality enlisted to persecute, discipline, and even kill black and brown bodies. Here illicit love and sex become the precondition for paradise.

Du Bois announces the reunion of the two estranged lovers in a marriage ceremony, after Mathew's divorce from his wife, Sara. Here the preacher's text is instructive. Upending articulations of the imminent race war found in black radical and white supremacist discourses during the first two decades of the century, Du Bois limns his new political geography with an apocalyptic vision of paradise. Supplementing the biblical imagery of resurrection and rebirth, drowning and revelation, which make up the symbolic grammar of the novel, the minister reads from St. John's apocalyptic vision in Revelation. The verses from the seventh chapter recall God's promise to preserve the faithful, a body that will be drawn from "every nation, from all tribes and peoples and tongues."[78] Straddling political, ethnic, and religious traditions, baby Madhu (Matthew) embodies Du Bois's, Kautilya's, and Matthew's Pan-African and Pan-Asian fourth dimension; he is "Messenger and Messiah to all the Darker Worlds!"[79] Stripped of locatives—name, age, or hometown—the 100 children pictured on the pages of the October *Crisis* (1916) are likewise not "individual children." Rather, they pointedly "belong," in the words of Du Bois, to no persons and no families; they belong to a great people, and in their hands is that people's future."[80]

Du Bois's internationalism admittedly provides a literal and figural conceptual model for cooperation among the "darker world" that reinstalls U.S. supremacy and risks provincializing race. Nonetheless, his portrayal of children as world citizens is strategic and valuable.[81] Du Bois's insistence on the redemptive character of babies was certainly both a symptom of his cultural moment and an intervention in it. The children that Du Bois celebrated—Madhu, the young adults of the Paris albums and *Health,* the infants featured on the pages of the *Crisis*—reprimand social and scientific charges of black inferiority. More urgently, his prophetic equation—child equals world citizen—renders children blank slates for a range of sexual, political, and economic orthodoxies that tend to determine material conditions confronting the dark world. These accumulating representations of the redemptive child offer a shorthand and a method for enunciating a cosmopolitan future. Citing the photographed young men and women in *Health* as evidence of race-mixture, Du Bois predicts:

> Upon the whole, if we consider (1) that the most mixed and most civilized races are those which are soonest acclimatized, (2) that the tendency of races to intermingle, and of civilization to develop, goes on increasing every day in every part of the world, we may affirm without being accused of exaggeration that the cosmopolitanism of mankind, if it does not yet exist today in all races . . . will develop as a necessary consequence of the facility of acclimatation. For it to become general is only a matter of time.[82]

Children become the buds with which Du Bois will propagate his agenda.

Children alone, however, are not sufficient cause for a new world. Educational reform and democratized industrialism are also needed to realize his ambition. The cathexis of child with world citizen extends the humanism that supplements Du Bois's rooted cosmopolitanism.[83] Accordingly, if children belong to no one, if children belong to the world, then to be a world citizen expresses an ethical and social philosophy of shared humanity, of shared life, and of mutual obligation. Within the Christian imagery suffusing *Darkwater* and *Dark Princess*, these primary social obligations are a postscript to "I am my brother's keeper." And although the name "world citizen" confirms the secondary role of national and ethnic differences to human rights, Du Bois refuses to demean the material effects and value of identity politics. While he might argue that state sovereignty should not curtail human development or imperil human life, either at home or abroad, ethnic, gender, racial, religious, and generational differences nevertheless continue to form the core of his democracy. His just world surfaces through the complex negotiations that must occur when all knowledge traditions are voiced and respected.

RACE AND THE PROBLEM OF PEACE

The interest in an alternative political space and praxis announced in the visions of Banneker, Griggs, and Du Bois constitutes a utopian call for asylum. The black emigrationist projects that began in the late eighteenth and continued through the nineteenth century are among the imagined and realized ventures for an alternative black space. Texts like Martin R. Delany's *The Condition, Elevation, Emigration, And Destiny of the Colored People of the United States Politically Considered* (1852) and the *Official Report of the Niger Valley Exploring Party* (1861) are part of more than a century of writings entertaining the possibility of black emigration to states such as Liberia, Nigeria, and Haiti. They reflect more than a century of pleas for sanctuary—relief from the indignities, prohibitions, and assaults of racism. James T. Holly's "Thoughts on Haiti" of 1859 urged black expatriation to the island. Printed during the U.S. Civil War, James Redpath's *Guide to Hayti* (1861) echoed Prince Saunders's 1818 claim that Haiti indeed presented an "asylum" for black people. With chapters on climate, geography, natural resources, vegetation, and available land, Redpath's *Guide* encouraged emigration to Haiti.[84] By 1900 President Theodore Roosevelt had sent T. Thomas Fortune to scout and assess the prospects for black resettlement in Hawaii, Puerto Rico, and the Philippines.[85] Emigrationist responses to U.S. racism persisted throughout the twentieth century, capturing the support of thousands of black American who invested in the Universal Negro Improvement Association's (UNIA) Black Star Line, the fleet of Marcus Garvey's "Back-to-Africa" movement.[86]

As Michele Mitchell posits, emigrationist campaigns betray the conjunction of territory and civil identity.[87] Space is about privilege and access. Writing in a tradition that includes Sutton Griggs's *Imperium in Imperio*, George Schuyler's *Black Empire*, and Chester Himes's *Plan B*, Du Bois's democratic experiment equally resonated with the ambitions of the Exodusters;[88] Zora Neale Hurston's Eatonville, Florida; Francis Boyer's Blackdom, New Mexico; and Kendleton, Texas; Boley, Creek Nation Indian Territory (now Oklahoma); Lovejoy, Illinois; and Princeville, North Carolina—an imagined territory beyond racism. Blacks within the United States have long understood and lived David Delaney's "geographies of race," and this geography remains sensitive to economic, social, and political crises. The topography of African American utopian discourses is marked by the imperative to rearticulate space, to reimagine black futures that are otherwise denied by racism. Although Du Bois might have proclaimed the world citizen as the resident of his fourth dimension, our contemporary moment demands a further particularization. What is at stake here is the status of black life within the United States and within the world. If the problem of the twentieth century has been the problem of the color line, then I hazard that the problem of—and the figure for—the twenty-first century is the refugee.

Du Bois opens *Dark Princess* with a recurring theme of dislocation. Sailing aboard the *Orizaba* (named after the ship Du Bois took to the Paris Peace Conference and Pan-African Congress), Matthew is literally and figuratively unmoored. He is an "exile," stationed at "the edge of the world": "Where *was* he going?"[89] His watery isolation confirms his political provisionality, his alienation from a homeland that more than disapproves of—in fact, persistently reprimands—him for his blackness. Although Du Bois redefines black Americans as semicolonials, Matthew's liminality, however brief, signifies upon stateless persons, exiles, and refugees. A disruptive social force, the refugee is a liminal figure inhabiting a political narthex, the threshold between nation-states. The refugee challenges the borders of state power and state law. It has been more than eighty years since Du Bois first outlined his plan. The "children's children" that Du Bois expected to achieve his "fourth dimension" are now nearing retirement age. They are the generation of civil rights activists from the 1950s and 1960s. And yet, if we read his world citizen as a figure to whom we are all responsible—whose condition challenges poverty, racism, sexism, colonialism, religious intolerance, illness, disease, privatized resources, economic exploitation, industrial monopolies, political tyranny, and defense mechanisms—then perhaps we should stop gazing forward like Du Bois's "immortal child," and attend to our own citizens of the world: refugees and stateless persons.

Du Bois's persistent articulation of the primacy of African Americans and colored peoples within global debates on governance, law, capital, and culture, and their entailments, intervenes in debates on cosmopolitanism and human rights, while engaging the figure of the refugee, a category that includes black diasporic peoples. To this end, I urge a reexamination of what Du Bois meant when he insisted that not only democracy, but also global legal and political cultures and global peace are risked by the presence of disenfranchised black peoples within the United States. Two years before drafting his petition to the United Nations on behalf of Rosa Lee Ingram, Du Bois served as the editor for, and wrote the introduction to, the National Association for the Advancement of Colored People's (NAACP) U.N. petition titled *An Appeal to the World: A Statement on the Denial of Human Rights to Minorities in the Case of Citizens of Negro Descent in the United States of American and an Appeal to the United Nations for Redress* (1947).[90] Turning his attention to the Congressional elections of 1946, Du Bois vividly graphed the failures of a representative government in which the majority of the population remained either disenfranchised or "discouraged" from voting. Tracing the racial, gendered, and economically driven voting disparities that enabled Congressional representatives from states like South Carolina to gain office with only several thousand votes— compared to the more than 100,000 needed for Midwestern seats[91]—Du Bois located black people outside of U.S. political culture and exposed segregation as an example of a state of exception. In keeping with his other writings, his introduction to *An Appeal to the World* reviews a history of "unhomeliness";[92] forced migration; and lost political, economic, and social futures experienced by blacks in the United States. This history should be read alongside the writings of intellectuals and political theorists similarly engaged with questions of human and civil rights intensified by the mass populations of displaced, "rightless" persons whose numbers rose in the aftermath of the two world wars. When Du Bois contended in 1947 that the disenfranchisement of more than "three-fourths of the Negro population of the nation" was in fact as much an international as national crisis, he intervened in a larger discourse on human rights for refugees, stateless persons, and colonial and semicolonial peoples, communities collectively outside of the law and within what Hannah Arendt labeled the "law of exception."[93] It is anything but incidental that in the aftermath of a war for democracy, black civil rights, decolonization struggles, and debates over human rights intensified. I am neither dismissing nor arguing against the agency of black peoples in the New World (specifically the United States) or the kinds of communities, institutions, and cultural expressions shaped by the experience of disenfranchisement. Rather, I am seeking to underline the history of reprisals, violence, and prohibitions systematically deployed in hopes of curtailing, if not completely disabling, these same social, political, and cultural formations. Indeed, the social, political, and cultural formations they have historically produced mark convergences of blacks, stateless persons, and refugees, and offer a testament to the agency and political possibility that Arendt's writings seem to foreclose.

According to Du Bois, black semicoloniality commands international attention not merely out of sympathetic or empathetic identification, but in part because discriminatory policies seep into—withholding and imperiling—the rights and lives of colored foreigners living in or traveling through the United States.[94] For Arendt, the law of exception (i.e., U.S. segregation, in this context) produced to negotiate the presence of the stateless person or refugee means that the civil rights and liberties of all persons within the polis are at risk. On this matter she writes:

> The nation-state cannot exist once its principle of equality before the law has broken down. Without this legal equality . . . the nation dissolves into an anarchic mass of over-and underprivileged individuals. Laws that are not equal for all revert to rights and privileges, something contradictory to the very nature of nation-states. The clearer the proof of their inability to treat stateless people as legal persons and the greater the extension of arbitrary rule by police decree, the more difficult it is for states to resist the temptation to deprive all citizens of legal status.[95]

The way in which a governing body responds to refugees does indeed serve as a litmus test for the stability of the political rights and privileges enjoyed by the polis as a whole. Du Bois said that peace can never come in a world that remains captivated by racism; peace can never come in the absence of worldwide democracy. Written in the midst of India's struggle for colonial independence, *Dark Princess* critically dismissed Garveyism, revolutionary black militancy, and a professed U.S. republicanism, and instead advocated the civil disobedience best practiced by Mahatma Gandhi.[96] Access to Du Bois's fourth dimension is predicated on civil disobedience and on the expansion of human rights, rights that continue to be affected by the proliferating presence of the refugee.

In his testimony to the Senate Foreign Relations Committee gathered on July 11, 1945 to deliberate the ratification of the United Nation's founding charter, Du Bois underscored how human rights, the promised work of this international body, remained compromised in this proposed agreement. He pinpoints his "reservations" with respect to the millions of colonized people worldwide, a community virtually unrepresented by the draft. The question of "representation" and "recognition" threads through his remarks, and stitches together an outline of the problem of incorporation, which is the predicate for human rights. It is a problem intimately connected to what Arendt describes as "legal personality." The failure to grant representation on the Trustee Council to "native colonial peoples" whose countries remained under the administration of the United Nations, or "even of giving them the right of oral petition, or of making any investigation into colonial conditions except under the eye of the governing power," undercut in Du Bois's estimation the very logic of this international governing body. The shape and substance of the promise to "reaffirm faith in fundamental human rights" and to "promote and encourage respect for human rights and for the fundamental freedoms for all without distinction as to race, sex, language or religion" announced in the Preamble to the charter was compromised by this symbolic disenfranchisement of colonies.[97] Common to both his remarks before the Senate Foreign Relations Committee and his *Appeal* two years later to the U.N. Human Rights Commission, is the larger question of legal recognition necessary for meaningful incorporation within a political body. The history of the state's conjunction of "rights" to "recognition" and of its refusal in turn to imagine black Americans as bearers of a legal personality has helped shape a state of exception in the U.S. that began with slavery.

The conception of human rights, based upon the assumed existence of a human being as such, broke down at the very moment when those who professed to believe in it were for the first time confronted with people who had indeed lost all other qualities and specific relationships—except that they were still human. The world found nothing sacred in the abstract nakedness of being human.
HANNAH ARENDT, *The Origins of Totalitarianism*

American humanity hates us, scorns us, disowns and denies, in a thousand ways, our very personality.
FREDERICK DOUGLASS, "A Nation in the Midst of a Nation"

3

Sanctuary

WHEN THEY ARRESTED and held him for four days in the spring of 1854, Anthony Burns had been walking a familiar route from his laundering and clothing repair job. He was simply and significantly a black fugitive.[1] His capture inspired the Boston slave riot, drawing several thousand to the courthouse square where he was interned, guarded by marines, city militia, police personnel, newly deputized civilians, and a U.S. marshal, Watson Freeman. Within hours the mayor had called upon the military, and militias stationed nearby began to guard the courthouse. Standing before congregants at a black Baptist church in New York a year later, Burns would recall the events of that night, a night leading to his reenslavement and later to his freedom, purchased for $1,300:

> When I was going home one night I heard some one running behind me; presently a hand was put on my shoulder, and somebody said: "Stop, stop; you are the fellow who broke into a silversmith's shop the other night." I assured the man that it was a mistake, but almost before I could speak, I was lifted from off my feet by six or seven others, and it was no use to resist.... I told them I wanted to go home for supper. A man then come to the door; he didn't open it like an honest man would, but kind of slowly opened it, and looked in. He said, "How do you do, Mr. Burns?" And I called him as we do in Virginia, "master!"[2]

Burns's exchange with the slave catchers is instructive, pointing to the larger protocols of misrecognition, criminalization, linguistic dissemblance, and power structuring black encounters with the law. It is an encounter that points to a legal demeanor Paul Laurence Dunbar would characterize almost fifty years later, stating, "No one has the right to base any conclusions about Negro criminality based on the number of prisoners in the jails and other places of restraint. Even in the North the prejudice against the Negro reverses the precedents of law, and everyone accused is looked upon as guilty until proven innocent."[3] At each point, Burns is thwarted. The certainty of his guilt marked in his accusers' declarative—"You are the fellow who broke into a silversmith's shop"—registers the ways in which the legal presumption of innocence is suspended for African Americans. His speech resembles a kind of linguistic dissemblance: it is stunted and interrupted not simply by the imposition of hands carrying him presumably to jail, but also disregarded because of his blackness. His capture, trial, and subsequent remanding back into slavery speak to a failure to recognize his personhood, which expresses the fundamental problematic of the black body—slave, fugitive, or free. His case rehearses a racialized syntax of legal personhood and political recognition shaping the body of this chapter, namely the anopticism that both obscures and dehumanizes black subjectivity, the instability of black speech, and the criminalization of the black body. And although Burns's voice does not appear within the trial transcripts and social texts surrounding his arrest (the legal prohibitions against slave testimony gagged him), his compliance with the required racial protocols of self-deprecation ("I called him as we do in Virginia, 'master!'") only further indicted him: both the plaintiff's attorney and Commissioner Edward Loring interpreted the social etiquette as a confession of ownership. The false pretenses under which Burns was captured calls attention to the politics of legal recognition outlined in his arrest.

This chapter addresses the material consequences of denying legal subjectivity and political recognition to individuals, namely dehumanization. For it is when persons no longer appear as such—when their humanity is no longer apprehended or recognized—that they fall outside the precincts of law and are increasingly at risk of assault, if not murder. They no longer count. With a reading of Herman Melville's 1855 novella, "Benito Cereno," I examine what it means to be outside of the law and thus outlawed. Relying on a repertoire of racialized visual codes, Melville takes on the effects of what Maurice Wallace called "spectra-graphia," a "doubly spectral and spectacle perceptibility in the public eye," posited by a simultaneous visual excess and insufficiency that produces "a chronic syndrome of inscripted misrepresentation."[4] This scopophilic preoccupation with the black body sets the pace for the forms of racial profiling, withheld legal protections, and legal depersonification that will mark the inscriptional moment of Melville's story. These spectragraphic investments obscure the visibility of the black body, tilting perception away from, if not completely disavowing, the humanity of the enslaved. "Benito Cereno" offers a rubric for reading the relationship of the law to the black body that will continue to inform our legal culture even after emancipation. This point cannot be overstated, particularly if it is our hope to more fully appreciate the manner in which slavery survives within the constitutive makeup of U.S. legal and political culture as the interface through which rights became contingent on political membership and the subsequent acknowledgment of a legal personality.[5] Drilling down on the substantive social and political implications of legal recognition, Melville mines this central problem that has shaped the relationship between blacks and U.S. legal culture (i.e., law and jurisprudence). He reveals how legal recognition serves the state as an instrument buttressing rights and conferring citizenship. Melville's attention to the racial politics and political effects of legal recognition adumbrates the critique written by Supreme Court Justice John Marshall Harlan in his 1883 dissent to the Civil Rights Cases in which Harlan opined that challenges to black civil liberties have arisen from a failure to recognize blacks' "legal right" to citizenship, to see "them as a component part of the people for whose welfare and happiness government is ordained."[6]

Melville's story grapples with the social and legal dislocation of the black body, figured in practices of misrecognition and disarticulation, of which Anthony Burns's case is a historical example. Melville's text examines the bankruptcy of a social economy in which the value of human life is predicated on civil identity, the social and legal legibility of injury is dictated by racialized protocols for citizenship, and race dictates legitimacy and mitigates forms of legal competency. A story tracking U.S. imperial ambitions and slave culture during the first half of the nineteenth century, "Benito Cereno" speaks to the geopolitical scales of race: in other words, its international and domestic character. It wrestles with the consequences of colonialism and slavery in the formation of national bodies (citizens) that the slaver and its cargo belie. Studying the homology that emerges between sanctuary and asylum in "Benito Cereno," this chapter focuses on the figure of the refugee, pointing to the resemblance between this figure and communities of black people throughout the Atlantic world, but most specifically those in the United States.

FUGITIVE

"Slavery was in the *Government of the land*," preached Samuel Johnson at the Free Church in Lynn, Massachusetts, two weeks after Burns's incarceration. "Massachusetts had her hand clasped in the slaveholder's clutch; she dared not withdraw it, because the *Slaveholder was the Government.*"[7] For many, Burns's captivity in the courthouse showed a state transformed by the 1850 Fugitive Slave Act. This legislation transformed judicial institutions into "garrisoned slave pens," purchased government officials for its cause, secured military and police support for "kidnappers,"[8] promised the assistance of every American in identifying and remanding slaves back to their masters, and created a new breed of legally unassailable civil servants who would arbitrate life and death for the enslaved. Before a crowd of more than 4,000 gathered at Faneuil Hall two days after Burns's arrest, Wendell Phillips argued, "There is now no law in Massachusetts. . . . The people may act in their own sovereignty."[9] Weeks after Burns's arrest Thomas Wentworth Higginson reframed the political stakes of these events for the Boston public, arguing that democracy had been supplanted by martial law, the State by "military despotism":

> If we are all Slaves indeed—if there is no law in Massachusetts except the telegraphic orders from Washington—if our own military are to be Slave-catchers—if our Governor is a mere piece of State ceremony, permitted only to rise at a military dinner and thank his soldiers for their readiness to shoot down his own constituents, without even the delay of a riot act—if Massachusetts is merely a conquered province under martial law—*then I wish to know it*, and I am grateful for every additional gun and sabre that forces the truth deeper into our hearts. *Lower, Massachusetts, lower, kneel still lower!*[10]

"In view of these facts," Higginson demanded, "what stands between us and a military despotism? . . . What is your safeguard? Nothing but a parchment Constitution which has been riddled through and through whenever it pleased the Slave Power."[11] This singular act—the 1850 Fugitive Slave Law—deformed legal culture. Yet, casting abolitionists and the white body politic as "all Slaves" was more than simply an effective rhetorical device for Higginson.

Although this collapsed identification between white and black, free and fugitive, unquestionably supplants the subject of his polemic, Anthony Burns, it also recalls the problem of sovereignty advanced by Wendell Phillips. Phillips and Higginson both describe a lawlessness produced by the suspension of law, that in and of itself creates an alternative set of norms. To suspend law is to revise and install a different legal order—in this context, martial law.

There were many remarkable additions to the 1850 law against which Phillips and Higginson railed. Like the predecessor it amended, the 1850 act significantly failed to mention either slavery or race, carefully defining fugitivity instead as an escape from "labor service."[12] Passed in the midst of France's decade-long revolution, only four years after its Declaration of the Rights of Man and of the Citizen and two years after the Haitian Revolution had begun, the Act Respecting Fugitives from Justice and Persons Escaping from the Service of Their Masters (1793) reflected the ideological disconnect of a State seemingly disarticulated from the globally felt campaigns for political and racial equality being waged throughout the Atlantic world. For although black Jacobins were transforming the nature and condition of citizenship within France's shifting political system, the United States was recodifying the status of the black body, free or otherwise, as slave. The 1850 revisions to the first Fugitive Slave Law should be considered in relation to Britain's abolition of the slave trade (1807) and slavery throughout the commonwealth and Britain's colonies (1833), the Haitians' independence (1804), and the struggles for independence in Latin America (Bolivar's War, 1811–1825). With the 1850 Fugitive Slave Law, the United States further abrogated human rights, promised State assistance in the capture and sale of slaves, facilitated the kidnapping and sale of free people, and suspended legal protections, including habeas corpus, trial by jury, and rules of evidence.

Required by law to assist in the kidnapping, detention, and remanding of reported fugitive slaves, by 1850 all citizens became potential slave catchers, subject to fines and jail time if they refused or failed in their civil obligation.[13] Government officials, police personnel, and the military were now the sanctioned arm of slaveholders. They were required to "hunt men and women and children, as wild beasts, and to restore them to slavery."[14] The law also engendered a value system in which money outweighed ethics. U.S. marshals were subject to $1,000 penalties for failing to execute a warrant or successfully secure a fugitive, whereas the commissioners in charge of these proceedings were paid $10.00 for every case settled in favor of the slaveholder and $5.00 for every outcome favorable to the fugitive.[15] The financial disincentives transforming civil servants into bounty hunters were comparable to the altered role of the judiciary. Armed with the same jurisdictional reach and privileges of judges, the commissioners' decisions were final. In his history of constitutional law and congressional legislation, D. M. Dewey would write in 1854, "Not only does this law take from all Northern men every legal right, but it forbids all the tribunals of the country, whether state or nation, to interfere in their behalf if demanded as Slaves, by any perjured scoundrel who may have the audacity to make the demand and swear to it."[16] Denied due process, the writ of habeas corpus, and the right to testify on their own behalf, and confronted instead with diluted evidentiary standards, black defendants were not simply voiceless, but legally without recourse. In its protection of slaveholders, the Fugitive Slave Act evacuated constitutional privileges and reframed political power. Reducing state and federal courts to advisers, the law stripped the courts of their role as legal interpreters and lawmakers. We cannot underestimate the significance of this moment and its mimetic replays during states of war, states of emergency, and perhaps most discomfitingly, in the United State's dealings with immigrants, refugees, and the ill.

Restructuring the law, its institutions, and the role of its administrators, the 1850 law yielded a variant of Gerald Neuman's "anomalous zones." Anomalous zones create extralegal spaces. They are sites where the suspension of law replaces one juridical code with another. Anomalous zones are state sanctioned, frequently cordoned or mappable spaces in which substantive legal, social, and cultural norms are suspended. According to Neuman, anomalous zones impose a peculiar breed of law and order, singularly affecting those within its jurisdiction. They are areas that include, by Neuman's account, New Orleans's Storyville, a sanctioned red-light district created in 1897, that strictly regulated and restricted to a twenty-block area the bodies and residences of prostitutes. Under the ordinance, which remained in effect until 1917, it was "'unlawful for any public prostitute or woman notoriously abandoned to lewdness to occupy, inhabit, live, or sleep in any house, room, or closet situated' outside the district."[17] The compass of the Fugitive Slave Law extended to wherever the fugitive traveled. The anomalous zones that contained fugitive slaves, wherever they might flee, are properly described as sanctuaries: spaces that mirror and sustain the violence that erected them. Further extending the legal reach of the slave codes, the fugitive slave acts (e.g., the Black codes and Jim Crow laws that came later) halted constitutional law and produced a racialized set of norms that helped bring to fruition the state's vision of an ideal polity—its vision of a political paradise.

Denied access to his client, Burns's attorney, Richard Dana, had been retained less than a day when he went before the court on the fugitive's behalf.[18] Outlining in his argument the gravity of these "examinations" whose outcomes were final, he "urged delay." "This is not a case of extradition, and the prisoner goes to no other court," insisted Dana. "He is given to the man who calls himself his master, and in his custody he remains."[19] Without evidence beyond a statement of ownership and without prior knowledge of those presenting their claims, commissioners sat in judgment on the lives of the enslaved. Their deliberations were undoubtedly influenced by the promised fee, which all but ensured a favorable outcome for the claimant. The fugitivity of the runaway slave was marked more emphatically by a law that remained fugitive to them—perpetually deferred, detained, and withheld.

According to Herman Melville's biographer, Hershel Parker, the circumstances of Burns's arrest and trial in May of 1854 were of little moment to the writer, whose summary response to the events matched Parker's own sardonic frame: "He was a galley-slave himself, in the grim pun, and a slave to secret debt. 'Who ain't a slave?' he had asked."[20] Parker claims that Melville not only removed himself from this case and the national slavery debate, but subscribed to a belief that mixing politics with craft was an occupational hazard. In the margins of his copy of Milton's "Lycidas," Melville wrote, "'Mark the deforming effect of the intrusion of partisan topics and feelings of the day, however serious in import, into a poem otherwise of the first order of merit.'"[21] Parker's biography, however, intimates a political consciousness that both he (and Melville himself) refuse to acknowledge in the writer:

Like poverty, slavery was not an imaginary evil, but it was not the evil Melville focused on, even when a Boston mob stormed his father-in-law's bastion, the courthouse. . . . Melville was not oblivious to what was going on in Boston, and not blind to the great national sin of slavery, but he was a man with obligations as a husband, father, son, son-in-law, and brother (a condition he always viewed in the light of the New Testament's absolutism).[22]

The proximity of Melville to these historic events troubles, if not undermines, Parker's assessment of Melville's absolutism. Its proximity, when read alongside "Benito Cereno," complicates our understanding of Melville's reputed response, his marginalia, and Parker's interpretation of the writer's relationship to slavery. By Parker's own admission, the *Boston Investigator* recorded the Burns dispute as "perhaps unparalleled by any event since the revolutionary war," a sentiment reiterated in many of the surviving social texts.[23]

Burns's kidnapping and arrest resulted in the Boston slave riot, garnered national interest, and prompted sufficient anxiety within the administration to require a presidential dispatch. The ensuing legal transformations raised by the proceedings required the attention of Melville's father-in-law, Lemuel Shaw, chief justice of Massachusetts's Supreme Judicial Court. Although Shaw had long been a respected abolitionist, his moral and political convictions became casualties when he unequivocally upheld the rule of law. "After his appointment as chief justice in 1830," notes Robert Wallace, "Lemuel Shaw 'defined the law of freedom and bondage in Massachusetts.' He became known as the judge eager to free any slave who had been brought voluntarily by an owner onto Massachusetts soil."[24] The same Shaw who earlier in his career denounced slavery in the *North American Review* but insisted that the South settle on its own its "internal trade," and who had secured the freedom of a six-year-old slave girl transported into Massachusetts by her master, scrupulously enforced the 1850 Fugitive Slave Act.[25] Shaw was involved in the adjudication of at least two earlier proceedings in Boston against fugitive slaves, Frederick Wilkins Shadrach (1846) and Thomas Sims (1851).[26] In the Sims incident, witnesses recalled the judge bending under the chains encircling the court building in consequence of the fugitive's arrest, a posture he was forced to resume because of Burns. Coming on the heels of Shadrach's and Sims's recent remands into slavery, Burns became a litmus test for New Englanders on their commitment to liberty and on their willingness to defy a federal and local government that had increasingly succumbed to Southern demands. In defiance of the verdict in Burns's case, in 1855 Massachusetts passed a personal liberty law similar to the Pennsylvania ordinance vacated in *Prigg* v. *Pennsylvania* (1842). And although personal liberty laws would continue to appear in states throughout the Union in response to the Fugitive Slave Law, the passage of such a law in Massachusetts prompted the ire of Lemuel Shaw. Committed more to the idea of a Union than its realization, Shaw bent once again before slavery, offering a formal apology to Southern slaveholders.[27]

Although Hershel Parker argues that the historical record preserves few of Melville's reactions to these events or to the national slavery crisis (further enflamed by the Compromise of 1850, the Fugitive Slave Law, and the Nebraska Bill of 1854), Melville's fiction gives us insight into the writer's politics. How can we take seriously Parker's remarks that "Melville's way of responding to the Burns case was to reflect more deeply on the American national character rather than on the specific issue of slavery"?[28] Melville understood that slavery could not be separated from the "national character," and further, that it figured centrally in the ambit of expansionist projects in the South and West. His writings confirmed slavery's role as the hinge upon which the Union turned. The legal and social landscape of Melville's Massachusetts was transfigured by the recurring spectacle of the fugitive slave body, a body literally conveyed through city streets by throngs, whose face and condition plastered walls, attracted mobs, and incited violence.

The problem of fugitivity articulated in the slave body was familiar to Melville, who first broached the topic in his writing the year before he penned "Benito Cereno." Melville condensed the history of a slave revolution, slave insurrections on the Spanish *Tyral* (1805) and *Amistad* (1839), and the 1817 travel memoirs of the American ship Capt. Amasa Delano (*Narrative of the Voyages and Travels*) in his account of the politics of freedom and empire building. Published in installments in *Putnam Monthly* one year after the Boston slave riot and half a century after the Haitian Revolution, Melville's "Benito Cereno" (1855) translated domestic unrest along transnational axes, situating the problem of slavery at the heart of what Parker called the "national character" and teasing out the relationship between fugitivity and political recognition. Writing before the specters of Anthony Burns, Frederick Wilkins Shadrach, and Thomas Sims and in the midst of continued kidnappings aboard merchant ships of free black seamen from Massachusetts and the Northeast,[29] Melville's novella was an explicit response to globally felt political shifts. Locating his novella in the 1790s, Melville engaged the political conflicts of his contemporary moment—slavery and fugitivity—in relation to an abolitionist movement influenced by the Enlightenment discourse on citizenship and political rights that emerged out of the French and Haitian Revolutions. He rendered the implicit (and frequently explicit) interconnections between domestic policies and international relations. Melville's dating of his story in 1799, the year the Haitian Revolution formally began, and his decision to name the Spanish slaver *San Dominick*, an allusion to Haiti's colonial name—St. Domingue—reveal "Benito Cereno" to be a revisionist history of Haiti.[30] Critics' unwillingness to read the political framing of "Benito Cereno" until the last several decades is symptomatic of the same refusals that surrendered the role of Haiti in modernity, in the Age of Revolution, and in international politics to a footnote while overwriting her place in histories of disease.[31]

The politics of captivity demonstrated in Melville's imbricated histories of slavery—the *Tryal,* the *Amistad,* and the Haitian Revolution (and their related economies of capital and power)—represent a broader cultural logic of citizenship. Chronicling the encounter of an American sea captain with a seemingly abandoned, but in fact badly undermanned, Spanish schooner after a slave mutiny, "Benito Cereno" is a fictional treatise on the politics of asylum. Melding the *Amistad* trials of the 1840s into the historical syntax of his novella, Melville stages both the status of stateless persons and refugees, and the contingencies of asylum. A proceeding marked by the petitions for freedom and repatriation to what we now describe as a "safe third country," the *Amistad* hearings prefigure the immigration policy of political asylum cases after World War II.[32]

INTERNMENT

"Let the slave-holders in our Southern states tremble," declared William Wells Brown, "when they shall call to mind these events. . . . Who knows but that a Toussaint, a Christophe, a Rigaud, a Clervaux, and a Dessalines, may some day appear in the Southern States of this Union?"[33] Brown would give his lecture on "St. Domingo: Its Revolutions and Its Patriots" twice in 1854, once before the Metropolitan Atheneum in London and again at St. Thomas's Church in Philadelphia. That same year, Theodore Holly spearheaded the Negro National Emigrationists' plans to resettle in Haiti and began talks with the island's administration to secure black American immigration to the island.[34] Haiti, an island roughly 700 miles from the United States, inspired abolitionist propaganda at the same rate that slaveholders sought to suppress news of her existence. For politicians like Thomas Jefferson, Haiti portended a resolution to racial tensions. She stood as an expected sanctuary, an emigration site for freedmen in the inevitable event of slave emancipation. Haiti offered an example of a successful insurrection to slaves like Nat Turner and gave hope to an enslaved Frederick Douglass. Read as the standard of possibility for blacks, her sovereignty provided the theme for a fundraiser in 1841 intended to offset the expense of building an orphanage for 800 African American children in Philadelphia.[35] Her revolutionary history contested theories of limited "Negro capacity." Like Liberia and Ethiopia, Haiti became and remained a sanctuary within the political and cultural imaginary of the Americas throughout the eighteenth, nineteenth, and the early twentieth centuries. In his 1818 address to the American Convention for Promoting the Abolition of Slavery and Improving the Condition of the African Race, Prince Saunders characterized Haiti as "an Asylum." To the crowd he stated, "Among the various projects or plans which have been devised or suggested, in relation to emigration, there are none which appear to many persons to wear so much the appearance of feasibility, and ultimate successful and practical operation, as the luxuriant, beautiful and extensive island of Hayti (or St. Domingo)."[36] Saunders's Haiti reads like pages torn from a Fodor's travel guide—"paradise of the New World" with its "28,000 square kilometers; its 84,617,328 pounds of coffee; 217,463 casks of sugar, white and brown; and 5,836 casks of molasses." His Haiti would be a refuge for freed and newly emancipated African Americans. Forty-two years later, James Redpath would make a similar plea in his *Guide to Hayti* (1860), first printed by Thayer and Eldridge in Boston and reprinted the following year by the Haytian Bureau of Emigration:

> There is only one country in the Western World where the Black and the man of color are undisputed lords; where the White is indebted for the liberty to live to the race which with us is enslaved; where neither laws, nor prejudices, nor historical memories, press cruelly on persons of African Descent; where the people whom America degrades and drives from her are rulers, judges, and generals; men of extended commercial relations, authors, artists, and legislators; where the insolent question, so often asked with us, "What would become of the Negro if Slavery were abolished?" is answered by the fact of an independent Nationality of immovable stability, and a Government inspired with the spirit of progress. The name of this country is Hayti.[37]

Redpath's guide bore a striking resemblance to the guide Thomas Jefferson drafted to encourage emigration to Virginia, *Notes on the State of Virginia*. Replete with chapters ranging from "The Geography of Hayti," "The Animal Kingdom," "The Vegetable Kingdom," and "The Mineral Kingdom," to "Vacant Lands" and "How to Go, and What to Take to Hayti," Redpath's manual encouraged African American colonization. By 1860 the Haitian government had assured Redpath that newly emigrating blacks would enjoy religious freedom, "access to the land, liberal political privileges, and free passage to the island if desired."[38] The following year, Frederick Douglass, whose support of emigration was brief at best, lent pages of the *Douglass' Monthly* to this recruitment project, routinely featuring advertisements on the island's government in an effort to inspire interest in and immigration to Haiti.[39] In the spring of 1861, the *Pine and Palm*, the official serial of Redpath's Haitian colonization scheme, was in circulation with Redpath and George Lawrence, Jr., respectively, acting as its Boston and New York editors. Committed to "the triumph of the Democratic Idea in this Continent and its islands . . . the elevation of the Negro to a position of perfect Social, Political, and National Equality and Power with the Whites," the editorials in the *Pine and Palm* regularly critiqued U.S. slavery and failed national politics, while pushing Haiti as the seat for a new black republic. "I hope, my friends, you will not stay in America, and die under the influence of the word negro, as you are called" implored an essayist writing from St. Marc in the *Pine and Palm*.[40] Within a year the emigrationist efforts of Redpath and his agents had inspired Haiti emigration clubs in various parts of the United States. Between December 1860 and 1862 an estimated 2,000 to 3,000 African Americans set sail for Haiti as part of Redpath's St. Marc colony experiment. Despite the failure of this and other colonization experiments on the island—like the misguided project at Ile á Vache—the revolutionary sentiments and promise held within the first sovereign black nation and second state of the New World would continue to hold claims on the U.S. political and cultural imagination well into the nineteenth and twentieth centuries.

Melville turned his attention to the historical topography of this imagined refuge for black fugitives and freed persons alike. A study on the interplay between injury and political recognition, "Benito Cereno" opens with a vision of sanctuary. Yet to read sanctuary is to read a crisis of political recognition produced through legal and historical misrepresentations, misprisions, and anopticisms. Melville's iconography of political recognition is built of tropes on vision and perception. The question of vision—literally and figurally translated in the text as apprehension, recognition, or discernment—appears in the opening paragraphs of the story in connection to sanctuary. Melville presents us with Capt. Delano, an American, anchored off the coast of St. Maria, and he cannot see ahead because of dense fog. And although his vision is challenged in these opening sequences, it is his naiveté that impairs his perception throughout the story. Collectively, this shortsightedness engenders sympathy for and identification with his failure or refusal to recognize the authority of the slaves aboard who, having revolted, are now in charge of the Spanish *San Dominick*. Responding to his first mate's observation of a "strange sail . . . coming into bay," Capt. Delano boards a whale-boat to gain a "less remote view." The narrator observes:

> The morning was one peculiar to the coast. Everything was mute and calm; everything gray. The sea, though undulated into long roods of swells, seemed fixed, and was sleeked at the surface like waved lead that has cooled and set in the smelter's mould. The sky seemed a gray surtout. Flights of troubled gray fowl, kith and kin with flights of troubled gray vapors among which they mixed, skimmed low and fitfully over the waters, as swallows over meadows before storms. Shadows present, foreshadowing deeper shadows to come.[41]

In these early moments of the story two elements become critical, namely, Delano's telescoping vision as the whale boat draws closer and closer to the "strange sail" and the shifting impressions produced by his fluctuating perspective. For it is here aboard this smaller boat, which affords him a "less remote view," that Delano characterizes the "stranger" before him as a floating "monastery."[42] Delano assures his reader that indeed this was no mirage on his part, no "purely fanciful resemblance." "[P]eering over the bulwarks" he observes, "were what really seemed, in the hazy distance, throngs of dark cowls; while fitfully revealed through the open port-holes, other dark moving figures were dimly descried, as of Black Friars pacing the cloisters." Of singular interest here is the notable shift in tenor that the succeeding observation instantiates for the remainder of the story.

"Upon still nigher approach, this appearance was modified, and the true character of the vessel was plain—a Spanish merchantman of the first class, carrying negro slaves, amongst other valuable freight from one colonial port to another."[43] That the *San Dominick* is a slave trader neither threatens nor discomfits Delano. Rather, at the precise moment Delano recognizes the ship as a slaver, this sanctuary shifts shape: "death" and "blackness" become synonyms. I will postpone addressing the comprehensive critique of imperialism embedded in this slaver and instead turn to how the vision Melville presents to his reader in this scene represents the costs of empire building. He reveals the unquantifiable loss realized in the marriage of imperialism, empire building, and stripped political recognitions in an iconography of internment, burial, and skeletons. After Delano discovers the "true character of the vessel," the ship takes on a spectral presence, transformed from "whitewashed monastery" into "Ezekiel's Valley of Dry Bones." It is a ship whose architecture manifests the death it realizes: outfitted with "dead lights" and a human skeleton masthead, the ship breaks the waters with a "hearse-like roll," "mourning weeds" fastened onto her sides, while her captain with his "distempered frame . . . almost worn to a skeleton," navigated onward. A slaver serving as a proxy for Haiti and for blackness writ large, the *San Dominick* traffics in, and becomes a synecdoche for, death.[44] This ship he initially identifies as the spiritual counterpart to his physical haven—the "small, desert, uninhabited" St. Maria—is now marked by images of death.

Fastening death and burial to blackness, Melville ties "whiteness" to a state of sympathetic perpetual victimacy, particularly regarding expansionist projects. More precisely, this collocation emphasizes the "burden" that writers like Rudyard Kipling, almost half a century later, quipped that whites willingly carried on behalf of empire building. It is the immortal threat Thomas Dixon and D. W. Griffith argued the black body posed in *The Clansman: An Historical Romance of the Ku Klux Klan* (1905) and *Birth of a Nation* (1915). For Melville, the encounter with blackness is the collateral cost of empire, a cost he further translates into the U.S. legal and political culture and one to which I will return. This encounter, however, equally revives the "signifying property *plus*," Hortense Spillers's claims as the burden attached to blackness, a category pregnant with meanings that disfigure, if not completely disrupt, understanding of the very subject it seeks to name—the black body.[45] That blackness signifies death recalls the colonial rhetoric of slavery and imperialism that marked these darker skins in tropical medicine as vectors of disease and death and in criminal and medical sciences as a pathogen for which the social order needed a prompt cure.[46] More immediately, by equating blackness with death, Melville mirrors a U.S. legal culture whose refusal to confer a civil existence to blacks casts this community among Orlando Patterson's "socially dead."[47] It is a maneuver that points all the more emphatically to the patterned similarities between U.S. legal culture and Roman law outlined by legal theorist Douglas Smith. Citing Justinian's *Institutes*—"'We compare slavery closely with death'"—Scott argues, "This concept of slavery as absence of civil existence was the foundation of the decision in *Dred Scott v. Sanford*."[48] If "Benito Cereno" gives us any indication, Melville well understood the constitutive relationship between the legal desubjectivation of the black body and the production of a rightlessness so complete that injury is no longer legally legible for this community: the (social and civil) dead cannot be harmed.[49]

In the intricate relationship between blackness and death, between fugitive slave and captive captor, signified by the skeletal *San Dominick*, Melville complicates our understanding of captivity, pointing to its racial and political structures.[50] Melville's language in the opening paragraphs of "Benito Cereno" adumbrates the reciprocal relationship between sanctuary and political recognition. As quickly as he exploits the cultural associations attached to sanctuary (i.e., safety and paradise), he disabuses the reader of this mythology. Delano is in a sanctuary: a space occasioned in part by the fraternal space of the ship (the *Bachelor's Delight*), but elaborated and sustained by the location at sea, afield of the state. The geographic isolation of this deserted island produces a suspension of law aggravated, if not facilitated, by their distance from the United States. The arrival of the *San Dominick,* though initially welcomed, interrupts and revises the relationship of the *Bachelor's Delight* and its crew to "paradise." That this "monastery" is in fact a slaver, and that the dark cloisters where Delano imagines friars pacing back and forth is in fact a slave hold, refashions the slave ship and its subterranean vault into an ecclesiastical refuge. Melville positions these sites of refuge—slave hold and the blackened space of the slaver—in line with cultural understandings, and the cultural work of asylums: sites for managing unmanageable populations.

He continues to string homologies, comparing the slave hold to "the belittered Ghetto." Melville's ghetto resists being read as a benign reference to an ethnic or racial enclave, but rather serves as a synecdoche for the entire slaver and its subterranean vault—the slave hold. The racialized spatial equation constructed—sanctuary equals slaver/slavehold equals ghetto—revises cultural understandings of the racialized nature of sanctuary. His use of the loaded term "ghetto" represents a peculiar domestication of the black body, fixing it within a specific ethnic enclave, while rendering a culturally familiar space strange. As Melville's text demonstrates, two qualitatively different kinds of sanctuary necessarily operate in tandem: The first denotes the idealized state, which the maintenance of the second understanding of sanctuary—"the belittered ghetto," the detention camp, the "anomalous zone"—partially enables.[51] It is within this second order of sanctuary—the space of the legally anomalous— that African Americans have historically been locked. These sanctuaries are places of arrest, sites of stasis that, like Delano's "whitewashed monastery," have been politically whitewashed as places of detainment, obscuring the forms of indefinite incarceration that occur in them. Resembling "the state of exception" that political philosophy describes as a space demarcating the threshold between what is inside and outside the law, this supplemental or subjacent sanctuary is the byproduct of a suspension of legal norms. However, although the sociojuridical condition—sanctuary—that I am claiming in culturally and racially nuanced terms is of a different order of magnitude from the "state of exception" featured in political philosophy, there are revealing correspondences between the two. Part of an ontology on sovereignty, by Giorgio Agamben's measure "the state of exception" is a "state of emergency" or "siege" whereby not only law but distinctions among governing branches (legislative, judicial, and executive) are suspended.[52] Agamben continues, "The state of exception is not a dictatorship ... but a space devoid of law, a zone of anomie in which all legal determinations— and above all the very distinction between public and private—are deactivated."[53] In turn, what I, in a seeming paradox, name "sanctuary" is in fact a nonlocalizable space—a "zone of indistinction," in Agamben's words[54]—that is produced through an ongoing breech of law focused on African Americans rather than the entire political structure. Moreover, this disruption of law constitutes a new/revised/different juridical order—in other words, slave laws, Black Codes, Jim Crow. Simply put, sanctuary is an anomic legal state predicated on the rupture of blackness from legal personality that is achieved by denying the humanity of the black body. In this sense, sanctuary, as an "anomalous zone" or a "state of exception," guarantees black rightlessness. Sanctuaries are spaces that mirror the violence that constitute them.

Like the legal corridor in which they are contained, black Americans are simultaneously a part of, yet substantively outside, the national body. With bodies that slave law codified in U.S. legal custom and culture as "uniquely human"—ruled rational and sensate only when it benefitted a master[55]—black Americans suffered a kind of postemancipation second-class citizenship that is best described as the intermediary space between slave and citizen. Agamben's logic for the state of exception provides an analogue for this sociopolitical reality: "*Being-outside, and yet belonging.*"[56] Beyond its spatial characteristics—the marginal, the interstitial, the border—sanctuary also signals a temporal disruption.

Confronted by a set of sociolegal and political realities that disavow the accuracy of modernity's linear developmental model of human progress toward freedom, the black modern subject—the refugee, the asylee, the exile, and the stateless inhabitant of sanctuary—occupies a space that is, in Claude McKay's words, "out of time."[57] Or, as Ralph Ellison suggests in perhaps the most poignant expression of black alienation penned in the twentieth century,

> Invisibility, let me explain, gives one a slightly different sense of time, you're never quite on the beat. Sometimes you're ahead and sometimes behind. Instead of the swift imperceptible flowing of time, you are aware of its nodes, those points where time stands still or from which it leaps ahead. And you slip into the breaks and look around.[58]

Having slipped out-of-time and into the "breaks," the figure of the black refugee calls attention to the uses of freedom and citizenship as instruments of state alienation. They are representations that at their most generous fail to account sufficiently for the rightless, and in their most insidious uses, place these communities at further risk. The 1883 Supreme Court's reliance on a developmental model of citizenship to substantiate its rejection of black anti-discrimination claims and, subsequently, to overturn Reconstruction-era civil rights legislation in the Civil Rights Cases, provides a compelling example of the use of time as a strategic device for state alienation. Declaring the 1875 Civil Rights Act—promising "full and equal enjoyment of the accommodations and advantages of inns, public conveyances, etc."—unconstitutional, the Court's majority opined:

> When a man has emerged from slavery, and by the aid of beneficent legislation has shaken off the inseparable concomitants of that state, there must be some stage in the progress of his elevation when he takes the rank of a mere citizen, and ceases to be a *special favorite of the laws*, and when his rights as a citizen, or man, are to be protected in the ordinary modes by which other men's rights are protected.[59]

In language as explicit as its ruling was damaging for black antidiscrimination claims, the Court latticed citizenship, diluting the political and legal substance of this category for black Americans. Imagining civic progress as a series of stages, they insisted that blacks had already attained citizenship and that the equal enjoyment of its privileges and protections was certainly not guaranteed. Branding postbellum civil-rights legislation as racialized legal favoritism, they dismissed the ongoing state of legal exception confronting freedmen, and racially codified rights as a form of privileged or preferential black exemption from an imagined pool of norms for civic life. Yet, whether we are speaking of Neuman's "anomalous zones," Agamben's "state of exception," Judith Butler's military war camps (e.g., Camp Delta), or sanctuary, each houses a power that "derealizes the humanity" of its occupants. We cannot neglect the tragedy: refugees' vulnerability only deepens with desubjectivation, and that refugees' suffering and injuries become increasingly unrecognizable within the normative constraints of the law because their humanity has been devalued.[60]

The ecclesiastical imagery suffusing the opening sequence in Melville's novella, connects the concept of the "safe haven" with the sacred. Albeit fleeting, Delano's troubled comparison of the San Dominick and her occupants—monastery and slave ship, friars and chattel slaves—cracks at the exploited labor and degraded human life constituting (the state's vision of) paradise. My use of the term sanctuary as the central theme in this book places in relief a discourse on safety and the sacredness of human life essential to any interrogation of rightlessness, while respecting, as a powerful constant, both the desire and the necessity for refuge repeated throughout the history of African American writings and expressive traditions. The architectural design of a church narthex lends visual and semantic density to this definition, offering a means through which the structural qualities of sanctuary for the African American may be apprehended because these spaces point to the interstitial quality of black life within the U.S. political unconscious. A junction between private and public, between sacred and secular, the narthex acts as a metaphor for the political and cultural vestibularity experienced by black Americans. Sanctuaries, I argue, are better described as narthexes: throughways, interregnums, thresholds, the "between" that African American theorists from blues singers to philosophers have named the "junction"—corridors ineluctably demarcating boundaries.[61] To continue with the metaphor of traditional church architecture, just as the narthex is placed before the nave, sanctuaries are the spaces that precede the actual worship area, the "sanctuary" proper. Here design replicates experience: The spaces that come before signify the legal and social dislocation of the refugee or the stateless whose rights remain perpetually deferred.

Sanctuaries are spaces of internment in the fullest sense: they are spaces realizing social—and sometimes literal—death. Melville's late eighteenth-century slaves of the Middle Passage, like the slaves of the mid-nineteenth century that he refuses to explicitly name, are among Agamben's "sacred," of whom Agamben writes, "When their rights are no longer [or have never been] the rights of the citizen, that is when human beings are truly sacred, in the sense that this term used to have in the Roman law of the archaic period: doomed to death."[62] The curious naming of this category—the sacred—retains the cultural associations with safety that obscure the material violence experienced by these communities. As Melville demonstrates, it is a death achieved through a politics of visibility, a politics that reveals the anxieties underlying whiteness, and the limits of a white national imaginary. The structure of this opening scene—a movement from occluded vision to black death—mimics the structural progression of Melville's argument. He begins with the problem of recognition that by the novella's end necessarily culminates with death.

REFUGEE

The aftermath of World War II included a crisis in governance aggravated by the massive presence of refugees and stateless persons. Postwar reconstruction projects would have to account for these new persons, confronting the challenges they posed to civil identity and civil rights and to an ill-defined prescription for human rights.[63] I want to return briefly to Arendt's orthodoxy on statelessness as outlined in chapter 1 in order to tease out the bond between black bodies and statelessness and the discordant relationship between blacks and the law. For Arendt, statelessness is marked by first, a profound social and legal dislocation realized in the loss of and inability to procure a home; second, in an anomalous relationship to law; and, finally, in a devalued civil identity that gives way to assaults against life. It is a rightlessness resulting from the absence of a national, and consequently, a legal identity.[64] I offer Arendt here as an interdiction, a crossroads pointing both to the conditions of the rightless and to the ways in which the convergences between this community and African Americans have been misrecognized—the very politics of misapprehension depicted in Melville's text.

For Arendt, it is the absence of a national identity that *bares* individuals, rendering them simply and transparently human. Of the rightless, she laments, they "appeared to be nothing but human beings whose very innocence—from every point of view, and especially that of the persecuting government—was their greatest misfortune. Innocence, in the sense of complete lack of responsibility, was the mark of their rightlessness as it was the seal of their loss of political status." It is, she reasons, "the loss of a polity itself [that] expels him from humanity." By this logic, Arendt insists, "Man . . . can lose all so-called Rights of Man without losing his essential quality as man, his human dignity. Only the loss of a polity itself expels him from humanity."[65] Arendt's definition of statelessness, however, demands historical and racial particularity. By sidestepping her own rubric for defining the polis, Arendt insists that slaves fail to qualify among the stateless. In the case of the slave, Arendt reduces the value of what it means to be constituted as "human," reading instrumentation—slaves' role as laboring devices—as sufficient evidence of their status within a larger human (re: political) community: "It is possible to say that even slaves still belonged to some sort of human community; their labor was needed, used, and exploited, and this kept them within the pale of humanity. To be a slave was after all to have distinctive character, a place in society—more than the abstract nakedness of being human and nothing but human."[66] Arendt's ahistorical summary mistakes "the body" for "the flesh," to borrow Spillers's useful formulation, and disregards the progressive character of slavery, an institution that, in Frederick Douglass's assessment, itself makes slaves of men: "The dark night of slavery closed in upon me; and behold a man transformed into a brute!"[67]

Spillers's "Mama's Baby, Papa's Maybe" proves the inaccuracy of Arendt's claim. She cites the gross medical experimentation endured by the enslaved among the processes engineering the dehumanization of slaves. The perfection of surgical procedures, involuntary vaccinations with unproven drug therapies, organ harvesting, and autopsies transformed the enslaved into a "living laboratory." Spillers writes,

> This profitable "atomizing" of the captive body provides another angle on the divided flesh: we lose any hint or suggestion of a dimension of ethics, of relatedness between human personality and its anatomical features, between one human personality and

another, between human personality and cultural institutions. To that extent, the procedures adopted for the captive flesh demarcate a total objectification.[68]

Spillers's "divided flesh" captures an essential aspect of black life, concentrating in an image of partition the formal and informal techniques administered to uncouple personality from black bodies. It is a trope remembering the proprietary relationships of slavery, which counted men like Douglass among the property to be "equally divided"[69] by beneficiaries of an estate. That divided flesh returns us to the apportioned black body reproduced through the federal ratio, a crass calculation that provides some of the most compelling evidence of state-sanctioned and administered devaluation of black life. This tally of a slave as three-fifths of a free person was applied beginning in 1783 to apportion taxation and expanded four years later to formulate political representation.[70] The fractioned slave body parceled, divided, multiplied, and tabulated with this arithmetic always fails to measure up to the whole number reserved for persons. It is, however, to the remainder—to the missing two-fifths—that we must look to fully understand and gauge how the redaction of life into something *less than* literally subtracted a class of humans from the province of law. In exacting sums, the enslaved are worth less. Blacks bore the levy of this calculus for taxation and representation, a singular example of the structurally designed and deployed techniques recalibrating black life.

Arendt's unwillingness to recognize the slave body among the stateless speaks to the difficulties inherent in her proposition. New World slaves were not only stateless, but also representatives of a ruptured humanity. Although Arendt rightly notes the interdependent relationship between civil and human rights—that the absence of one guarantees the absence of the other[71]—rightlessness not only encapsulates slave identity, but was elaborated and sustained through the dehumanization of slave bodies. Citizenship remains a graduated political category in the United States, as the histories of African, Asian, and Mexican Americans demonstrate, not simply guaranteed through birth (*jus soli*) or naturalization. For African Americans it is a category that has been calibrated largely in response to the question of humanity. Differently put, because the humanity of black bodies during and after slavery was ignored, the civil rights of African Americans have remained a legal and political fiction. Again, Melville's text seems precursive, tracking the link between legal subjectivity and rights.

Melville's repeated references to vision and its epistemological work in "Benito Cereno" (e.g., "spectacle," "scene," "look," "gaze," "watch") cluster around two related consequences arising from misrecognition: First, individuals are placed outside the precincts of law, and, second, their injuries become legally illegible and thus irremediable. I am writing not only of the references to troubled vision that open the novella, but to the spectacle of captivity performed by the enslaved, and to the persistent references to sight that suffuse the narrative. These expressions of vision consolidate into a family of images, phrases, and verbal interchanges among characters. For example, this range of significations includes references to "natural sights," attempts to "change the scene," and quips like the following from Benito Cereno to Delano: "I have to thank those negroes you see, who though to your inexperienced eyes appearing unruly, have, indeed, conducted themselves with less of restlessness." They are equally found in Delano's repeated "enchantment" with blackness: "As master and man stood before him, the black upholding the white, Captain Delano could not but bethink him of the beauty of that relationship which could present such a spectacle of fidelity on the one hand and confidence on the other. The scene was heightened by the contrast in dress."[72] Caricatures come to mark within this narrative the impalpability of blackness, what Spillers describes as its "confounded identities, a meeting ground of investments and privations in the national treasury of rhetorical wealth."[73] Melville demonstrates how the inability to rec-ognize—or the refusal to acknowledge—an individual's humanity casts bodies beyond the parameters of law. He anticipates the effects of what Du Bois in 1894 called the single most crucial issue at stake in the constellation of social problems falsely labeled "the Negro Prob-lem." Du Bois wrote, "We [African Americans] regard the Negro problem proper as nothing more nor less than a question of humanity and national morality. . . . This is the kernel of the Negro problem and the question which the American people have never boldly faced, but have persisted in veiling behind other and dependent problems."[74]

The *San Dominick* is a living spectacle. It is a tableau of civil authority performed by for-merly captive slaves holding captive the Spanish officers and their crew—after having killed their owner, Aranda, and making his body the ship's skeletal figurehead—while holding Delano's imagination captive through their performance. It is a tableau stabilized, neverthe-less, through scripted racial ideologies that collectively transfigure blackness into representa-tions of the primordial and the pathogenic. With the exception of a farce in which one slave, Atufal, is shackled and presented before Cereno at regular intervals so that he might be com-pelled to plea for forgiveness for some transgression, slaves freely roam the deck unchained, "flourishing hatchets and knives, in ferocious piratical revolt."[75] Yet, despite the fraught per-formance of these fugitives, the risks to white subjectivity that recognition of the enslaved's "captive power" would produce outweigh the costs to "character" that must arise in the per-formance of an equally incredulous state of ignorance. Evident in the mentally unstable Cer-eno, Delano's psychic integrity depends upon representations of the black supplicant body. Melville's emphasis on the spectacle aboard this slave-commandeered ship underlines the visual politics surrounding blackness, preparing readers for one of the signal encounters rei-fying Delano's sense of this slaver as his sanctuary. Curiously, Melville sketches the ways in which blindness precipitates racialized vision, as Delano contemplates a nursing African mother:

> His attention had been drawn to a slumbering negress, partly disclosed through the lace-work of some rigging, lying with youthful limbs carelessly disposed, under the lee of the bulwarks, like a doe in the shade of the woodland rock. Sprawling at her lapped breasts was her wide-awake fawn, stark naked, its black little body half lifted from the deck, crosswise with its dam's; its hands like two paws, clambering upon her; its mouth and nose ineffectually rooting to get at the mark; and meantime giving a vexatious half-grunt, blending with the composed snore of the negress.[76]

"It is on that other being," writes Franz Fanon, "on recognition by that other being that his own human worth and reality depend." What, then, is the outlay of Delano's blindness toward the Negress's humanity? Dana Nelson's reading of this scene offers at least one solu-tion: shoring up white masculinity. The slumbering mother and child become the locus for a consolidated white masculinity achieved, according to Nelson, through the enjoyment gained in the "anthropological dissymmetry of looking on the African woman and her child."[77] I want to linger for a moment longer with Nelson's critique of this sequence, as a way to begin to adduce the effect of withholding recognition of black legal subjectivity. A proxy for Delano's desires, Nelson remarks on how this woman elicits the captain's prompt identification with the colonial explorer Mungo Park. Referencing Delano's bemusement ("'Ah!... These perhaps are some of the very women whom Mungo Park saw in Africa, and gave such a noble account of.'"), Nelson argues, "We can see how Delano's 'republican' subjectivity is consolidated through a triangular structure, in imagined affiliation with other men who have power over groups of people—the power to objectify, to identify, to manage."[78] Yet, the stability purchased through this "anthropological dissymmetry"[79] guarantees that which the Negress's abject form is denied—humanity. If Fanon's calculation that identity formation is predicated on recognition is correct, then in Melville we see the consequences of a closed visual circuit. It is a consequence Fanon defines as the loss of individuality and liberty, a retrofitting of the visual object into an instrument exclusively for self-realization and "subjectivity security"—Nelson's consolidated white masculinity.[80] Although the psychology of colonialism and identity formation performed here aids our understanding of how a racialized civil identity is produced, I want to read past Nelson's investment in the colonial and masculinist dimensions of this scene, and shift our focus away from Delano and direct it to the slave woman, whose desubjectivated black body buys Delano's stabilized white masculinity. If this moment replays in Technicolor the discursive and visual relays mooring a specific brand of masculine identity, then what of the Negress?

As a story restaging the grounds of political revolution—*freedom*—"Benito Cereno" projects the legal and civil conundrum of the fugitive slave body. The story challenges the rationale of fugitivity as a sign of disobedience, legal breech, or criminality, and anticipates the effects of precedent-setting nineteenth-century cases on citizenship—*Dred Scott* (1857), the *Civil Rights Cases* (1883), and *Plessy* v. *Ferguson* (1896). Melville opens a space for understanding the process by which the postemancipation black body came to inhabit the intermediary slot between slave and citizen: the sanctuary that is the "belittered ghetto" of the rightless. By turning our gaze toward the Negress, we are reminded of the contingent relationship between citizenship and rightlessness. The see-saw effect of Delano's gaze reminds us that it is not simply a white masculinity gained at the expense of a black woman's humanity, but a civil identity whose configuration installs the appearance of its most profound "other"—the rightless (e.g., refugees, stateless persons, and the displaced). We see just how expertly Melville exposes, in Paul Downes's words, "the lines of association and identification that tie vulnerability to power, revolution to violence, and citizenship to rightlessness."[81]

Nineteenth-century ideologies of race anchored in the biological and social sciences appear in "Benito Cereno" as visual metaphors. Within the space of a paragraph, as Delano ogles the sleeping woman, Melville recasts the visual politics underlying blackness. He tracks the differentiation, if not complete excision, of black life from the categorically human, distilling the labor performed by the taxonomic enterprises of racial sciences during the nineteenth and early twentieth centuries. Delano's gaze is scapellic. It strips away the mother's humanity with surgical precision. She quickly shifts from "slumbering negress" to "doe in the shade of a woodland," and finally two paragraphs later to "naked nature." By his second encounter with the woman, later in the day, he simply refers to her as "nature." This slip mirrors the regression attributed to black bodies. Sleights of pen and fantasy, Melville's transpositions condense blackness, thickening the cultural fictions that bury the woman's identity. In three turns—Negress, doe, nature—Melville isolates a historical perjoration of blackness that habitually results in attenuated black flesh: the painful microphysics of autopsy replayed in pernicious visual and verbal play. The ethnographic aspects of the moment enact a kind of anthropometry: despite unspecified facial angles and ear, lip, nose, and eye socket dimensions, Delano measures and summarily judges the "Negress" inadequate.

To read this scene only as a rehearsal of cultural and scientific fictions regarding blackness, however, risks overlooking the larger political stakes in the derealization of black humanity. Melville uses the image of a screen—"partly disclosed through the lace-work of some rigging," "the screened sun," and "the charmed eye"[82]—in each of Delano's encounters with the African mother to emphasize the artifices through which black humanity could be resisted and ultimately denied. Melville's descriptions of black primordiality mark more than Delano's rejection of black humanity. They summon the normalizing and normativizing effect of these representations on civil identity and rights, and emphasize the boundary between protected and unprotected.

There is nothing innocent about this carefully crafted revision of the black seductress trope, although the expected sexual overtones are muted. This cultural myth characterizes the black woman as a temptress and credits her for inciting white male desire. Only part of its harm is gauged in the alibi this myth lends white male aggression. Effectively racializing injury, the black seductress trope ensures her assailants' perpetual innocence—even allows them to paint themselves as victims—and propels ensuing moments of sexual violence beyond the precincts of law and into the protected sphere of purported consensual sex. Although there is no sex here, there is seduction, violence, and white innocence. Yet, the erotics within this scene that mark the "slave Negress" as a territory ripe for possession are not all that is laid bare. Her nakedness has a double assignment, signifying her status as *bare* humanity, as the stateless or the refugee. She stands as yet another element within the text's signifying chain on black primordiality. As "doe," she is the female equivalent to the black rebel leader whose name, "Babo," mocks his person and, in its resemblance to a circus chant, claims him as a "freak." That this woman captivates Delano further marks the colored space she occupies—the *San Dominick*—as his "monastery," his sanctuary. This image of a prostrate, supplicant black body signifies the Enlightenment-influenced discourse on blackness and attests to the Hobbesian state of nature present aboard the slaver, and echoed in her abbreviated name: "naked nature." As an example of what Michelle Stephens describes as "the trope of the ship of state,"[83] Melville's repetitive descriptions of black primitivism aboard the *San Dominick* signal the lawlessness Hobbes ascribes to prepolitical existence. These rebel slaves are outside the law—they are fugitives.

The Negress's nakedness remarks on a vulnerability sanctioned through the denial of a legal personality fashioned by marking the Africanized body *uniquely human*. Jurist Leon Higginbotham's and Barbara Kopytoff's assiduous reading of nineteenth-century Virginia slave law remind us that these concessions to the slave's capacity to reason, to feel, indeed, to express his or her "unique qualities as a human being," were acknowledged only if it benefitted the master.[84] Her unclad body anticipates the extreme vulnerability of the refugee, the semiotics of the flesh: denied legal personality, refugees are merely flesh. They may be excluded from due process and civil and human rights and their entailments; they must endure restricted access to social space. Indeed, her bare flesh marks the woman's status as a refugee, just as it locates her within a white political imaginary as more than a ripe conquest. Indeed, she is territorial expansion's ideal aftermath—a utopic (nation) space. But, as Melville impresses upon the reader, the effects of this politics of recognition impugn the humanity of the individual. Its consequences at best include the indignity of dehumanization and unredressed grievances and injuries; at worst, premature death.

LEGAL COMPETENCY

What had, perhaps, seemed a purely symbolic interest, a simple preoccupation with the semiotics of sight and the black body, or even confirmation of the scopophilic pleasure of the white gaze and its unequivocally disastrous effects for black representation, becomes more concrete and urgent by the novella's end. During the criminal proceedings against the slaves in the regal court of Lima, Peru, following Delano's successful recapture of the *San Dominick*, Melville offers his most explicit exegesis on slave law. He suggests the lethal effect of withholding political recognition and outlines the significant legal consequences to the derealization of the black body, a dehumanization undertaken in the slavery that engineered expansionist projects—indeed, he articulates the life-and-death stakes of scopophiliac investments in blackness. Melville casts a shadow on a juridical consciousness and legal culture that abetted the state's construction of an ideal polity by denying blacks the legal subjectivity requisite for incorporation into the political body and the human and civil rights that membership guaranteed.[85] Within the context of this hearing, Melville's descriptions of the Negress's nakedness and comparison of the besieged slaver to Hobbes's state of nature gain significance: blacks are extralegal and as such are among the rightless. The fugitive slave body (e.g., Anthony Burns, Shadrach, Wilkins) taunts these passages, calling into question what constitutes fugitivity in a society constituted and preserved by rendering the black body *fugitive* or *excessive* to the law. Melville's metered interest in the relationship of the law to the black body is measured in the narrowness of these proceedings, a narrowness of both the hearings' structure and content. He admits offering only a "partial translation" of the deposition of only one witness to the mutiny and its subsequent suppression by Delano; he casts this moment singularly through Cereno's dictated testimony.[86]

Melville's rehearsal of the deposition manages readers' understanding of the effects realized by the absence, or veiled assertion, of legal protection. He strategically orients our reading of the deposition, carefully framing Cereno's testimony in relation to three legal resonances: the troubled credibility of a witness "not undisturbed in his mind"; the corroborating evidence required and supplied; and the oaths taken to ensure the deponent's honesty. He writes,

> Some disclosures therein were, at the time, held dubious for both learned and natural reasons. The tribunal inclined to the opinion that the deponent, not undisturbed in his mind by recent events, raved of some things which could never have happened. But subsequent depositions of the surviving sailors . . . gave credence. . . . So that the tribunal, in its final decision, rested its capital sentences upon statements which, had they lacked confirmation, it would have deemed it but duty to reject.[87]

Melville's insertion of the deposition highlights the racial predicates managing legal evidence during the nineteenth century. Race continued to structure legal culture, serving as an underlay circumscribing legal presumptions, curtailing due process, and challenging convictions and sentencing. Cereno's fragmented testimony stands in for his fractured psyche and points to an absent testimony—Babo's. Melville punctuates this absence in his closing reference to Babo's willfully stilled tongue and his "voiceless end." The elision in the juridical record becomes all the more acute in the nature of the account Cereno shares. His solipsistic testimony transfers responsibility for the events aboard the *San Dominick* to Babo, who he accuses of being "the plotter from first to last," having "ordered every murder," and having pointed daggers to intimidate and coerce Cereno's compliance in his "design" against Delano. Babo was, in Cereno's words, at "the helm and keel of the revolt."[88] That the executed Babo remains immured, fixed in a sense within Cereno's testimony, is the result—as the text suggests—of a legal displacement that hinges on race.

We cannot afford to underread the structure Melville deploys to introduce this hearing. His attention to legal formality betrays the larger stakes surrounding legal subjectivity and political recognition that underlie this scene. The opening moment is a set piece on witness competency: state evidentiary regulations determining the kinds of testimony that could be admitted into legal proceedings. Cereno's sanity, the substantiating testimony, the necessity of a notary, the oaths taken by both the notary and Cereno—all reflect on the procedures adjudicating the competency of witnesses. According to Thomas Morris, evidence laws barring slave testimony during the seventeenth century hinged on a secondary witness and the oath. Of this legal history he writes, "Two rules used in seventeenth century English criminal trials were of significance in the trials of slaves. Both derived from Christian doctrine. The first was the two-witness rule found in Deuteronomy 17: 6. The second rule was that witnesses had to take an oath before they would be admitted to testify."[89] The slave's oath lacked legal standing because slaves were not recognized as credible. The religious sanctions reflected here operated on two registers, signaling a belief in immediate "divine judgment" if a witness committed perjury and calling attention to a requisite for oath taking. In many states only Christians were permitted to take oaths.[90] That these laws initially found sanction in scripture offers an additional motive for the vehemence with which many slave masters prevented blacks from being proselytized.

Melville's juxtaposition of Cereno's questionable sanity with references to supplemental testimony shifts this moment from a sufficiency guarantee (a matter of corroboration) to the question of the "competency" of black speech and representability. Higginbotham explains,

> Originally, a 1705 statute prohibited all blacks, slave or free, from giving evidence of any kind under oath. Blacks accused of criminal acts, some punishable by death, had no right to testify under oath in their own defense. Although a court might permit them to speak, their words were considered wholly unreliable, as their testimony was unsworn."[91]

In many states, slaves eventually gained testimonial privileges in slave trials and, later, in proceedings involving free blacks, mulattoes, and Indians, but even in these cases, many states prohibited blacks from being sworn in.[92] Blacks, slave or free, however, were not permitted to testify against whites. By the 1860s all but four Southern states continued to use race as a preclusion to testimony.[93] In Thomas Cobbs's words, blacks simply were not "oathesworth." "Mendacious" and "ignoble," blacks were frequently harassed in judicial proceedings and endured stiffer penalties for the crime of perjury.[94] As late as 1866, Virginia passed legislation preventing African Americans from drafting depositions, stating that "The testimony of colored persons shall in all cases be given *ore tenus* and not by deposition."[95] Competency was the hinge anchoring racial preclusion in evidence law, as well as a major way in which jurisprudence helped secure the depersonification of African Americans. If slavery destroyed the reputation of the slave as human, then surely the law was her handmaiden. Melville's text reflects and engages nineteenth-century legal culture, and anticipates what would become the central debate of 1865, a debate in which the North would intervene, using the stripped testimonial rights of all criminal defendants as leverage.[96]

Although Massachusetts senator Charles Summer's 1864 amendment granted blacks testimonial privileges in federal courts, state evidence rules remained intact.[97] This withheld legal privilege meant that black injuries risked being unredressed. According to Kentucky Circuit Justice Noah Swayne in *United States* v. *Rhodes* (1866), "Crimes of the deepest dye were committed by white men with impunity."[98] In *Blyew* v. *United States* (1872), the Supreme Court dismantled the partial protections assured by the 1866 Civil Rights Act, an act authorizing federal jurisdiction for improperly tried state cases involving black claimants. With *Blyew,* African Americans lost their short-lived right to seek federal adjudication in cases where race trampled due process in state courts, increasing the likelihood that white assailants would continue to be prejudicially tried.[99] The Tennessee Supreme Court's 1887 reversal of Ida B. Wells' suit against the Chesapeake and Ohio Railroad Company (*Chesapeake, Ohio & Southwestern R.R. Col.* v. *Wells, 1884*), after she was forcibly removed and dragged from the train because she refused to relinquish her seat to a white patron and take a seat in the smoky, filthy, overcrowded "Jim Crow" car, demonstrates the racialized inequities of U.S. legal culture.[100] The 1875 Civil Rights Act had promised "the full and equal enjoyment of the accommodations, advantages, facilities, and privileges of inns, public conveyances on land or water, theaters, and other places of public amusement," regardless of race, a promise that proved short-lived. (By 1883, the U.S. Supreme Court deemed these protections unconstitutional in the *Civil Rights Cases*.) In one brushstroke, the court dismissed her injuries and the $500.00 in damages she had been awarded by the lower court, and demolished Wells's confidence in the legal system. It was a disheartened Wells who privately pleaded in her diary in 1887, "O God is there no redress, no peace, no justice in this land for us."[101]

The stakes of Melville's seemingly parochial rehearsals of popular supremacist rhetoric become all the more apparent when measured against this legal history of racial preclusion. His attentiveness to the judicial protocol of the oath revises how we read the recurring textual references to confidence, trust, and black loyalty. Understood within the skein of evidence law, Melville's seemingly straightforward presentation of black primordiality bears a double assignment. Melville observes, "Delano took to negroes, not philanthropically, but genially, just as other men to Newfoundland dogs." Delano's awe over the spectacle of Babo shaving Cereno protracts his already extended descriptions of the enslaved:

> The negro . . . performing these and similar offices with that affectionate zeal which transmutes into something filial or fraternal acts in themselves but menial; and which has gained for the negro the repute of making the most pleasing body servant in the world; one, too, whom a master need be on no stiffly superior terms with, but may treat with familiar trust; less a servant than a devoted companion.

And again: "As master and man stood before him, the black upholding the white, Captain Delano could not but bethink him of the beauty of that relationship which could present such a spectacle of fidelity on the one hand and confidence on the other."[102] The insistent rhetoric of "Negro capacity" belying the bestial iconography of the novella thickens, creating a stew of social meanings regarding blackness, while foregrounding the problem of legitimacy that structured legal interdictions on black testimony.

The absence of Babo's perspective, of his testimony, equates with the refusal to recognize his injuries. Although Melville calls attention to the translation of the document—"the following extracts, translated from one of the official Spanish documents"—the framework of the deposition as a legal document summons an additional, and arguably more devastating, transliteration. Melville encodes these events in legal discourse, embracing all the filtering, suppression, and rearticulation required to cast a criminal occurrence within the precincts of law. The shifted syntax and redacted text of the final pages signal this encoding, starkly contrasting with the casual, memoiristic idiom of the first two-thirds of the novella. The legal translation of events is further mediated by race. Melville's frequent narrative interruptions in Cereno's deposition finger the grain of this problem: "Here, in the original, follows the account of what further happened at the escape. . . . From this portion is the following" and "Various particulars of the prolonged and perplexed navigation ensuing here follow . . . from which portion one passage is extracted."[103] Melville highlights how the legal process must be interrupted—how due process is in fact interrupted—when race mandates justice, when race overdetermines the possibilities governing speech, and when race measures injury. We are left, literally, with a singular reading of Babo. This exclusive framing prohibits access to, sympathy with, and reparations for the suffering endured by this black slave and his fugitive compatriots. Within this fragmented legal text, Babo is simply a murderer.

Melville's concluding descriptions of Babo take on new meaning when read against these racial fictions of law: "Seeing all was over, [Babo] uttered no sound, and could not be forced to. His aspect seemed to say, since I cannot do deeds, I will not speak words." The U.S. political and legal histories embedded within "Benito Cereno"—the *Amistad* revolt and trial, the Fugitive Slave Acts of 1793 and 1850, and the United State's imperial interest toward Latin America during the mid-nineteenth century—attest to Melville's sustained interest in U.S. domestic and international affairs, despite the Spanish colonial setting of the narrative. The moral bankruptcy of U.S. legal culture that Melville stages becomes all the more explicit in the succeeding lines: "Don Benito did not visit [Babo]. Before the tribunal he refused. When pressed by the judges he fainted. On the testimony of the sailors alone rested the legal identity of Babo."[104] Don Benito's repeated refusals to "see" Babo cap the politics of recognition featured throughout the novella, a politics precipitated by the loss of Babo's legal identity. A year after this story's publication, legal theorist William Goddell wrote that slaves only transform into "'*a person*' whenever he is to be *punished!* . . . He is under the *control* of law, though *unprotected by* law, and can know law only as an enemy, and not as a friend."[105] His legal identity, the identity for which he was summarily convicted and executed, was as a murderer.

Babo is never *seen* in this text. By likening Babo to a "Newfoundland dog" in one of the few descriptions of him, the story marks off a liberal descriptive and representational excess that simultaneously renders the black body concealed and hypervisible. It is a problem Ellison places under the heading of invisibility:

I am an invisible man. . . . I am invisible, understand, simply because people refuse to see me. Like the bodiless heads you see sometimes in circus sideshows, it is as though I have been surrounded by mirrors of hard, distorting glass. When they approach me they see only my surroundings, themselves, or figments of their imagination—indeed, *everything and anything except me.*[106]

Ellison introduces this anopticism with an epigraph drawn from "Benito Cereno," and with opening lines confirming Melville's consequence for political recognition. He pointedly cites an exchange between Cereno and Delano from the final moments of Melville's narrative: "'You are saved,' cried Captain Delano, more and more astonished and pained; 'you are saved: what has cast such a shadow upon you?'" Ellison's distorted mirror remembers Delano's, Cereno's, and the Lima court's disfiguring lenses. His "bodiless head" is a visual dagger violently cutting to the lethal consequences Melville prefigures in the conclusion to "Benito Cereno": the executed and decapitated Babo. Withholding his name, Melville completes the rebel leader's effacement, repeatedly referring to him as merely "the black." Of Babo's execution, Melville writes, "Some months after, dragged to the gibbet at the tail of a mule, the black met his voiceless end. The body was burned to ashes, but for many days, the head, that hive of subtlety, fixed on a pole in the Plaza, met unabashed, the gaze of the whites."[107]

In Ellison, this narration foreshadows the lynching in his closing depiction of the Harlem race riot (1943).[108] Within the U.S. legal economy that Melville depicts, that Babo and the other fugitives aboard the *San Dominick* were kidnapped persons illegally trafficked and sold in the New World never mattered. Recognizing Babo's violence as a legitimate response to his captivity—an act of self-defense—is never entertained. The symmetries between this story and historical events, specifically the *Tyral* and *Amistad* trials, are here even more aligned. As his gratuitously violent punishment confirms, this framing—Babo as murderer, rather than kidnapped victim—bears a lethal charge. Melville's circumscribed description of Babo calls attention to the effects of racialized state evidence laws on witness competency. This legal silencing dictated the terms under which slaves could be indicted and mitigated the nature and possibility of their defense. Babo is our Anthony Burns, and he is our slave murderess Celia. The 1855 murder trial of Celia, a nineteen-year-old slave, rested on this question of testimony. After five years of repeated sexual assault by her widowed master, Robert Newsom, Celia killed him. She was fixed in a triangulated power structure between her slave lover, George, and her master. George, emasculated by a system that refused to respect his relationship with Celia and guaranteed severe corporeal punishment if he should intervene on her behalf, laid the burden of punishment and suffering on Celia. George offered an ultimatum. Celia must either end her "relationship" with Newsom or consider theirs over. Although this case gathered a complex of legal questions, not the least of which were Missouri's recently passed prohibitions on rape (1850) and legislation permitting slave self-defense, I want to focus on the ways in which Celia's absent testimony mattered.

A history fragmented by lost legal documents, summarized court testimonials, and absent or unrecorded public and private testimonies by Celia, this case mirrors the silencing of the black body in Babo's voiceless death. From the perspective of the authorities, Celia was an unlikely suspect in Newsom's murder: a slave, not to mention a woman, she was assumed to lack the competence to execute murder. The slave codes that gagged her, rendering it unlawful for her to testify against a living or deceased white person, dictated the terms of Celia's indictment and her legal defense. She was admitted as a slave witness in a proceeding she was not legally permitted to testify in, and charged the 5-cent fee for swearing in persons serving as witness.[109] Her irregular treatment testifies, in ways that Celia could not, to the dense social and legal exchanges that further circumscribed her status as an article, as property.

Although Missouri slave law provided for a self-defense plea in capital crimes, this plea would require Celia's firsthand testimony, a condition prohibited by the same slave statutes. The prosecution circumvented Missouri's prohibitions of rape, insisting on Celia's legal status as property. It was a maneuver that erased her injuries and placed her outside the protection of law. Fixed within Neuman's anomalous zone—slave jurisprudence—Celia's injuries did not simply transfer to her master (as the protocols of slave law dictated), recast as an expression of trespass whose effects may only be suffered by a property owner, but instead became legally illegible. Because Newsom owned her, even the crime of trespass could not stand. Like Melville's Babo, *Missouri* v. *Celia* distills the nexus between law and the black body, revealing how race renders personhood, like property, alienable. The status of "person" is a privilege, and a privilege that may be granted or withdrawn in law. The court's failure to acknowledge Celia's rape compounded the sexual trespass she experienced and warranted her conviction for murder and eventual hanging on June 23, 1855. Celia's body, like Babo's and like the countless other raped slaves whose injuries were never redressed, calls out for the question: How could jurisprudence sacrifice so many bodies in order to secure the identities of others?

Celia inhabits the anomalous jurisprudence of the slave codes. It is because she could not testify, because she could not bear witness to her own assaults, that a deferred act of self-defense that would now fall under the legal heading of battered women's syndrome, was prosecuted as first-degree murder. Her case points to the estranging effects of a legal system that, at the risk of positioning a slave as a gendered human subject, undermined its own system of civil protections. To legally cite Celia as a "woman" under second section article twenty-nine of the Missouri statutes of 1845 threatened property relations and risked the sanctity of what had been a racially exclusionist category: womanhood. Working against a social and legal economy that linked propriety with property, Celia's lawyer struggled to extract secondhand testimony from Newsom's neighbors and others of the repeated sexual assaults against this slave woman that began the evening of her sale, when she was fourteen. And although some reluctantly attested to this abuse, stating that Celia asked Newsom's daughters to intervene on her behalf, even requesting on the night of his murder that they encourage him to stop "visiting her," these tellings were tempered. In the absence of her direct testimony, the jury could and did easily acquit itself of any feelings of wrongdoing inflicted against Celia, a slave. Her absent testimony starkly contrasts with the voluminous documents reproducing her status as slave: records documenting ownership transfers replace a birth certificate, mooring her fungibility as a commodity within slavery's pecuniary economy of property loss and accumulation.[110] The judge upended the defense attorney's attempt to craft jury instructions that would call attention to Celia's abused body and legally construct her as a "woman" and subsequently entitled to exercise self-defense, dismissing Celia's motive for her crime—the "imminent danger of forced sexual intercourse." In one stroke he eliminated the possibilities of an acquittal or a conviction for a lesser crime.

Celia's case offers the material expression of loss that Melville fictionalizes in the decapitated slave. Her case calls attention to a class of distinctions affixed in slave jurisprudence that cluster under the heading of humanity. It is the "inferiority precept" that Higginbotham argued underwrote slave jurisprudence, the Black Codes, and post-Reconstruction and Jim Crow U.S. legal culture. Higginbotham reminds us that it was this same precept that Thurgood Marshall specifically challenged in his arguments in 1953 before the U.S. Supreme Court in *Brown* v. *Board of Education of Topeka*,[111] in which Marshall reasoned:

> So whichever way it is done, the only way that this Court can decide this case in opposition to our position, is that there must be some reason which gives the state the right to make a classification that they can make in regard to nothing else in regard to Negroes, and we submit the only way to arrive at this decision is to find that for some reason Negroes are *inferior* to all other human beings.[112]

And it is because of this class of distinctions that *Plessy* v. *Ferguson* could offer legal sanction to the construction of race as property:

> How much would it be worth to a young man entering upon the practice of law, to be regarded as a white man rather than a colored one? ... Probably most white persons, if given a choice, would prefer death to life in the United States as colored persons. Under these conditions, is it possible to conclude that the reputation of being white is not property? Indeed, is it not the most valuable sort of property, being the master-key that unlocks the golden door of opportunity?[113]

It is a construction licensing white claims during the twentieth century for damages against train lines when individuals were wrongfully "Jim Crowed." It is a construction that would warrant $1,495 compensation in 1923 to a white police officer who was offended by the conductor's request that he sit in the Jim Crow section of a train car while transporting an African American prisoner across state lines (*Illinois Central Railroad Company* v. *Cox*). The illegitimacy of the black body before the law that *Plessy* reinvigorated rendered the slave body more than an ideograph of his or her moment. The slave body is a veritable case study for the juridical hangover of this institution; indeed, slavery installed a set of rigorously maintained legal protocols against whose persistence and reinvention the civil rights movement fought.

More than a decade before *Plessy* v. *Ferguson*, Supreme Court Justice John Marshall Harlan fastened onto the problem of (legal) recognition that Melville's "Benito Cereno" so deftly illustrates, outlining its determinative effects on the relationship between blacks and U.S. legal culture. His dissent in the *Civil Rights Cases* (1883) rejected a Court that, through its refusal to weigh "legal intent" as it determined the constitutionality of the Civil Rights Acts (1866, 1875), wrongly judged black petitions for equal accommodation, service, and access based on this legislation, legally indefensible. Harlan reasoned:

> The one underlying purpose of congressional legislation has been to enable the black race to take the rank of mere citizens. The difficulty has been to *compel recognition* of their legal right to take that rank, and to secure the enjoyment or privileges belonging,

under the law, to them as a component part of the people for whose welfare and happiness government is ordained.[114]

Significantly, Harlan's recitation of the politics of recognition marks the literal and symbolic end to his argument. Citing the Fugitive Slave Acts, *Prigg* v. *Pennsylvania*, *Dred Scott* v. *Sandford*, *Ableman* v. *Booth*, the Civil Rights Act, and the *Slaughterhouse Cases* among others, Harlan's narrative of U.S. legal history vis-à-vis the black body dilated a particular juridical and social consciousness that diminished citizenship by transforming it into a tiered racial category that wielded little, if any, real capital for African Americans during the late nineteenth through the twentieth century despite the legislated promises and civil protections and immunities installed with the Fourteenth and Fifteenth Amendments and the 1866 and 1875 Civil Rights Acts. By summoning *Dred Scott* v. *Sandford* (1856) for his case study, Harlan confirmed the ways in which the legal conception of the slave body—the body devoid of legal personality and rights and branded unsuitable for citizenship—carried forward after slavery and continued to shape legal culture.[115] The *Scott* ruling remains a potent reminder that 1) political membership has historically been a prerequisite for rights, an understanding echoed in the writings of contemporary political theorists like Seyla Benhabib, and 2) human rights are contingent on legal personality. The Court's refusal to "recognize" Scott as a lawfully entitled petitioner rested on a rejection of blacks' legal personality. Through their radical effacement of a legal black subjectivity, the Court concurrently barred Scott's access to civil rights and protections and to the range of human rights that fall under the heading of "freedom," not least of which being the enslaved Scott's fundamental right to his own person. If *Dred Scott* further normalized who would come to signify as human, it also revealed how figurations of the human would determine both legal personhood and political membership, and, consequently, access to human rights.

RECOGNITION AND EMPIRE

Melville's prose is unrelenting. He extends his graphic portrait of the corporeal manifestations of dehumanization for black bodies and legal culture to U.S. foreign relations. Addressing the global character of race, "Benito Cereno" translates U.S. political cartography, placing in relief the international dimensions of U.S. race culture on state imperial interests, specifically on its neighbor, Haiti. "Benito Cereno" is also a story about empire building and the United States's supremacy over Spain, a country caricatured in an insipid, frail, mentally overwrought Spaniard, Capt. Benito Cereno. The novella reveals the imperial ambitions of the United States toward Spanish territories that long anticipated the Spanish-American War of 1898, ambitions fashioned in the mid-nineteenth century over the slave body. Both Cereno and Delano personify larger national and international contests over space and bodies. According to Eric Sundquist, representations of a "failing" Spain found a home within discourses of expansionism and Southern destiny, both frequently touted by proslavery factions, and both suggesting the annexation of Cuba and eventual occupation of Central America.[116] Proslavery Democrats James Buchanan, John Y. Mason, and Pierre Soulé traveled at Secretary of State William Marcy's request to Belgium in 1854 to draft a "secret agreement allowing the United States to take Cuba by force if Spain refused to sell it" (i.e., the Ostend Manifesto).[117]

Although a plan that went unrealized until the Americans' turn-of-the-century defeat of Spain, the Ostend Manifesto made the Pierce administration's colonial ambitions toward the Caribbean all the more explicit. The March 1855 edition of *De Bow's Review* included a piece purportedly reflecting Spanish and Cuban views on the annexation of the island in an essay bearing the self-explanatory title "Spanish and Cuban Views of Annexation." Presented as extracts from a soon-to-be-published Spanish text on Cuba, *Llamamiento a la nacion Española* (1855), this essay appeared amid fears of an "Africanized island" generated in part by rumors of a Spanish and English plot to free Cuban slaves in order to secure black rule. "Spanish and Cuban Views on Annexation" curiously propped up what Sundquist characterizes as a circulating Southern racialist rhetoric. According to the *De Bow's Review* article, "The future destiny of Cuba, under the domination of Spain, presents in perspective a precarious existence of decadence and ruin; and, on the other hand, all its inquietudes and embarrassments to production cease with its annexation to the United States."[118]

This Southern expansionist project, both domestic and international in kind, persisted and was articulated in journals like the *Southern Quarterly Review*. Outlining the "causes, conditions and influences . . . which are giving her people a character, an interest and a destiny of their own" the *Review* included "the territorial and industrial expansion of the South, by force of her own efforts, and under the sanction of her own authority," as critical to the well-being of this community.[119] During the Democratic convention of 1860, at which Stephen Douglas, author of the Kansas-Nebraska bill (1854), received the party's presidential nomination, Democrats adopted a six-resolution platform that included the acquisition of Cuba: "Resolved, That the Democratic party are in favor of the acquisitions of Cuba on such terms as shall be honorable to ourselves and just to Spain."[120] Yet the petitions for Cuba's annexation and the racialist imperial imagination that these demands betray are all the more fraught, as self-determination and freedom within this discourse are contingent on slavery and are singularly reserved for Cuba's U.S.-educated aristocracy. This was a community "so imbued with American ideas, with a social institution identified with that of all the Southern and Southwestern States," wrote Samuel Walker in *De Bow's Review*, that for "this race [to be] ruled simply by the force of the bayonet, is, in this age, an anomaly too monstrous to be borne."[121] Here the black rule of emancipated slaves is injurious to freedom and governance, whereas slavery ironically is imagined as the key to securing self-determination. Southern fears engendered by the freeing of Cuban slaves and the institution of black rule announced in the rumored Spanish and English conspiracy rested in no small part on U.S. access to commercial markets.[122]

Walker warned,

> "Let Cuba be Africanized, and then with another San Domingo blocking the mouth of the Mississippi, all we can do by internal improvements will help us little [. . .]." He continues, "We well know that a feeling is rife at the North antagonistic to the institution of slavery. . . . They make the same error . . . in regarding the negro as a white man—in speaking of him and arguing of him thus. . . . The safety of the South is to be found only in the extension of its peculiar institutions and the security of the Union in the safety of the South—towards the equator."[123]

Unsurprisingly, the revolutionary impulse captured in Walker's essay failed to recognize the project of freedom as the project of slave emancipation; revolution remains frustrated, extended only to a Cuba myopically envisioned as a white aristocracy supplicant beneath Spanish rule. He rhapsodized,

> It is the sound of the struggle of despot with despot; and although the strife goes on Freedom will raise her bowed head, and the downtrodden people, brutalized by ages of oppression, will rise in the rude majesty of their ungovernable might.... The seeds of liberty, it seems, must be won in blood, even as man's redemption was purchased by its price.

Ending as polemically as he began, Walker challenged:

> What, then, will America do? What will the United States, the center from which these rays diverge, be willing to contribute to the cause of Freedom and humanity? Will she, while absolutism wars with itself, stand like a sentinel on a hill to perpetuate the existence of the worst despotism on this continent which exists on the face of the whole earth? Will she forge the fetters for men striving to be free, or rivet the chains already fastened on their limbs?[124]

The irony of Walker's use of slave metaphors to suggest an embattled slaveholder, and in his prescription of slavery as a condition for revolutionary freedom turns on a specific relationship to the slave body. That the slave body fails to warrant an appearance here (except metaphorically) speaks to the derealized humanity of chattel flesh within the imagination of Walker and his cohort.

Substituting international waters for domestic soil, Spanish slavers for U.S. plantations, and Haiti for the United States, Melville's "Benito Cereno" becomes as much the utopic "haven" to a U.S. political culture interested in domestic and international expansion as the island St. Maria was to Delano's ship. Having permitted Delano to restore control of the ship for Spain, Melville grants in one stroke white supremacy and U.S. imperial mastery across three sites: blacks, Spain, and the sovereign black nation—Haiti—that the group of slaves symbolizes. Returning the ship, its remaining crew, and its cargo literally to the law—the Peruvian shores and court—reconstitutes these fugitive slaves as disposable, fungible property, and seemingly reaffirms faith in a white supremacy contested with each slave insurrection and Haiti's continued independence. It is a moment in Melville's text that disrupts the image of the sovereign black nation that the *San Dominick* symbolizes. In this strategically manipulated revision of the Haitian Revolution, the United States accomplishes what neither France, England, nor Spain could: the reconstitution of slavery in Haiti.

"Benito Cereno" refutes Hershel Parker's reading of Melville. For Melville is firmly situated in a debate whose dimensions would be solidified two years later in *Dred Scott* v. *Sandford*, the case whose verdict offered legal precedent for the partial citizenship that *Plessy* v. *Ferguson* confirmed. In addition to referencing slave revolts and their violent suppression, including those aboard the *Amistad* and the *Tyral*,[125] Delano's mastery over the ship indexes Haitian and U.S. diplomatic relations at this historic juncture. The United States, like Delano, refused to recognize Haiti's sovereignty. Such an acknowledgment would have been read as the administration's endorsement of and tacit support for black self-determination and a direct assault against slavery and plantations in the United States. Recognition implied support for this black nation and acceptance of black self-rule, a political gesture that would have undermined the fictions of black inferiority that supported the social and legal mechanisms that sustained Southern plantocracies, slavery, and the legal prohibitions on black political and civil rights. It would have been a gesture that might have either foreclosed or initiated the Civil War.[126]

The significance of this political omission cannot be overstated. It would damage Haiti's political leverage in the international scene, impair her ability to negotiate treaties and trade agreements, and complicate the procurement of loans for badly needed funds to rebuild. The anxieties expressed in the refusal of formal recognition suggest a dawning awareness of the larger political influences of this revolution and this nation, the lone country in the Americas, as Sibylle Fischer reminds us, to abolish slavery before the 1830s. According to Fischer, the revolutionary effects of this island exceeded both the French and Spanish revolutions, influencing the revolutions, smaller slave insurrections, and resistance practices that appeared throughout the Americas in the late eighteenth and early nineteenth centuries. Most Southerners nursed the impulse to suppress or rework the facts of Haiti's revolution into barbarous acts of unimaginable and inhuman cruelty in order to contravene the black political and social freedoms of the island and to further license theories of racial inferiority. This impulse stood in lockstep with Haiti's prominence in many of the emigration schemes of white colonization societies, plans that had been debated since the beginning of the nineteenth century. For many this call for black deportation articulated fears over the status of freedom and its entailments. Did emancipation mean that blacks were fully human, and if so, were they necessarily entitled to the privileges of citizenship?

By 1801 Thomas Jefferson, who had already suggested in *Notes on the State of Virginia* that slaves be deported because of the threat their continued presence posed to the "purity" of blood lines and to the mortality of slaveholders, had decided upon St. Domingue (Haiti) as the "'most probable and practicable retreat.'" In an 1824 letter to Jared Sparks, Jefferson considered deporting child slaves to St. Domingue, where President Pétion had offered "to pay their passage, to receive them as free citizens, and to provide them employment."[127] St. Domingue's determinate blackness enticed Jefferson: as a supposedly all-black nation, the anticipated and worrisome hazards of racial dissolution posed by the inevitable intermixture among the newly exiled and the native populations would not be an issue. Haiti would assist in the production of a U.S. haven: a utopia from which blackness had been deported. These proposals for black emigration coincided with ongoing domestic expansion efforts. In the first published use of the term, John O'Sullivan would, in an article for the *Democratic Review* in 1848, describe "Manifest Destiny" as the project of curtailing "foreign impediments" through westward expansion. The domestic version of the Monroe Doctrine, Manifest Destiny signaled a concerted political effort to define the native vis-à-vis the alien. As the Congressional debates that ensued in 1848 over the status of newly incorporated territories such as Oregon, Texas, and Arizona demonstrated, freedom continued to be mapped across the black body. In this sense, the colonial ambitions that underlie Delano's fascination with "naked nature" are direct transcriptions of the domestic political scene's imperial dimensions.

POSTSCRIPT: PHANTOMS

I want to return to the figure of the ghetto that opened this discussion of "Benito Cereno," rethinking the terms of Melville's equation—blackness equals death—for which the slaver became the locus. Organized through parallelisms—the floating monastery of the *San*

Dominick reworked into Cereno's restorative monastery in Lima, the Spanish and American captains—the story, with its lynched Babo, retools the threat attached to black bodies in the opening moments of its narrative. The spectral presence of black flesh embodied by the skeletal slaver has a different meaning by the end of the novella. That which had been marked as a threat throughout the novella, in stilled and silenced tongue, and in severed and mounted head, appears endangered. Melville refuses the solace imagined—and perhaps anticipated among his contemporaries—in executing slave rebels. Babo's death troubles these final moments, remaining one of the text's lingering images. His interminable gaze, his persistent look, memorializes all the black subjectivities previously denied, both within and beyond this fictive narrative space: the African mother, Atufal, the named and unnamed slaves documented in Cereno's deposition, Frederick Douglass, and Celia. In the midst of an ongoing student activism shaping the civil rights movement, James Baldwin wrote, "What students are demanding is nothing less than a total revision of the ways in which Americans see the Negro, and this can only mean a total revision of the ways in which Americans see themselves."[128] The essay from which these lines are drawn, aptly entitled "They Can't Turn Back," carries the injunctive force of Melville's executed Babo, of the silenced Celia. These deaths represent the damage of withheld recognition whose effects exceed its primary victims. Delano and Cereno's final exchange hardens the logic of the text.

> "You generalize, Don Benito; and mournfully enough. But the past is the passed; why moralize upon it? Forget it. See, yon bright sun has forgotten it all, and the blue sea, and the blue sky; these have turned over new leaves."
>
> "Because they have no memory," he dejectedly replied; "because they are not human."[129]

The troubled Cereno's final recrimination posits the problem of failed political recognition, while pointedly offering a concluding reminder to readers of the distinction between nature and the human, a distinction whose collapse anchors Amasa's racialism. It is because the past can never be simply passed that this novella remains relevant. The timelessness and timeliness of the proscription of U.S. legal and political culture embedded in its pages calls attention to the danger of absent perspective housed in the refusal to grant political recognition. It is a problem Du Bois describes as the "tyranny of the Majority," whose hegemony over political ideas risks democracy and it calls forth Arendt's description of the troubling stasis experienced by the refugee and the stateless.[130] To refuse recognition, to refuse to incorporate alternative perspectives into the process of social meaning making and social memory, is—in Cereno's words—"to clutch for a monster," remaining yoked to cultural myths.

The Negro finds himself an unprotected foreigner in his own home.

SUTTON GRIGGS, *Imperium in Imperio*

4

Graphic Inscriptions of Power: The 1919

Chicago Race Riots

IN AN ARTICLE in *The Chicago Defender* on August 9, 1919, William Howard Taft[1] offered the body of a black teenager, Eugene Williams, and urban congestion as causes for the Chicago race riot of 1919: "The evidence seems to show, as is usually the case, that in Chicago the whites were the aggressors in stoning a negro lad into a watery grave because he had passed a supposed line of segregation between white and negro bathers on a city beach."[2] Perhaps he was seeking relief from the heat of a late July afternoon in the city, or simply the pleasure of a relaxing swim in Lake Michigan. In either case, before the day's end Williams was dead. He had erred. Drifting on his raft, Williams floated across a racial border that though unmarked, remained nonetheless fixed in the eyes of his attackers. For the white youth who battered him with rocks and killed him, the border for this segregated white and black Chicago beach divided land and water in kind. During the ensuing weeklong summer riot, from July 27 to August 2, hundreds of African Americans in Chicago were wounded, many fatally; jobless, following layoffs by frightened employers; hungry from a reduced food supply in the communities of Chicago's "Black Belt"; and homeless, surrounded by cemeteries of collapsed brick, gutter graves, and streets piled with salvaged items that in their uselessness, they regretted having cared enough to save.[3] By July 30, the Black Belt was cordoned off by police and 6,000 military personnel, armed with 15,000 guns, equipped with military trucks and machine gun regiments, and commanded by adjutant generals. Eugene Williams was mauled with stones for gliding on a raft that crossed an imaginary boundary, a line of racial segregation that wavered with each ripple and wave. The specter of his trespass is a haunting reminder of the provisional political status of blacks within the United States.[4]

This devalued political status speaks to the critical distinctions between place and placelessness, a distinction that Houston Baker marks as the qualitative difference between being in control of, or being controlled by, boundaries.

74

For place to be recognized by one as actually PLACE, as a personally valued locale, one must set and maintain the boundaries. If one, however, is constituted and maintained by and within boundaries set by a dominating authority, then one is not a setter of place but a prisoner of another's desire. Under the displacing impress of authority even what one calls and, perhaps, feels is one's own place is, from the perspective of human agency, placeless. Bereft of determinative control of boundaries, the occupant of authorized boundaries would not be secure in his or her own eulogized world but maximally secured by another, a prisoner of interlocking, institutional arrangements of power.[5]

Baker's idiom of loss characterizes the kinds of deaths or extinctions that necessarily frame the experience of political provisionality. This figural marker for placelessness (a characterization that arguably names the conditions of black space) was violently realized during the race riots of 1919. The material losses exceeded the absence of law, home, and job, reflecting more than simply the structural expressions of disenfranchisement. Indeed, the damaged and disabled flesh of the injured, maimed, tortured, and dead became yet another script testifying to the provisionality of these persons within social space.

For Williams's death on July 27, 1919 expresses a violence that exceeded his dying, not only because it provoked four days of unmitigated racial violence, but also because it articulated a deliberate ungrounding of blacks within U.S. borders. Williams's death offers a social text for reading the material experiences of blacks within the United States. That he passed and was killed for crossing an imaginary water boundary testifies to the fluidity and permeability of borders, to the instability of the devices used to erect these boundaries, and to the violence that preserves them despite their structural and cultural flaws. His body, floating in a Chicago lake, symbolizes the social and legal vestibule that blacks occupy within the United States, a political narthex discomfittingly resembling the condition of the refugee, in which full civil entitlements, privileges, and protections remain suspended.[6] His watery grave becomes an unsettling refutation of black access to nation-space that speaks as much to blacks living in the 1920s as it does to the imperiled Haitian immigrant body of the 1980s and 1990s floating in the Windward Passage.

To read this, a moment so marked by lynching and a rising tide of race riots that James Weldon Johnson would call 1919 the "Red Summer," is also to read U.S. international liberalism backward and forward in history. The Chicago race riot reflects a moment grounded in the global shifts in world power that culminated in World War I. In the closing years of the nineteenth century and the opening decades of the twentieth, two contradictory but nonetheless cooperative strands of political ideology emerged. Similar in effect if not expression, they may be grouped under the heading of "containment." Colonialism's rubrics of containment were necessarily expressed domestically and internationally, as social space became recodified and as the national body, in turn, was further defined. That the bloody summer of 1919 bears a name matching the fluids that soaked the streets of our nation's cities highlights a telling coincidence of events: Red Summer references the communism and Bolshevism that were increasingly being linked to radical African American nationalisms as much as it names the riots and the blood. Yet the larger national and international landscape articulated in this conjunction of events is frequently lost. Although race riots are often understood in relation to domestic labor and economic upheavals, they are absent from studies of

U.S. foreign policy, denying us opportunities to trace a political unconscious revealed in the coordination between domestic and international state interventions. The violence and military intervention that occurred in July 1919 are part of a larger, historical campaign against black radicalism and blackness.

This chapter, like the chapter that follows on the United States's first Haitian occupation (1915–1933), traces the shared condition of blacks in and beyond the United States's borders, demonstrating the imperialist practices of a United States that could imagine Chicago as its heartland and Haiti as the outermost limits of its geographical claims. The drowned teenage boy whose body floating across an imaginary line of segregation instigated the riot; the literal and figural maps produced after the riot by the *Chicago Daily Tribune* betray a state of rescinded citizenship[7] that was endemic to segregation. The *Tribune* would go so far as to cast blacks as foreigners. My primary interest here is in the *Tribune*'s reporting on the riot. The written and visual narratives the paper produced borrow from an idiom of war to rehearse tropes of blackness prevalent in the political and cultural unconscious of the United States. To this end, the war writings of Sigmund Freud, Lothrup Stoddard, Randolph Bourne, and W. E. B. Du Bois do not simply explain the psychosis of post-Reconstruction white supremacy, the exclusionist immigration politics of the early twentieth century, and the politics of McCarthyism and the Cold War, they also help us assess a historically coordinated relationship between U.S. domestic practices and international interventions.

One corner of the first moment of U.S. global ambition, which began with the acquisition of Puerto Rico, Cuba, Guam, and Hawaii following the end of the Spanish-American War, is our beginning.[8] Analyses of World War I should include the U.S. invasion and military occupation of Haiti and the race riots, lynchings, and radical domestic insurgencies that came to mark our domestic landscape. The war's relevance to our changing global environment is reflected in the emergence of a discourse on war psychology that also reads as a primer on ethnic and racial profiling, new forms of state-supported surveillance, and an international liberalism that would produce the United Nations's precursor, the League of Nations. World War I was a moment of geopolitical pulsation, an international expansion and intracolonial contraction that made possible the American Century and its increasing privatization of resources.

TROOP MARCH

On July 30, 1919, the third day after the riots erupted in Chicago, the *Tribune* featured on its front page the march of national guardsmen to the armory, the new makeshift military headquarters for the North Side (see Figure 4–1). These troops arrived a little more than twenty-four hours after what would become four days of violent, bloody assaults within the Black Belt. The photograph captures not simply the state of U.S. race relations in the first decades of the twentieth century, but also the displacement of an international battlefield onto a domestic home front and the commensurate remapping of urban spaces and inhabitants into managed sites of containment. The photograph's wide angles resemble the aerial reconnaissance photography that would emerge during the war. The *Tribune*'s representation of orderly, bayonet-armed troops marching through the city does more than aestheticize violence. By engaging the visual repertoires of war and colonial photography, as well as parades and pageants, the photograph depicts the visual codes of war spelled out in the headlines and articles that serve as both its extended caption and frame: "Negroes Storm Own Hospital after Battle," "One Death in 14 hours puts Total at 26," "Rioters Ignore Overseas Negro Wound Stripes," "Combine Orders To Police and Troops To Combat Riot," "Downstate Troops Called to Aid Chicago: Local Militia Ready; Lowden Defers to Mayor," and "Loop Emptied of 250,000 in Record Speed." It is a "battle" that implicates, prolongs, and reinforces the racial undertones and anxieties over the status of black Americans and immigrant bodies, which was frequently the undercurrent of the violent conflagrations appearing in the aftermath of World War I.

The bold line used to offset photo from text is a visual design that ironically states the terms of Chicago's violent clashes—racial trespass. The dark frame suggests the problem of racialized space, the nature of war, and the visual absence to which this photograph inadvertently calls attention. For although the photographs's cropping constructs the perception of an unending line of troops, the bold frame calls attention to the artifice of the cut, casting the surrounding text as the natural extension of the image. The cut memorialized in the dark framing line amplifies what is absent from this image—the black body, the putative cause of the riot—and augments the representational density of this profile of U.S. troops bisecting a

FIGURE 4.1 "Troop March."
Chicago Tribune, July 30, 1919.

city. Part of the ideological work of the photo is meted out in the shot's perspective. Panning the expanse of a city street, this shot suggests the politics of war reconnaissance, while interpolating photographer and audience into both the soldier and his forward march toward an unspecified mission or enemy. In its ideological aestheticization of the riot, the photograph betrays a war psychology that remaps domestic space as a battlefield and black Americans as a foreign enemy. That blackness marks an excess already cued by the absence of black soldiers within the troop march is attested to in both the article beneath the photo's edge and in other representations to which the image syntactically gestures: the Silent Parade of 1917 and the military parades lauding both soldiers' departure and return from battlefields overseas.

In 1936, Walter Benjamin discussed the transformed relationship between "the masses" and art realized in reproducible arts like photography and film, mediums whose focalizing capabilities manufacture responses comparable to the effects of psychoanalytic theory on human consciousness:

> Since the *Psychopathology of Everyday Life* things have changed. This book isolated and made analyzable things which had heretofore floated along unnoticed in the broad stream of perception. For the entire spectrum of optical, and now also acoustical, perception the film has brought about a similar deepening of apperception.[9]

Yet part of this deepening of apperception necessarily includes an awareness of what Benjamin calls the "optical unconscious," an unconscious placed in at least partial relief by the details the camera highlights when it is fixed on a subject. The photograph becomes both the evidence of and the symbol for the mechanical ability of the camera to exhaust the visual scene, capturing the material available to its lens, a gathering that cordons off sites of excess. And that which remains excessive to the "Troop March," suppressed or perhaps repressed within the textuality of this optical unconscious, is precisely what Zahid Chaudhary characterizes as the "phantasmagoric aesthetics" underwriting colonial photography.[10] It is an aesthetic realized here in the phantasmagoric presence of the African American soldier that haunts the image.

An article describing the brutal beating of Frederick Smith, a thirty-three–year-old black veteran of World War I who served three years overseas as a member of the Canadian Army, rests beneath the figure of the troops' march, gesturing toward the buried racial politics within the image and the race riot that occasioned its capture. Having survived being "gassed and wounded," the fragile, injured Smith readily succumbed to the brutal attacks of Chicago's white youth gangs, gangs later credited in the report issued by the Chicago riot commission as principally responsible for the spread of interracial violence across the city. Smith himself encapsulated the tragic irony of his postwar injury in Chicago, an irony barely admitted by the article's headline, "Rioters Ignore Overseas Negro Wound Stripes." Distilling the terms of engagement underwriting the bloody scene, Smith declared, "I don't see why they wanted to bother a fellow like me . . . I did all I could to help make this old country safe for just such men as these. I call this a pretty poor welcome home." That Smith in his military uniform should be a victim of the flaying hands of white teenaged boys reinscribes the lengthened line of the troop march captured in the photo, for which it becomes a figural caption. Who and where is the enemy against whom these troops are setting up headquarters in the city armory?

The photograph, maps, and articles that make up the *Tribune*'s history of this violence share a synoptic register. Collectively they suggest an urban battlefield soon to be secured. Photojournalism here operates as more than simply an expression of the documentary, more than simply an illustration, but as a Derridian supplement:[11] the *Tribune*'s photographic coverage of the riot is both compensatory and substitutive. It both calls attention to what is missing, namely a visual narrative of the conflict and its participants, and offers another set of subjects in its place, namely patriotism and law and order. The phantasmagorical aesthetic of the image—like the others that preceded and succeeded it during the days of rioting—extends the work of intracolonialism for which the image is both evidence and memorial. The restoration of law and order visualized here compromised and endangered the black bodies who inhabited the city. Their "absent presence" in this photograph is a haunting reminder of the violent regulation, if not complete erasure, of black life that precipitated the bloody conflict.

The *Tribune*'s portrait of marching soldiers eerily resembles, and certainly cues within the cultural memory of many African Americans, photographs of the Silent Protest parade (see Figures 4–2 and 4–3) in Harlem, organized by the NAACP in response to the East St. Louis race riots of 1917. The riots in East St. Louis left 125 African Americans dead, hundreds tortured and disfigured, homes destroyed, and suspended and in some cases permanently ended,

FIGURE 4.2 Silent Protest Parade, Brownies Book, 1917.
Courtesy of the Photographs and Prints Division, Schomburg Center for Research in Black Culture, The New York Public Library, Astor, Lenox and Tilden Foundations.

FIGURE 4.3 Silent Protest Parade, 1917.
Courtesy of the Photographs and Prints Division, Schomburg Center for Research in Black Culture,
The New York Public Library, Astor, Lenox and Tilden Foundations.

black employment opportunities. The losses and grief were unremarked upon by a government that refused to investigate or condemn the events.[12] The deafening silence of hundreds,
coupled with the white dress and diminutive size of the child participants who marched
with, but were separate from, the mass of uniformly suited black males, articulated the frustration of black communities throughout the United States confronted by the bitter terms
and violent consequences of Jim Crow. Indeed, the children's white smocks, like the men's
dark suits, were traditional vestments of mourning. The marchers' silence held the weight
and stilled the moan of grief for the lives lost, not only in East St. Louis, but also through
lynching, the war, and rising mortality rates in urban centers.

What escapes the frame in the *Tribune*'s front-page image is the figure of the embattled
black body: the uniformed solider returning home from the war (reputedly on behalf of
democracy) confronted by unchanged segregation, the infant dead because of the diseases
and inadequate medical care that characterize poverty, and the lynched body murdered
in illegitimate reprisal for an alleged crime. The Silent Protest parade marked a shift in black
Americans' relationship to a state that demanded their participation in, and loyalty to, a "war
for democracy" and yet refused to condemn or to prosecute those responsible for the East
St. Louis massacre.[13] Although W. E. B. Du Bois and James Weldon Johnson believed black
participation in the war offered an oppportunity to highlight the loyalty, patriotism, and
value of blacks to the United States and to challenge prevalent racialized social and scientific
theories on "Negro capacity," the 1917 race riot proved the durability of racism and offered
evidence of a state that intended to maintain the status quo. For a community that was
already perceived as dangerous to the social and political fabric, the increasing militancy,

civil disobedience, and public critiques against the state indexed by the black children and adults of the Silent Parade were met by intensified surveillance of black life and suggestions of potential "Negro subversion."

The photograph of the Chicago riot reflects the idiom of war and the psychology of warfare. Mapped in the diagonal of bayonets and polished boots is the reconfiguration of a U.S. city into a policed territory. This representation of city life punctuated by the soldier's march distills the work of war. Yet understanding the *Tribune*'s coverage of the race riot depends upon the structures of intelligibility governing the image, what W. J. T. Mitchell characterizes as the "ground" that enables the photograph to appear.[14] The photograph functions as both metaphor for and symbol of the sociopolitical arrest experienced by the inhabitants of sanctuaries: refugees, stateless persons, colonials and semi-colonials.[15] Offering a visual syntax for the critical concepts to be discussed in this chapter—war, enemy, surveillance, spectacle, and cartography—the troops marching through Chicago begin an interlocution on war psychology and the transformation of the black body from native to foreigner/refugee, and the subsequent transformation of black space into sanctuary.

WAR PSYCHOLOGY

Six months into World War I, Freud asserted that "[w]e cannot but feel that no event has ever destroyed so much that is precious in the common possessions of humanity, confused so many of the clearest intelligences, or so thoroughly debased what is highest."[16] He attributed this intensifying social "disillusionment" to our altered relationship with morality and death necessitated by warfare. For Freud, the battlefield would provide the ground for developing his theories on repression and the unconscious, built around figurations of primitivism. Weighed and tempered by national and ethnic prejudice, Freudian primitivism became the undercurrent for a presumptive crisis in (white) civil society. "[War] strips us of the later accretions of civilization," he wrote, "and lays bare the primal man in each of us. It compels us once more to be heroes who cannot believe in their own death; it stamps strangers as enemies, whose death is to be brought about or desired; it tells us to disregard the death of those we love."[17] According to Freud it is not merely that war exposes the fragility of human life, but that this loss reflects a lost supremacy; it is not merely that war reveals the hypocrisy of a state that skirts as much as it flirts with the law, but that moral codes relax and civil societies regress into their primitive psychological states, states that are not readily overturned, yet absolutely essential for successful conflict.[18] And as morality and law collide, he argued, conscience and the moral and legal obligations it produces become flexible. In his words,

> our conscience is not the inflexible judge that ethical teachers declare it, but in its origin is "social anxiety" and nothing else. When the community no longer raises objections, there is an end, too, to the suppression of evil passions, and men perpetrate deeds of cruelty, fraud, treachery, and barbarity so incompatible with their level of civilization that one would have thought them impossible.[19]

That Freud's writings on war devolve into a discourse on civilization is critical to understanding the labor performed by and consequences of war psychology.

Civility in Freud's theories is predicated on sanctioning hatred. The community, the constitutive unit for the nation, requires aggression: "We have seen that a community is held together by two things: the compelling force of violence and the emotional ties (identifications is the technical name) between its members."[20] Rising fears over human mortality became space filler for white supremacy, referencing a specific anxiety over a vanishing white race aggravated by the war. Yet, these concerns about mortality and a weakened moral order (possibly leading to anarchy) that were prevalent during World War I equally spoke to the force of hatred in war: a hatred that when unleashed promises death, and whose propensity increases because moral codes are relaxed. According to Freud, "The individual who is not himself a combatant—and so a cog in the gigantic machine of war—feels bewildered in his orientation, and inhibited in his powers and activities."[21] And it is perhaps through shifting the terms and sites of battle that this frustration finds relief. Denied bayonet, the noncombatant may adopt hatred as a uniform. This hatred may manifest itself in any one or a combination of -isms and phobias: nativism, racism, sexism, xenophobia, or homophobia. In a kind of geographic and demographic transmigration, U.S. urban centers came to resemble European battlefields: twenty-five race riots within six months in 1919. And Gallipoli's fields of blood were reenacted in the bloody slow drip of dangling tree-, pole-, or bridge-hung black flesh: seventy-eight blacks lynched in 1918. In the United States these anxieties would rework themselves into dangerously productive ends offering imperative, subtext, and legitimation for public policy agendas, domestic surveillance strategies, campaigns opposing immigration, increased lynchings and race riots, and a burgeoning postwar foreign policy of international liberalism.

It was to this supposed liberalism, marketed as U.S. transnationalism and effected within the violence of a war waged internationally and domestically through segregation, vigilante violence, and formal and informal surveillance practices, that intellectuals like Randolph Bourne would turn their attention. Having already distinguished himself as an activist and intellectual in essays featured in *The Atlantic Monthly, The Dial,* and *The New Republic,* Bourne's antiwar protest essays in *The Seven Arts* critiqued not only the motives undergirding, but also the promises of democracy used to support, the war. Both Freud and Bourne were equally worried about the future that the war promised. What Freud perceived as a dissolving civility, Bourne read as the fortification of the state. According to Bourne, the expanding national technologies of control, containment, and surveillance ensured political consensus and solidified state power, and produced a political geography that removed civil liberties and protections under the rubric of preserving a national family. Of this situation, Bourne wrote, "War is the health of the State. It automatically sets in motion throughout society those irresistible forces for uniformity, for passionate cooperation with the Government in coercing into obedience the minority groups and individuals which lack the larger herd sense."[22] Indeed, the state's deep-seated interest in war shapes and foments hatred in the public imagination toward an enemy, a myth-making that produces consent and depends on a rationale of danger and peril for the nation-turned-homogeneous (white, middle-class, heterosexual) family. "In general," wrote Bourne, "the nation at war-time attains a uniformity of feeling, a hierarchy of values culminating at the undisputed apex of the State ideal, which could not possibly be produced through any other agency than war."[23] These processes of patriotism are so refined and replete that critiques of the administration often find little or no public space, let alone support, for their articulation. Campaigns for peace are muted beside a more vehement war propaganda machine or reimagined as assaults against the state, and socioeconomic, political, gender, sexual, religious, racial, generational, and ethnic differences are corralled by the shared specter of an evil enemy. Yet it is a hatred that, in failing to dissipate immediately, finds a postwar locus at home.

THE SEEDS OF DISUNION

Beginning the preface to *The Rising Tide of Color Against White Supremacy* with a line that directly draws upon—and quickly distorts—W. E. B. Du Bois's turn-of-the-century characterization of the preeminent problem of our times, Lothrup Stoddard wrote, "More than a decade ago I became convinced that the keynote of twentieth-century world politics would be the relations between the primary races of mankind."[24] A political theorist, Stoddard's preoccupation with war and revolution, particularly World War I, is attested to in the recurring topography of his writings. Yet, with titles including *The French Revolution in San Domingo* (1914), *The Revolt against Civilization: The Menace of the Under Man* (1922), and *Re-Forging America: The Story of Our Nationhood* (1927), Stoddard rendered palpable his fear of a specific brand of war: an impending race war. Offering a revisionist political geography in *The Rising Tide of Color against White World Supremacy* (1920), Stoddard traced a global racial imperialism that, although fueled by subsistence demands rather than strategic necessity, nonetheless promised the dissolution of white civilization.

Like his contemporary, Freud, Stoddard read World War I as a crucible for whiteness. And although their methodological approaches differed, the two cartographic projects that resulted are strikingly similar. For both men, the war marked a singular, unparalleled moment in their racially particularized versions of world history: the moment that revealed a (white) human vulnerability portending the dissolution of civilization (read here as a specific brand of whiteness). In *The Rising Tide of Color,* Stoddard constructed a pan-whiteness, ignoring ethnic and national distinctions among whites as he examined the effects of World War I on a global scale. Tapping into the political and cultural currency of geography, he regraphed the globe, creating a political geography already made possible through imperialism's racial topography. Stoddard placed race at the center of a global politics reduced to primordial pressures: fertility, demography, and geography. Mass replaced military, economic, or political might as the sheer magnitude of the colored races increased because of putatively higher fertility rates, rates that stood fair to destabilize existing power dynamics, ultimately promising to displace the political authority of whites around the globe.[25]

World War I rearticulated colonial fears of revolution, fears that within the United States amplified state and civilian concerns regarding black citizenship and the lengths blacks might go to secure these rights and to deconstruct segregation. The myth of white supremacy and invincibility—the foundation of colonial rule—dissolved before rising casualty lists, so that although war continued to expand white political control by broadening the "territorial basis of its authority," the "immutability" of white hegemony was nonetheless compromised.[26] Transformed into relations of intimacy and performance, supremacy, according to Stoddard, resides in the capacity to have sex and birth babies:

There can be no doubt that at present the colored races are increasing very much faster than the white. Treating the primary race-stocks as units, it would appear that whites tend to double in eighty years, yellows and browns in sixty years, blacks in forty years. The whites are thus the slowest breeders, and they will undoubtedly become slower still, since section after section of the white race is revealing that lowered birth-rate which in France has reached the extreme of a stationary population.[27]

By representing a demographic expansion as a "rising flood of color," Stoddard refuses to imagine the possibility of a politically ambitious, deliberative black world engaged in a countercolonial project. Instead, he frames this threatened shift in global power within the racially and culturally saturated discourse of instinct and self-preservation. This turn to breeding within racial communities as a measure of political health nevertheless rehearses a historic white claim that gained currency during World War I with D. W. Griffith's use of the racialized family as social barometer in the film *Birth of a Nation* (1915).

Representations of black pathology concomitantly emerged in the popular culture of the day. By the turn of the century, Lost Cause writers like Thomas Dixon were referencing microscopy and footprint analysis in their texts, capitalizing on the conjunction of science and race to manage black bodies and resolidify a nation that remained fractured by emancipation. Ten years after the publication of Dixon's immensely popular novel, *The Clansman* (1905), his thesis of white femininity imperiled at the hands of black males, which underwrote his account of a nation compromised by the threatening presence of the black body, resonated with a country anxiously watching the outbreak of a war cast as a crusade to "make the 'World Safe for Democracy,'" while rigorously seeking to sustain segregation.[28] Dixon's text moved from page and stage to big screen as D. W. Griffith's *Birth of A Nation* (1915), capturing the attention of millions worried about the stability of their own home (fronts).

Among the nation's first movie blockbusters, earning $18 million, *Birth of a Nation* offered a revisionist history of antebellum culture and the post-Civil War United States that installed a new rubric for national identity and national unity for the early twentieth century. The primer for films like *Hallelujah!* (1927), *Gone with the Wind* (1939), *Jezebel* (1940), and *Song of the South* (1946), *Birth of a Nation* refused sympathetic discourses that blamed contemporary national discord on the Civil War and the question of slavery, instead locating the source of national rupture and disunity in the initial encounter and continued presence of the enslaved (and now former slaves). Reading beyond Dixon's *Clansman*, the significance of Griffith's opening scene to these supremacist thematics resonates in the beating tom-toms, a rhythm that frequently interrupts a score otherwise composed of patriotic tunes.[29] Music condenses Griffith's project: the bombastic drumbeat operates outside and in deliberate contradistinction to the recurring patriotic song. The musical misalignment, and what was intended to be read as dramatic racial and cultural differences between the two musics, underscores an impassable divide reiterated in the subtitles and the images that ensue: glistening black bodies crowned and waisted with feathers, standing otherwise naked, follow an intertitle that reads, "The bringing of the African to America planted the first seed of disunion."

A film eventually used to enlist members to the Ku Klux Klan,[30] *Birth of a Nation*'s role within the national imaginary cannot be understated. Appearing within months of the beginning of the United States's violent eighteen-year military occupation of Haiti and only one year after the country entered World War I, the film offered a solution to regional and class fissures widened by the Civil War. *Birth's* musical score transformed Griffith's film into a national anthem, enabling the nation at war to cohere, tethered by mesmerizingly familiar songs that celebrated an imagined quintessential American culture. Although "Dixie" and "Turkey in the Straw" would serve as social glue, the true adhesive gathering Griffith's public lay in the promised possibility of eclipsing regional, religious, class, and gender differences with a shared enemy: the black body.

Part of the film's appeal and persuasive force as a propaganda instrument for what had been an almost extinct Klan lay in the particularities of the political moment—an occasion of global warfare. It is easy to imagine the effects upon sympathetic viewers of Griffith's anthems, articulating as they do the very patriotism that Bourne characterizes as both requisite for state health and the means for achieving a herd instinct used to solidify and secure state power. The success of the film's narrative was generated, in part, through a patriotism wedded to and welded through excised blackness, a fantasy of racial genocide rendered all the more urgent amid intensifying fears of white racial dissolution through the war casualties and the imminent race war. As intimated in the opening depiction of slaves arriving in the New World, blacks both within and beyond the United States threatened the Union. And "the seeds of disunion" that they embodied engulfed all of their biological materiality: semen and womb.

Framed within the genre of the sentimental romance, both the family and the South are visual shorthand for the nation: the crisis in national political culture was cast as a threat against family, ripening racial anxieties. The film's title discloses the stakes: the domestication of civil identity. Griffith imagined a nation literally and symbolically birthed by the white female body, a telling attentiveness to and participation in the sanctioned paranoias of U.S. civil identity. As foremother of the national body—and invariably the site of its foreclosure—white female sexuality compromised by the specter of black maleness equaled social dissolution. Framed by the intertitles, "The Aftermath at the sea's edge, the double honeymoon" and "*Liberty and union . . .* inseparable *now and forever,*" the fertility images depicted in the closing moments of the film—the Cameron and Stoneman couples dressed for their weddings—symbolize a future for the nation, a future that the continued unregulated presence of blacks supposedly risked.

This birthing of the nation along racially restrictive lines naturalized citizenship in precise ways. It defined race biologically, reserving access to the full social and cultural, let alone political, privileges of citizenship for white Americans. The racially and ethnically centered anti-immigration debates and proliferating immigration laws of the late 1910s and 1920s further confirm the wide-ranging, legislated effects of this racially coded geneticism for the national body. The appeal and stability of such images for many Americans is evident in the Chicago Censor Board's response to independent black filmmaker Oscar Micheaux's 1919 critique of Griffith's project in *Within Our Gates.* Three months after the Chicago race riot, Micheaux sought permission to release his film to Chicago audiences. His countermand to *Birth's* representations of black sexual predation and predators sought to supplant this mythology with depictions of black victimacy, of a capricious, routine ritual racial violence that included not only the murder and rape of black men, women, and children, but also incest executed by white fathers on their black daughters. According to Chicago's film board,

Micheaux's movie risked inciting yet another riot, a fear that Griffith's film failed to warrant.[31] In order to air the film, Micheaux was forced to remove more than 1,200 feet of putatively incendiary material.[32]

A MAN'S CHANCE

The years surrounding World War I provided the foundation for late-twentieth and early
twenty-first century hypervigiliance campaigns. Domestic combat took the form of a viru-
lent and vigilant white supremacism cloaked in antisedition and anti-communism campaigns. It would be difficult to overstate the tenacity and elasticity of the "herd instinct," this
abandonment of self and refrain from critique for the sake of the state. Cultivated by and for
the preservation of the state at war, Bourne's version of the "herd instinct" embodies the hate
generated during the manfacturing of an enemy, a lethal disdain that endures and extends,
joining disparate collectives together. Although the Army, Navy, and Marine Corps fought
abroad, many civilians would become a kind of parapolice force, relentlessly scouting and
surveying for potential threats—spies, seditionists, and subversives—to national security.
They would become primary instruments and agents for redacting civil liberties, forming
their own intelligence-gathering organizations such as the American Protective League,
American Defense Society, National Civic Federation, and the National Security League for
spying on neighbors, friends, and associates while federal agencies proliferated and
expanded.[33]

   The gateway to securing a reconfigured United States, national security during and after
the war limited immigration patterns, foreclosed naturalization, restricted inheritance and
property ownership, stripped U.S. women married to Asian foreign nationals of their citizenship, renewed a long-defunct Enemy Aliens and Sedition Act (Alien Act and Espionage Acts
of 1918), and led to the passage of the Trading-with-the-Enemy Act (1917), the Sabotage Act
(1918), the Passport Act (1918), and extended formal and informal strategies for surveillance.
I want to emphasize the political and cultural moment of this a hypervigilance that installed
the Bureau of Information, the precursor to the FBI, and that produced a policing force for
almost every branch of the federal government, including the Postal Service: this is the
moment of war. We need to understand this "brotherly watchfulness" as a symptom and
expression of a war psychology. The vigilance it demanded bred vigilantism. Aggravating
existing fears over the nature and extent of democracy at home, World War I offered a convenient platform for staging and protracting an already active white supremacism at home.
In a country whose national stability was already tensely held by segregation's legal and social
codes, the war threatened to widen racialized political divides. Significantly, white supremacist activity rose during a war that was understood by many as a crucible for whiteness and by
black political activists as an opportunity to campaign for political rights. This period witnessed President Wilson's celebration of Griffith's *Birth of a Nation,* President Harding's
admittance into the Ku Klux Klan while in office, and proliferating work in, and attention
to, eugenics in criminology, behavioral, social, and biological sciences, and even in the formulation of federal immigration law.[34] The failed passage of federal antilynching legislation
(the Dyer Bill of 1922) amid a lynching rate that rose during the war and the enactment of
some of the most egregiously restrictive immigration laws in U.S. history (the Quota Act of

1921 and the Johnson Reed Act of 1924)[35] capped a shared cultural fear of difference. The democratic initiatives at stake in the war worried our own domestic politics, engendering fear among whites that black soldiers campaigning for self-determination abroad would seek and expect the same civil entitlements at home. For an already frustrated black population, the war underscored the hypocrisy of a state that battled for democracy abroad while continuing to withhold it at home.

"If we must die, let it not be like hogs/Hunted and penned in an inglorious spot/While round us bark the mad and hungry dogs,"[36] cried Claude McKay. Written in the aftermath of twenty-five race riots during a six-month period, McKay's "If We Must Die" (1919) was less a battle cry than a call for self-defense. Tethering a discourse on primitivism and warfare, on captivity and violence, McKay's poem testifies to an intractable violence whose predatory intensity necessarily revises the terms of black life and black masculinity. Although marked as hog, the black body remains singularly human in these lines, as McKay reserves grotesque epithets for the white assailants. McKay's retreat to, and revision of, racial biologisms and racist logics restructures this battle into a campaign for human dignity and human life. Decoupling cultural representations of savagery from blackness, he reimagines the corruption of racial violence as the degradation of whiteness into monstrousness. And his image for the slaughtered and captive body—the hog—describes the carceral, violent conditions of black life and the imperative for a self-defense upon which black masculinity is necessarily hinged. "Like men we'll face the murderous, cowardly pack." To the extent that the "hunted and penned" black body promises to remain impugned—"What though before us lies the open grave?"—black dignity and black humanity rests on a defensive, decisive response. The figural and literal insistence of blood produces a poetic cadence that remembers life's fragility ("So that our precious blood may not be shed/In vain"), outlines the dangerous stakes of this race war ("Though far outnumbered" blacks must "for their thousand blows deal one death-blow!"),[37] and confesses the spectral presence of death. Yet "If We Must Die" is not simply a testament to black humanity, but also a primer outlining the constitution of black masculinity. The references to manhood, self-defense, and cowardice capture the debates surrounding the Negro soldier in World War I, debates locating the uniformed black man as a synecdoche for larger concerns about black citizenship for the African American community. Writing at the end of the war, McKay's representation of this international conflict as a battle for humanity both domesticates and extends this global conflict to U.S. shores. His poem refuses the idea of a war ended, claiming instead a battle as yet to be joined, one in which black soldiers—literal and symbolic—must transfigure the U.S. political landscape.

"I am but one of many victims of my people who are paying the price of America's mockery of law and dishonesty in the profession of a world democracy," said Sgt. Edgar Caldwell to the crowd of 2,500 gathered on July 30, 1920, to witness his execution. Du Bois would characterize Caldwell's death as a "legal lynching." The sergeant's wrongful murder conviction, his illegitimate judicial proceedings, and his failed U.S. Supreme Court appeal are more than footnotes in the historiography of World War I and African American history, but document the greater problem of the black male body in U.S. politics and social life. Caldwell was a victim of segregationist regulations over space. Boarding the Oxford streetcar line in Anniston, Alabama, on December 24, 1918, Caldwell mistakenly secured a seat in the whites-only section, an error that—in addition to a dispute over fare—prompted the conductor, Cecil Linton, and the motorman, Kelsie Morrison, to assault and throw him from the train. While face down on the ground, Caldwell was repeatedly beaten and kicked by the two train representatives, an attack that triggered the soldier's defensive reflex. Enacting his combat training, Caldwell rolled and shot. Morrison was dead, and Linton injured. Indicted less than a week later, his trial, conviction, and sentence to death came within weeks of the event.[38]

Following the persistent petitions of a local minister, R. R. Williams, Caldwell's case gained the attention of the NAACP and its legal defense team, who not only questioned the legality of the defendant's summary trial and its all-white jury, but also the indictment and venue for the proceedings. His conviction for murder effectively erased the primary injuries and provocation Caldwell suffered, injuries dictating the nature of his crime. Beaten both on the streetcar and the street, Caldwell's crime failed to meet the premeditation requisite for the legal definition of murder. At worst his violent response fell under the legal heading of self-defense or manslaughter. His appeals and first scheduled execution date ran parallel to the Chicago and Washington riots of 1919.[39] Caldwell was pummeled by white fists, Jim Crow, and a judicial system that tried him in a kangaroo court and denied him access to a military trial, which held at least the possibility of clemency. His case captures the peculiar situation of the black American (male), for whom the figure of the soldier stood as symbol and agent of promise during the first half of the twentieth century.

In his brief address at the Calhoun County prison before his execution, Caldwell claimed the victimhood that the legal system had denied him and rendered his case banal: "I am but one of many victims."[40] Compelling for the indictment they serve up, and perhaps more significantly for the forgiveness they refuse, Caldwell's words distilled the payment in flesh made by blacks on the battlefield. "I am but one of many" becomes shorthand for the African American soldiers beaten, tortured, maimed, and lynched for having worn their uniform too long, or for having worn one at all.[41] The disillusionment couched in these lines tempers how we must read the war in relation to black Americans. "This is the crisis of the world," wrote Du Bois in his July 1918.[42] "We of the colored race have no ordinary interest in the outcome. That which the German power represents today spells death to the aspirations of Negroes and all darker races for equality, freedom, and democracy." Resisting provincial political ideologies of race and race relations, Du Bois focused on the so-called "Negro problem" within international strife. In the midst of the Paris Peace Conference during the spring following the Armistice, he wrote,

> Some Americans may think that Europe does not count, and a few Negroes may argue vociferously that the Negro problem is a domestic matter, to be settled in Richmond and New Orleans. But all these careless thinkers are wrong. The destinies of mankind for a hundred years to come are being settled to day in a small room of the *Hotel Crillion.*[43]

In words grievous to many black intellectuals and uncannily reminiscent of Booker T. Washington's 1895 Atlanta Compromise speech, Du Bois concluded his essay with a petition: "Let us not hesitate. Let us, while this war lasts, forget our special grievances and close our ranks shoulder to shoulder with our own white fellow citizens and the allied nations that are fighting for democracy. We make no ordinary sacrifice, but we make it gladly and willingly with our eyes lifted to the hills."[44] The future imagined in the "hills" was to be realized through a simplified prescription: black loyalty to the war.

In the words of an African American soldier in France, "We came to France and won a man's chance."[45] His remark anticipates the entitlement that would undergird black nation-alisms, radicalisms, and militancy during the 1920s while realizing white supremacist fears of black demands for fuller participation in U.S. political and social life. Like Abraham Lincoln's anthropometric studies conducted on Civil War soldiers, the Stanford-Binet intelligence tests administered to U.S. Army soldiers in 1917 and 1918 would mark yet another installment of U.S. nativism.[46] The work of eugenicist Lewis Terman, these tests conceived of fitness as a racialized determinant of "Americanness," highlighting the frequent coincidence of xenophobia and racism. A putative competency test, ability did not simply measure skill for armed service, but also serviced the historical problem of black and immigrant fitness for civil life. Administered in English, the tests reflected linguistic, regional, and class biases. According to Richard Slotkin,

> Success in answering the questions depended on the subject's recognition of terms and figures from professional baseball and football, medicine, commercial trademarks, and advertising slogans—information familiar to English-speaking middle-class urban whites, but likely to be unfamiliar to non-English speakers and to Blacks and Whites from rural districts.[47]

Correlating numeric scores with coded categories—"superior," "inferior," and "subnormal"—the findings of these deeply flawed tests aided the work of anti-immigrationists and sanctioned competency and heredity theories founded on race.[48]

Labeled by Mississippi senator James Vardmann the single greatest threat to the South,[49] African American soldiers experienced the full assault of Jim Crow, ranging from public censure to brutal beatings, court martials to hangings, medical treatments withheld to leaves and weekend passes denied, segregated regiments to a complex of substandard living conditions including inferior housing, equipment, supplies, training, and transportation outlets. When a medical sergeant in Manhattan, Kansas, was prohibited from entering a local movie theater by its owner because his presence might discourage business from white patrons, the sergeant's commander, Gen. C. C. Ballou, issued Bulletin No. 35, a corrective for black behavior. Prohibiting black soldiers from fraternizing among whites, Ballou's five-point memorandum openly confessed the necessity of suspending legal rights in the interest of preserving the comfort of white southerners: "It is not a question of legal rights, but a question of policy, and any policy that tends to bring about a conflict of races, with its resulting animosities, is prejudicial to the military interest of the 92 Division, and therefore prejudicial to an important interest of the colored race." He insisted that black troops under his command "refrain from going where their presence will be resented," arguing that "no useful purpose is served by such acts that will cause the 'color question' to be raised."[50] Prompting the ire of black presses and further dampening the morale of black troops, Ballou's mandate was of a piece with the policy practices of the armed services. But it is the second point of the bulleted memorandum that most tellingly discloses the nexus between law, policy, and prejudice in the promulgation of Jim Crow. A gesture that recalls Paul Laurence Dunbar's assertion that the black body is always presumed guilty,[51] Ballou acknowledged his sergeant's legal right to enter the theater, yet condemned him nevertheless: "He is strictly within his legal rights in this matter, and the theater manager is legally wrong. Nevertheless the sergeant is guilty of GREATER wrong in doing ANYTHING, NO MATTER HOW LEGALLY CORRECT, that will provoke racial animosity."[52] Civil rights are trumped precisely because law and social custom sanction segregation. The bulletin, like segregation, produces Neuman's anomalous zone of legal practice: the dislocation of law that produces an alternative legal structure.[53]

Du Bois wrote in June 1919:

[T]ransported bodily from America sits "Jim-Crow"—in a hotel for white officers only; in a Massachusetts colonel who frankly hates "niggers" and segregates them at every opportunity; in the general from Georgia who openly and officially stigmatizes his black officers as no gentlemen by ordering them to never speak to French women in public or receive the spontaneously offered social recognition.[54]

After visiting African American troops in France for several months, Du Bois catalogued the litany of abuses suffered by black regiments as a consequence of a Jim Crow politics, by which it was "thoroughly understood . . . that the Negro had to be 'properly handled and kept in his place.'"[55] Bearing a title almost as ominous as the indictments it would list, Gen. John G. Pershing's military directive, "Secret Information Concerning Black American Troops" (1918), was intended by the Army as a cautionary note for French officers and personnel working and living with these soldiers. Stating that "American opinion is unanimous on the 'color question' and does not admit of any discussion," the Army demonized African Americans as a "menace of degeneracy" to the "Republic." The radical distance effected in the taxonomic distinctions made between American and African American in this message performed a kind of linguistic denationalization. The gulf between these identities deepened with the catalogue of offenses presented. Named a racial inferior, blacks lacked "intelligence and discretion . . . civic and professional conscience." And as the repeated rape allegations in France demonstrated, they must be "repressed." Remembered by Du Bois as the circular of American Negro prejudice, this document demonstrated the international stakes of domestic race relations. Claiming that the French needed to have "an exact idea of the position occupied by Negroes in the United States," military officials insisted that blacks must not only be prevented from intimate contact and association with the French, but also that the "familiarity" demonstrated by the French toward black soldiers was of "grievous concern" and considered by Americans to be an "affront to their national policy."[56]

The relatively few African Americans promoted to officers were among the most vigorously challenged. The circular called for the shared management of black troops by white and French soldiers. Its pleas to decline eating and socializing with black officers and its recommendation not to "commend too highly the black American troops," but rather to "moderately" acknowledge their efforts, were part of a larger campaign to discredit black troops, and black Americans in turn. And it was perhaps because African American officers most emphatically embodied the "fitness" and equality of black Americans symbolized by black soldiers that African American officers received some of the most brutal recriminations by the services. "The campaign against Negro officers began in the cantonments," wrote Du Bois. "Most of the Colonels began a campaign for wholesale removals of Negro officers from the moment of embarkation."[57] Commanding officers submitted numerous letters to Army headquarters requesting the replacement of black officers with under qualified white personnel. Citing cowardice, untrustworthiness, incompetence, and an inability to lead and control black soldiers, black officers became the ground on which a battle against black men could be waged. Accused of routinely failing "in all their missions," of "[sneaking] off to the rear, until they were withdrawn," of "numerous accidental shootings, [and] several murders," and of being suited to do "anything but fight," black officers and soldiers were frequently court-martialed and even hung on specious evidence and allegations, most particularly for rape and fraternization with French women.[58] "The undoubted truth," wrote Col. Allen J. Greer to Senator Kenneth D. McKellar, "is that the Colored officers neither control nor care to control the men. They have in fact been engaged very largely in the pursuit of French women." With more than thirty allegations of rape in their collective record, the black soldiers of the 92nd regiment were, in Greer's words, "dangerous to no one except themselves and women."[59] The necessity of a Military Morale Branch to rally African American military and civilian support for the war testifies to the climate of assault against black life. "It would seem in this great American melting pot," wrote R. S. Abbott, publisher and editor of the *The Chicago Defender,* "we are a little closer to the flame than any other class, but perhaps this fire test makes us the best and most loyal American citizens."[60] Through a mass of letters, addresses, poems, essays, books, and photos, African Americans vehemently petitioned against the disfigured character of the black soldier, marshalling the logic of racial pride and the achievements of black regiments as their evidence.

The more than 1,000 letters received by the Bureau of Investigation in 1917 voiced prevailing fears about subversion and national security, which fed suspicion of the black armed body. The image of a black male ape common in nineteenth-century anthropometric studies, restaged in the ethnographic exhibitions at world fairs, and bolstered by the caging of Belgian Congo native Ota Benga in the primate cage of the Bronx Zoo (1906), received new license in contemporary caricatures of German spies as gorillas.[61] The collapsed distinctions between German enemies and black bodies thickened a discourse on Negro subversion and lent apparent credibility to Griffith's dangerous black soldier.[62] The same racial prejudice that laughed at the subversive Negro or blackened German ape ironically precipitated the disillusionment in U.S. politics that risked African American allegiance to the state and rendered this community vulnerable to anti-American German war propaganda. If the black soldier worried white America, he emboldened black America.

"[T]he imperative duty of the moment," wrote Du Bois in the Loyalty issue of *Crisis* (May 1919), "is to fix in history the status of our Negro troops," against the rising tide of articulations that the "black officer was a 'failure.'" Photography and illustrations substantively aided the work performed by texts like Kelly Miller's *History of the World War for Human Rights* (1919), Emmett Scott's *Official History of the American Negro in the World War* (1919), and Du Bois's preliminary essays and research toward what he had hoped would become the larger volume, *The Negro in the Revolution of the Twentieth Century.* Visual shorthand, the photograph captioned black loyalty, and helped to redeem the caricatured black male body (see Figures 4–4 and 4–5). Scott's promise of an "Authentic Narration, from Official Sources" that is "Profusely Illustrated with Official Photographs" cues the competing visual narratives saturating representations of the black body. For the recursive presence of the photographed figure of the black soldier in African American newspapers and periodicals, and in bound volumes of African American war history, worked much like Du Bois's war-era campaign to publish photographs of fit black babies: Displacing the mugshot and the lynched black body, the uniformed black body in combat and still pose, and in cantonments and military parades, troubled articulations of black subnormality, degeneracy, and death.

For African Americans the conjunctions among black conscription and compelled loyalty, rising black lynching rates, and increasing domestic violence were hardly lost. "On the eve of a great patriotic parade, while the members of our $300,000 police force are making a house-to-house canvas in order to begin registering the Race manpower of Memphis and Shelby country for selective conscription," wrote an outraged *Chicago Defender* staff correspondent, "A MOB OF 3,000 OF THE NATION'S RULING CLASS, SHERIFFS, JUDGES, EDITORS, LAWYERS, PRIESTS, PREACHERS, PHILANTHROPISTS, MILLIONARIES AND MERCHANT PRINCES deliberated" and planned the lynching of Eli Persons.[63] Sadly, the double headline preceding the article—"Horrible Memphis Lynching Astounds Civilized World" and "Tenth Cavalry to France"—betrayed a domestic norm: lynchings continued as troops marched. The coverage of these two events frequently coincided, appearing in tandem in articles and headlines in the African American press.[64]

FIGURE 4.4 1st Lt. James E. Scott, 367th Infantry, Camp Upton, N.Y.

From W. E. B. Du Bois's photograph collection, ca. 1917–1918. Courtesy Special Collections and University Archives, W. E. B. Du Bois Library, University of Massachusetts, Amherst.

FIGURE 4.5 Needham Roberts.
From W. E. B. Du Bois's photograph collection, ca. 1917–1918. Courtesy Special Collections and University Archives,
W. E. B. Du Bois Library, University of Massachusetts, Amherst.

The evidentiary weight of photographs as proof and social history cannot be overstated. Du Bois would cite the repeated refusal by the Chief of Staff to permit photographers to record the war work of black troops,[65] while remarking elsewhere that Army photographers were enlisted to capture the lynching of a black soldier in France by the U.S. Army. These writings and images itemizing the awards and assaults against black military life further mediated the response of black Americans to the war and to U.S. political culture.

In direct response to what one *Crisis* writer would describe as the "unvoiced determination to belittle our [African American] efforts, to mock and to refuse to recognize all that is black,"[66] African American newspapers covered the achievements of black regiments and the war hardships borne by black civilians. Increasing in number and subscribers partly because of this population concentration, black presses proliferated alongside nationally felt black radicalisms and nationalisms. Creating a national audience, black presses orchestrated the dissemination of political ideas by black intellectuals and radicals across the country, which was crucial to the civil rights mobilizations afoot. The emergence of the NAACP (1910), black women's clubs, the National Urban League (1910, 1920),[67] Garvey's Universal Negro Improvement Association (UNIA) (1914), and A. Philip Randolph's Brotherhood of Sleeping Car Porters (1925), across a roughly fifteen-year span reflects concerted, engaged, and organized efforts demanding political and social reform. Figures like Claude McKay would find themselves wrestling with the political and social possibilities forecast by communism but foreclosed because of race. But for readers of *The New York Times,* who credited the riot to German-"duped" blacks and Bolshevism, blacks were decidedly, if not dangerously, un-American.

FOREIGN IN A DOMESTIC SENSE

Thus, the 1919 race riots were part of a postwar ethos that solidified and licensed what had already begun legally in 1896 (*Plessy*) and 1901 (*Insular Cases*)[68] and had been carried further in 1915 with the Haitian occupation. Chicago's riot-ravaged streets bore the remnants of a war psychology that reflected white supremacism, for which war had offered sanction and to which segregation was afforded the protection of the law. The postwar riots of 1919 stood in marked contrast to the violent racialized conflagrations of the turn of the century, specifically the Wilmington (1898) and Atlanta (1906) race riots. The increasing social and economic pressures produced by war, segregation, new migratory patterns, demographic changes, increased immigration, and densely populated urban centers amplified cultural attention to race. Mass migrations out of the South to the Midwest and the North precipitated by wartime labor demands altered the character of these riots. Most notably, the populations at risk and the sites of engagement had shifted since previous race conflicts. As anticipated in the labor difficulties undergirding East St. Louis (1917), race riots were now no longer Southern in their geography, and their "victims"—the mass of migrating laborers from the South—were often the poorest of the poor.

Each of the twenty-five race riots of 1919 speaks in its own way to racial conditions during and following the war, yet collectively these histories attest to the vestibule that was black life—a corridor between international and domestic space, whose structure and condition is best understood through extranational state practices. The corridor that segregation would make legally and geographically visible, however, continues to persist today, surrendering its residents to the status akin to occupants of extranational U.S. territories: "foreign to the United States in a domestic sense."[69] This colonial logic was cemented into legal thought by the *Insular Cases* (1901–1922). These thirty-five Supreme Court cases tested the applicability of the Constitution to U.S. territories, consistently labeling these sites as both unincorporated and subject to separate legal customs. A lawsuit addressing import duties owed on oranges imported into the United States, *Downes* v. *Bidwell* (1901) decided the peculiar status of Puerto Rico, and later all unincorporated U.S. territories. Specifically, international threats against these islands were perceived as threats against the United States, but in all other ways these unincorporated spaces were, in Chief Justice Edward Douglass White's opinion, "foreign to the United States in a domestic sense."[70] Although the inhabitants of U.S. territories were considered citizens, they were denied many of the privileges of citizenship, among them representation and participation in a representative government secured through voting. Their anomic citizenship effectively rendered them unincorporated members of the body politic—citizen.

Not insignificantly, the *Insular Cases* exposed a juridical and political consciousness that regulated political incorporation based on a perceived foreign threat during an historic era in U.S. empire building. The recodification of black and brown communities into foreign spaces and peoples during both the early decades of the twentieth century was neither new nor benignly intentioned. Rather, it reflected a much more intransigent racializing practice.[71] Explicitly signaling the imbricated relationship among imperialism, civil identity, and race, Justice White's articulation of an alternative political identity—"foreign in a domestic sense"—speaks to the state's ability to internally displace and/or colonize its own citizens. It was a brutal reminder of the ways in which the dispossession judicially sanctioned in *Plessy* could effectively be translated and revised to apply to other communities. "Foreign in a domestic sense" names the dialecticism within black American political identity—legally a citizen but nonetheless politically and legislatively disenfranchised. Although White's appellation serves as sufficient shorthand for understanding black American political identity, this designation is driven and shaped by the complex legal, political, and social matrices constituting the institution of slavery. The *Insular Cases* are but a reminder of the ways in which state power relies on the relationships established in *Dred Scott*. Justice White contended that to count Puerto Ricans among the citizenry of the United States would mean that U.S. citizenship was "precarious and fleeting, subject to be sold at any moment like any other property. That is to say, to protect a newly acquired people in their presumed rights, it is essential to degrade the whole body of American citizenship." Amy Kaplan's reading of Justice White's opinion reconfirms what nineteenth-century jurisprudence on citizenship consistently revealed—blackness stands among the critical axes against which civil identity takes it shape. It was this very legal orthodoxy that Melville unpacked in "Benito Cereno" and Justice Harlan railed against in the *Civil Rights Cases* (1883). Fastening onto Justice White's arguably strategic recourse to metaphors of a degraded political body and a citizenship rendered precarious because it had been reduced to a commodity object—transferrable property—Kaplan rightly accuses Justice White of "resurrecting" the "memory of slavery." Having intimated "a moral and racial tainting" through the invocation of "physical degradation," Kaplan insists that Justice White managed to connect "the inclusion of nonwhite citizens from abroad" with "the enslavement and darkening of white Americans." By her measure, "according to White's logic, the notion of 'foreign' in 'a domestic sense' maintains Puerto Rico as a 'possession' and its people as quasi-slaves 'acquired' to differentiate U.S. citizenship from the degradation of slavery."[72] Unsurprisingly, a similar recalibration of black Chicagoans into domestic foreigners and later slaves inflected the *Tribune*'s cultural narrative of the race riot.

Within the climate of fear, xenophobia, and heightened white supremacism that gathered its force in the summer of 1919, African Americans' status as "domestic foreigners" efficiently captured the correlation between state racism and immigration policy. The mass migrations of blacks in response to the labor demands of war and to the sociopolitical conditions of Jim Crow quickly transformed these economic migrants into "foreigners." It is hardy incidental that black Chicagoans were described as foreigners, refugees, and eventually slaves in the *Tribune*'s reportage, in an historic moment when civil liberties were suppressed through civilian-led task forces and surveillance agencies.[73] Three years later the Chicago Commission on Race Relations, a group formed by Chicago governor Frank Lowden in 1919 to investigate the causes of the riots, would consistently label African American neighborhoods "colonies."[74] Such a designation, at the very least, placed black citizens-turned-refugees squarely within the politics of immigration. The anti-immigrant sentiment mapped onto black Chicagoans colonized their bodies and mirrored federal legislation restricting naturalization and immigration along racial and ethnic lines. According to the Chicago Commission on Race Relations, more than half a million African Americans left the South between 1916 and 1918. They were part of the Great Migration, a mass exodus of African Americans fleeing the neocolonial conditions of a post-Reconstruction South. Labor demographics shifted with the onset of World War I. Thousands left industry to participate in military campaigns abroad, and the steady stream of new laborers typically guaranteed through immigration ran dry. The loss of laborers to military campaigns, coupled with a reduction in foreign immigration, produced a labor crisis that opened up employment options to black Americans in major industrial centers throughout the country. Labor agents actively canvassed black workers throughout the South, promising better wages and, in some cases, train tickets to relocate. Chicago alone saw an increase of 50,000 in the black population from 1917 to1918.[75] In their landmark study *Black Metropolis: A Study of Negro Life in a Northern City* (1945), St. Clair Drake and Horace Cayton documented the effects of this massive influx of black laborers from the rural South on urban landscapes, tracking the emergence of Chicago's residentially segregated "Black Belt," or what they referred to as "the Black Metropolis."

Admittedly, not all stayed who arrived in Chicago, for the city served as a kind of urban depot for other points north and west. Chicago, along with other Northern cities, nonetheless continued to be imagined in African American presses like *The Chicago Defender* as "the Promised Land": higher wages, more "permanent prospects," and as Richard Wright said of his initial encounter with the city, a place without "racial fear."[76] Of this enthusiasm for the city the commission would write,

> The stimuli of suggestion and hysteria gave the migration an almost religious significance, and it became a mass movement. Letters, rumors, Negro newspapers, gossip, and other forms of social control operated to add volume and enthusiasm to the exodus. Songs and poems of the period characterized the migration as the "Flight out of Egypt," "The Escape from Slavery," "Bound for the Promised Land," and "Going to Canaan."[77]

With headlines such as "Frozen Death Better," "Good-bye, Dixie Land," and "Determined to Go North," *The Chicago Defender* encouraged black flight by restaging abolitionist rhetoric that compared migration from the South to an exodus from racial tyranny. "To die from the bite of frost is far more glorious than that of the mob. I beg of you, my brothers, to leave that benighted land. You are free men," urged the *Defender*, and "You see they are not lifting their laws to help you, are they? Have they stopped their Jim Crow cars? Can you buy a Pullman sleeper where you wish? Will they give you a square deal in court yet?"[78] Yet, as the race riots throughout the North from 1917 well into the mid-1930s would attest, the sanctuary that the North promised was hardly free from racial violence and discrimination.

Framed by such *Tribune* headlines as "3,500 Troops Ready to Go into Riot Zone: Daybreak May See Black Belt Under Military Rule," "Patrol Burned Homes to Foil New Terrorism: Troops Act on Hint of Revenge Raid on Black Belt," "Negroes Seek Safety Haven At Milwaukee: Hundreds Flee from Chicago to Escape Rioters," and "Troops Armed, Ready to Act; No Order Given," the Chicago race riots amounted to a series of killings, arsons, and robberies that led to military intervention within black residential space. Published maps of each day's events supplemented the *Chicago Daily Tribune*'s coverage of the riots. Like the photograph of the "Troop March," the maps borrow from, and accrue intelligibility through, a semiotics of war that translates domestic events into a racial battlefield. The visual vernacular shared among these maps and those published to chart the progression of the recently settled global conflict casts Chicago's Black Belt as a war zone marked for territorial conquest, transforming its inhabitants into refugees desperately searching for sanctuary. Initially intended to chart the sites of racial infighting ("The Riot Area Extending Over the Black Belt"),[79] these maps and the news articles that ensued created an itinerary of war that, by the end of the riots, reflected the colonization of space that is a by-product of military conquest (see Figures 4–6 and 4–7). The maps' Germanic crosses resemble military targets more than clashes. They were replaced with so-called flags and shading as a sign not only of their presence, but also of the appropriation and subsequent erection of "protected" borders (see Figures 4–8, 4–9, and 4–10).

The maps and surrounding text frame an accounting of war mediated through terminology that progresses from anti-immigrationism mimicry, blaming the riots on "aliens" ("Hoodlums—newcomers—drifters, who have come to Chicago with the influx from the south. No permanent resident of the black belt is involved in these riots"), to increasing militarism ("a front line of battling whites and Negroes, with spurts of fire in the Chicago avenue district" and "troops readied for riot") (see Figure 4–11). The nature of the riots shifted within the *Tribune*'s coverage, from the local competition and frustration with access that Eugene Williams's crossing of the water border marked, to the larger questions of borders and national bodies anticipated in racial segregation. Blacks are identified as exiled, as seeking extraterritorial refuge in neighboring states ("South Offers Chicago Negro Exiles Homes"), and as refugees pleading with police powers for shelter and protection ("Riot Refugees Flee to Police Fearful of Mob"). Occurring alongside the presence of federal troops, arms, and war maps, the riot coverage both visually and linguistically makes black bodies alien in an emerging contest over national bodies and spaces.

We need only return for a moment to the Commission's description of Negro flight from the South to understand the collapsed distinction between an anti-immigrant and anti-black sentiment that labeled blacks as foreigners. The *Chicago Tribune*'s initial distinction between native black Chicagoans and newcomers begins a narrative that culminates in the misrecognition of the legal status of black citizens and constructs Chicago as a

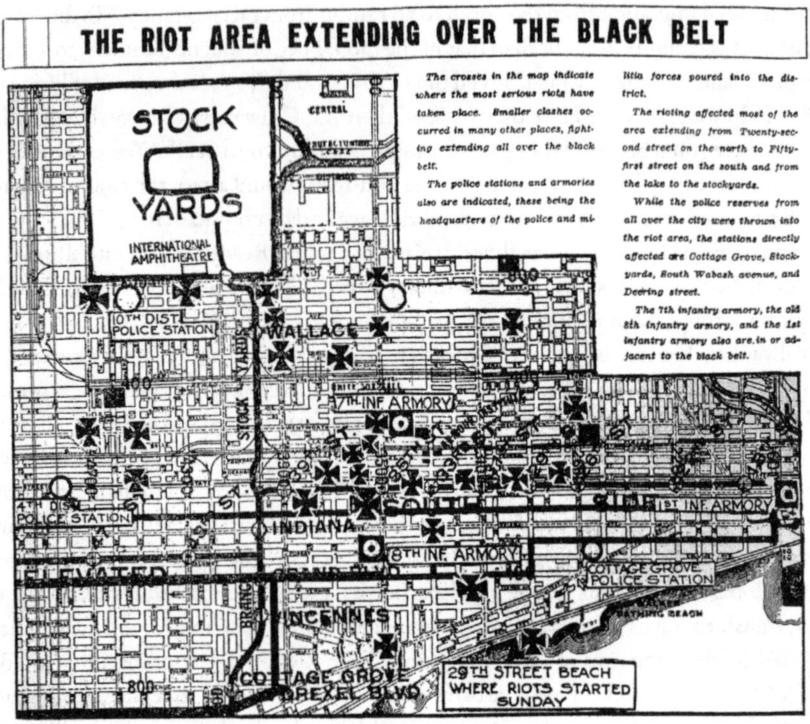

FIGURE 4.6 "The Riot Area Extending Over the Black Belt."
Chicago Daily Tribune, July 29, 1919.

nation within a nation. The Commission, like the *Tribune,* consistently refers to these economic migrants as "immigrants": "Chicago was a re-routing point, and many immigrants
went on to nearby cities and towns." Even more pointed, however, are the Commission's
concluding remarks. Summarizing its findings in the foreword to the report, the Commission argued, "It finds that in that portion of Chicago in which colored persons have lived
the longest and in the largest numbers relatively there has been the minimum of friction.
This is a fact of the first importance. For it tends to show that the presence of Negroes in
large numbers in our great cities is not a menace in itself."[80] Focusing on long-standing
black residents of Chicago intimates a distinction between native and newcomer, which
replayed a cultural logic of assimilation circulating through much of the discourse on the
Great Migration.

As the *Tribune*'s maps and articles moved from the initial reports to military notes, the
Black Belt was renamed a slave quarter, and the stakes of this interracial engagement became
more explicit: the reappropriation of black bodies into human cargo. Mocking the real terror
of blacks during the riot, the *Chicago Daily Tribune* provided supposedly phonetic representations of black speech, reporting:

"Uncle Tom's Cabin" in a modern setting—that was central police station yesterday.
Like fugitive slaves of the ante-bellum south, colored citizens huddled in the squad
room and awaited their turn to be taken home under escort.

FIGURE 4.7 "Where the Races Rioted Yesterday."
Chicago Daily Tribune, July 30, 1919.

WAR MAP OF THE BLACK BELT

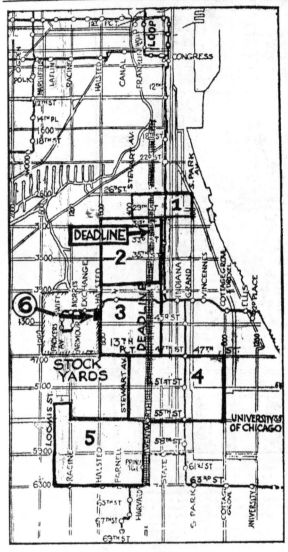

Three Illinois national guard and three Illinois reserve militia regiments took over the south side race riot area last night, shortly after 9 o'clock. The disposition of the troops follows:

1. Second Illinois reserve, Col. Joseph E. Wilson; South Park to Stewart avenue, Twenty-sixth street to Thirtieth street.

2. Third Illinois reserve, Col. Anson L. Bolte; State street to Halsted street, Thirty-first street to Thirty-eighth street.

3. Eleventh Illinois national guard, Col. James E. Stewart; State street to Halsted street, Thirty-ninth street to Forty-seventh street.

4. Tenth Illinois national guard, Col. O. P. Yeager; Cottage Grove avenue to Stewart avenue, Forty-eighth street to Fifty-fifth street.

5. First Illinois reserve, Col. A. F. Lorensen; Fifty-fifth street to Sixty-third street, Wentworth avenue to Loomis street.

6. Ninth Illinois national guard, in reserve at Dexter pavilion, stockyards; Col. Frank L. Taylor in command of base.

FIGURE 4.8 "War Map of the Black Belt."
Chicago Daily Tribune, July 31, 1919.

All day long they streamed into the station. Some came of their own accord. Others, too timid to venture out by themselves, telephoned for a bluecoat escort.

Belle Lawton of 4431 South State Street, a chambermaid at the Hotel Sherman, was sitting apprehensively on a bench between two colored men yesterday afternoon.

"Ah've been alahmed all day," she quavered, "an' fin'ly Ah just phoned Main 13 an' told 'em to come an' get me."

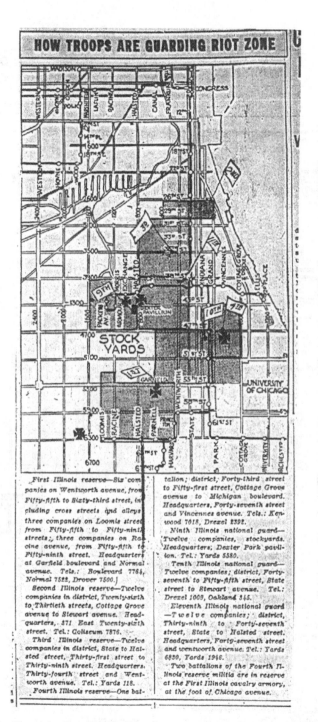

FIGURE 4.9 "How Troops Are Guarding Riot Zones."
Chicago Daily Tribune, August 1, 1919.

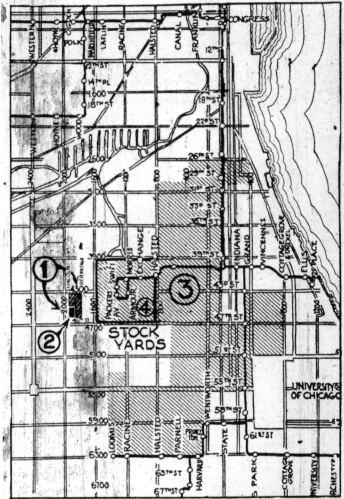

MAP OF RIOT AND FIRE ZONES

Shaded Area Shows Part of City Where Race Troubles Occurred—Black Area Marked by Arrows Shows Territory Burned Over.

1. The fire zone is bounded on the north by West Forty-third street, on the east by South Hermitage avenue, on the south by West Forty-sixth street and on the west by South Lincoln street.

2. The conflagration was at its worst in Honore street, between Forty-fifth and Forty-sixth streets, although many homes were damaged or destroyed in other parts

of the zone. The stricken families are encamped on the prairie land immediately west of the ruined district. There was a lesser conflagration at Forty-third and Wood streets

3. The large shaded zone indicates the riot district, which is now being patrolled by the militia.

4. Shows the location of the stockyards.

FIGURE 4.10 "Map of Riot and Fire Zones."
Chicago Daily Tribune, August 3, 1919.

THE ANSWER

[Copyright: 1919: By John T. McCutcheon.]

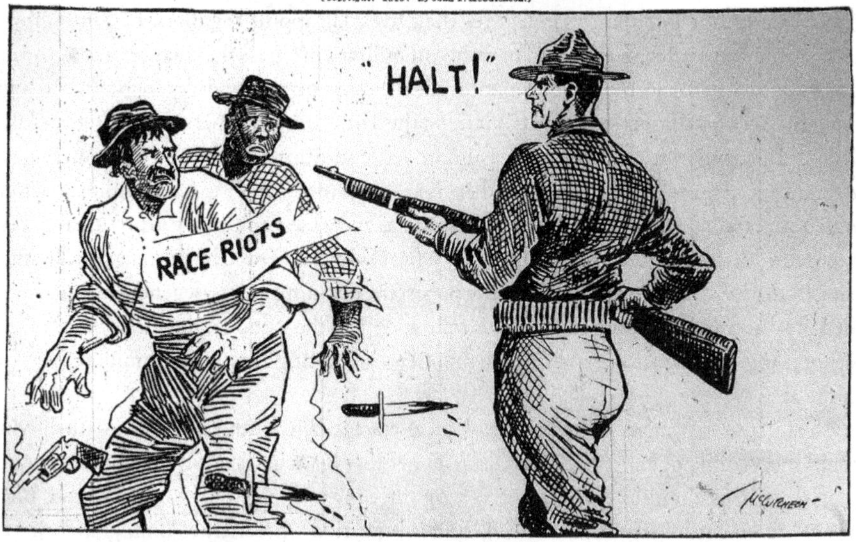

FIGURE 4.11 "The Answer."
Chicago Daily Tribune, July 31, 1919.

> Not far away stood a middle aged colored man whose costume was topped with an old black derby.
>
> "No, suh, Ah'm not takin' no chances," he said. "If Ah was bullet proof, like one of them there dugouts, it'd be diff'rent. Somethin' tells me Ah better stick right here with the perlice." [81]

That Harriet Beecher Stowes's *Uncle Tom's Cabin,* a text that Lauren Berlant persuasively argues in "Poor Eliza"[82] cannot help but revive racialized questions of domesticity and domesticated bodies, would be cited here is not surprising. The textual movement—from black neighborhoods to slave quarters—that the evocation of Stowe enabled underscores a social unconscious already coded within the maps and the accompanying news article narratives of war, that explicitly remands black bodies back into slavery.[83] With a shift in pronouns and nominatives, the *Tribune* revived slavery, characterizing the escorting of blacks to their homes as the movement of articles and transforming these persons into fungible property: "At long intervals a closed delivery auto from one of the downtown department stores would halt at the curb and the *human merchandise* would climb aboard. . . . 'We've *handled* over 400 of *them,*' stated Capt. Morgan Collins."[84]

In their work of surveying and containing, the riot maps merge the visible and the invisible. In their daily representations of the spectacle of violence, they chart sites of territorial penetration—zones of occupation that illustrate the nationalist dimensions of war strategies. Maps disseminate an epistemological power that colonizes not only spaces, but also the occupants of the sites they chart. The riot maps offer an itinerary that renders invisible the causes of the riots and fails to document the conditions within the black community—the starvation, the blood-streaked streets, the burned and pillaged homes, the battered and dismembered flesh paraded on sticks, the unemployment, and the darkness concealing African Americans hiding in buildings in fear for their lives. Chopping the Black Belt into military sectors, the maps offer an extended narrative of military progress that may be traced through points of successful access and occupation identified in map legends by numbers ("1" signifying the Second Illinois reserve; "2" marking the Third Illinois Reserve), shading, and flags. This is a progress intended to reflect "improved conditions" through coded messages of assurance and public safety, conveyed in map deadlines[85] for expected military activity, which succeeding maps faithfully demonstrate as met. Law and order is presumably being restored with increasing numbers of troops, a process documented by the daily thickening of zone lines, the shading of sectors, and the persistent recoding of map legends that on one day identify the various regiments, on the following list the commanders in charge of each armory, and on August 1 list telephone numbers, suggesting a permanent military presence in the area.

Thus, these riot maps reflect an ideological engagement with blackness as alien, which could successfully operate despite its fallacies because blackness continued to register not as a characteristic found in persons but as a signifier for property to be appropriated. Blacks needed to be cordoned off, "quartered," and inventoried—precisely as immigrants and foreign nationals were actively monitored, harassed, and arrested during the war for the threat they posed to national security. The *Chicago Daily Tribune* represented blacks as fungible "human merchandise." According to the *Tribune*, blacks were ultimately transportable, like Michel de Certeau's axiom on national borders: "Boundaries are transportable limits and transportations of limits; they are also metaphorai."[86] African Americans in 1919 Chicago were indeed in a political vestibule: subject to law but, with the increasing fungibility of their bodies and military management of their property, no longer subjects of the law. Their predicament ironically mirrored the conditions of sanctuary that, from the perspective of the *Tribune,* they were moving toward, as the Black Belt became putatively safer under the military's management. By August 1, the *Tribune* would boast, "The soldiers of the state are in full control."[87]

SOME RESIDENTS IN TROUBLE

On their final day of riot coverage, the *Tribune* replaced the war maps with a different icon of racial symbolism, the black Madonna and child. Framed by the headline and supporting subtext, "A Gleam of Silver Shows in Clouds of Riot: Long Awaited Food and Milk Supplies Bring Hope and Happiness to Some Residents in Trouble," a smiling black mother, Eloveize Simmons, holds her daughter, Eloveize Ball, while the infant eagerly clasps a jug of milk. This symbol of contentment and stability deepens with the presence of young Ernestine Fambro, a girl carrying a basket filled with needed supplies (see Figure 4–12).[88] These carefully aligned portraits produce an image that corroborates the headline's assurance that help has arrived for this beleaguered black community. Yet, this soothing representation flattens the real starvation, unemployment, and homelessness occurring in black Chicago communities and renders appropriate the single paragraph treating relief measures in the two-page article on the riot. The cultural power of the Madonna icon is such that readers do not wonder, as they

A Gleam of Silver Shows in Clouds of Riot

Long Awaited Food and Milk Supplies Bring Hope and Happiness to Some Residents of Trouble Zone.

ERNESTINE FAMBRO.

*ELOVEIZE SIMMONS
AND NAMESAKE,
BABY ELOVEIZE BALL.*

FIGURE 4.12 Eloveize Simmons, her daughter Eloveize Ball, and young Ernestine Fambro. *Chicago Daily Tribune,* August 3, 1919.

should, whether this mother and child have a home. The Madonna becomes the mechanism for dulling memory, producing like slavery's "happy darky"—a comforting illusion that the "quarters"/Black Belt have returned to their (impoverished) normality. Both her iconographic status and the ideological work attached to Ernestine are braced by the relative interchangeability of their portraits. That they are "cut outs"—Derridian supplements pasted, applied, and affixed beside one another—speaks to the labor the photographs perform to make the riot palatable. The Madonna image operates as a spectacular moment of ideological success: all the aggression and violence located in the riot and its cultural narratives are funneled into a single pleasing image, and any burden of social and structural responsibility disappears. It is a photograph that confirms Kaplan's assessment of the domestic as always already invested in a nationalist venture—a complex of territorial expansionism read as conquest, and occupation read as spatial and bodily colonialization that implies the violent insertion of borders.[89] Literally inserted into this text, Simmons, her namesake, and Ernestine are neither non sequitors nor misplaced, but extend the work produced by the maps of the preceding days, supplementing their discourse of custodial care.

As much as Bourne speaks of the state configured as mother during a state of war, and as much as Berlant reminds us of the figurations of women within national fantasies, this black woman and these children, by virtue of their blackness, are not the historically imagined or accepted national family. They do, however, reframe the geopolitical terrain of a deeply political, racially fractious contest and offer an alternative accounting for the violence. The photograph of Eloveize Simmons and her baby are part of a genre influenced by Christian imagery taken up in nineteenth-century photography, but the discursive codes it reveals are more complex.[90] The circulation of versions of the image in both the *Tribune* and the Chicago Commission's report suggests the liberal excesses for which they were employed (see Figure 4–13).[91] Although more readily discernible in the Commission's reprinting, these snapshots resemble portraits in a family album, which they likely were (see Figure 4–14). Again, the young mother posed with her daughter revives a comforting domestic sentimentality. The photo's resemblance to representations of black nursemaids and their charges in bourgeois family portraits of the nineteenth century forestalls the racial discrepancy of the baby depicted here. Cultural critic Laura Wexler reminds us that middle-class U.S. households had been constructed through and in relation to family photographs. To *Tribune* readers, this strangely familiar image would be reassuring, but also would frame their interpretations of the race riot through the lens of domestic space and custodial care.[92]

The visual density of the images reprinted in both publications—the *Tribune* and the Commission Report—displaces the economic and racial foundations of segregation and of this local instance of race war. Instead, they offer a surrogate history or cultural frame for deeply political, racially incisive events: the five-day conflict was an assault against home. These final moments of the *Tribune*'s reporting highlight the restoration of the black community—a restoration realized in the groomed mother and her fed baby and the young child and her heavy load of supplies—effacing and replacing the conditions of the conflict. This aesthetization moves the terms of engagement, reinscribing the race riot as a conflict over home. Custodial care is carefully rescripted as nation-state and home collide. And the enemy alleged in the prior days of reporting is even further stabilized: the black (American) foreigner.

The black Madonna and child call attention to the remaining graphic inscription deployed by the *Tribune* to tell this history of racial violence—photography. As forms of intertextual articulation, these modes of communication—linguistic, cartographic, and photographic—are more than simply mediators or frames posing for one another, for none completely inhabits or exhausts the meaning of the other. What interests me here is the peculiar labor of the photograph in the discursive fiction of war created by the *Tribune*. The photograph rehearses a narrative of safety and assurance secured through military force that compromised black humanity. This sleight of hand required the absence of the black male soldier's body, replacing him with the politically defused image of a black mother. Although unmistakably the product of segregation, the Chicago riot offers us more than a simple case

FIGURE 4.13 Milk was distributed for the babies.
From *The Negro in Chicago: A Study of Race Relations and a Race Riot*. Chicago Commission on Race Relations.
Courtesy General Research and Reference Division, Schomburg Center for Research in Black Culture,
The New York Public Library, Astor, Lenox, and Tilden Foundations.

FIGURE 4.14 Provisions Supplied by the Red Cross to Hundreds of Negro Families.
From *The Negro in Chicago: A Study of Race Relations and a Race Riot*. Chicago Commission on Race Relations.
Courtesy General Research and Reference Division, Schomburg Center for Research in Black Culture,
The New York Public Library, Astor, Lenox, and Tilden Foundations.

study on segregation. This is a history of the ways in which native sons and daughters were reimagined as outsiders, their civil status coextensive with the black and brown communities occupying the United States's extraterritorial claims, and the dire consequences of such a redrafting. Conscripted like the custodial bodies her presence is intended to conceal, the Madonna/Eloveize Simmons/mother flattens the custodial effects of violence, and the violent effects of custody. She obscures the custodial relation imposed on Eugene Williams, on segregated black Chicagoans, and on segregated black Americans held as bodies in custody whose access to civil space and its privileges remained withheld.

One cannot begin to understand U.S. foreign policy during the past century without contemplating race and racism, or understanding the ebb and flow of race and racism in this nation, without contemplating the global context.

GERALD HORNE, "Race from Power: U.S. Foreign Policy and the General Crisis of White Supremacy"

5

"I Dream a World": Occupied Haiti and

African Americans

"THE UNFITNESS OF the Haitian people to govern themselves has been the subject of propaganda for the last century," wrote James Weldon Johnson in a special issue of *Crisis* in September 1920.[1] Following a three-month investigation conducted on behalf of the NAACP, Johnson authored a four-article series on the ongoing occupation, which was published by both *Crisis* and *The Nation*.[2] His essays attracted the attention of the Republican Party, whose campaign slogans would come to include "Self-determining Haiti as a ploy for securing African American votes." His probe netted the first Senate hearings in 1922 to address U.S. Marine practices on the island, following the slaughter of 3,000 Haitian Caco insurgents by U.S. soldiers in 1918 who were protesting military-enforced labor conscription (*corvee*). The investigation included allegations of U.S. Marine kidnappings, and the wrongful imprisonment of Haitian civilians.[3] Johnson's precise language—"the unfitness of the Haitian people"—betrays the colonial motivations underpinning the U.S. occupation. This racially charged discourse on fitness circumscribing political, social, and cultural histories of the island is part of a larger, historic debate about "Negro capacity" that would burden the question of black self-determination through World War II. Sanctioned by techniques in medicine, forensics, ethnology, anthropology, and psychology that proliferated in the late nineteenth and early twentieth centuries, the discourse on Negro capacity suffused colonial practices both domestically and abroad. Driven by economic imperatives but shaped by a war psychology birthed in global conflict, the Haitian occupation offered fertile ground for both white supremacists and black intellectuals engaged in the problem of African American civil rights. Haiti became the crucible around which supremacist anxieties, regarding the domestic reach of U.S. constitutionalism that deepened with World War I, continued to be forged.

Seven years earlier, Du Bois offered a different petition on behalf of the besieged island. Writing directly to President Wilson weeks after Marines invaded the island, Du Bois fastened onto the importance of fair dealing with Haiti in "establishing the moral hegemony of the United States in the western hemisphere," and more interestingly, in relation to black Americans. "The United States has throughout the world a reputation for studied unfairness toward black folk," critiqued Du Bois. Slinging guilt to incite a different approach in the United States's dealings with her neighbor, Du Bois inveighed:

> The political party whose nominee you are is historically the party of Negro slavery. Is this not a peculiarly opportune occasion to attack both these assumptions by doing, in the words of your letter . . . to Bishop Alexander Walters, "not mere grudging justice, but justice executed with liberality and cordial good feeling," to the only independent Negro government in the New World?[4]

Yet, Du Bois's claims on Haiti had as much to do with his investment in self-determination as a fundamental human right as it did with a quintessentially U.S. sensibility that perceived a connection between Haiti and the political future and social life of black Americans. "She is almost the sole modern representative of a great race of men among the nations. It is not only our privilege as a nation," urged Du Bois to Wilson, "to rescue her from her worst self, but this would be in a sense a solemn act of reparation on our part for the great wrongs inflicted by this land on the Negro race."[5]

This chapter discusses an internationalism that functions not simply in name, but in the political unconscious of a nation state whose domestic politics are mirrored in its international interventions. The hangover of a war psychology couched in a paternalist discourse shaped U.S. relations with Haiti along two related lines: U.S. domestic and foreign relations, and black American claims for civil rights. Against the United States's imperialist occupation and cultural fetishization of Haiti, African Americans wielded the revolutionary history of the island as an instrument for extending African American civil rights within a global crisis over race and colonialisms.[6] Their revisionist aesthetic for Haiti became part of a civil rights discourse on peace and democracy, on sovereignty and equality, after World War I. This turn to Haiti's history during the occupation functioned on no fewer than four registers: as counterclaim to Western histories pathologizing blackness, as a challenge to the problem of sovereignty for black peoples, as a catalyst for domestic Black civil rights, and as another set of recuperative black histories emanating from postwar black nationalism. Apparent here is a black internationalism that refuses to disassociate black Americans from a globally waged assault against black life.

Turning to Langston Hughes's play turned opera, *Troubled Island, Emperor of Haiti,* (1936), I limn Haiti's role as a vehicle for further mobilizing the interwar civil rights movement in the United States, and outline a black internationalism that yoked domestic racial policies to the threatened sovereignty of Ethiopia and Haiti and the rise of fascism in Western Europe. The figure of the slave anchors Hughes's charges, unleashing an acerbic critique of modernity and, perhaps more significantly, an indictment of the shifting political landscape announced by the rise of fascism and by the sustained colonialism in Africa, India, the West Indies, and a segregated United States. Slavery—the signal shared experience among blacks in the New World, an event that installed the social and legal dislocations that became normative for blacks in the United States—with its ensemble of discursive and material practices, defined black life. In Paul Gilroy's words, "It is . . . the relationship between masters and slaves that supplies the key to comprehending the position of blacks in the modern world."[7] Toni Morrison goes further: "It's not simply that human life originated in Africa in anthropological terms, but that modern life begins with slavery."[8] The retreat to the revolutionary past by many black intellectuals during this period disrupted geographical and national distances and canceled ethnic and historical particularities among blacks in the Atlantic, and emphasized a shared history of New World enslavement. These revisionist histories did more than adjudicate a set of social and political symmetries across the black Atlantic, and did more than supply a corrective to traditional historiography on the black body: they posited an ineluctable *changing same* within something that may be classed as the modern black condition. Their restagings refused the partitive approach of history. Casting the Haitian Revolution as a scene of black possibility and hope, a political manifesto, and an international call for black political solidarity, they recalled the island's utopian promise for black civil life despite its present attenuation. In their resurrection of the figure of the (Haitian) slave body, black intellectuals articulated the necessity of new forms of social and political relations for a world wedded to the sociopolitical and economic gains supported by black disenfranchisement and colonialism. The figure of the slave became a supple trope for unpacking the problem of sovereignty and freedom placed in crisis by Du Bois's semi-colonial black Americans.

FITNESS TO RULE

When the United States invaded Haiti on July 15, 1915, they camouflaged their political and colonial ambitions on the island. The administration framed the incursion as a mission intended to stabilize the government following the murder of President Vilbrun Guillaume Sam and several political prisoners.[9] The United States had spent the previous year attempting to gain a more permanent entry into Haitian economic and administrative affairs, hoping to expand and solidify its own commercial interests on the island.[10] The occupation convention that followed, sanctioning both a U.S. military presence and federal oversight until 1936, bore remarkable similarities to the administrative terms the United States sought in 1914 with the substantive addition of control over Haiti's military, as well as its financial affairs. Haitians were stripped of their land, legislature, military, finances, voice, and sovereignty. It was a violence mediated for both the U.S. public and military by a discourse of familial protection. After nineteen years, the United States withdrew its troops from the island in August 1934.

With his invasion of the first black nation in the Western hemisphere, Woodrow Wilson furthered his version of a new world order. From the turn of the century through the 1930s, U.S. colonial projects were masked by a foreign policy of international liberalism that caused social historians to credit this interval, particularly the interwar years, as the United States's period of isolationism. Yet this policy of neutrality in international affairs licensed interventions that transformed countries in the Caribbean and Latin America into permanent or "temporary" dependencies. Despite the apparent contradictions between speech act and political practice, U.S. engagements and occupations in this region adhered to an imagined political map: isolationism effectively only applied to U.S.-European relations. From 1898 to 1922, the administration reinterpreted the meaning of the Monroe Doctrine, conveniently extending its interests in the Americas under the aegis of assisting border countries to secure or maintain their sovereignty. Under the pretext of protection and with the promise of aiding in the discharge of national debts, the United States corralled Haiti (1915–1934), Nicaragua (1912–1925), the Dominican Republic (1916–1924), and Honduras (1924–1925). By 1914, the United States was intimately involved in the affairs of the Mexican government, removing then-President Victoriano Heurta, in addition to dispatching U.S. troops to Cuba (1917), Panama (1918), and El Salvador (1932).[11]

The Monroe Doctrine legitimated these aggressive interventions, remembered as the Banana Wars, as well as extended periods of occupation that were couched as defensive measures against an unwanted European presence in the Western hemisphere. Strengthened by the Roosevelt Corollary of 1904, which proclaimed the United States an "international police power," the Monroe Doctrine enabled the United States to acquire the benefits of colonial rule without the stigma. Treaty agreements, like the one brokered with Panama authorizing the United States to act "as if it were the sovereign of the territory,"[12] confirmed the ways in which extranational territories were framed and incorporated into the political consciousness. Aid became a convenient ruse for ensuring hemispheric hegemony. Vulnerable countries in the Americas such as Haiti were convenient outlets for a United States anxious to reap the benefits of a white supremacism renewed by the *revanche* of the Versailles Treaty and the Paris Peace Conference. With the restoration of control over colonial possessions by European powers, decolonization was sacrificed for the maintenance of white (political) supremacy at home and abroad. The war psychology embraced by soldier and civilian during World War I extended into a Pax Americana whose effects were felt in sites as near as Chicago or as distant as Haiti, Mexico, and Panama. Haiti's occupation reflects the first actualization of Wilson's planetary ambition. The successful invasion and military occupation gave force and substance to Wilson's claim that the United States had entered a new age.[13]

Although the opening years of the United States's military takeover garnered little attention in a mainstream press, which remained riveted by the military campaigns and political outcomes of World War I, during the interwar period representations of Haiti saturated U.S. popular culture. "It is interesting to speculate," wrote the anthropologist Melville Herskovits, "just why the life of the Haitian peasant . . . became a subject for lurid description."[14] Haiti became a fetish for cultural productions and an object of social scientific and pseudoethnographic memoirs stimulated by the U.S. Marine presence on the island. Works by both U.S. and European authors found a ready audience in the United States. Texts like William Seabrook's *Magic Island* (1929), Faustin Wirkus's *The White King of La Gonave* (1932), John Craige's *Black Bagdad* (1933) and *Cannibal Cousins* (1934), Richard Loederer's *Voodoo Fire In Haiti* (1935), Edna Taft's *A Puritan in Voodoo-Land* (1938), and Philippe Thoby-Marcelin's *Beast of the Haitian Hills* (1946), emerged alongside Anna Julia Cooper's history of the Haitian revolution, Charles Gilpin's and Paul Robeson's performances in Eugene O'Neill's *Emperor Jones* (1920, 1925), Melville Herskovits's and Zora Neale Hurston's anthropological studies, Jacob Lawrence's *Toussaint L'Ouverture* series (1937–1938), C. L. R. James's *Black Jacobins* (1938), Langston Hughes's play, libretto, and juvenile fiction on the island, Josephine Baker's portrayal of a caged Haitian songstress in *Zou Zou* (1934), Orson Welles's Federal Theater Project staging of *Black Macbeth* (popularized as *Voodoo Macbeth*, 1936), and William Du Bois's *Haiti* (1938).[15] Projecting themselves as pseudoscientific studies, the fictions by figures like Seabrook, Taft, Craige, and Loederer stabilized images of black primitivism, gaining further ground for proponents of paternalism—the grease lubricating the axle of imperialism[16] and aiding the political reconfiguration of extranational space—and recruited the public into the project of empire building.

Ethnographic narratives of Haiti participate in a conceptualization of freedom that depends on the discourse of racial subjection—the social and linguistic codes Saidiya Hartman delineates as the fuel for slavery and, later, for the new forms of racial bondage that emerged post-Emancipation. Seabrook repeatedly turned to what would become a kind of primal scene for Haiti in the U.S. imaginary—the occult, specifically voodoo.

"The colored people of the United States should be interested in seeing [the removal of U.S. troops] ... ," Johnson petitioned, "for Haiti is the one best chance that the Negro has in the world to prove that he is capable of the highest self-government."[17] To lose in Haiti, Johnson insisted, meant that blacks would lose their greatest hope for an alternative to segregation—indeed, an alternative to their political voicelessness.[18] The political and social rationales servicing U.S. martial law and segregation abroad drew from the repertoire of representations of black inferiority: the child, the coward, the buffoon, the idiot, the criminal, the diseased, the savage, and the slothful or indigent black person. Operating at the expense of black dignity, these representations managed and disguised fears over black enfranchisement that, as this episode in Haiti demonstrated, were not merely provincial in nature. These racist anxieties crossed the Atlantic, underwriting the violence in Chicago (1919) that ran concurrently with the occupation of Haiti. The discourse on black fitness in World War I included Haiti among its expressed sites. During this period of armed conflict, debates over fitness went beyond the familiar categories of physical, sexual, and moral hygiene to include a prescription for manhood. Collectively, these categories supported theories of governance and political participation predicated on racial capacity.[19] The taxonomic efforts supported by anthropology, sociology, and psychology sought to discount the legitimacy of black claims for self-determination in the United States and in Haiti. As a *New York Age* editorial remarked in the days immediately following the invasion, "We long to see Haiti demonstrate to the world the capacity of the Negro for self-government and self improvement ... each time she suffers from revolution and lawlessness we experience a feeling of almost personal disappointment over it."[20] Although the chief administrator for the U.S.-run Haitian government, Gen. John B. Russell, argued that Haitians held the mental intelligence of seven-year-olds, Secretary of State Robert Lansing insisted on the propensity of black Americans, Liberians, and Haitians to "revert to savagery," an insurmountable fact that "makes the negro problem practically unsolvable."[21] Haitian's infantalization ran lockstep with the race intelligence tests being conducted on black Americans through the military and in experiments like M. K. Trabue's at Columbia University on 4,730 blacks and 28,052 whites, which putatively established the black mental age at nine.[22] The discourse on black criminality, first solidified by an influential study by Prudential Insurance Company statistician Frederick L. Hoffman, *Race Traits and Tendencies of the American Negro* (1896), with Charles McCord's *The American Negro as A Dependent, Defective, and Delinquent* (1914), further coupled an impugned black Americanness to the delinquent Haitian body.[23]

A U.S. Marine commander and head of the Haitian gendarmerie, Gen. Smedley Butler's testimony before the Senate Select Committee on Haiti and Santo Domingo, which was convened in 1922 to investigate the U.S. occupation of the island, clarifies the stakes of Russell's and Lansing's appraisals. Encoding the logic of racial subjection used to promote the capitalist enterprise attached to U.S. imperialism, Butler creates a bridge between the infantalization of Haiti and nineteenth-century slavery. Terms like "minors," "wards," "develop," "docile," and "harmless" work in concert with "horrible atrocities," "cannibals" and "voodoo" to form a collocational set—a vocabulary on primitivism and underdevelopment—in Gen. Smedley's remarks on Haiti and her people. For this general, who imagined that U.S. Marines in Haiti, and by extension America writ large, "were trustees of a huge estate that belonged to minors," Haitians were in fact a "most gentle" people "when in their natural state." He surmises,

> Ninety-nine percent of the people of Haiti . . . are most gentle when in their natural state. When the other 1 percent that wears vici kid shoes with long pointed toes and celluloid collars stirs them up and incites them with liquor and voodoo stuff, they are capable of the most horrible atrocities; they are cannibals. They ate the liver of one marine. But in their natural state they are the most docile, harmless people in the world.[24]

Two interdependent strands of racial thinking are present here. On the one hand, clothing within Butler's statement to the Senate becomes the vehicle through which racial anxieties and economic ambitions are unleashed: Haitians in Western dress resemble equals in a social economy executed by martial law where even a semblance of equality cannot afford to be legitimated. Butler later admits that teachers wore vici kid shoes with long pointed toes, whereas barefooted farmers enacted his celebrated "natural state." This celebration of the Haitian farmer laboring for U.S. sugarcane companies over the educator stresses the radical opposition between economic imperialism and republicanism—the campaign, in fact, for economic underdevelopment that Neil Smith argues motivated empire building.[25]

Addressing a body convened, in part, to respond to the U.S. Marine-led massacre of several thousand insurgents rebelling against the conscription of Haitian labor, Butler justifies U.S.-imposed neo-slave labor arrangements by invoking the racial ideology that buttressed U.S. slavery. Here, the second-order racial logic emerges. Butler's clothing-driven racial caricature expresses the putative psychological, social, political, and economic underdevelopment of the Haitian. His repeated references to and promotion of some alleged (and conveniently raced) "natural order" are a swift shorthand for the nature-versus-nurture/divine-order-versus-learned-behavior claims that provided much of the foundation for slavery. For a people described by H. M. Pilkton, a technical expert and vice president of the American Development Company of Haiti, as "naturally and inherently cultivators of the ground" who "became exceptionally good plantation operators to the extent of planting, cultivating, and cutting the cane" with "a very slight outlay of patience and a very slight exercise of friendly discipline," the alleged agrarian proclivities of the Haitian translated into opportunities for exploitive U.S. commercial arrangements and suppressed Haitian civil rights. Collectively, the comments of U.S. military informants like Russell, Lansing, and Butler conjoin with the racist play operating in popular representations of Haiti to deprive the nation of her sovereignty. Part of a reservoir of pathologizing images used to discredit blacks, this discourse helped to fuel and secure the successful transplantation of Jim Crow to Haiti.

In an article for *Crisis* in 1920, Episcopal Bishop John K. Hurst read in the occupation the transatlantic transplantation of a domestic problem. Simply put, the occupation was "but the

Negro question in a new form."[26] According to Hurst, Haiti's historic role within the black Atlantic as a site of refuge and a beacon for black potential and black sovereignty—denied within the United States—was short-circuited by the U.S. invasion. Glossing the cultural and social devastation wrought by the U.S. Marines, Hurst's final words cued the supremacist logic that managed the occupation and that made its racial violence immediate to his black American audience. "The Haitian people find themselves violently arrested, the work of their fathers pulled down, their traditions shattered, and now," he pleaded, "at the mercy of those whose only right to manage their affairs is that they are strong."[27] Hurst summoned the sympathies of a black audience attuned to the long arm of U.S. racism, for which ethnic, geographic, political, social, and gender particularities always lagged behind a shared experience of white supremacism. For black Americans traveling to Haiti, Jim Crow was ever-present.

The backdoor etiquette of segregation, with its separate entries, separate facilities, and lethal recrimination for the slightest social misstep, took residence in Haiti. In Gruening's words, the "social line between Haitians and Americans [was] rigidly drawn."[28] "Americans have carried American prejudice to Haiti," James Weldon Johnson reported for *Crisis* readers.

> Before their advent, there was no such thing in social circles as race prejudice. Social affairs were attended on the same footing by natives and white foreigners. The men in the American occupation . . . have set up their own social circle and established their own club to which no Haitian is invited, no matter what his social standing is."[29]

Rayford Logan and Langston Hughes shared Gruening's and Johnson's critique. Yet, the peregrinations of a Jim Crow that traveled on military cruisers and that accompanied U.S. soldiers, diplomats, government administrators, and financial and business experts was in fact a kind of border crossing. It enhanced the solidarity of and emphasized commonalities among the experiences of blacks living domestically and those in the extraterritorial United States. By 1915 Haiti's role as case study had shifted. With the ability to disprove theories on racial capacity in jeopardy, Haiti reenacted the role that World War I had played for many African Americans. The island became a crucible for the racial ideologies delimiting the borders of democracy. Erupting in the midst of a war for global democracy and continuing well past the founding of the League of Nations, the U.S. occupation worried the legitimacy of democracy. According to radical leftist Hubert Harrison, "As long as such things can be done without effective protest or redress, black people everywhere will refuse to believe that the democracy advertised by lying white politicians can be anything but a ghastly joke."[30] Understanding the significance of the occupation for many black Americans, who saw their political futures interlocked with Haiti's, demands reading the occupation within the context of the failed promises and hopes of political enfranchisement that marked the aftermath of World War I.[31] It demands reading the invasion within the framework of a eugenics movement that was taking shape and gaining momentum in the early decades of the twentieth century, whose call to arms was the perfection of a master race. For black Americans the Haitian crisis routed the campaign for human and civil rights into a politically tenuous, racially inscribed global arena. By the early 1930s, the fascism underwritten by eugenics that was sweeping across continental Europe had already brutally undone Ethiopian sovereignty. Traces of the entailments of statelessness—derealization of humanity and legal personality,

stripped human rights, ruptured state and disrupted civil protections, and unredressed murder—that would transform the political landscape a decade later, with the massive post-
World War II explosion of refugees, had already reworked the landscapes of what had been
imagined black political utopias: Ethiopia and Haiti.

TROUBLED ISLAND

While continuing his coverage on the Spanish Civil War for the Baltimore *Afro-American,*
the Cleveland *Call and Post,* and *The Globe,* in 1938[32] Langston Hughes traveled from Madrid
to Paris for the meeting of the International Writers Association for the Defense of Culture.
Reading from an essay, "Writers, Words, and the World," it was the politically uncompromis-
ing and socialist Hughes who proclaimed,

> Because our world is . . . so related, and inter-related, a creative writer has no right to
> neglect to understand clearly the social and economic forces that control our world.
> No matter what his country or what his language, a writer, to be a good writer, cannot
> remain unaware of Spain and China, of India and Africa, of Rome and Berlin.[33]

Black intellectuals like Hughes cited Haiti's occupation in their writings as not simply
another occasion of U.S. imperialism, but as the violent evidence of an earlier historical problem. In turn, many engaged in a revisionist historiography on the island that placed the sentient slave body at the center of contemporary civil rights claims. This return to the Haitian
revolution was as much a call to a kind of revolutionary praxis and race pride as it was a repudiation of scenes like Marlene Dietrich's performance of "Black Voodoo" (*Blonde Venus,*
1933) and of texts like Faustin Wirkus's internationally acclaimed memoir and John Craige's
Black Bagdad (1933) and *Cannibal Cousins* (1934). Part of a larger, anticolonial campaign,
Hughes's writings accentuated Du Bois's description of a "color-line [that] belts the world."
Hughes anticipated African American petitions for human and civil rights before the United
Nations and the U.S. president (1940s–1960s) and decolonization struggles that would mark
the aftermath of World War II. By the late 1930s, his writings already demonstrated an even
more public and explicitly named connection between colonialism and segregation. Hughes's civil war reports articulate a sensitivity to the global character of race. For readers already
familiar with "The Negro Artist and the Racial Mountain," featured in Alain Locke's *New
Negro* (1925) anthology, which prompted George Schuyler's acerbic "Negro Art Hokum"
(1926), Hughes's interweaving of the political with the aesthetic in 1938 further punctuated
an already actively practiced aesthetic.[34] Now, however, the signature rubric of his writing
was more direct and decidedly internationalist in scope. Hughes's radical socialist politics
fused the consequences and rationales underpinning domestic racial policy to international
political movements, yoking blacks worldwide to a struggle for freedoms withheld by colonialism, imperialism, fascism, and—in the United States—Jim Crow.

Although Hughes remained mostly silent on the question of Spanish colonialism[35] in
his coverage of the war—relaying instead to his black American audience a country unbelted
by the color-line, where black soldiers of the Fifteenth International Brigade were treated
with respect, where the directives of black officers went unchallenged, and where interracial

medical corps shared the labor of caring for the wounded—it was nonetheless a frustrated Hughes who complained of the limited compass of translated books on black life available in Spain. "Seabrook's *Magic Island*, Peterkin's *Scarlet Sister Mary*, and Paul Morand's bad short stories of stavism," he wrote, all exoticized the black body.[36] The character of his remark is hardly isolated. Hughes's defensive injunction gestures toward the stakes of his presence in Spain as an African American reporter articulating yet another instance of compromised democracy and suggesting the risks fascism posed to blacks worldwide. Amidst falling mortars and aerial raids, night bombings and food shortages, Hughes's sustained attention to the stubborn exoticization of the black body expresses his conviction that words held the possibility of radical political and social transformation, of impelling "people toward the creation of a good life." Simply put, "Writers have power."[37] Urging writers to uphold the ethical demands of their craft, to recognize and to wield responsibly the power of language, he charged, "Words have been used too much to make people doubt and fear. Words must now be used to make people believe and do. Writers who have the power to use words in terms of belief and action are responsible to that power *not* to make people believe in the wrong things."[38] In the midst of Mussolini's conquered Ethiopia, Batista's Cuba, Vincent's Haiti, and Franco's Spain, "wrong things" amounted to the continuance of "death instead of life, suffering instead of joy, oppression instead of freedom."[39]

Hughes's essays, poetry, and dramatic works signaled yet another intervention in the ongoing campaign for black civil and economic rights. Arguably, the arrest and convictions of eight out of nine African American males for the alleged sexual assault of two female riders on a Southern Railroad freight train heading to Memphis in the spring of 1931 marked a turning point in Hughes's politics. For writers like Hughes, Countee Cullen, and Richard Wright, the racial and gendered politics, and confluence of social and legal failures surrounding the Scottsboro incident spoke to the economic and legal import of Jim Crow on black and white lives in the South, and to the raced and gendered effects of the Great Depression on the working class. To avert being suspected of prostitution and possible prosecution under the Mann Act (1910) for having traveled unescorted among male riders, Ruby Bates and Victoria Price lied. Their allegations resulted in death penalty verdicts for eight young men, twenty years of legal wrangling that included two U.S. Supreme Court hearings (*Powell* v. *Alabama*, 1932; *Norris* v. *State of Alabama*, 1935), and in challenges to the racist application of due process in the trials. In a moment when the swift and illegal work of kangaroo justice permitted courtrooms to replace lynch mobs, and guarantee legally sanctioned summary executions, Bates and Price's complaint rehearsed the familiar myth of an endangered white femininity savaged at the hands of menacing black males.[40] The judicial miscarriages within this incident challenged the credibility of U.S. democracy and drew increasing numbers of black Americans toward the left, among them Langston Hughes.

An event Arnold Rampersad credits as "the driving public force in Hughes's move to the left,"[41] for this poet, essayist, and dramatist, Scottsboro measured the depth of U.S. racial and gender inequalities, confirmed the criminalization of African Americans, and revealed the racialized character of U.S. jurisprudence. By October 1931 Hughes had written and published a one-act agitprop play, *Scottsboro Limited* for *New Masses*. Two years later he repackaged this dramatic critique of the Jim Crow court. Printed now as a pamphlet that included illustrations by Prentiss Taylor and Hughes's four poems on Scottsboro, the poet allocated the proceeds from the publication to the Scottsboro Defense Fund. Scottsboro was not simply a watershed case in U.S. legal and social history—a moment encapsulating the shift from lynch mob to kangaroo justice, from extralegal vigilante justice to the sanctioned violence of the executioner's chair—but a watershed moment in Hughes's own political development and radical aesthetics. Hughes went to Kilby, Alabama, to meet with some of the incarcerated Scottsboro defendants during a trip he took across country in 1931.[42] His visit produced "Brown American in Jail: Kilby," an essay in which Hughes takes aim at the disproportionate imprisonment of black Americans, the use of prison bars and chain gangs to conscript black labor, and the labor performed by the U.S. legal system, federal government, and capitalism to actively dispossess black Americans. Hughes returned to the Scottsboro tragedy again and again in his writings, allowing the issues this case raised to broaden the campaign for African American civil rights. He would be one of numerous black artists and intellectuals directly or indirectly affiliated with the Communist Party (CP) during the 1930s and 1940s, and come to serve as honorary president of the CP's League of Struggle for Negro Rights (LSNR) (1930–1936). Boasting "ten thousand [members] at its peak," the LSNR pressed nationalist claims of self-determination expressed in the Black Belt thesis, advocated for black civil rights, and stridently protested lynching.[43] Perhaps it was the CP and CPUSA's (Communist Party USA) sustained involvement in the legal defense of the eight condemned that spring in 1931 that deepened Hughes's interest in and appreciation of communism and Marxist ideology. It is likely that Hughes recognized and sympathized with the same elements that Richard Wright felt moved by: the interdependency of the laboring class, the global problem of imperialism and fascism, and the ever-present need to address racial and social inequities. Communism provided black leftists with an international platform for engaging with revolutionary labor movements, for addressing symmetries among black Americans and colonial people worldwide, and for extending the campaign against imperialism and fascism.

Under the weight of federal surveillance and investigation and of public and (potential) political reprisals for "Goodbye Christ" (1932), his socialist poem written during a trip to the Soviet Union shortly after the Scottsboro death penalty verdicts, Hughes apostasized his relationship to communism, disavowing the poem and denying any formal affiliation with the CP.[44] It might be fair to imagine his actions as compelled conservatism in the early 1940s and increasing disengagement from the leftist politics that had dominated so much of his writing and affiliations up to and through World War II, but they should not be seen as Hughes's attempt to remove politics from his aesthetic. Although perhaps less willing to be identified or seemingly associated with the Left and communism, Hughes remained steadfast in his criticism of U.S. race relations, in his demands for black civil and human rights. In the words of Hughes's biographer, Arnold Rampersad, "The political fervor that had served radical socialism in the thirties would be rechanneled toward the greater specificity of black civil rights and to fresh explorations of the blues idiom, which Hughes had played down in the thirties in favor of radical political verse."[45] And although his politics became more focused after World War II, the socialist period of the 1930s charts his heightening awareness of this "inter-related world" and its consequences for blacks in and beyond the United States. Hughes certainly began to view the United States as a colonial power during the Spanish Civil War, whose fascist dimensions foreshadowed for writers like C. L. R. James the possibilities of things to come for blacks and colonial peoples, but it was in response to a U.S.-occupied Haiti that Hughes decried a colonial United States.

For an artist committed to labor rights and to the "Negro masses," Haiti placed in relief the intersections of race and class in accepted social and political structures. "It was in Haiti," Hughes recalled, "that I first realized how class lines may cut across color lines within a race, and how dark people of the same nationality may scorn those below them."[46] The writings that emerged from his summer on the island in 1931 betrayed a sociological enterprise decidedly different in character and imperative from the pseudoethnographic narratives produced by travel writers like William Seabrook.[47] The U.S. occupation remained a powerful subcurrent in Hughes's fiction and nonfiction on Haiti, even managing an appearance in *Popo and Fifina* (1932), a children's story on the Haitian laboring class coauthored with Arna Bontemps. His essay for *New Masses,* "People Without Shoes" (1932), restaged the means by which shoes functioned as a shorthand for the racialized caste system documented in Gen. Butler's testimony before the Senate a decade earlier, "People Without Shoes" effectively rebuts the racist imagination that Butler's testimony emblematizes—an imagination that validated a racially inscribed primitivism and that strategically employed a defunct rhetoric of "natural order" used historically to validate slavery in order to affirm U.S. neocolonialism on the island. That shoes document class in Haiti—that their presence or absence announces social position within an economy of social relations overdetermined by a theory of race managed through blood quantum—advances the logic of slavery, according to Hughes. Black Haitians were barefoot, whereas Haitian mulattoes, the community who dominated the island's business and administrative class, were among the privileged who could afford shoes. In Haiti a sociopolitical distance managed through blood and chromatics was replayed symbolically in costume.

"Haiti is a land of people without shoes," Hughes reported. "Yet shoes are things of great importance in Haiti. Everyone of any social or business position must wear them. To be seen in the streets barefooted marks one as a low-caste person of no standing in the community."[48] Although in Hughes's words this preoccupation with dress is "a little pathetic" in "an underdeveloped land where the average wage is thirty cents a day," it is as much a cultural retention of slavery with its "white masters who wore coats and shoes long ago," a symbol of a "leisure and rest and freedom" privileged along a racial axis, as it is a reflection of the mulattoes' ineffectual power. Haiti's economic fortune—the real power—lay in the hands of foreign interests:

> Practically all business there is in the hands of white foreigners, so one must buy one's shoes from a Frenchman or a Syrian . . . Haiti has no foreign credit, no steamships, few commercial representatives abroad. And the government, Occupation controlled, puts a tax on almost everything. . . . The laws are dictated from Washington. American controllers count their money. And the military Occupation extracts fat salaries for its own civilian experts and officials.[49]

Undervaluing the significance of the occupation on black Americans risks dismissing the historic role Haiti played in the promulgation of freedom and sovereignty across the New World and the purchase this revolutionary model held in the imaginations of the enslaved, the newly emancipated, and those in the early twentieth century pressing forward a civil rights agenda. Certainly the nation's poverty and tumultuous, violent political history embarrassed more than a few, and hastened the support some black Americans gave the occupation, which had been advertised by the U.S. government as an expression of aid.[50] The occupation threatened the more than century-long counterpoint Haiti's sovereignty had posed to supremacist notions of race. Like the Banana Wars, Haiti's subjection to U.S. military, economic, and administrative forces, exposed the tension among U.S. foreign and domestic policy and political rhetoric. The occupation also revealed the geographical scale and transnational reach of Jim Crow. For Hughes, occupied Haiti supplied fecund ground for reimagining both the semantic contours of a "dream deferred"[51] and of the world he dreamt.

"Imagine a country where the entire national population is colored, and you will have Haiti—the first of the black republics, and that much discussed little land to the South of us," wrote Hughes in *Crisis* in 1932, amid the illegalities of the Scottsboro convictions and economic hardships multiplied by the Depression. For black Americans hoping to escape a recalcitrant Jim Crow, Hughes's words conjured paradise.[52] It was a vision quickly dimmed, however; a dream brusquely ended. The title he affixed to the essay prefigures the devastation: "White Shadows in a Black Land." Homeliness, that condition of refuge Homi Bhabha defines as fundamentally absent or lost for the exile, is precisely what Hughes prescribed and simultaneously frustrated. He wrote, "To a Negro coming directly from New York by steamer and landing at Port au Prince, the capital, it is like stepping into a new world, a darker world where the white shadows are apparently missing, a world of his own people." In a handful of lines he named the impetus driving black expatriation, capturing the psychic relief realized by an absent terror. The calculated force of this image—"white shadows"—yokes the occupation to the cultural syntax of voodoo and zombies and to the deep psychological structure buoying Jim Crow. The southward gaze demanded here is interrupted by a U.S. South whose coordinates precede this "little land to the South," a South whose psychotopography incorporates the violence of white supremacy and haunts the black imagination. It is the South of Baldwin's gospel singer, Arthur Montana, in *Just Above My Head,* which prompts confusion, terror, and dread: "He has the feeling that he is losing his mind. The streets are bright and empty, stretching into a dreadful future. The houses are low, conspiratorial, trees are everywhere. . . . He is hanging from any one of them—from every one of them, turned, lightly, from moment to moment, by the still, heavy, ominous air."[53] Shuttering this vision almost as quickly as it could be shown, Hughes's succeeding lines and pages narrate a spoiled refuge. By employing a term that many black writers came to rely upon as a modifier for the modern black experience, Hughes initially tilted the cultural registers for "shadow" away from the black body. Here "shadow" refers to the colonial dimensions of a U.S.-run Haiti that likened Haitians to segregated black Americans. Nonetheless, Hughes reassigns the weight of shadow back onto the black body, for this "dark world" shatters, supplanted by an island of black shadows where the semblance of black business, a black political structure, and black financial centers point to colonialism's subterfuges.[54]

According to the poet, "The dark-skinned little Republic, then, has its hair caught in the white fingers of unsympathetic foreigners, and the Haitian people live today under a sort of military dictatorship backed by U.S. guns. They are not free."[55] Both an indictment and an injunction against the United States, Hughes's assertion that Haitians "are not free" raises the intractable question of what constitutes freedom—democracy?—particularly for blacks corralled within the extraterritorial and domestic spaces of the United States. If Haitians were not free, then what were they? In turn, what description adequately captures the role the United States played in their abject circumstances? By 1936, Hughes had sketched the scope of the problem in a play on the Haitian Revolution entitled *Troubled Island, Emperor of Haiti*.[56]

THE SHOW OPENS

"I dream a world where man/No other man will scorn," wrote Hughes as part of an aria for his opera with William Grant Still, *Troubled Island*. Although the opera is among the least remembered and studied texts in Hughes's oeuvre, it gave audiences a glimpse of the social praxis underlying his writings. He repeatedly closed his public speaking engagements with a reading of this aria, what Rampersad calls his "amen-piece," "I Dream a World."[57] Hughes's aria extended what was by then an emerging trope within his writings—figurations on the dream. Like all utopian literatures, "I Dream a World" bears a double assignment. It couples a future desired to a present condemned. Heard within the context of the opera, the aria suggests both the privileged space Haiti held in Black cultural traditions and its tragic untenability. "I dream a world where all/Will know sweet freedom's way," he mourns, "Where greed no longer saps the soul." It is against Haiti's U.S. occupation and her quick transition to the "semi-fascist dictatorship . . . of Vincent"; it is against Mussolini's Ethiopia, Franco's Spain, and Hitler's Germany; and it is against a segregationist United States that the aria gains historical legibility.

Hughes had begun to imagine a dramatic treatment of the island as early as 1928, perhaps in response to the Senate hearings of 1922 and the on-going demands of black Americans for the removal of U.S. troops from the island.[58] By the time his play, *Emperor of Haiti,* opened at the Karamu Theatre in November 1936, Hughes was already collaborating with Still on its adaptation into an opera (*Troubled Island*).[59] Hughes imagined Paul Robeson in the lead of a musical on the revolution. The imposing singer and civil rights activist had longed, even after his performances in O'Neill's play and DuBose Heyward's film adaptation of *Emperor Jones,* for a black-written theatrical piece on Haiti featuring an all-black cast.[60] With *Emperor of Haiti,* Hughes returned to what he had enthusiastically described elsewhere as the island's "splendid history studded with the names of heroes like Toussaint L'Ouverture, Dessalines, and Christophe—the great black men who freed their land from slavery."[61] They were men whose triumph on behalf of freedom, James Weldon Johnson boasted three years earlier, exceeded the simple emancipation gained by the Civil War, producing a "more complete social revolution."[62] In the fall of 1944, the conductor Leopold Stokowski committed to staging the Still and Hughes opera the following spring. The opera promised to upset color lines that had all but barred black performers from serving as principal opera singers, but Still and Hughes would have to wait another three years for their opportunity to make operatic news.[63] Opening at the New York City Center on March 31, 1949, *Troubled Island* featured Robert Weede in the leading role of Jean Jacques Dessalines, and included several black singers in the chorus and black dancers, with the remaining cast members in blackface.[64] For Hughes the staging signaled that "the race is a-rising."[65] Although poor reviews closed the curtains on *Troubled Island* after the third performance, the U.S. State Department recorded the April 19, 1949 staging for international circulation. Audiences in Paris and Brussels listened in 1950 to this opera based on his 1936 play. The international reach of this opera, however, was short lived. Undoubtedly, Hughes's radical leftist politics informed the State Department's unexpected decision to stop sharing this work throughout the world.[66]

With the Haitian Revolution as its historical backdrop and narrative thrust, *Emperor of Haiti* engages the conditions of violence constitutive of political freedoms, the violence and oppression of war, and the racialized dimensions of betrayal that persist among the legacies of colonialism. This play, like the countless black histories and histories of the Haitian Revolution published from the 1920s through the 1940s (including Carter G. Woodson's *The Negro in History,* Benjamin Brawley's *A Social History of the American Negro,* W. E. B. Du Bois's *Black Reconstruction,* Anna Julia Cooper's *Slavery and the French Revolutionists,* C.L.R. James's *Black Jacobins,* and James Vandercook's *Black Majesty: The Life of Christophe, King of Haiti*), upsets the discourse on "Negro capacity," serving much like Jesse Owens's four gold medal wins during Berlin's "Hitler Olympics" in 1936 or like boxer Joe Louis's defeat of the German Max Schmelling in 1938: as a finger in the face of white supremacism. Both Hughes's investment in history and his antifascist critiques coincided with the cultural revolution advanced in the Communist Party's (CP) 1935 shift to a "Broad People's Front" (a.k.a., the Popular Front) to combat fascism and encourage a global movement toward democracy. As Bill Mullen reminds us, the CP attempted to facilitate the broad-based coalition prescribed in the Popular Front by concurrently advancing what it termed "people's culture."[67] For African Americans, the National Negro Congress (NNC), a racially and political heterogenous body formed in 1936, spearheaded this cultural nationalism, ostensibly realizing a "black 'cultural front'" to borrow from Mullen.[68] Their cultural nationalism featured a brand of civil rights that included the active deconstruction of racial stereotypes, the celebration of black culture, and the promotion of human rights.

In *Emperor of Haiti* Hughes refuses the accepted, popular narrative of a savage and brutal black violence, which had become the tradition of histories of the Revolution. He challenged the circumscription of these histories, whose harm extended beyond caricaturing the Haitian (that is to say, black) body to influencing political affiliations with the island.[69]

Emperor of Haiti traces the history of the revolutionary slave leader-turned-emperor Jean Jacques Dessalines, whose portrait here condenses the slave revolutionaries Boukman and L'Ouverture. Divided into three acts, the play opens on the eve of the slave rebellion in 1791, shifting quickly to Dessalines's reign as Haiti's first emperor and concluding with his betrayal and eventual overthrow by mulatto members of the royal court in 1806.[70] The play refuses any nostalgia for selfless heroism common in many black treatments of the revolution, a perspective perhaps explained by a too-narrow focus on the genuinely heroic Toussaint. Hughes instead plots the grounds of civil war, an internecine battle waged along lines of racial caste. He dramatizes the profound consequences of what Fanon characterizes as black colonial neuroses—a self-abnegation arising as slavery and colonialism's damaging by-product— that threatened the sovereignty of this black empire. Proponents of the very white supremacy that judged them inferior, mulattoes came to share the hatred for blackness. In Hughes's theatrical account, this loathing fuels their conspiracy against Dessalines and their eventual assassination of him. I want to focus on two of what Hortense Spillers has called "impression points" in the play, in order to dilate the operative hermeneutics of slavery: 1) the Haitian Revolution and, 2) the final staging of Dessalines's desecrated slave body. Hughes's turn to this specific slave history as a rubric for reading the modern black condition is a concern of the first order. If we concede Toni Morrison's assertion that slavery is the architectural ground for modernity, then the slave body is its documentary evidence. The curtain drops on Dessalines's dead, mutilated body, restaging what Saidiya Hartman calls the troped spectacle of tortured blackness.[71] Sometime in 1896, Du Bois wrote:

> The role which the great Negro Toussaint, called L'Ouverture, played in the history of the United States has seldom been fully appreciated. Representing the age of revolution in America, he rose to leadership through a bloody terror, which contrived a Negro "problem" for the Western Hemisphere, intensified and defined the anti-slavery movement ... and rendered more certain the final prohibition of the slave-trade by the United States in 1807.[72]

To return to this moment of the Haitian Revolution is to return to the Enlightenment and to the problem of colonialism and the black body, which were also the crux of the French Revolution.[73] It is to return to a revolution that Du Bois insisted produced the "Negro problem" for the Western hemisphere, a revolution around which a body of U.S. slave jurisprudence would take shape and through which the United States would expand geographically with the acquisition of Louisiana, and a revolution that would inspire the insurrectionary plans of Gabriel Prosser, Nat Turner, Denmark Vessey, and David Walker. As a revolution responsible for the wave of slave rebellions erupting across the Americas in the late eighteenth and early nineteenth centuries, Haiti's black slaves held France accountable for her boast of Liberty, Equality, and Fraternity. And finally, to return to this history is to recognize how questions regarding Negro capacity helped justify the U.S. invasion and nineteen-year occupation of Haiti and forestall black civil rights throughout the United States and its dependencies. The cultural and black nationalisms emerging in the aftermath of World War I, which came to mark a burgeoning repertoire of black expressive and intellectual productions during the Harlem Renaissance, shared an interest in repairing the tarnished and trampled cultural image of the black body.

Hughes's decision to feature Dessalines over the widely revered Toussaint speaks to the recuperative investments of—and critique housed within—his play. In a move that anticipates the distinction between emancipation and social revolution that James Weldon Johnson claimed as the critical factor that dictated the differing outcomes for black American and black Haitian slaves, Dessalines campaigned for a "Black Empire."[74] In short, Dessalines, not Toussaint, imagined, fought for, and declared Haiti independent, a sovereignty boldly claimed in his reinscription of her precolonial Arawak name, "Haiti."[75] Hughes's turn to Dessalines confronted the problem of a historical tradition that plagued the island in ways that a retreat to the conventional hero Toussaint could not. In a colonial moment when black demands for French political accountability and the rebels' willingness to die for freedom were read as symptoms of a black grotesque,[76] Dessalines's military stratagems anchored this interpretation. He not only participated in the well-remembered fires that razed Haiti in order to defeat French arms, but also ordered the massacre of whites in 1805.[77] The fires and massacre confirmed many onlookers' theories of racial degeneracy, and opened the way to challenges of black fitness to rule, and affected Haiti's economy for generations.[78] As the civil war raged on, William Wells Brown offered a counterpoint against which the revolutionary Dessalines might be reimagined: "Nearly all historians have set him down as a bloodthirsty monster, who delighted in the sufferings of his fellow-creatures. They do not rightly consider the circumstances that surrounded him, and the foe that he had to deal with."[79] Hughes risked confirming representations of the menace of black political power in order to expose the "circumstances that surrounded him" and to broker a reading on political ethics grounded in human rights.

Although the first third of the play depicts the slave conspiracy for freedom, the remaining two-thirds traces the transformation of a slave into a dictator. Hughes sympathetically frames this progression as a response to corporal assaults and the legal and political dislocations of slavery. Hughes introduces the man history remembers as "the Tiger"—the revolutionary who espoused the motto "Koupe tet, boule kay" (Cut off the head, burn down the house)[80]—as a slave who cannot legally marry his helpmate Azelia. He has been repeatedly beaten for his unauthorized late-night escapes to conspire against slave masters and was systematically deconstructed into a slave. It is Dessalines the Emperor who laments, "I keep remembering back to when I was a little naked slave among the slaves. Every day an old man came to dump a pot of yams into a trough where we ate, and the pigs and the dogs, they ate, too. And we got down alongside 'em, on all fours, and ate—us and the dogs. I thought I, too, was a beast."[81] The acute attention Hughes brings to Dessaliness humanity by repeated emphasis of his scarred "raw flesh" and by descriptions of how his gaze mobilized the emperor's psychological retransformation from a slave back into a man ("Then I lifted up my head and looked him in the eyes, and I knew I was a man, not a dog!"[82]) levels the weight of evidence against the indictment lodged in the black grotesque. Sensitive to the dialectic surrounding this iconic figure—a man both admired and loathed—Hughes's complex portrait captures an ambitious, misguided power succumbing to corruption and degrading influences.

With his signature iconography of the dream, Hughes repeatedly dramatizes the black sanctuary Dessalines imagined, but could not accomplish, because of the disfiguring effects of race. Anxious to create an infrastructure that supports commerce and education, Dessalines "dreams for Haiti" include "roads, and docks, and harbors fine as any country in the world." "I've told them [the peasants] of this Haiti I would make," Dessalines confides, "—where every black man lifts his head in pride, where there'll be schools and palaces, big armies and a fleet of boats, forts strong enough to keep the French forever from our shores."[83] The corollary costs attached to Dessaliness ambition—forced labor that essentially reinstitutes slavery—mocks a hard-won emancipation, as well as his proclamation, "But I am their Liberator."[84] By introducing Martel, a former slave and a cabinet advisor to the emperor, Hughes foregrounds the challenges to freedom and sovereignty that sour Dessaliness dream. "Now free men can dream a bigger dream than mere revenge," Martel forcefully replies. "A dream of an island where not only blacks are free, but every man who comes to Haitian shores. . . . I dream a world where no man hurts another. Where *all* know freedom."[85] Martel's corrective to the racialized limits of Dessalines ambition highlights the widening gap between the emperor's interests and those of his constituencies, a fissure channeling Hughes's larger political critique. The disinclination to support a universal freedom—to understand, in Martel's words, that "swords won't solve all problems"—unmasked within Dessaliness agenda outlines the work slavery performs within this drama. This biodrama about a mass murderer, which Hughes wrote in the aftermath of Mussolini's genocide in Ethiopia and the U.S. Marine's massacre of Caco insurgents, clarifies the Haitian Revolution in ways that are immediate and urgent. Indeed, the treatment of slavery in *Emperor of Haiti* suggests an already active opposition to fascism in Hughes, which would become all the more explicit during and after his coverage of the Spanish Civil War.

TIGHTROPE

Martel's caution in the second act, "It's not wise to ever be a master, Jean Jacques," shows the stakes in *Emperor of Haiti*. Dessalines's confused reply, "What do you mean, Martel? A master?" only engenders confirmation from Popo, the royal page, "Here, sire, is your hat! Your sword!"[86] A scene among former slaves, Martel's assailing being a "master" stands as an indictment for what would have been to these former slaves the most criminally egregious offense. It is an allegation whose validity Popo's seemingly innocuous "sire" makes stick, an allegation hardened subsequently by Dessalines's unapologetic donning of his "plumed helmet."[87] Like Martel's frequent humanitarian correctives, this scene fastens onto the character of the play. The invocation of slavery tethers the contemporary to the historic, rendering slavery a supple trope leveling expressions of difference in order to reflect continuities in racialized violence across time. Haitian history became for Hughes a vehicle for addressing a U.S. occupation that overlapped with the earliest moments of World War II—Mussolini's invasion of Ethiopia—and that ended within two years of Franco's march into Spain. Slavery continued to exert an undisputed semantic pull as a metaphor for—if not, in fact, a definitive forecast of—contemporary political shifts. For Hughes and C. L. R. James, the Haitian Revolution offered insight for their times. Hughes demonstrated that the present historical moment could be read through a strategic rescripting of Dessalines. In the Haitian Revolution, slavery signified the problem of trampled sovereignty emerging in Mussolini's conquered Ethiopia, Franco's interest in and promise for a defeated Spain, and the unstated dimensions of Hitler's three-pronged campaign of genocide, Aryanism, and fascism. Slavery became the glue connecting the circumstances of black, colonial, and oppressed peoples on a global scale.

Although the play opens with slaves conspiring to overthrow the plantocracy, the sustained references to slavery even in the aftermath of liberation redefine the contours of freedom for an emancipated community. Freedom means more than broken shackles. The rebel password, "Once . . . a slave . . . but soon no more!" is muffled in the confines of a black empire qua dictatorship. A quizzical Dessalines remonstrates, "They think I'd make them slaves again. And those to whom I gave the land, they call me tyrant now."[88] Hughes's representation of an embattled Dessalines, bitterly characterized as a "power-longing tax-hungry tyrant," a "black monster who cares not at all for us, or for Haiti, or for our people, but only for himself," and a "presumptuous Negro who dares call himself 'His Majesty,'" magnifies the problem of a totalitarianism that corrupts sovereignty, that mocks emancipation, and that muddies the meaning of freedom.[89] It is a problem of governance, however, that is not removed from the effects of race. The depiction of Dessalines's threat to compel work at gunpoint—"I've made up my mind to tell my soldiers to *make* you work from now on!"—adheres to the historical record as much as it expresses a veiled, chilling reminder of the U.S. Marines' recent conscription of Haitian labor under the corvee system.[90] To Dessalines's demands the chorus tellingly replies, "Huh! I'm no slave."[91] In what becomes an increasingly disparaging portrait, Hughes layers references to slavery. In an early moment with his adviser

Martel, a frustrated Dessalines threatens, "Too much freedom—if they no longer obey me, their liberator."[92] His tyranny reflects a contemporary global political culture that Hughes recognized as being steadily transformed by the presence of dictatorships.[93] These anxious references remind the audience of the grip of an imperial U.S. commercialism that unraveled Haitian sovereignty and, for black Americans like James Weldon Johnson, announced a political orthodoxy remanding blacks back into slavery. Supplementing the "virtual slavery" of the *corvee* was the U.S.-drafted treaty sanctioning the occupation that, Johnson observed, "kept a people enslaved by the military tyranny which it was [Woodrow Wilson's] avowed purpose to destroy throughout the world."[94] Thus, to fully appreciate the manner in which slavery functioned as a hermeneutic for modern black life and as a vehicle for critiquing contemporary politics requires reading Hughes in the context of the Spanish Civil War, for it is here that his recurring use of slavery as a surrogate for sundered civil and human rights is most explicit.

Reflecting on history, Lucien Febvre wrote, "The Past is a reconstitution of societies and human beings engaged in the network of human realities today."[95] C. L. R. James's 1938 history of the Haitian Revolution, *Black Jacobins,* deftly draws connections between the Revolution and his contemporary moment. *Black Jacobins*'s parallels between the late-eighteenth and early-twentieth centuries are such that we might just as fittingly read his "War is a continuation of politics by other means"[96] as "Occupation is a continuation of politics by other means." James's contemporary Walter Benjamin shared his perspective, contending:

> The tradition of the oppressed teaches us that the "state of emergency" in which we live
> is not the exception but the rule. We must attain to a conception of history that is in
> keeping with this insight. . . . One reason why Fascism has a chance is that in the name
> of progress its opponents treat it as a historical norm. The current amazement that the
> things we are experiencing are "still" possible in the twentieth century is not philo-
> sophical. This amazement is not the beginning of knowledge—unless it is the knowl-
> edge that the view of history which gives rise to it is untenable.[97]

Hughes's antifascism was evident to the audience of the Baltimore *Afro-American.* His comparisons of the circumstances in Spain and Ethiopia to slavery, and of the Klu Klux Klan and segregation to fascism, during his coverage of the Spanish Civil War confirmed his commitment to Black civil rights and a political aesthetic that was shared by a black internationalist discourse. When read alongside the political tumult of the 1930s, black intellectuals' recuperation of the Haitian revolution seems less curious. It was because, in de Certeau's words, "In periods of movement or revolution, ruptures of individual or collective action become the principle of historical intelligibility."[98] Thus writers like Hughes and James cast their eyes on revolutionary Haiti in the light of recent occupations, martial law, invasions and massacres (Ethiopia), civil war (Spain), labor revolts throughout the West Indies, anticolonialist struggles, and a resilient Jim Crow.

Spain's civil war erupted only months before the premiere of *Emperor of Haiti* in November 1936. The following year, Hughes left California where he had been working with William Grant Still on the libretto *Troubled Island,* to begin on-site coverage of the war, setting sail for Madrid aboard the *Aquitania.*[99] Fusing memoir and journalism, Hughes's essays on the war reconfigure the dimensions of violence with an eye to the larger stakes wagered here for black people around the globe. Describing fascism as a politics that "creeps across Spain, across Europe," Hughes predicted an intractable reality, preparing his black American audience for an inevitable arrival: it will "then [creep] across the world, there will be no place left for intelligent young Negroes at all. In fact no decent place for any Negroes—because Fascism preaches the creed of Nordic supremacy and a world for whites alone."[100] In one of many attempts to outline black participation and investments in the Spanish Civil War, Hughes repeatedly tackled the Moor's problematic alliance with Franco, revealing the dimensions of a colonial power that compelled colonized black Africans to ally against democracy and freedom. Sensitive to the interests of his black audience, Hughes deftly situated Moorish war casualties in the context of segregation, reporting in September 1937, "The Moors die in Spain, men, women, and children, victims of Fascism, fighting not for freedom—but against freedom—under the banner that holds only terror and segregation for all the darker peoples of the earth."[101] Segregation indicates the absent freedoms and social divisions that marked fascism. Thickening the comparison, Hughes turned to the grammar of slavery as an analogue for a range of political practices that exhaust the possibility of freedom. His use of slavery mirrored a dynamic black political discourse in which slavery bore a double assignment: first, as metaphor, and second, as a presumptive telos toward which, it was imagined, political landscapes were actively being reshaped.

By late October, Hughes recapped for his *Afro-American* audience a second encounter with the only black member of the ninth medical unit of the American Medical Bureau to Aid Spanish Democracy, C. G. Carter, a medical student from the University of Minnesota whom he had first met during his transatlantic voyage. For Carter, the stakes of this conflict were clear: "Who wants to be a slave to Mussolini?" Reserving his response to Carter's query for the paper's audience, a pensive Hughes wrote, "As our car sped southward toward Valencia . . . I could see quite plainly for myself that the Spanish people didn't want to be enslaved to anyone, native or foreign." This was the Spain for which, Hughes recounted, Josephine Baker and Paul Robeson performed benefits. It was a country fighting against the same "forces that have raped Ethiopia, and that clearly hold no good for any poor and defenseless people anywhere," and Franco was the man "hired . . . to put the country back in chains again."[102] This harnessing of Spain to Ethiopia lent immediacy to the violence being waged in Europe. For a persecuted and embattled community, Ethiopia signified Zion on earth.[103] The nation was a cherished refuge in the history of black letters, and its sovereignty, like Haiti's and Liberia's, supplied a necessary counterbalance to the glut of representations of black inferiority.

Mussolini's invasion of Ethiopia in 1935 marked the first battleground of World War II, where the devastating techniques of extermination—gassing—that made the war notable among the most vile conflicts in human history were perfected on black bodies. A powerful image of what Hughes described as an attempt to "smash . . . democracy," the figure of the chain used to describe the status of occupied Spain signifies a ruptured freedom while enchaining similarly situated communities in a sympathetic posture. Confronting similar concerns, but with a different geographical marker, Du Bois addressed the ways in which slavery's past continued to matter in the United States. He concluded his 1935 history on Reconstruction, "Today, in the face of new slavery established elsewhere in the world under other names and guises, we ought to emphasize this lesson of the past. . . . It is not well to be reticent in describing the past. Our histories tend to discuss U.S. slavery so impartially, that in the end nobody seems to have done wrong and everybody was right."[104] It was not only the new slavery that was disguised, but its progenitors. "Give Franco a hood," wrote Hughes, "and he would be a member of the Ku Klux Klan, a kleagle. Fascism is what the Ku Klux Klan will be when it combines with the Liberty League and starts using machine guns and airplanes instead of a few yards of rope. Fascism is oppression, terror, and brutality on a big scale."[105]

Recalling his final days in Spain, Hughes replaced the belt Du Bois used to signify the color line with the figure of a tightrope fashioned by class and race. "I stood alone on the platform of the little station at Tour de Carol that bright December day and looked down the valley into Spain," Hughes remembered, "and wondered about borders and nationalities and war. I wondered what would happen to the Spanish people walking the bloody tightrope of their civil struggle." The tightrope cuts through the isolation of this solitary moment with a solidarity born of the shared experience of civil strife. "In the last few years," he continued, "I had been all around the embattled world, and I had seen people walking tightropes every-where—the tightrope of color in Alabama, the tightrope of transition in the Soviet Union." The perils of Haiti, Ethiopia, and Spain, and of the Soviet Union, Japan, China, and France were as real for black Americans like Hughes as the lynching rope and its accomplice, the tree. "Anybody is liable to fall off a tightrope in any land . . . and God help you if you fall the wrong way."[106] Targeted assaults against human and civil rights were proliferating in Europe and around the world. Hughes raised the stakes of this new slavery, outlining indiscriminate violence that cut across color, ethnicity, and class. "Democracy is going to wreck itself if it continues to approach closer and closer to fascist methods in its dealings with Negro citizens—for such methods of oppression spread, affecting other whites, Jews, the foreign born, labor, Mexicans, Catholics, citizens of Oriental ancestry—and, in due time, they boomerang back at the oppressor."[107] Hughes, however, prefigures the tightrope tethering communities of suffering together in his representation of the slave body in *Emperor of Haiti*. Indeed, the disfigured slave body levels differences of history, ethnicity, language, gender, and culture, exposing the relationship between freedom and death.

THE HERMENEUTICS OF SCARS

Reflecting on the question of sovereignty, Agamben reminds us that part of the intellectual labor at stake for fascism and Nazism necessarily included enforcing new thinking on "the relations between man and citizen,"[108] the fundamental fissure distinguishing political from natural rights. If we forget the intimate relationship between racial sciences and eugenics during the 1920s and 1930s—not to mention the ways in which the U.S. eugenics movement underwrote U.S. immigration policy and offered reservoirs of supposed evidence for German fascism[109]—we risk missing the uses to which racialized ideologies of human capacity (a syntax familiarly marked by a rhetoric of fitness and pathology) continued to underwrite international political systems. Like Agamben, Arendt, Benjamin, and James, Hughes understood the political consequences of this moment, when racial sciences reinvested blood quantum with the power to delineate civil, political, and human rights. Hughes located these political consequences in the figure of the slave, where the relation of history to death could be made plain.

De Certeau also drew a helpful analogy between death and history. "Death obsesses the West," he reasoned. "In this respect, the discourse of the human sciences is pathological: a discourse of *pathos*—misfortune and passionate action—in a confrontation with this death that our society can no longer conceive of as a way of living one's life."[110] Death emerges as a central trope animating de Certeau's theoretical exegesis of historiography. Here death signifies chronological distance, a past that has literally passed on and its incumbent loss—the absent interlocutor and the complexities of making meaning out of loss. Yet, although pathology continues to operate largely on the level of abstraction in de Certeau, for blacks it is an exegetical expression of an existential reality. Black histories are necessarily suffused by death, because black humanity remained perennially in question and persistently discounted. To limn, then, the racial contours of this analogy is to redistribute the force of de Certeau's understanding of how pathos mediates histories and the project of historical representation. The problem of the sentient, pathos-bearing slave body is at the crux of abolitionist and pro-slavery debates, functioning at one level as the organizing principle around which the concentrated force undermining black humanity could be gathered. This is an acknowledged fact. Hughes's writing, however, posits another related set of lexical and ethical dimensions for pathos within black expressive culture. Etymologically linked to a class of signifiers that includes pathogen, pathogenic, and pathological, "pathos" translates in Hughes into a mechanism pointing to, in Baldwin's words, the "human validity" of the black body that death simultaneously troubles and confirms.[111] And although the connection between pathology and history has overdetermined how the Haitian Revolution has traditionally been read, Hughes recuperates this alignment in order to question the freedom assumed to ground this historic episode.

By the end of *Emperor of Haiti*, we are confronted with Dessalines's prostrate body, an image that returns us to the problem of sovereignty and the divisive character of race mobilizing this drama. The assassination scene signals the beginning of the second rebellion figured in the play, a coup d'état carried out by mulattoes. *Emperor of Haiti* chronicles more than the rise and fall of a man. In the recurring spectacle of the abused slave body, Hughes posits a closed economy. Although the play does not precisely repeat its opening, instead following a linear progression of time, it does reconfigure the terms of emancipation on which it found its initial ground. Dessalines is shot in the back by his mulatto adviser Vuval, and his abandoned body is stripped. Stenio, Vuval's accomplice, craves a souvenir of the killing. It is a moment restaging the photographic and material souvenirs collected and preserved by lynch mobs and spectators. The crude proprietary tone of the scene opens the possibility of reading the assassination as a lynching, a reading further prompted by an earlier reference to the burning of the eighteenth century slave rebel, Mackandal.[112]

However, despite the symmetries within these acts of violence, I want to impress instead, the significance of Hughes recasting of Dessalines back into a slave. His stage instructions are relevant here:

(*The fallen ruler lies alone, in the dust, on his back. From either side of the square come the same RAGMUFFINS who earlier plagued the market women. They steal in awe around the body, then silently creep up and touch it . . . jabbering in wonder at the tassels of gold on his shoulders, the heavy golden cords at his cuffs, his shiny boots. One of the RAGMUFFINS picks up the EMPEROR's hat with the purple plume and puts it on his head.)*

. . .

(Two of the BOYS begin to turn the body over as they unbutton his coat and take it off. While they squabble over the coat, a third removes his silken shirt, the color of wine, and rubs it against his face.)

. . .

(The body of the EMPEROR now lies on its face, back bare to the sun. The old welts of his slave days stand out like cords across his shoulders.)[113]

Significantly absent are any signs of respect for his status on the part of the ragmuffins. Their disrobing of his corpse captures Dessalines's declension back into slavery. In a culture where clothing dictates social position, where Dessalines's imperial costume had become for the masses symptomatic of state corruption, his stripped body returns to the "naked slave" of his childhood. Indeed, Hughes supplants the "golden cords" of his epaulets with the "cords across his shoulders," a brisk shorthand for the slave-turned-emperor: the old slave with the scars across his back.[114] An exchange between two curious fishermen carries the weight of this transformation: "Who's that laying over there?" "He musta been a slave once," responds the other, "from the looks of his back."[115]

This swift slide from emperor to slave, initiated by a homicide that can never be named or prosecuted, reflects more than the collateral damage and concomitant spoils of war. Beyond the punishment recorded on the desecrated body, Hughes's concluding representation of scars represents an instance of the preoccupation with mutilated flesh that permeates the entire drama. Dessalines's scars recall institutional injuries and elicit terror in his enemies, while concentrating loathing that is directed toward the black body. This final staging of flayed flesh layers the consequences Spillers suggests in proposing a generational dimension to slave scars: "We might well ask if this phenomenon of marking and branding actually 'transfers' from one generation to another, finding its various *symbolic substitutions* in an efficacy of meanings that repeat the initiating moments?"[116] That this harm carries forward in chromosomal matter, in family mythologies and the like is understood. The spectacle of the slave corpse refuses the selective amnesia and aphasia Du Bois and Baldwin ascribe to a U.S. culture that conceives history as dead, revealing instead the impossibility of such an ambition precisely because scars *do* carry forward. That Dessalines is unrecognizable as "Dessalines" in this moment, that recognition among the unfortunate observers of his abandoned corpse is predicated on and limited to marks on his flesh (what Spillers labels the hieroglyphics of the plantocracy), speaks to the leveling effects Hughes intends for this figuration.

The spectacle of the mutilated slave body erases geographical, historical, political, religious, social, national, and lingual particularities, standing in for the new brands of slavery—camps, detention centers, prisons, traffic in women and children—that marked the twentieth century. In other words, that the slave body is ahistorical and crosses lines of difference. *Emperor of Haiti* rehearses the recurring articulations of death within the black imaginary, a tradition according to Paul Gilroy that "is integral . . . to the narratives of loss, exile, and journey which ... serve a mnemonic function: directing the consciousness of the group back to significant nodal points in its common history and its social memory."[117] Dessalines's bare back reflects the forms of exposure borne by the enslaved. The bared slave is a sobering reminder of the violence of modernity, which Du Bois attested transformed an island in the eighteenth century into "a gold mine for white folk and a burial ground for black folk." The occupation was but another expression in the continuum of modern violence, but sadly here, Du Bois wrote, "Murder is naked and unashamed."[118] Indeed, the bared slave symbolizes a constitutive moment in the history of the U.S. republic when, according to James Baldwin, "the idea of black persons as property" was first formulated within a system of valuation that "decided that the concept of Property was more important—more real—than the possibilities of the human being."[119] Hughes's slave body sounds off on the problem of exploited and expropriated labor, the crisis in human and civil rights, and the substitution of totalitarianism for democracy. Of this, Hughes's fictional proxy, Dessalines declaimed,

> Look what they've done to me! Look at my scars! ... The sacks of sweet white sugar the French ship off to Paris go stained with our blood ... The soft white cotton the French weave into garments is red with my blood! ... The coffee our masters sup in the cool of evening on their wide verandas is thick with blood! ... Our masters live on blood!"[120]

Hughes's representation of the slave rails against a freedom yet unattained. The slave's body redefines freedom as more than simply the literal release of shackles, insisting that emancipation entailed the very thing Arendt marked as denied to refugees and stateless persons: political rights. Unrecognizable and "unhomed," with a body that may be killed and desecrated without remorse or redress, Hughes stages the slave in exile. The leveling effect of the sacred, scarred flesh tilts the play away from civil rights—rights moored in nation-states—to the larger issues of human dignity and human rights looming over the 1930s. Some years later, in the aftermath of Hiroshima, Hughes revisited the equalizing effects of death, observing in the *Chicago Defender*, "There is no color line in death. In spite of each other, we die for each other—poor whites—Negroes—soldiers—sons—heroes of the Purple Heart 'for wounds received in action.'" He continued, "Eligible for medals, eligible for tears at death—as at departure. Eligible to shake hands tomorrow—when we grow big enough to know how to live for each other. Eligible for friendship then—not hate."[121] This need to learn to live for one another rests with Hughes's prostrate Dessalines, whose death returns us to the spirit of intraracial cooperation and human rights that motivate the first rebellion in the play—the slave battle for freedom.

CODA: CUSTODIAL CARE

Readers of the *New York Amsterdam News* were greeted on July 28, 1934 by a barrel-waisted, club-and-tote-carrying grim-faced figure, the composite of two former U.S. presidents, Herbert Hoover and Theodore Roosevelt. Ironically captioned "Coming Home," the *New York Amsterdam News* political cartoon sidesteps teary reunions, publicly staged celebrations,

Coming Home   By CHASE

FIGURE 5.1 "Coming Home." Reproduced with permission of the *New York Amsterdam News*. *New York Amsterdam News*, July 28, 1934.

and parades featuring triumphant marines, soberly capturing the nature of U.S. aid (see Figure 5–1). This image upends the discourse on state aid, a discourse that also circulated in the final days of the Chicago race riot when the *Chicago Tribune* suppressed the material conditions following the week-long melee beneath calculated visual and discursive representations of state aid. In "Coming Home," it is not simply the U.S. Marines who are returning home—they do not even manage an appearance here—but a U.S. dictatorship whose double-nature exposes the contingency of U.S. relief. Aid and dictatorship go hand in hand: packaged as relief, iron-fisted rule necessarily accompanies the U.S. medical/money bag. In its similarities to a medical bag, the tote reminds readers of the manner in which Haiti was configured among the outermost geographical claims of the United States: here, humanitarian aid is redefined as part of a "house call." The pendular swing of the president's arms signal the reciprocal flow between relief and governance.[122] Through perspective and visual cues, the artist shifts our attention from the micropolitical—Haiti and the United States—to the global, signaled by the topography this figure so easily traverses. His broad-toed black and white shoes call attention to the weight of the U.S. impression: on Haiti, on an unmarked world far in the background, and on the United States itself. Most telling, however, is the failed transformation of power articulated in this image. African Americans, like the *New York Amsterdam News* artist, understood that the racialized dictatorial force in the guise of aid that stomped across Haiti was returning unchanged and unweakened, exerting its weight at home. The sustained political climate of racial segregation forecast by the cartoonist signaled that a black refuge constituted on human and civil rights would continue to remain a dream.

Epilogue: Requiem

THE CITY CARE FORGOT

"I GUESS IF you could kill this city, you could kill any city," remarked a Hurricane Katrina survivor.[1] Months after the storm surge, after the floods broke levees still incomplete forty years into their construction, and after the winds subsided and the water receded, the obituaries in New Orleans remained 30 percent higher than average.[2] Late August 2005 witnessed one of the costliest natural disasters in U.S. history, supplanting the 1927 flood of the Mississippi River into New Orleans that rendered more than 1 million persons homeless and placed 200,000 in tent cities after the state bombed the levees surrounding St. Bernard Parish in order to protect wealthier sections of the city. Forty minutes into his four-hour, award-winning film documenting the devastating aftermath of Hurricane Katrina, *When the Levees Broke: A Requiem in Four Acts,* Spike Lee's cameras pan the masses of survivors huddled in an emergency shelter. In a movement as slow as the repeated funeral dirges that punctuate the film, Lee inserts Eric Gay's photograph of an elderly African American woman, Milvertha Hendricks's, blanketed in a U.S. flag. It is an image that recalls Gordon Parks's "American Gothic," his 1942 portrait of an African American cleaning woman for the Federal Security Administration, Ella Watson (see Figure 6–1). Parks's photograph testifies against black, female poverty in the wake of A. Philip Randolph's plan to march on Washington in 1941 and Roosevelt's subsequent passage of the Fair Employment Act that same year. It is an image that preserves the dignity of a black womanhood repeatedly assailed under Jim Crow. In Parks's photograph the flag hangs behind Watson's wiry frame. Her slightly downcast eyes betray sadness, a loss and hurt echoed by her missing buttons—telling symptoms of black female poverty—on her otherwise tidy dress. Her concealed hands clench a broom and mop, whose straight lines aesthetize her captivity. Literally boxing her in, these instruments of labor stand in for the economic opportunities delimited by race and gender during segregation. A woman whose father was lynched, whose husband abandoned her, whose daughter died young after giving birth to a second child—leaving her at once

FIGURE 6.1 Ella Watson.
Gordon Parks's "American Gothic." Courtesy of the Library of Congress, Federal Security Administration
(LC-USF34–013407-C).

mother and grandmother—this cleaning woman confronts the camera, embodying the contingencies of U.S. citizenship that Judith Shklar argues continue to be organized around job
opportunity and electoral privilege.[3] Silent in Shklar's assessment, however, is the manner by
which citizenship in the United States trades on human rights. The relationship between
these three categories of natural and legal privilege underlies Lee's anonymous figure.

The flag that framed Watson in Parks's "American Gothic" serves as veil and figural shroud
for Gay's elderly woman (see Figure 6–2). Watson's neat, polka-dot shirtwaist is supplanted
in the shot of Hendricks by a flag that covers what may be imagined as garb bearing evidence
of the storm—winds, flood waters, and debris. Yet, the shared critique against the state
lodged within these portraits upends the differences in time, geography, and circumstances
leading to their production. Gay's veiled woman amplifies Du Bois's turn-of-the-century

FIGURE 6.2 Milvertha Hendricks, 84, center, waits in the rain with other flood victims outside the convention center in New Orleans, Thursday, September 1, 2005. Officials called for a mandatory evacuation of the city, but many residents remained in the city and had to be rescued from flooded homes and hotels and remain in the city awaiting a way out.

AP Photo/Eric Gay. Used with permission of AP/WIDE WORLD PHOTOS. Spike Lee included this photograph among the images he reproduced in *When the Levees Broke: A Requiem in Four Acts.*

trope for black American life—the veil. A memorable symbol of the divide between black and white American social, political, and cultural thought and experiential realities, the veil is simultaneously a sign of mourning and death.[4] A macabre cultural fascination—no less striking, despite the popularity of U.S. procedural dramas like *CSI: Crime Scene Investigation*—became ever more transparent in the repeated images of dead hurricane victims casually strewn about, which were broadcast and published as evidence of the storm's devastation in the media coverage following the disaster. Spike Lee carefully restages these scenes of desiccating flesh in *When the Levees Broke,* coupling images of human remains to narratives by family members compelled by state authorities to abandon dead and dying loved ones and to the performance of a staged funeral march for Katrina victims, a formal recognition of national grief and mourning. Lee's use of Gay's still life captions the actual and felt disposability of black people. Studies by the Pew Foundation and the Center for the Study of Race Politics and Culture at the University of Chicago shortly after the hurricane exposed what Melissa Harris Lacewell describes as the racially uneven, debilitating psychic consequences of this disaster and the state's failures for black Americans. Forty-two percent of blacks surveyed reported that "their negative emotions had interfered with their life activities," and the anxiety, discomfort, depression, and distress experienced by black respondents was not restricted to victims of Katrina, betraying the ways in which many Blacks in the United States fasten their life chances to other members of their racial group.[5] According to the 2005 *Racial Attitudes and Katrina Disaster Study* conducted by the Center for the Study of Race Politics and Culture, 84 percent of African Americans surveyed believed that if the majority of storm sufferers were white there would have been prompt federal assistance.[6]

Lee's use of Hendricks's portrait, this black grandmother-mother-aunt-wife-sister-neighbor, articulates grief and a grievance. The flag upon this woman's back testifies in ways her silent figure cannot to a state that neglected black hurricane victims, and to the shrouds inaction made necessary as tens of thousands languished—homeless, starved, dehydrated—in the five-day wait for federal assistance. It is difficult to miss the acerbic irony of Hendricks's image: in the shadow of needless deaths caused by absent medical care, delinquent federal assistance, and underfunded and incomplete infrastructure intended to guard against the environmental vulnerabilities faced by communities seated below sea level, the woman's flagged body bespeaks absent protections. Literally a blanket, this flag that flies over all fails to offer much security beyond a basic cover. However, Gay's camera dislodges even this limited defense. The short-sleeved crowd surrounding Hendricks reminds us of the inconvenience and discomfort of the flag blanketing a victim who was enduring sweltering late August heat that reached the upper nineties in the days following the storm. In a scene rehearsing the spectacle of patriotic celebration performed by athletes at the close of a competition, Hendricks siphons the hope and possibility located in the flag. Her covered body points instead to the fictions of U.S. political ideology and social life for which the flag stands, and from which the black body has been historically routinely repelled. Her body repudiates the criminalizing presuppositions betrayed by the armed military personnel stationed throughout the city. Hendricks's image resists the defamiliarization common to other representations of the storm's victims, such as the distended corpses blighting the evening news. Instead, she lends a face to some of the most vulnerable populations in this storm: black women and the elderly.[7] Gay's' and Parks's depictions of black women focus on the racial and gender inequalities that would strip African Americans of their dignity, humiliate and destroy their character, and consign them to a second-class citizenship that permits—even sanctions—comparisons of these citizens to refugees.

In December 2005 the *Washington Post* announced that, in the aftermath of Hurricane Katrina, "refugee" was the word of the year.[8] The term catapulted into the public's imagination due to the media's framing of the natural disaster. Terms like "victim" and "evacuee" would not only have been more accurate, but carried less racial and ethnic baggage, and perhaps would have engendered greater sympathy and support from the American public. Before the storm, African Americans had made up 67 percent of the population of New Orleans. According to 2000 census data, "More than one in four individuals living in the city . . . lived below the federally defined poverty line: $16,000 for a family of three," and 84 percent of the poor were black.[9] With limited resources, the poor in New Orleans were less able to evacuate before the storm. In a city where poor and black were so desperately intertwined, it was these citizens who suffered Katrina's most grievous effects. In a storm disproportionately affecting black Americans, the mainstream newspapers[10] references to hurricane victims as refugees points to the resilience of this disposition toward the black body. The distinctions between the two terms—"evacuee" and "refugee"—exceed the semantic, retreating to the larger historical, social, and political protocols that make "refugee" more than an expression, but a sufficient description of the material reality of black Americans.

"Refugee" in Katrina became telling shorthand, signaling the distance of the state and the national polity from poor, black Americans. The aftermath of this hurricane laid bare a public and political demeanor toward black Americans frequently unacknowledged. A study conducted by the Center for the Study of Race Politics and Culture weeks after the storm revealed a perceptual gap between blacks and whites that should directly affect national social welfare agendas and public policy strategies. According to Michael Dawson, one of three principal investigators, "nearly four-fifths of Blacks (78%) believe that Blacks will either never or not in their lifetimes achieve racial equality in the United States. On the other hand, nearly two-thirds of Whites (66%) believe that Blacks have either achieved or will soon achieve racial equality."[11] Katrina represented a watershed in black political sensibilities toward the state, reifying across the socioeconomic and geographic spectrum of this population widespread distrust, alienation, and unease toward the federal government. Although the September 11 attacks fostered a bridge—however fleeting and artificial—across racial, ethnic, religious, regional, generational, gender, and economic divides in this country, the national tragedy of the hurricane failed to produce a comparable result.[12] The profound homelessness that marks the condition of the stateless and the refugee—the severed social relationships, the stripped political and legal privileges, the alienation from both the public sphere and the nation-state—was precisely what these survivors refused, but what their experiences nonetheless evidenced. "Refugee?" remarked a quizzical Katrina survivor. "When the storm came it blew away our citizenship too? . . . I thought those were folks that didn't have a country?"[13]

The repeated references to refugees carried forward the indictments simultaneously waged against brown and black refugees seeking asylum on U.S. shores, who have been increasingly marked as criminals over the last two decades. The collapsed distinctions among blacks, stateless persons, and refugees worldwide further sutured black Americans to a global community steadily at risk and reinforced the primary role that immigration law and policy serve in testing pending civil rights agenda.[14] At the same time that global capitalism, uneven distributions of goods and resources, civil wars, and pandemics have progressively displaced people around the world, refugees—who now represent a significant and steadily rising portion of the world's population—face increasingly strict conditions for asylum, intensifying violence against immigrants, and growing barriers to naturalization. As Europe moves away from granting permanent residence to refugees, constructing temporary relocation centers from which asylum seekers are repatriated in spite of the continued dangers to their lives,[15] the United States has responded in kind. Ronald Reagan's and George Bush's Haitian Interdiction program during the 1980s and early 1990s was one such successful attempt to bypass asylum conventions and the legislated guarantees prohibiting refoulement outlined in the Refugee Act (1980).[16] These changing approaches to global governance have had a direct, immediate affect on U.S. legal institutions, operating in tandem with transformations in the penal and social welfare systems that have unduly affected black and brown people in the United States.[17] In the context of Katrina, "refugee" summoned up the all-too-familiar rubric of cultural associations for national security and economic liabilities fastened onto asylum seekers and illegal immigrants—homelessness, poverty, unskilled labor, criminality, and disease—and sanctioned the transmogrification of acts of subsistence into expressions of criminality.

Consider the following storm-related anecdotes. The frequently revisited verbal missteps of the AP newswire service in the aftermath of the storm read like Freudian slips; they unconsciously project a larger social consciousness around black people. With a subtle shift in nominatives the wire service transformed a description of subsistence in the case of white survivors—"finding bread and soda from a local grocery store"—into an act of criminality when referencing a similarly situated black male—"A young man walks through chest deep water after looting a grocery store." In both instances the photographed scenes depict victims struggling to survive in the absence of federal support in a city more than 80 percent under water.[18] Likewise, the *Baltimore Afro-American* reported on an incident in which a black man saved more than forty hurricane victims, transporting them to safety in a public school bus, was disparagingly described in the media as a "thief" driving a "renegade bus."[19]

In studies testing the effects of racial markers on public support for federal assistance, white respondents consistently downgraded the level of federal aid needed to rehabilitate the city and address humanitarian needs.[20] In their 2005 study *Racial Attitudes and the Katrina Disaster,* Michael Dawson, Melissa Harris-Lacewell, and Cathy Cohen found,

> White respondents who are exposed to the media frame pairing a black family with the description "refugee" are less likely to believe that the federal government should spend whatever is necessary to rebuild the city and restore the victims. . . . This result suggests that the dominant frame of early reports, which showed African American victims and referred to them as refugees, may have reduced the political will among white Americans to hold the federal government responsible for rebuilding.[21]

Indeed, their study found that only 33 percent of whites, compared with 79 percent of blacks, believed the government "should spend whatever is necessary" for Gulf Coast recovery and reconstruction.[22] These responses attest to a social and juridical unconscious[23] that fails to consistently apprehend and consequently redress injuries to black bodies. They reflect the manner in which cultural assumptions regarding black criminality continue to inscribe black life as pathogenic to national security, national health, and the nation's economic, political, and social welfare.

By January 2006 a lawsuit had been filed against the Louisiana city of Gretna and its police department for having created a human barricade reinforced with gun barrels across the Crescent City Connection Bridge to prevent hurricane evacuees from finding safe harbor in their city in the days after the hurricane. Beneath the "unreasonable, unnecessary, and excessive force" used to deter victims from finding asylum in this adjoining municipality lay the presumption that these victims bore criminal designs.[24] Gretna had offered a hardhearted answer to the question Bill Torpy posed in the *Atlanta Journal Constitution* on September 4, 2005: "Where do the people nobody wants go?"[25] In Gretna, property and supposed public safety outweighed human life.[26] We need only remember how the property value of each race stabilized after emancipation with the Supreme Court's verdict in *Plessy* v. *Ferguson* to understand how human life has been measured in the United States. A century after the court codified segregation with its decision in the New Orleanian Homer Plessy's case, this city reminded the national public that segregation lives on.

While serving as Senate majority leader, Mississippi Senator Trent Lott expressed his nostalgia and support for the preintegration United States by praising Strom Thurman and, implicitly, the former candidate's 1948 presidential platform to keep "Negroes" from white homes, schools, and churches. Lott's remarks are one in a long list of examples of a counterpolitical backlash to the civil rights movement. On a radio program broadcast only weeks after Katrina, former Secretary of Education William Bennett argued that, although "morally reprehensible," "you could abort every black baby in this country, and your crime rate would go down."[27] Consider former First Lady Barbara Bush's remarks on the relocation of Katrina survivors to Houston: "What I'm hearing, which is sort of scary, is they all want to stay in Texas. Everybody is so overwhelmed by the hospitality. And so many of the people in the arenas here, you know, were underprivileged anyway. This is working very well for them."[28] The politics bared here recalibrate what had simply been a descriptor of time—*post-*civil rights—into an alternative political scheme, which David Theo Goldberg characterizes as "undoing the laws, rules, and norms of expectation that the civil rights movement managed to put in place."[29] Glossing the fracturing U.S. social life—churches, fraternal and civic organizations, schools, housing—Michael Dawson questions, "To what degree does it make sense to talk, either theoretically or empirically, about a single *American civil society?*" The presence of multiple political publics parallels and partially explains the dissolution of black political power in the United States.[30] Black Americans' inability to exert their political opinions and social needs meaningfully in the political sphere is marked in expanding urban gentrification, recurring accounts of electoral disadvantage and disenfranchisement in local and national elections, and continuing forms of racial and ethnic profiling across a range of sectors and institutions.[31]

African American civil rights campaigns have encompassed more than a demand for civil liberties, but an assertion of black humanity—a humanity challenged by the kinds of racial mythologies that bolster the rhetoric of the refugee—always plays a signal part. Indeed, human rights are already implied in the demands for fair labor, access to social welfare institutions, and equal treatment before the law. As Hurricane Katrina proved, despite the significant legal and social inroads of the Civil Rights Act (1964), black Americans remain among the most vulnerable communities in the United States. Kevin Shulman's 1999 study, *The Effect of Race and Sex on Physician's Recommendations for Cardiac Catherization,* which led to the Health Care Fairness Act in 2000, and surveys like the Institute of Medicine's 2002 *Unequal Treatment: Confronting Racial and Ethnic Disparities in Health Care* only further elaborate the mortal payments that have been collected in the twentieth-and twenty-first century against black Americans. Race and ethnicity, even more than socioeconomic status, continue to determine access to medical care and the parameters of medical research.[32] Narratives of adulterated care, though neither new and nor unfamiliar, are part of the cultural memory of black Americans. They recall a litany of abuses ranging from the 200 slaves Jefferson used to test a smallpox vaccine, to the blacks killed before their time or stolen from graves to support medical colleges, to the prisoners used in experimental medicine, to the poor injected with live cancers without their consent, to the patients left untreated for forty years during the Tuskegee syphilis experiment, to the women who were involuntarily sterilized throughout the twentieth century.[33] These histories remind us of the ways in which race informs sociomedical discourse and influences public policy, and they remind us that the racialization of disease and managed care continues to serve as an instrument of denaturalization and geopolitical containment.[34]

For some, the more than 3,000 children separated from their families in the days and months following the flood, evacuation, and relocation of Gulf Coast residents stand among the most shameful evidence of the administrative failures that compounded this natural disaster. For some, the way survivors were piled onto buses and airplanes during the massive evacuation without being told, let alone given the option to decide, where they were going mark the government's most disappointing intervention. Although some neoliberals have urged the erasure of "race" and its corollary syntax from our cultural vernaculars, this storm manifested the material impasses that continue to make race central to our cultural and national politics. Lee closes one of the four acts of his documentary on Katrina with a set of moving images. By filming survivors holding portrait frames around their faces while sharing their names and hometowns, Lee limns the questions of identity and home raised by this national disaster (Figure 6–3). Like the framed family portraits that were swept away in the flood, these living portraits stress the displacement—indeed, the homelessness—that is the condition of so many of these survivors. These still photographs point to the fiction of the frames—the media and the state—that have historically deepened the social and legal dispossession experienced by black Americans.

The divisive character of race as it operated in New Orleans is tragically apparent. Failure to acknowledge the racialization of poverty, crime, and civil and human rights exposed by this event jeopardizes the ability to apprehend these problems as the United States's tragedy. It is not simply the degrees of separation between collateral and protected, between

FIGURE 6.3 Three-Time Grammy Award Winner Terence Blanchard and his mother, Wilhelmina Blanchard. Courtesy HBO.®

imprisoned and free, and between refugee and black American citizen that are shrinking. Risking the human and civil rights of one community undermines the stability of these privileges for all. Since its application by the federal government in 1865 to describe emancipated slaves aided by the Bureau of Refugees, Freedmen, and Abandoned Lands (the Freedmen's Bureau), "refugee" has continued to cling to black Americans. Its historic peroration transformed it into a signifier for a political ethos invested in separating, differentiating, and disenfranchising blacks from the larger polity. In the fall of 2005, winds, flood waters, administrative failures, and media insensitivity were potent reminders of the currency of James Baldwin's claim, "Blacks have never been, and are not now, really considered to be citizens here."[35]

NOTES

PREFACE

1. Frederick Douglass, *Narrative of the Life of Frederick Douglass, An American Slave, Written by Himself*, ed. David W. Blight (Boston: Bedford/St. Martins, 1993), 47.

2. Deirdre Mullane, "The Great Migration, 1910–1920" *Crossing the Danger Water: Three Hundred Years of African-American Writing*, ed. with intro. Deirdre Mullane (New York: Anchor Books, 1993), 455–456.

3. Richard Wright, *Black Boy*, intro. Jerry Ward (New York: Harper Perennial, 1993 [1944]), 307.

4. Carter G. Woodson, "Fifty Years of Negro Citizenship as Qualified by the United States Supreme Court," *Journal of Negro History* 6 (1) (1921), 1–53.

5. 8 U.S.C.§1101 (42)(A)(B)(1998) (Supp. covering 1971–1997).

6. Hortense Spillers, "Mama's Baby, Papa's Maybe: An American Grammar Book," in *Black White and in Color: Essays on American Literature and Culture* (Chicago: University of Chicago Press, 2003), 203.

7. Toni Morrison, *Paradise* (New York: Plume Books, 1997), 8, 12.

8. Ibid., 16.

9. My paraphrase is borrowed from the title of an edited collection by Christina Duffy Burnett and Burke Marshall, *Foreign in a Domestic Sense: Puerto Rico, American Expansion, and the Constitution* (Durham, N.C.: Duke University Press, 2001).

10. W. E. B. Du Bois, *Color and Democracy: Colonies and Peace* (New York: Harcourt, Brace, 1945), 91–92.

11. This work is entitled "Words like Freedom" in both the *Collected Poems*, ed. Arnold Rampersad and David Roessel (New York: Vintage Books, 1994) and *The Collected Works of Langston Hughes*, Vol. 3, *The Poems: 1951–1967*, ed. with intro. Arnold Rampersad (Columbia: University of Missouri Press, 2001).

145

12. Hughes, "Song of the Refugee Road," in *Collected Works of Langston Hughes*, Vol. 3, 265.

13. Ralph Ellison, "Harlem is Nowhere," in *The Collected Essays of Ralph Ellison*, ed. John F. Callahan (New York: Modern Library, 1995), 325.

14. Homi Bhabha, *The Location of Culture* (New York: Routledge 1994), 153. Emphasis in original.

15. Ibid., 236. Emphasis in original; Author's conversations with Shelley Wong, October 2007.

16. Author's conversation with Shelley Wong October 2007.

17. Ann Stoler, "Tense and Tender Ties: The Politics of Comparison in North American History and (Post) Colonial Studies," in *Haunted by Empire: Geographies of Intimacy in North American Empire*, ed. Ann Stoler (Durham, N.C.: Duke University Press, 2006), 40.

CHAPTER 1

1. Gerald Horne, *Communist Front?: The Civil Rights Congress, 1946–1956* (Rutherford, N.J.: Fairleigh Dickinson University Press, 1988), 205.

2. *Ingram v. State*, 204 GA. 164, 48 S.E. 2d 891 (1948).

3. Charles Martin, "Race, Gender, and Southern Justice: The Rosa Lee Ingram Case," *American Journal of Legal History* 29 (3) (1985), 252.

4. "My Children Need Me: 'Please Get Me Out' Doomed Mother Cries," *Pittsburgh Courier*, February 21, 1948. The Ingrams were also jailed in separate towns to reduce the risk of lynching.

5. W. E. B. Du Bois, "Race Relations in the United States: 1917–1918," *Writings by W. E. B. Du Bois in Periodicals Edited by Others*. Vol. 4, *1945–1961*, ed. Herbert Aptheker (Millwood, N.Y.: Kraus-Thomson, 1982), 69. Paul Robeson echoed Du Bois's sentiments on the case. In his words, the trial and its outcome was nothing short of a "legal lynching" of Ingram and her sons. These were young people who had been "jailed for life in Georgia for protecting her honor." Philip S. Foner, ed., *Paul Robeson Speaks: Writings, Speeches, Interviews 1918–1974* (Secaucus, N.J.: Citadel Press, 1978), 218.

The law recognizes a child's right to aid a parent whose life is in danger as justified presuming the child used "just such force and means as would seem necessary and proper to a reasonable person to prevent the assault in the protection of the mother." "Charge of the Court" *The State v. Rosa Lee Ingram, Wallace Ingram, Sammie Lee Ingram*, Supreme Court—Clerk of Court-Criminal Appeal Case, RG-SG-S 92-1-3; Georgia Archives.

6. *Brief of Evidence The State v. Rosa Lee Ingram, Wallace Ingram, Sammie Lee Ingram*, Supreme Court—Clerk of Court-Criminal Appeal Case, RG-SG-S 92-1-3; Georgia Archives.

7. Martin, "Race, Gender, and Southern Justice," 252.

8. "Judge Silent on Ingram Plea: Takes Case Under Advisement; Jury Erred, Court Told" *Pittsburgh Courier*, April 3, 1948; cited in Horne, *Communist Front*, 205.

9. The National Association for the Advancement of Colored People (NAACP), the Civil Rights Congress (CRC), and the *Pittsburgh Courier*, and other groups raised more than $100,000.

10. Charles Washington, "Ingrams Have Spent Eight Months in Jail," *Pittsburgh Courier*, June 26, 1948.

11. "'He Tried to Go with Me'" *Pittsburgh Courier*, March 20, 1948. Emphasis in original.

12. "Mrs. Rosa Lee Ingram Tells Her Own Story," *Pittsburgh Courier*, July 10, 1948.

13. *Brief of Evidence The State v. Rosa Lee Ingram, Wallace Ingram, Sammie Lee Ingram*, Supreme Court—Clerk of Court-Criminal Appeal Case, RG-SG-S 92-1-3; Georgia Archives.

14. Ibid.

15. Cited in Horne, *Communist Front*, 205.

16. Ibid., 204.

17. Horne, *Communist Front*, 209.

18. "Georgia Jury Assailed as 'Hog Wild'" *Washington Post*, March 26, 1948.

19. Here I am troping on Ruth Wilson Gilmore's definition of racism as the movement toward premature black death. "Fatal Couplings of Power and Difference." *Professional Geographer* 54 (1) (2002), 16.

20. W. E. B. Du Bois, "Colonialism, Democracy, and Peace after the War," *Against Racism: Unpublished Essays; Papers, Addresses, 1887–196*, ed. Herbert Aptheker (Amherst: University of Massachusetts Press, 1985), 229.

21. Horne, *Communist Front*, 206.

22. W. E. B. Du Bois, "Georgia: Invisible Empire State," *Writings by W. E. B. Du Bois in Non-Periodical Literature Edited by Others*, ed. Herbert Aptheker (New York: Kraus-Thomson, 1982), 138, 140.

23. "'He Tried to Go With Me,'" *Pittsburgh Courier*, March 20, 1948.

24. Horne, *Communist Front*, 200.

25. Ibid., 205.

26. "Doomed Georgia Widow Has Never Been Out of State," *Pittsburgh Courier*, April 3, 1948.

27. Martin, "Race, Gender, and Southern Justice," 261, 264.

28. "Text of the Communist Party's Platform for the Presidential Election" *The New York Times*, August 7, 1948; Martin, "Race, Gender, and Southern Justice," 251–268; Horne, *Communist Front*, 209.

29. Cited in Horne, *Communist Front*, 204.

30. Between 1947 and 1961, Du Bois drafted four petitions: two were dedicated to the United Nations, and two were intended for the sitting president.

31. Although Du Bois penned this petition, it was Mary Church Terrell who presented this document before the United Nations on September 21, 1949. W. E. B. Du Bois, "A Petition to the Human Rights Commission of the Social and Economic Council of the United Nations; and to the General Assembly of the United Nations; and to the Several Delegations of the Member States of the United Nations." In *Against Racism: Unpublished Essays, Papers, Addresses, 1887–1961*, ed. Herbert Aptheker (Amherst: University of Massachusetts Press, 1985), 261–263.

32. Horne, *Communist Front*, 167. Horne records an essay by Harry Haywood in *Political Affairs* featuring a letter from Dean Acheson, stating that "The existence of discrimination against minority groups in this country has an adverse effect upon our relations with other countries."

33. Carol Anderson, "The NAACP and Black Communists," in *Window on Freedom: Race, Civil Rights, and Foreign Affairs 1945–1988* (Chapel Hill: University of North Carolina Press, 2003); and Horne, *Communist Front*, 167.

34. J. Richardson Jones, "'Please Get me Out!' My Children Need Me, Doomed Mother Cries" *Pittsburgh Courier*, February 21, 1948. Emphasis added.

35. In her first-hand account for *Courier* readers, dictated to the publication's news editor, Robert M. Ratcliffe, Lee complained that the injury to her head resulted in pain that lingered for two months after the event. "Mrs. Rosa Lee Ingram Tells Her Own Story," *Pittsburgh Courier*, July 10, 1948.

36. Gerald Neuman, *"Anomalous Zone," Surveying Law and Borders: Anomalous Zones* 48 STANFORD LAW REVIEW (1996) WL 1197* 1197.

37. See Nahum Chandler's "The Economy of Desedimentation: W. E. B. Du Bois and the Discourses of the Negro" for a thorough analysis of "between" and the labor performed by this prepositional proposition in Du Bois. *Callaloo* 19 (1) (1996): 78–93.

38. Hannah Arendt, *The Origins of Totalitarianism* (San Diego, Calif.: Harcourt, [1968] 1976), 297.

39. Homi K. Bhabha, *The Location of Culture* (New York: Routledge, 1994); Edward Said, "Reflections on Exile," *Reflections on Exile and Other Essays* (Cambridge, Mass.: Harvard University Press, 2000), 173–186.

40. Arendt, *Origins of Totalitarianism*, 293.

41. Ibid., 294.

42. To cite Arendt's orthodoxy on the stateless and the refugee within the African American context is to immediately confront the fact that the communities she references describe individuals displaced or expelled respectively from their homelands. Although it's certainly true that the loss of a nation-state rests among the numerous losses endured by the African slave body, black Americans, however, arguably never had a nation-state to lose. My thanks to R.A. Judy whose consistent insight reminded me of the need for clarification on this point.

43. In addition to the petitions brought forward by the NAACP and other civil rights organizations, see, for example, W. E. B. Du Bois, "A Petition to the President of the United States, The Honorable John F. Kennedy, February 1961"; "Petition of Right to the President, the Congress and The Supreme Court of the United States of America, 1957," *The Papers of W. E. B. Du Bois* (Sandford, N.C.: Microfilming Corporation of America, 1980).

44. Karla Holloway, *Moorings and Metaphors: Figures of Culture and Gender in Black Women's Literature* (New Brunswick, N.J.: Rutgers University Press, 1994); Paul Gilroy, *The Black Atlantic: Modernity and Double Consciousness* (Cambridge, Mass.: Harvard University Press, 1993).

45. Arendt, *Origins of Totalitarianism*, 297.

46. W. E. B. Du Bois, *Black Reconstruction in America: 1860–1880*, intro. David Levering Lewis (New York: Atheneum, 1992), 39. I want to thank Nahum Chandler for sharing this passage with me.

47. Richard Wright, "I Choose Exile," Richard Wright Papers. Yale Collection of American Literature, Beinecke Rare Book and Manuscript Library, Yale University, New Haven, Conn., 1–3. Undated manuscript.

48. Said, "Reflections on Exile," 173–176.

49. Wright, "I Choose Exile," 1.

50. Richard Wright, "The Man Who Went to Chicago," *Eight Men* (New York: Perennial Press, 1996).

51. The FBI's investigations of Wright for sedition began with the publication of *12 Million Black Voices* in 1942, a sociological photo-essay collection on black life, and continued until his death in 1960. See Hazel Rowley, *Richard Wright: The Life and Times* (New York: Henry Holt, 2001), 275.

52. James Baldwin, "The Price of the Ticket," *James Baldwin: Collected Essays*, edited by Toni Morrison. (New York: Library of America, 1998), 837.

53. Wright, "I Choose Exile," 2. Emphasis in original.

54. Baldwin, "The Price of the Ticket," 837.

55. Wright, "I Choose Exile," 8.

56. Ibid., 12.

57. Ibid., 10, emphasis in original.

58. Frantz Fanon, *Black Skins, White Masks* (New York: Grove Press, 1967), 109.

59. William Faulkner, *Absalom, Absalom!* (New York: Modern Library, 1993); Toni Morrison, *Playing in the Dark: Whiteness and the Literary Imagination* (New York: Vintage Press, 1993), 71.

60. Alphonse Bertillon, *Signaletic Instructions: Including the Theory and Practice of Anthropometrical Identification*, edited by R. W. McClaughry. (Chicago: Werner, 1896), 151. Emphasis in original.

61. Ibid., 183.

62. Although "refugee" would also occasionally be used to describe Gulf Coast evacuees generally, the term was more frequently applied, and seemed to adhere more rigidly, to black Americans.

63. *Associated Press*, August 30, 2005.

64. Quoted in Robin D. G. Kelley, "'But a Local Phase of a World Problem': Black History's Global Vision, 1883–1950," *Journal of American History* 86 (3) (1999): 1045–1077. The alienation Douglass felt in the mid-nineteenth century recurs, appearing during World War I among 1) blacks who felt that they had no country for which they should be compelled to fight; 2) black activists such as Ida B. Wells, Du Bois, Paul Robeson, and William Patterson, whose passports were either seized or threatened by the state; and 3) black expatriates like Richard Wright, Chester Himes, and James Baldwin.

65. W. E. B. Du Bois, *The Suppression of the African Slave-Trade* (New York: Library of America, [1896, 1946]1986), 74.

66. Frederick Douglass, "Lecture On Haiti at the World's Fair," January 2, 1893.

67. Hortense J. Spillers, "Who Cuts the Border? Some Readings on 'America,'" in *Comparative American Identities: Race, Sex, and Nationality in the Modern Text*, edited with an introduction by Hortense J. Spillers, 1–25. (New York: Routledge, 1991), 16.

CHAPTER 2

1. Sutton E. Griggs, *Imperium in Imperio*, intro. Cornell West (New York: Modern Library, 2003), 6.

2. Ibid., 125.

3. Frederick Douglass, "A Nation in the Midst of a Nation: An Address Delivered in New York, New York, on May 11, 1853," in *The Frederick Douglass Papers, 1847–1854*, Vol. 2, ed. John Blassingame, 423–440. (New Haven, Conn.: Yale University Press, 1982), 425.

4. This term is taken from the title of George M. Fredrickson's chapter, "The Vanishing Negro: Darwinism and the Conflict of the Races," where he addresses an active late nineteenth-century discourse espousing the degeneracy and eventual extinction of African Americans. This discourse anticipates the rhetoric of social Darwinists, refashioning the logic of proslaveries to argue that African Americans were degenerating and suffering higher mortality rates because of the absence of white custodial care. Figures like Fredrick Hoffman refined racial Darwinism, attributing the inferiority of the black body as the cause for poverty, illness, and disproportionate mortality rates experienced by this community. George M. Fredrickson, *The Black Image in the White Mind: The Debate on Afro-American Character and Destiny, 1817–1914*. (New York: Harper Torchbooks, 1971), 228–255.

5. Howard Bell, "Introduction," in *Black Separatism and the Caribbean 1860*, by James Theodore Holly and J. Dennis Harris, ed. with intro. Howard H. Bell (Ann Arbor: University of Michigan Press, 1970), 1; Michelle Stephens. *Black Empire: The Masculine Global Imaginary of Caribbean Intellectuals in the United States, 1914–1962* (Durham, N.C.: Duke University Press), 2005.

6. Griggs, *Imperium in Imperio*, 6.

7. Ibid., 150; William Seraille, "Afro-American Emigration to Haiti during the American Civil War," *The Americas* 35 (2) (1978), 200.

8. Griggs, *Imperium in Imperio*, 177.

9. Robin D.G. Kelley, "'But a Local Phase of a World Problem': Black History's Global Vision, 1883–1950," *Journal of American History* 86 (3) (1999), 1064.

10. Kelley, "But a Local Phase of a World Problem," 1064.

11. Janken, "New Introduction," xxi–*xii.

12. W. E. B. Du Bois, "Flashes from Transcaucasia," in *Against Racism: Unpublished Essays, Papers, Addresses, 1887–1961*, ed. Herbert Aptheker (Amherst: University of Massachusetts Press, 1985), 257.

13. W. E. B. Du Bois, *Color and Democracy: Colonies and Peace* (New York: Harcourt, Brace and Company, 1945), 92.

14. Kenneth Robert Janken, "New Introduction," in *What the Negro Wants* (Notre Dame, Ind.: University of Notre Dame Press, [1944] 2001), *xvi,*vii,* x,* xv–xvi.

15. W. T. Couch, "Publisher's Introduction," in *What the Negro Wants* (Notre Dame, Ind.: University of Notre Dame Press, [1944] 2001), xxii.

16. Quoted in Janken, " New Introduction," * xx.

17. Ibid., xix.

18. Herbert Aptheker, Editorial Notation, "Flashes from Transcaucasia," in *Against Racism: Unpublished Essays, Papers, Addresses, 1887–1961*, ed. Herbert Aptheker (Amherst: University of Massachusetts Press, 1985), 254–260.

19. Ibid., 255.

20. Quoted in Marable, *W. E. B. Du Bois: Black Radical Democrat*, 100.

21. W. E. B. Du Bois, "News from Pan-Africa," in *W. E. B. Du Bois Papers*, 1887–1968. (Sandford, N.C.: Microfilming Corporation of America, 1980), 1389.

22. Du Bois's long standing commitment to, and substantive participation in the Pan-Africanist movement has been well documented, from his participation in the Pan African Conference that met in London in 1900 to his participation in the fifth Pan-African Congress in 1945. Manning Marable reminds us that the 1906 meeting of the Niagara Movement included the establishment of a "standing committee on Pan Africanism." According to Marable, Du Bois's sense of the primary role that Africa would play as a global actor was reaffirmed during the 1911 Universal Race Congress in London. This pan-Africanist sensibility is all the more explicit in Du Bois's seminal text on Africa, *The Negro*, published in 1915. In Marable's assessment, "Its theoretical departure was Pan-Africanist: no study of African history and culture could ignore both the impact of the transatlantic slave trade, and the extensive links between the continent and the peoples of African descent in the Caribbean and the Americas." Manning Marable, *W. E. B. Du Bois: Black Radical Democrat* (Boston: Twayne Publishers, 1986), 92.

23. Janken, "New Introduction," *xv.

24. Quoted in Janken, "New Introduction," *xvi–xvii.

25. Ibid., *xvi.

26. W. E. B. Du Bois, "My Evolving Program for Negro Freedom," Ed. Rayford Logan. New Intro. Kenneth Robert Janken, *What the Negro Wants* (Notre Dame, Ind.: Notre Dame University Press, [1944] 2001), 40.

27. Ibid., 40–41.

28. Ibid., 42.

29. See Saidiya Hartman, *Scenes of Subjection: Terror, Slavery, and Self-Making in Nineteenth Century America* (London: Oxford University Press, 1997).

30. Frederic Jameson, *Archaeologies of the Future: The Desire Called Utopia and Other Science Fictions* (New York: Verso Press, 2005), xiv. My use of the term critical cosmopolitanism draws from Walter Mignolo who defines this practice as a critique of modernity lodged from outside. Walter D. Mignolo, "The Many Faces of Cosmo-polis: Border Thinking and Critical Cosmopolitanism," *Public Culture* 12 (3) (2000), 724.

31. Neil Smith, *American Empire; Roosevelt's Geographer and the Prelude to Globalization* (Berkeley and Los Angeles: University of California Press, 2003), 56.

32. See Du Bois, "My Evolving Program"; and *Dusk of Dawn* in *W. E. B. Du Bois Writings*, edited by Nathan Huggins (New York: Library of America, 1986), 590.

33. Smith, *American Empire*, 25–26; and see Smith, "Revolutionarily Yours: The New World, the Council on Foreign Relations, and the Making of Liberal Foreign Policy," *American Empire*, 181–207.

34. Ibid., xiii.

35. W. E. B. Du Bois, *Darkwater: Voices From Within the Veil* (Mineola, N.Y.: Dover Publications, [1920], 1999), 27.

36. Ibid., 20.

37. W. E. B. Du Bois to *New York Age* editor concerning the Pan African Movement, 1919, *The Papers of W. E. B. Du Bois, Correspondence, 1887–1932* (Sandford, N.C.: Microfilming Corporation of America, 1980).

38. W. E. B. Du Bois, "Worlds of Color" *Du Bois: Writings in Periodicals Edited by Others*, ed. Herbert Aptheker (Millwood, N.Y.: Kraus-Thomason, 1982), 241.

39. Among the corpus of Du Bois's writings on this subject see, *Darkwater: Voices from Within the Veil*, in *Dark Princess*, with an introduction by Claudia Tate (Jackson: University of Mississippi Press, [1928] 1995); "Prospect of a World Without Race Conflict," *American Journal of Sociology* 49 (5) (1944), 450–456; "Colonialism, Democracy, and Peace after the War (Summer 1944)," *Against Racism: Unpublished Essays, Papers, Addresses, 1887–1961*, ed. Herbert Aptheker (Amherst: University of Massachusetts Press, 1985), 229–249; "Roosevelt," Manuscript. Manuscripts, Archives, and Rare Books Division, Schomburg Center for Research in Black Culture, The New York Public Library, New York, N.Y., 1–25.

40. Du Bois, *Darkwater*, 56.

41. Ibid., 58–59.

42. Du Bois, *Darkwater*, 35.

43. Hortense Spillers, "Mama's Baby, Papa's Maybe," *Black White and in Color: Essays on American Literature and Culture* (Chicago: University of Chicago Press, 2003), 207.

44. Du Bois, *Darkwater*, 86.

45. Ibid., 89.

46. Ibid., 87–89.

47. W. E. B. Du Bois, *The Souls of Black Folk. In Du Bois Writings*, edited by Nathan Huggins (New York: Library of America, 1986), 372. I want to emphasize two points here; first that Du Bois repeats this statement, articulating it initially in the preface and again in the second chapter of *Souls of Black Folk*. On this second occasion he expanded on the first articulation, which is cited here and represents the global reach and coordinated relationship among racial discriminations.

Second, and more significant, although I have indexed *Souls* here, this phrase, among the single most noted lines by Du Bois, and a crucial claim within African American political thought, was in fact, according to the work of Nahum D. Chandler, first stated at the turn-of-the century during an address Du Bois gave to the American Negro Academy (1899). Chandler traces this earlier statement and its subsequent publication the following year in a piece entitled, "The Present Outlook for the Darker Races of Mankind." He is the first scholar to my knowledge to map the history of this line, thickening in kind the ways in which we might approach and understand the significance of Du Bois's work to African American political and social thought, and to global political relations. See Nahum D. Chandler, "The Figure of W. E. B. Du Bois as a Problem for Thought," *New Centennial Review* 6 (3) (2006): 29–55.

48. W. E. B. Du Bois, "The Color Line Belts the World," in *W. E. B. Du Bois: A Reader*, ed. David Levering Lewis (New York: Henry Holt, 1995), 42.

49. W. E. B. Du Bois, "Prospect for a World Without Race Conflict," *American Journal of Sociology* 49 (5) (1944), 453; 450–456; emphasis mine.

50. Du Bois, *Dark Princess*, 257.

51. Harcourt, Brace and Howe to W. E. B. Du Bois "Re: publication of *Darkwater*," in *The Papers of W. E. B. Du Bois, Correspondence, 1887–1932* (Sandford, N.C.: Microfilming Corporation of America, 1980).

52. Du Bois, *Darkwater*, 89.

53. This rhetoric permeates colonial discourse and accounts for much of the legal and social rigor placed on sexuality, while informing nationalist movements in the United States like the "Lost Cause."

54. W. E. B. Du Bois, "The American Negro in Paris," *American Monthly Reviews* 22 (November) (1900), 576–577. Du Bois who was working as a professor of sociology at Atlanta University during the time of the exhibition, was already conducting his sociological studies on black life whose findings were regularly presented at conferences he directed at the University. Between 1896 and 1914 he conducted eighteen sociological studies. *Mortality Among Negroes in Cities* and *Social and Physical Condition of Negroes* were among the first of these projects (1896–1897), but his publications for the conference series began with his next investigation, *Some Efforts of American Negroes for Their Own Social Betterment* (1898). Ernest Kaiser, "Introduction," *Atlanta University Publications* (New York: Arno Press, 1968), iv.

55. See Deborah Willis, "The Sociologist's Eye: W. E. B. Du Bois and the Paris Exposition," *A Small Nation of People: W. E. B. Du Bois and African American Portraits of Progress* (New York: Amistad Press, 2003), 56. Although the names of the photographers whose work supported this exhibition have been unknown, Deborah Willis has identified one of the contributors, Thomas Askew. The charts Du Bois compiled reflected the contributions of blacks in agriculture and manufacturing, the scale of black property ownership, and the population size of black Americans. Du Bois, "American Negro in Paris," 575–577.

56. Du Bois, "American Negro in Paris," 577.

57. Shawn Michelle Smith, *Photography on the Color Line: W. E. B. Du Bois, Race, and Visual Culture* (Durham, N.C.: Duke University Press, 2004), 6, 9, 89.

58. Smith, *Photography on the Color Line*, 7.

59. Zahid Chaudhary, "Phantasmagoric Aesthetics: Colonial Violence and the Management of Perception," *Cultural Critique* 59 (Winter) (2005), 71.

60. Du Bois, *Darkwater*, 120–121.

61. Ibid., 121, 123.

62. Ibid., 122.

63. Ibid., 123.

64. Du Bois, *Darkwater*, 114.

65. Rebecka Rutledge Fisher, "Cultural Artifacts and the Narrative of History: W. E. B. Du Bois and the Exhibiting of Culture at the 1900 Paris Exposition Universelle," *Modern Fiction Studies* 51 (4) (2005), 750. Rutledge Fisher's thoroughgoing essay on Du Bois's participation in the exhibition as a critique of various sociological theories and methodologies, reminds us of the effects that Paris, a "cosmopolitan world capital" that nonetheless remained wedded to "a narrow nationalistic insistence upon the metaphysics of race and society" would have on Du Bois's approach to the exhibit (741–742).

66. Michele Mitchell, *Righteous Propagation: African Americans and the Politics of Racial Destiny After Reconstruction* (Chapel Hill: University of North Carolina Press, 2004), 75.

67. Ibid., 80.

68. W. E. B. Du Bois, *The Health and Physique of the Negro American* (Atlanta, Ga.: Atlanta University Press, 1906), 37; quoted in Smith, *Photography on the Color Line*, 55.

69. Mitchell, *Righteous Propagation*, 210.

70. I want to thank Masako Nakamura for suggesting that I look at the *Crisis* Education numbers.

71. Mitchell, *Righteous Propagation*, 76–102.

72. For additional examples of the use of this oceanic metaphor to evince race relations see Lothrup Stoddard, *The Rising Tide of Color Against White World Supremacy* (New York: Charles Scribner's Sons, 1920); and Charles Johnson, *To Stem This Tide: A Survey of Racial Tension Areas in the United States* (Boston: Pilgrim Press, 1943).

73. W. E. B. Du Bois, *The Autobiography of W. E. B. Du Bois: A Soliloquy on Viewing My Life from the Last Decade of Its First Century* (New York: International Publishers, 1968), 284.

74. Due to high infant mortality rates, African American parents had customized postcards and portraits taken either depicting their child laying in state, or being held by a parent. Frequently, these images concurrently served as both the birth and death announcement for a newborn or a toddler. See James Van der Zee's *Harlem Book of the Dead* and Karla Holloway's *Passed On: African American Mourning Stories*.

75. Du Bois, *Darkwater*, 120.

76. The pictures of young children filling the pages of the Children's numbers were similarly intended as defensive evidence against circulating theories of "Negro" pathology that sought to present blackness as a site of exhaustive difference. Having begun collecting infant and toddler portraits in 1911, by 1914 Du Bois would explicitly attribute this testamentary function, writing, "The pictures which we have published may be considered from many points of view. The students of a great social problem will look upon them first as physical types. No sooner had he looked with this in mind than certainly the fiction of the physical degeneracy of American Negroes must disappear." W. E. B. Du Bois, *Crisis* 8 (6) (1914), 298.

77. W. E. B. Du Bois, Editorial, "The Immortal Children," *Crisis* 12 (6) (1916), 267–268.

78. Rev. 7: 9.

79. Du Bois, *Dark Princess*, 311.

80. Du Bois, "Immortal Children," 268

81. For a fuller discussion on internationalism, see Brent Edwards, *The Practice of Diaspora: Literature, Translation, and the Rise of Black Internationalism* (Cambridge, Mass.: Harvard University Press, 2003).

82. Du Bois, *Health and Physique of the Negro American*, 8; *The American Negro: His History and Literature. The Atlanta University Publications nos. 1, 2, 4, 8, 9, 11, 13, 14, 15, 16, 17, 18* (New York: Arno Press and The New York Times, 1906), 37.

83. For a theory on "rooted cosmopolitanism" see Kwame Anthony Appiah, "Cosmopolitan Patriots," in *Cosmopolitics: Thinking and Feeling Beyond the Nation*, ed. Pheng Cheah and Bruce Robbins (Minneapolis: University of Minnesota Press, 1998), 111.

84. James Redpath, ed. *A Guide to Hayti. Boston: Haytian Bureau of Emigration* (Boston: 1861), 9. Division of Rare and Manuscript Collections, Carl A. Kroch Library, Cornell University, Ithaca, N.Y. Both Saunders's and Redpath's texts are taken up in greater detail in chapter three, "Sanctuary."

85. Mitchell, *Righteous Propagation*, 64–65.

86. George Schuyler criticized the colonial dimensions of Garvey's plan in his serialized utopian science fiction novel, *Black Empire*. He would be one among many black voices of dissent critical of the UNIA and its leader.

87. Ibid., 16–50.

88. Nell Irvin Painter, *Exodusters: Black Migration to Kansas after Reconstruction* (New York: Alfred Knopf, 1977).

89. Du Bois, *Dark Princess*, 3, 5. W. E. B. Du Bois "Introduction," in *An Appeal to the World; A Statement on the Denial of Human Rights to Minorities in the Case of citizens of Negro Descent in the United States of America and an Appeal to the United Nations for Redress* (New York: NAACP, 1947).

90. Du Bois, "Introduction," in *An Appeal to the World.*

91. Ibid., 10–11.

92. Homi Bhabha, *The Location of Culture* (New York: Routledge, 1994), 9–11.

93. Du Bois, *An Appeal*, 6; Hannah Arendt, *On Totalitarianism*, 275.

94. Du Bois, *An Appeal*, 13.

95. Arendt, *On Totalitarianism*, 276.

96. After suggesting that Martin Luther King, Jr. could well be "the American Gandhi," Du Bois would rescind this praise, frustrated by the absence of an economic agenda in the civil rights leader's movement. David Levering Lewis, *W. E. B. Du Bois: The Fight for Equality and the American Century, 1919–1963*, 557.

97. W. E. B. Du Bois, "Testimony on the United Nations Charter Before the Committee on Foreign Relations," in *The Papers of W. E. B. Du Bois, Correspondence, 1877–1965* (Sandford, N.C.: Microfilming Corporation of America, 1980).

CHAPTER 3

1. Burns escaped from Virginia the year before, boarding a ship docked at the harbor that set sail for Massachusetts. For additional readings on these events see Charles Emery Stevens, *Anthony Burns A History* (New York: Arno Press, 1969 [Boston 1856]).

2. "Anthony Burns in New York," *Liberator*, March 9, 1855.

3. Paul Laurence Dunbar, "Is Higher Education for the Negro Hopeless," in *The Paul Laurence Dunbar Reader*, ed. Jay Martin and Gossie H. Hudson (New York: Dodd, Mead, 1975), 45–47.

4. Maurice Wallace, *Constructing the Black Masculine: Identity and Ideality in African American Men's Literature and Culture* (Durham N.C.: Duke University Press, 2002), 30.

5. On the contingent relationship between rights and political membership see Seyla Benhabib, *The Rights of Others: Aliens, Residents, and Citizens* (Cambridge: Cambridge University

Press, 2004); Frank Michelman, "Parsing 'A Right to Have Rights,'" *Constellations* 3 (2) (1996), 200–208.

6. The Civil Rights Cases, 109 U.S. 3, 3 S. Ct. 18 (1883) WL 18, * 34.

7. Samuel Johnson, *The Crisis of Freedom: A Sermon Preached at the Free Church, In Lynn, On Sunday, June 11, 1854* (Boston: Crosby, Nichols, 1854), 5. Division of Rare and Manuscript Collections, Carl A. Kroch Library, Cornell University, Ithaca, N.Y.

8. *Boston Slave Riot, and Trial of Anthony Burns. Containing the Report of the Faneuil Hall Meeting; The Murder of Batchelder; Theodore Parker's Lesson for the Day; Speeches of Counsel on Both Sides, Corrected by Themselves; A Verbatim Report of Judge Loring's Decision; and Detailed Account of the Embarkation* (Boston: Fetridge and Company, 1854), 25, 9.

9. Ibid., 9.

10. Thomas Wentworth Higginson, *Massachusetts in Mourning. A Sermon, Preached in Worcester, on Sunday, June 4, 1854 by Thomas Wentworth Higginson, Minister of the Worcester Free Church. Reprinted by Request, From the "Worcester Daily Spy"* (Boston: James Munroe, 1854), 5. Division of Rare and Manuscript Collections, Carl A. Kroch Library, Cornell University, Ithaca, N.Y.

11. Ibid.

12. This omission would prove strategically useful to abolitionists who incited public concern for fugitive slaves in part by arguing that the Fugitive Slave Law rendered everyone vulnerable. Because all fugitives were prohibited from testifying on their own behalf, anyone could now be indicted with fabricated affidavits claiming that services were owed, particularly minors. Moreover, the removal of constitutional privileges secured through this legislation was seen as the precursor for a dangerous military despotism that would further transform this country, its administrators and functionaries, and citizens into "slaves." *The Boston Slave Riot, and Trial of Anthony Burns*. Boston: Fetridge and Company, 1854; James Clarke Freeman, *The Rendition of Anthony Burns. Its Causes and Consequences. A Discourse on Christian Politics Delivered in Williams Hall, Boston, on Whitsunday, June 4, 1854*, (Boston: Crosby, Nichols/Prentiss and Sawyer, 1854), 14. Division of Rare and Manuscript Collections, Carl A. Kroch Library, Cornell University, Ithaca, N.Y.

13. *Fugitive Slave Law of 1850*. Thirty-First Congress. Sess. 1, 60, 1850, sec. 7, 22. Division of Rare and Manuscript Collections, Carl A. Kroch Library, Cornell University, Ithaca, N.Y.

14. *The Constitution of the United States with Acts of Congress Relating to Slavery Embracing the Constitution, The Fugitive Slave Act of 1793*, 20. In addition, under the law, marshalls were also "liable . . . for the full value of the service or labor of said fugitive in the State, Territory, or District whence he escaped." Ibid.

15. *Fugitive Slave Law of 1850*. Thirty-First Congress. Sess 1, 60, 1850, sec. 5., 20; "An Act to Amend, and Supplementary to the Act, Entitled 'An Act Respecting Fugitives From Justice, and Persons Escaping From the Service of Their Masters,' Approved February 12, 1793." Sec. 5 & 8. Ibid., 9. Division of Rare and Manuscript Collections, Carl A. Kroch Library, Cornell University, Ithaca, N.Y.

16. *The Constitution of the United States with Acts of Congress Relating to Slavery Embracing the Constitution, The Fugitive Slave Act of 1793, the Missouri Compromise Act of 1820, The Fugitive Slave Law of 1850, and the Nebraska and Kansas Bill* (Compiled by D. M. Dewey. Rochester (Arcade Hall, 1854), 25. Division of Rare and Manuscript Collections, Carl A. Kroch Library, Cornell University, Ithaca, N.Y.

17. Ordinance 13,032 January 29, 1897, cited in Gerald Neuman, *Surveying Law and Borders: Anomalous Zones*, 48 STANFORD LAW REVIEW (1996) WL 1197, *, 7, 19.

18. *Boston Slave Riot*, 26.

19. *The Boston Slave Riot, and Trial of Anthony Burns*, 15.

20. Hershel Parker, *Herman Melville: A Biography*, Vol. 2, *1851–1891* (Baltimore, Md.: Johns Hopkins University Press, 2002), 832; 220.

21. Hershel Parker, *Herman Melville: A Biography*, Vol. 1, *1819–1851* (Baltimore, Md.: Johns Hopkins University Press, 2002), 819.

22. Parker, *Herman Melville*, Vol. 2, 832, 221.

23. Ibid. Standing before thousands gathered at Faneuil to protest Burns's incarceration, Wendell Phillips compared this historic building—the "cradle of liberty"—to the courthouse-turned-slave pen that was freedom's tomb. The references to "liberty" and "76" on circulars, broadsides, and placards that papered Boston buildings were hardly casual. They highlighted not only the beginnings of U.S. democracy, but Boston's constitutive role in the formation of this country, a history many felt had been disparaged in Burn's arrest and continued captivity. "The rich Boston of 1854, with its two hundred millions, has not the same energy and patriotism as the poor Boston of 1776." Freeman, *Rendition of Anthony Burns*, 9.

24. Robert K. Wallace. "Fugitive Justice: Douglass, Shaw, Melville," in *Frederick Douglass and Herman Melville: Essays in Relation*, ed. Robert S. Levine and Samuel Otter (Chapel Hill: University of North Carolina Press, 2008), 43.

25. Robert Wallace speculates that Shaw's repeated attempts in the 1830s to sell the land he owned in Kentucky (land partially operated by at least one tenant who held slaves) "may indicate that being a landowner in a slaveholding state was an embarrassment for the chief justice of the Massachusetts Supreme Judicial Court, especially as he became increasingly known as a judicial opponent of slavery itself." Ibid. Wallace also notes that in his work as an attorney, Shaw also helped to prepare a contract related to the publication of the second edition of Amasa Delano's *Narrative of Voyages and Travels* issued in 1818, and that perhaps it was through Melville's father-in-law that he the writer first gained access to the American captain's autobiography. Ibid.

26. Parker, *Herman Melville*, Vol. 2, 221. On February 15, 1846, Frederick Wilkins (a.k.a. Shadrach), a waiter, was arrested as a fugitive. Melville's friend Richard Henry Dana pled Wilkins case before Lemuel Shaw, Melville's father-in-law. Shaw refused the petitioner's writ of habeas corpus. Captured on April 3, 1851, Thomas Sims was held in the courthouse, a building authorities summarily encircled in iron chains and guarded. The events of Shadrach's rescue from the courthouse by blacks who had gathered en masse are recorded in Leonard Levy's *The Law of the Commonwealth and Chief Justice Shaw* (New York: Harper & Row, 1967).

27. By 1861 Wendell Phillips would issue his argument against the repeal of this legislation. Wendell Phillips, Esq. *Argument of Wendell Phillips, Esq. Against the Repeal of the Personal Liberty Law, Before the Committee of the Legislature, Tuesday, January 29, 1861* (Boston: R. F. Wallcut, 1861). Division of Rare and Manuscript Collections, Carl A. Kroch Library, Cornell University, Ithaca, N.Y.; Parker, *Herman Melville*, Vol. 2, 457–458.

28. Ibid., 221.

29. *Proceedings of the U.S. Senate, on the Fugitive slave Bill, the Abolition of the Slave Trade in the District of Columbia, and the Imprisonment of Free Colored Seamen*. Division of Rare and Manuscript Collection, Carl A. Kroch Library, Cornell University, Ithaca, N.Y.

30. Critics like H. Bruce Franklin have identified Melville's *San Dominick* as a referent for the Dominican Republic, and consequently mapped the mythology of this story back to the Dominican Independence, an independence which did not in fact occur until 1844. However, I respectfully disagree with the conflation that Franklin makes when, in failing to acknowledge Haiti as a possible allusive cite, he condenses the Haitian and the Dominican Independence struggles as a single event, reading 1799 as the dating of Independence for the island which in fact it was not. Neither Haiti nor the Dominican Republic were independent at this point; however, as Joan Dayan's careful dating records, 1799 begins the civil war for independence between mulatto, Andre Rigaud and Toussaint L'Ouverture, and within a year the United States would offer assistance in the Revolution. Joan Dayan, *Haiti, History, and the Gods* (Berkeley and LosAngeles: University of California Press, 1995), Appendix.

31. Susan Buck-Morss, Sybille Fischer, Laurent Dubois, David Geggus, Carolyn Fick, Michel Rolp Trouillot, Robin Blackburn, have continued the early work of James Weldon Johnson, Frederick Douglass, and C.L.R. James in (re)articulating the saliency of this island to modernity, revolutionary history(ies), and the Americas. Buck-Morss, "Hegel and Haiti," *Critical Inquiry* 26 (4) (2000), 821–865; Carolyn Fick, *The Making of Haiti: The Saint-Domingue Revolution from Below* (Knoxville: University of Tennessee Press, 1990); Sibylle Fischer, *Modernity Disavowed: Haiti and the Cultures of Slavery in the Age of Revolution* (Durham, N.C.: Duke University Press, 2004); David Geggus, *Impact of the Haitian Revolution in the Atlantic World* (Columbia, S.C.: University of South Carolina Press, 2001); Laurent Dubois, *Avengers of the New World. The Story of the Haitian Revolution* (Cambridge, Mass.: Belknap Press of Harvard University Press, 2004), and *A Colony of Citizens: Revolution & Slave Emancipation in the French Caribbean, 1787–1804* (Chapel Hill: University of North Carolina Press, 2004); Robin Blackburn, *The Overthrow of Colonial Slavery* (New York: Verso, 1988).

32. The post-World War II policy history on political asylum is marked by the passage of two acts, the Displaced Persons Act (1948) and the Refugee Relief Act (1953). See also, Nicole Waligora-Davis, "The Ghetto: Illness and the Formation of the 'Suspect' in American Polity," *Forum for Modern Language Studies* 40 (2) (2004), 182–203.

33. William Wells Brown, *St. Domingo: Its Revolutions and Its Patriots. A Lecture Delivered Before the Metropolitan Atheneum, London, May 16, and at St. Thomas' Church, Philadelphia December 20, 1854*, with an introduction by M. Whiteman (Boston: Bela Marsh, 1855), 25.

34. Bell, "Introduction," 2. James T. Holly, along with John Brown Jr,. and J. Dennis Harris would be among those recruited by James Redpath to enlist blacks for settlement in Haiti. Bell, "Introduction," 4.

35. James McCune Smith, *A Lecture on the Haytien Revolutions; with a Sketch of the Character of Toussaint L'Ouverture. Delivered at the Styuvesant Institute (For the Benefit of the Colored Orphan Asylum), February 26, 1841* (New York: Daniel Fanshaw, 1841). Division of Rare and Manuscript Collections, Carl A. Kroch Library, Cornell University, Ithaca, N.Y.

36. Prince Saunders, *A Memoir Presented to the American Convention for Promoting the Abolition of Slavery, and Improving the condition of the African Race, December 11, 1818. Containing Some Remarks Upon the Civil Dissentions of the hitherto Afflicted People of Hayti, as the Inhabitants of that Island may be Connected with Plans for the Emigration of Free Persons of Colour as may Be Disposed to Remove to It, In Case Its Reunion, Pacification and Independence should be Established. Together with Some Account of the Origin and Progress of the Efforts for Effecting the Abolition of Slavery in Pennsylvania and its Neighborhood, and Throughout the World* (Philadelphia: Dennis

Heartt, 1818), 9. Division of Rare and Manuscript Collections, Carl A. Kroch Library, Cornell University, Ithaca, N.Y.

37. James Redpath, ed., *A Guide to Hayti. Boston: Haytian Bureau of Emigration* (Boston: 1861). Division of Rare Book and Manuscripts, Carl A. Kroch Library, Cornell University, Ithaca, N.Y., 9.

38. Bell, "Introduction," 3.

39. Ibid. Crippled by insufficient funds, and embattled by the tide of African American anti-emigrationist critiques, Redpath's colonization plan came to an end by the fall of 1862. William Sevaille recounts Frederick Douglass's dour response in the *Douglass' Monthly* to the news that Redpath's colonization career had ended: "We can express no regret, that Mr. Redpath has ceased to exert his talents in the cause of . . . colonization." "Afro-American Emigration to Haiti during the American Civil War," *The Americas* 35 (2) (1978), 200.

40. Quoted in Willis D. Boyd, "James Redpath and American Negro Colonization in Haiti, 1860–1862," *The Americas* 12 (2) (1955): 172. Second quotation cited in William Seraille, "Afro-American Emigration to Haiti during the American Civil War," *The Americas* 35 (2) (1978), 187.

41. Melville, "Benito Cereno," 161.

42. This imagery is also of singular significance for the immediate connection it creates among death, Spain, and the slave trade. The ecclesiastical imagery within this novella yokes this text to larger histories of violence and Catholicism, including the Spanish Inquisition and Spain's continued participation in the slave trade. Sundquist, *To Wake the Nations: Race in the Making of American Literature* (Cambridge, Mass: Harvard University Press, 1993), 137. See Sundquist for a detailed analysis on the role of religious imagery and imperialism within the novella. "Melville, Delany, and New World Slavery," in *To Wake the Nations: Race in the Making of American Literature* (Cambridge, Mass.: Harvard University Press, 1993), 135–224; and "'Benito Cereno' and New World Slavery," in *Reconstructing American Literary History*, ed. Sacvan Bercovitch (Cambridge, Mass.: Harvard University Press, 1986), 93–122. Gloria Horsley-Meacham offers an extended reading on Melville's "ecclesiastical imagery" in relation to the slave trade, tying the textual references to the monastic and friars to Bartholomew de Las Casa, the priest who advised Charles V to import African slave labor to Santo Domingo (95). "The Monastic Slaver: Images and Meaning in 'Benito Cereno,'" in *Critical Essays on Herman Melville's "Benito Cereno,"* ed. Robert E. Burkholder (New York: G. K. Hall, 1992), 94–98.

43. Melville, "Benito Cereno," 163–164.

44. Ibid., 165.

45. Hortense Spillers, "Mama's Baby, Papa's Maybe," in *Black, White, and In Color* (Chicago: University of Chicago, 2003), 203.

46. This equivalence between blackness and death precedes European colonialisms, and may be found in England at least as early as the thirteenth and fourteenth century.

47. Orlando Patterson, *Slavery and Social Death: A Comparative Study* (Cambridge, Mass.: Harvard University Press, 1982).

48. Douglas G. Smith, *Citizenship and the Fourteenth Amendment*, 34 SAN DIEGO LAW REVIEW (May–June 1997), WL 681, *28.

49. Ibid., 28. Threading the connections between U.S. slave and Roman law, Scott includes the following reference from Taylor's "Elements of the Civil Law": "'Slaves were held pro nullis. . . . They had no head in the state, no name, title, or register: they were not capable of being injured. . . .'" (28–29).

50. Ibid., 164–165.

51. Portions of this paragraph originally appeared as part of an essay, "The Ghetto: Illness and the Formation of the 'Suspect' in American Polity," published by the *Forum of Modern Language Studies*. Nicole A. Waligora-Davis, "The Ghetto: Illness and the Formation of the 'Suspect' in American Polity," *Forum for Modern Language Studies* 40 (2) (2004), 189–190.

52. Giorgio Agamben, *State of Exception*, trans. Kevin Attel (Chicago: University of Chicago Press, 2003), 23.

53. Ibid., 50. Speaking of Japanese internment during World War II, Scott Michaelsen reminds us that "the suspension of constitutional rights along racial lines is not an extraconstitutional matter" rather "racially based exceptionalism lies at the core of the U.S. version of the doctrine of sovereignty." Scott Michaelsen, "Between Japanese American Internment and the USA PATRIOT Act: The Borderlands and the Permanent State of Racial Exception," *Aztlan* 30 (2) (2005), 89.

54. Agamben, Giorgio, *Homo Sacer: Sovereign Power and Bare Life*, trans. Daniel Heller-Roazen (Stanford, Calif.: Stanford University Press, 1998), 19.

55. Leon Higginbotham and Barbara Kopytoff, *Property First, Humanity Second: The Recognition of the Slave's Human Nature in Virginia Civil Law*, 50 Ohio State Law Journal (Summer 1989), WL 511, *4.

56. Agamben, *State of Exception*, 35.

57. Claude McKay, "Outcast," in the *Complete Poems*, ed. William J. Maxwell (Urbana: University of Illinois Press, 2004), 173–174. "Time" within the framework of the poem is code for a specific tradition in western continental philosophy that located the African body outside (cast-out from) "History," the narrative of human progress. Georg Frederich Hegel, *The Philosophy of History*, intro. C. J. Friedrich (New York: Dover, 1956), 91–99.

58. Ralph Ellison, *Invisible Man* (New York: Modern Library, 1994), 8.

59. The Civil Rights Cases, 109 U.S. 3, 3 S. Ct.(1883), WL 18, * 15; emphasis added.

60. Addressing the nexus between vulnerability and humanization Judith Butler writes, "A vulnerability must be perceived and recognized in order to come into play in an ethical encounter, and there is no guarantee that this will happen. Not only is there always the possibility that a vulnerability will not be recognized and that it will be constituted as the "unrecognizable," but when a vulnerability is recognized, that recognition has the power to change the meaning and structure of the vulnerability itself. In this sense, if vulnerability is one precondition for humanization, and humanization takes place differently through variable norms of recogniztion, then it follows that vulnerability is fundamentally dependent on existing norms of recognition if it is to be attributed to any human subject." *The Precarious Life: The Powers of Mourning and Violence* (New York: 2004), 43. I take the phrase derealizing humanity from Butler who employs it in the aforementioned book.

61. In his essay, "Between," Nahum Chandler offers a rigorous reading of Du Bois's strategic employment of this preposition as the opening term in *Souls of Black Folk* in order to set forward a critique operating even at the level of the grammatical, the syntactic, as a challenge to a particular "logic *of being*." Nahum Chandler, "Between," *Assemblage* 20 (April 1993), 27.

62. Giorgio Agamben, *Means Without End: Notes on Politics*, trans. Vincenzo Binetti and Cesare Casarino (Minneapolis: University of Minnesota Press, 2000), 22.2.

63. See Arendt, *On Totalitarianism*.

64. Ibid., 293–294.

65. Ibid., 294–295, 297.

66. Ibid., 297.

67. Spillers, "Mama's Baby, Papa's Maybe," 206; Frederick Douglass, *The Narrative of the Life of Frederick Douglass An American Slave Written by Himself*, ed. David Blight (Boston: Bedford Books of St. Martin's Press, 1993), 74–75.

68. Hortense Spillers, "Mama's Baby, Papa's Maybe," 208.

69. Douglass, *Narrative of the Life*, 64.

70. For a history of the three-fifths clause see Donald L. Robinson, *Slavery in the Structure of American Politics 1765–1820* (New York: Harcourt Brace Jovanovich, 1971).

71. "The stateless people were as convinced as the minorities that loss of national right was identical with loss of human rights, that the former inevitably entailed the latter." Arendt, *On Totalitarianism*, 292.

72. Melville, "Benito Cereno," 198–199, 175–176.

73. Spillers, "Mama's Baby, Papa's Maybe," 203.

74. W. E. B. Du Bois, "The Afro-American," *in the Papers of W. E. B. Du Bois, 1877–1963* (Sandford, N.C., Microfilming Company, 1980), 15–16.

75. Melville, "Benito Cereno," 233.

76. For additional readings of this scene see Dana Nelson, *National Manhood: Capitalist Citizenship and the Imagined Fraternity of White Men* (Durham, N.C.: Duke University Press, 1998), 2–3; Melville, "Benito Cereno," 198.

77. Nelson, *National Manhood*, 3.

78. Ibid., 2, 3.

79. Ibid., 3.

80. Fanon, *Black Skin, White Masks*, 212.

81. Paul Downes, "Melville's Benito Cereno and the Politics of Humanitarian Intervention," *South Atlantic Quarterly* 103 (2/3) (2004), 479.

82. Melville, "Benito Cereno," 198, 230.

83. Michelle Stephens, *Black Empire: The Masculine Global Imaginary of Caribbean Intellectuals in the United States, 1914–1962* (Durham, N.C.: Duke University Press, 2005), 31.

84. Ibid., 4.

85. Of this Frank Michelman writes "As matters have actually developed . . . the having of rights depends on receipt of a special sort of social recognition and acceptance—that is, of one's juridical status within some particular concrete political community. The notion of a right to have rights arises out of the modern-statist conditions and is equivalent to the moral claim of a refugee or other stateless person to citizenship, or at least juridical personhood, within the social confines of some law-dispensing state." Quoted in Seyla Benhabib, *The Rights of Others: Aliens, Residents, and Citizens* (Cambridge: Cambridge University Press, 2004), 56.

86. Melville's singular focus on, and rescripting of, Cereno's deposition in the judicial records on the Tyral revolt (an account recorded along with two other depositions by Capt. Amasa Delano's in his *Narrative of Voyages and Travels* [1817]), further evince the carefully staged critique launched against U.S. legal culture. Melville biographer Laurie Robertson-Lorant recounts Putnam's editor, George William Curtis's annoyance with this lengthy legal section of the text, a section whose placement at the tale's end he read as "laziness on Melville's part." Laurie Robertson-Lorant, *Melville: A Biography* (New York: Clarkson Potter, 1996), 350.

87. Melville, "Benito Cereno," 238–239.

88. Ibid., 251.

89. Thomas Morris, *Southern Slavery and the Law 1619–1860* (Chapel Hill: University of North Carolina Press, 1996), 230.

90. Ibid., 230–1. Morris's texts reflect that there was already concern about the use of spiritual affiliation as a requisite for oath taking as early as the seventeenth century. Jurists were increasingly worried that criminals might escape punishment because the testimony of witnesses from different faith communities would be deemed less credible, if not wholly illegitimate by the court. See Morris, *Southern Slavery*, 231. In his essay, *The Jury's Rise as Lie Detector*, George Fisher demonstrates how this religious criterion continued to remain salient in the nineteenth century, emerging as a topic of concern during congressional debates regarding black testimony in 1862. Such that a Connecticut senator would assert "In most of the States, I think, the belief in the existence of God is required in order that man shall be admitted as a competent witness." By 1860 Massachusetts, for example, had already placed a prohibition on this criteria. George Fisher, *The Jury's Rise as Lie Detector*, 10 YALE LAW JOURNAL (7) (1997), 678.

91. A. Leon Higginbotham, Jr., *The 'Law Only as an Enemy': The Legitimization of Racial Powerlessness Through the Colonial and Antebellum Criminal Laws of Virginia*, 70 NORTH CAROLINA LAW REVIEW (April 1992), WL 969, *11.

92. Ibid., 12.

93. George Fisher, "Jury's Rise as Lie Detector," 684.

94. Quoted in Morris, *Southern Slavery*, 231–232.

95. Cited in Higginbotham, "'Law Only as an Enemy,'" WL *12.

96. Fisher, "Jury's Rise," 585–712.

97. By 1866, eighteen states had abolished their racial exclusion clauses from their regulations on witness testimony. See Ibid., 683.

98. Quoted in A. Leon Higginbotham, *Shades of Freedom: Racial Politics and Presumptions of the American Legal Process* (New York: Oxford University Press, 1996), 77.

99. Ibid., 79.

100. For Wells's account see *Crusade for Justice: The Autobiography of Ida B. Wells*, ed. Alfreda M. Duster (Chicago: University of Chicago Press, 1970), 18–20.

101. Ibid., xvii.

102. Melville, "Benito Cereno," 213, 169, 176.

103. Ibid., 250, 246.

104. Ibid., 258.

105. Cited in Thomas D. Morrison, *Southern Slavery and the Law: 1619–1860* (Chapel Hill: University of North Carolina Press, 1996), 229; emphasis in original.

106. Ellison, *Invisible Man*, 3, emphasis added.

107. Melville, "Benito Cereno," 258.

108. See Nicole Waligora-Davis, "Riotous Discontent,": Ellison's "birth of a nation," *Modern Fiction Studies* 50 (2) (2004): 385–410.

109. Missouri ends its racial exclusion laws regarding testimony in 1865. See Fisher, "Jury's Rise."

110. For a history of this case see Melton McLaurin, ed., *Celia: A Slave* (New York: Avon Books, 1991).

111. Higginbotham, *Shades of Freedom*, 95.

112. Cited in Ibid., 82, emphasis in original.

113. *Plessy* v. *Ferguson* 163 U.S. 537. U.S. Sup. Court. 1896. For more on the relationship between race and property see Cheryl I. Harris, "Whiteness as Property," *Critical Race Theory: The Key*

Writings That Formed the Movement, ed. Kimberle Crenshaw et al. (New York: New Press, 1995), 276–291.

114. The Civil Rights Cases, WL, *34; emphasis added.

On behalf of himself and his family, Scott sued his master for their right to freedom. Brought by his owner to the free state of Missouri where they resided for a period, Scott insisted that as a state citizen he and his family were entitled to their freedom. Speaking on behalf of the Court, Chief Justice Taney disagreed. He claimed that neither the terms "citizen" nor its constitutional synonym, "people of the United States," applied to blacks, rendering them ineligible for "the rights and privileges which that instrument [the Constitution] provides for and secures to citizens of the United States." Effectively dismissing the case, the court decided that based on his race Scott was not a citizen, and therefore lacked legal recourse. Ibid., WL *19.

In *Hobbs et al. v. Fogg* (1837) the Pennsylvania Supreme Court overturned a lower court ruling supporting William Fogg, a freeman's, political rights. Fogg had brought a suit against the election inspector, asserting that as a citizen of Pennsylvania he had a right to participate in the general election. The state supreme court argued that neither "a free negro or mulatto" was a citizen. Nebraska's Supreme Court ruled similarly in *Messenger* v. *State* (1889). Reversing a lower court's ruling in support of a black petitioner's right to service at a barbershop, they concluded that because the plaintiff failed to prove his citizenship, he was not guaranteed equal accommodation and service (3). See also Douglass Smith, *Citizenship and the Fourteenth Amendment*, 34 SAN DIEGO LAW REVIEW (May–June 1997), WL *681.

115. Scott underscores the role of legal personality as a precondition for human rights. In 1846, Dred Scott sued his master, insisting that as Missouri citizens he and his wife Harriet were entitled to their freedom.

116. Sundquist, *To Wake the Nations*, 146–148. In an essay in 1854 Samuel Walker would describe Spain as a "weak and enervate government." Samuel R. Walker, "Cuba and the South," *De Bow's Review* 17 (5) (1854), 520. As biographer Andrew Delbanco reminds us, Melville's demure at U.S. expansionism is hardly new, finding a presence in the writer's magisterial, *Moby Dick* (1851). Andrew Delbanco, *Melville: His World and Work* (New York: Knopf, 2005), 164.

117. Robertson-Lorant, *Melville*, 354–355.

118. "Spanish and Cuban Views on Annexation," *De Bow's Review* 18 (3) (1855), 305.

119. "The Destinies of the South," *Southern Quarterly Review* 7 (3) (1853), 202.

120. Henry Martyn Flint, *Life of Stephen A Douglas: To Which Are Added His Speeches and Reports* (Philadelphia: J. E. Potter, 1863), 213. For a detailed analysis of the role of Cuba, the Spanish Inquisition, Catholicism, Southern imperialism, the "1853 conspiracy" by Spain and England to "Africanize" Cuba, and the imperial tensions between the United States and Spain, see Sundquist *To Wake the Nations*, and "'Benito Cereno' and New World Slavery," In *Herman Melville: A Collection of Critical Essays*, ed. Myra Jehlen (Englewood Cliffs, N.J.: Prentice Hall, 1994), 174–186. For more information on Southern imperialism see C. Stanley Urban, "The Ideology of Southern Imperialism: New Orleans and the Caribbean, 1845–1860," *Louisiana Historical Quarterly* 39 (1) (1956), 48–73; Samuel R. Walker, "Cuba and the South," *De Bow's Review* 17 (5) (1854), 519–525; Robert E. May, *The Southern Dream of a Caribbean Empire, 1854–1861* (Baton Rouge: Louisiana State University Press, 1973).

121. Walker, "Cuba and the South," 521–522.

122. "Destines of the South," 202.

123. Walker., 523–524.

124. Ibid., 525.

125. See Nelson, *National Manhood*, 1.

126. Ironically, during the Haitian Revolution U.S. economic interests outweighed political and ideological fears. In 1799, the United States negotiated a trade agreement with Toussaint L'Ouverture, the act itself a tacit acknowledgment of St. Domingue's sovereignty and L'Ouverture's power to create and enforce diplomatic agreements. These ships became a critical "source of guns and ammunition" for St. Domingue in their continued fight against French colonialism. Laurent Dubois, *Avengers of the New World. The Story of the Haitian Revolution* (Cambridge, Mass.: Belknap Press of Harvard University Press, 2004), 224. Under Lincoln's administration the United States would finally formally recognize Haiti's independence in 1862.

127. Quoted in Joan Dayan, *Haiti, History, and the Gods* (Berkeley and LosAngeles: University of California Press, 1995), 189.

128. James Baldwin, "They Can't Turn Back," in *Collected Essays*, edited by Toni Morrison (New York: Library of America, 1998), 623.

129. Melville, "Benito Cereno," 257.

130. Du Bois, *Darkwater*, 87–92; Arendt, *Totalitarianism*, 296.

CHAPTER 4

1. Taft's assessment of the riot reflects more than the vantage point of a former U.S. president, but should also be read in relation to Taft's work as Roosevelt's secretary of war, and McKinley's chief administrator for the Philippines. Taft's article originally appeared in the *Chicago Daily Tribune.*

2. William Howard Taft, "Untitled article," *The Chicago Defender*, August 9, 1919.

3. During the riot thirty-eight people were killed, twenty-three of whom were black; an additional 537 were injured, 342 of whom were African American. For additional information regarding the gross injuries suffered, see the Chicago Commission on Race Relations report, *The Negro in Chicago* (Chicago: University of Chicago Press, 1922); Allan Spear, *Black Chicago: The Making of a Negro Ghetto 1890–1920* (Chicago: University of Chicago Press, 1967); William Tuttle, *Chicago in the Red Summer of 1919* (Urbana: University of Illinois Press, 1970); St. Clair Drake and Horace Clayton, *Black Metropolis* (Chicago, [1945] 1993); *The Race Riots: Biennial Report 1918–1919 and Official Record of Inquests on the Victims of the Race Riots of July and August, 1919, Whereby Fifteen White Men and Twenty-three Colored Men Lost Their Lives and Several Hundred Were Injured* (Cook County Coroner's Report).

4. It was not just Eugene Williams's murder that engendered anger within these communities, nor their congested living quarters, as Taft argued in the days immediately following the bloody skirmishes, but the unwillingness of the police to arrest the white youths involved in spite of numerous eyewitness accounts confirming both the events and identity of the killer. These testimonies incontrovertibly shifted this other young (white) boy from an *alleged* killer, to a murderer.

5. Houston Baker, Jr., *Workings of the Spirit: The Poetics of Afro-American Women's Writing* (Chicago: University of Chicago Press, 1991), 104.

6. It is with World War I that the figure of the refugee emerges as a legal category and a social concern. See Hannah Arendt, *The Origins of Totalitarianism* (New York: Harvest Books, 1968).

7. For black Americans, the freedom and citizenship constitutionally conferred and ostensibly protected with the Thirteenth, Fourteenth, and Fifteenth Amendments, and with the Civil

Rights Act of 1875 were not simply disregarded but systematically dismantled. The verdicts in *Civil Rights Cases* (1883) and *Plessy* v. *Ferguson* (1896) effectively defanged civil rights legislation passed in the aftermath of the Civil War.

8. Neil Smith, *American Empire: Roosevelt's Geographer and the Prelude to Globalization* (Berkeley and Los Angeles: University of California Press, 2003), xii.

9. Walter Benjamin, "The Work of Art in the Age of Mechanical Reproduction," *Illuminations*, ed. with intro. Hannah Arendt (New York: Schocken Books, [1955] 1968), 235.

10. Zahid Chaudhary, "Phantasmagoric Aesthetics: Colonial Violence and the Management of Perception," *Cultural Critique* 59 (Winter) (2005), 63–119.

11. Jacques Derrida, *Of Grammatology*, trans. Gayatri Chakravorty Spivak (Baltimore, Md.: Johns Hopkins University Press, 1974), 155.

12. Richard Slotkin, *Lost Battalions: The Great War and the Crisis of American Nationality* (New York: Henry Holt, 2005), 66; Mark Ellis, *Race, War, and Surveillance: African Americans and the United States Government during World War I* (Bloomington: Indiana University Press, 2001), 39.

13. Ellis, *Race, War and Surveillance*, 38–39.

14. W. J. T. Mitchell, *Picture Theory: Essays on Verbal and Visual Representation* (Chicago: University of Chicago Press, 1994), 31.

15. My reference to the semi-colonial is taken from W. E. B. Du Bois's essay "Colonialism, Democracy, and Peace after the War" in which he compares African Americans to other colonized peoples (229). W. E. B. Du Bois, "Colonialism, Democracy, and Peace after the War (Summer 1944)," in *Against Racism: Unpublished Essays, Papers, Addresses, 1887–1961*, ed. by Herbert Aptheker (Amherst: University of Massachusetts Press, 1985), 229–249.

16. "Thoughts for the Times on War and Death" is divided into two sections: "The Disillusionment of the War" and "Our Attitude Towards Death." Sigmund Freud, "Thoughts for the Times on War and Death," *Standard Edition of the Complete Psychological Works of Sigmund Freud*, ed. James Strachey. Vol. 14 (London: Hogarth Press, 1955), 273–300.

17. Freud, "Our Attitude Towards Death," 299.

18. Freud, "Disillusionment of the War," 285–286, 280.

19. Ibid., 280.

20. Freud's "Why War," 208.

21. Freud, "Disillusionment of the War," 275.

22. Randolph Bourne, *War and the Intellectuals: Essays by Randolph S. Bourne, 1915–1919* (New York: Harper and Row, 1964), 71.

23. Ibid.

24. T. Lothrup Stoddard, *Rising Tide of Color Against White Supremacy* (New York: Charles Scribner's Sons, 1920), v. Although Stoddard was almost certainly referencing a line found in the preface, and again as the opening to the second chapter of *The Souls of Black Folk*, this oft-quoted line was first articulated by Du Bois in 1899. See Nahum Chandler's "The Figure of W. E. B. Du Bois as a Problem for Thought," *New Centennial Review* 6 (3) (2006), 29–55.

25. Stoddard, *Rising Tide of Color*, 5–7.

26. Ibid., 4.

27. Ibid., 7–8.

28. Du Bois, *Darkwater*, 20.

29. For further reading see Linda Williams's *Playing the Race Card: Melodramas of Black and White from Uncle Tom to O.J. Simpson* (Princeton, N.J.: Princeton University Press, 2001);

Michael Rogin, "'The Sword Became a Flashing Vision' D. W. Griffith's Birth of a Nation," *Ronald Reagan, the Movie, and Other Episodes in Political Demonology* (Berkeley and Los Angeles: University of California Press, 1987), 190–235.

30. Linda Williams, *Playing the Race Card: Melodramas of Black and White from Uncle Tom to O.J. Simpson* (Princeton, N.J.: Princeton University Press, 2001), 128. See also Jane M. Gaines, *Fire and Desire: Mixed-Race Movies in the Silent Era* (Chicago: University of Chicago Press, 2001), 254.

31. Although Griffith's film did endure censorship on occasion, inciting race riots was not among the concerns engendered by the film.

32. Pearl Bowser and Louise Spence, *Writing Himself into History: Oscar Micheaux, His Silent Films, and His Audiences* (New Brunswick, N.J.: Rutgers University Press, 2000), 125.

33. Within their first year, the American Protective League's (APL) roster listed 250,000 volunteers. Encouraged by U.S. Attorney General Gregory's call for information on subversives, the APL assisted federal agencies in scouting out potential threats to national security. During "slacker raids" in New York City (1918), the APL were among a more than 4,000-member team that included military, police, and Bureau of Investigation officers who managed to rout and detain more than 50,000 persons for allegedly failing to register for the draft. Theodore Kornweibel, Jr., *"Investigate Everything": Federal Efforts to Compel Black Loyalty During World War I* (Bloomington: Indiana University Press, 2002), 14, 23.

34. Richard Slotkin, *Lost Battalion: The Great War and the Crisis of American Nationality* (New York: Henry Holt, 2005), 453, 459; 452–455.

35. Ibid., 458–460.

36. Claude McKay, "If We Must Die," *Complete Poems, Claude McKay*, ed. William J. Maxwell (Urbana: University of Illinois Press, 2004), 177.

37. Ibid., 177–178.

38. Mark Robert Schneider, *"We Return Fighting": The Civil Rights Movement in the Jazz Age* (Boston: Northeastern University Press, 2002), 97, 92–94. For additional readings see, *Caldwell* v. *State* 203 Ala. 412, 84 So. 272, and *Caldwell* v. *Parker, Sheriff* 252 U.S. 376, 40 S. Ct. 388, 64 L. Ed. 621.

39. Schneider, *"We Return Fighting,"* 95.

40. Quoted in Schneider, *"We Return Fighting,"* 97.

41. Countless articles in the black press covered the treatment of negro soldiers at home. Wilberforce University president W. S. Scarborough's piece in *The Chicago Defender* titled "Race Riots and their Remedy," August 30, 1919, Editorial page; W. E. B. Du Bois, "Our Success and Failure," *Crisis* 18 (3) July 1919: 127–131; "The Looking Glass," *Crisis*, 18 (3) July 1919: 144–8.

42. W. E. B. Du Bois, "Close Ranks," *Crisis*, 16 (3) July 1918: 111.

43. W. E. B. Du Bois, "My Mission," *Crisis*, 18 (1) May 1919: 7.

44. Du Bois, "Close Ranks," 111.

45. Emmett Jay Scott, *Scott's Official History of the America Negro in the World War* (Chicago: Homewood Press, 1919), 297. Division of Rare and Manuscript Collections, Carl A. Kroch Library, Cornell University, Ithaca, N.Y.

46. During the two moments in which the tests were administered (October–November 1917 and April–November 1918), the scores of well over 1 million men were taken.

47. Slotkin, *Lost Battalion*, 228–229.

48. Ibid.

49. Mark Ellis, *Race, War, and Surveillance: African Americans and the United States Government During World War* (Bloomington: Indiana University Press, 2001), 11.

50. Cited in Scott, *Official History*, 97–98.

51. In his essay, "Is Higher Education for the Negro Hopeless," Dunbar wrote, "No one has the right to base any conclusions about Negro criminality based on the number of prisoners in the jails and other places of restraint. Even in the North the prejudice against the Negro reverses the precedents of law, and every one accused is looked upon as guilty until proven innocent." Paul Lawrence Dunber, "Is Higher Education for the Negro Hopeless," in *The Paul Laurence Dunbar Reader*, ed. Jay Martin and Gossie H. Hudson (New York: Dodd, Mead, 1975), 47.

52. Scott, *Official History*, 97–98.

53. See chapter 2 for an additional explication of Neuman's "anomalous zones."

54. Du Bois, "An Essay Toward a History of the Black Man in the Great War," *W. E. B. Du Bois Writings*, edited by Nathan Huggins (New York: Library of America, [1919] 1986), 879. Essay first published in *Crisis*, 18 (2) June 1919.

55. Ibid., 882.

56. W. E. B. Du Bois, "Documents of the War Collected by W. E. B. Du Bois," *Crisis*, 14 (3) July 1917, 16–19. See also Du Bois, "An Essay Toward the History of the Black Man in the Great War."

57. Du Bois, "Black Man in the Great War," 892.

58. Du Bois, "Documents of the War," 19.

59. Ibid.

60. R.S. Abbot, "The Test," *The Chicago Defender*, April 28, 1917, Editorial page.

61. Slotkin, *Lost Battalion*, 219.

62. In the face of Bolshevism, the Red Scare, and an altered black consciousness following the war, concern over Negro subversion persisted. In the midst of the Chicago race riots, Charles Henry Phillips, Bishop of the Fourth District Colored Methodist Episcopal Church in Nashville Tennessee, rebuffed assumptions that "the negro was influenced by Bolshevist agents in the part he took in the rioting." "It is not like him to be a traitor," he insisted, "or a revolutionist who would destroy the Government." "Denies Negroes are 'Reds,'" *New York Times*, August 2, 1919.

63. *The Chicago Defender*, "Millions Prepare to Leave the South Following Brutal Burning of Human," May 26, 1917, 1.

64. James Weldon Johnson critiqued the failure of *The New York Times* to address the lynching of pregnant Mary Turner, and the valiant combat of African American war commendated soldiers, Henry Johnson and Needham Roberts, referenced in coinciding headlines: "Two Negroes Whip 24 Germans" and "Mob Lynches Negro and His Wife." Slotkin, *Lost Battalion*, 144.

65. Du Bois, "The Black Man in the Revolution of 1914–1918," *Crisis*, 17 (5) March 1919: 223.

66. "When Pride Becomes a Virtue," *Crisis*, 17 (5) March 1919: 217.

67. The National Urban League first began in 1910 as the Committee On Urban Conditions. By 1911 the group had changed to the National League on Urban Conditions, consolidating under this new heading two historic organizations, namely The Committee for the Improvement of Industrial Conditions Among Negroes in New York and the National League for the Protection of Colored Women. The National Urban League assumed its current, abbreviated name in 1920.

68. See chapter 2 for a discussion of *Plessy*. There were thirty-five *Insular Cases* in all, including *Armstrong* v. *United States*, *DeLima* v. *Bidwell*, *Downes* v. *Bidwell*, *Fourteen Diamond Rings* v. *United States*, *Goetze* v. *United States*, *Huus* v. *New York and Porto Rico S.S. Co.*

69. *Downes* v. *Bidwell* 182 U.S. 244, 21 S.Ct. 770 WL*56 (1901).

70. Ibid. Christina Duffy Burnett and Burke Marshall Eds. *Foreign in a Domestic Sense: Puerto Rico, American Expansion, and the Constitution* (Durham, N.C.: Duke University Press, 2001), 1. Amy Kaplan, *The Anarchy of Empire in the Making of U.S. Culture* (Cambridge, Mass.: Harvard University Press, 2002), 1–12.

71. Although the turn of the twentieth century is frequently misread as the beginning of U.S. imperialism, Amy Kaplan points to the connection between "continental expansion" and empire building, a process well underway during the early 19th century as evident with the Indian Removal Act (1830). Kaplan, *Anarachy of Empire*, 17. The transformation of indigenous communities into "domestic dependent nations," in *Cherokee Nation v. the State of Georgia* (1831) substantively marginalized these communities. In Kaplan's words, the indigenous population were now "neither foreign nationals nor U.S. citizens." They were "foreign to the rights guaranteed by states and territories, but domestic for federal purposes." This case serves as a pointed reminder of the instrumental effects of, and the efficiency with which, the state recalibrates native (read: internal) communities into aliens, and its substantive legal, political, and social consequence. Amy Kaplan, *Anarchy of Empire*, 27, 10.

72. Kaplan, *Anarchy of Empire*, 9.

73. R. S. Abbott's *The Chicago Defender* humanized the riot. The *Defender* provided not only detailed accounts of skirmishes ensuing in apartments and on street corners throughout the city, but listed the wounded and the dead. In its framing of this event, the *Defender* theorized this interracial violence, and included the response of the international community to the riots that had erupted across that summer. In the months that followed, their coverage included the arrests, indictments, and trial of those involved in the riot. See August 2, 1919, August 9, 1919, and October 4, 1919.

74. Chicago Commission on Race Relations, *The Negro in Chicago: A Study of Race Relations and a Race Riot* (Chicago: University of Chicago Press, 1922), 108.

75. Ibid., 79.

76. Ibid., 87, 79; Richard Wright, *Black Boy* (New York: Harper and Row, 1966), 307.

77. Cited in *Negro in Chicago*, 88.

78. Ibid.

79. "The Riot Area Extending Over the Black Belt," *Chicago Daily Tribune*, July 29, 1919.

80. *Negro in Chicago*, xii.

81. "Riot Refugees Flee to Police Fearful of Mob: Colored Citizens Jam Stations; Go Home in Closed Vans," *Chicago Daily Tribune*, July 30, 1919.

82. Lauren Berlant, "Poor Eliza," *American Literature* 70 (3) (September 1998): 635–668.

83. Peter Brooks, "The Idea of a Psychoanalytic Criticism," *Psychoanalysis and Storytelling* (Cambridge, Mass.: Blackwell, 1994); Claudia Tate, *Psychoanalysis and Black Novels: Desire and the Protocols of Race* (New York: Oxford University Press, 1998).

84. "Riot Refugees Flee to Police Fearful of Mob: Colored Citizens Jam Stations; Go Home in Closed Vans," *Chicago Daily Tribune*, July 30, 1919, emphasis added.

85. Map, "War Map of the Black Belt," *Chicago Daily Tribune* July 31, 1919.

86. de Certeau, *Practice of Everyday Life*, 129.

87. "Rioting Calms, But Problems are Unsolved. One Slain in Day: Troops in Full Control," *Chicago Daily Tribune*, August 1, 1919, 1.

88. "A Gleam of Silver Shows in Clouds of Riot: Long Awaited Food and Milk Supplies Bring Hope and Happiness to Some Residents in Trouble," *Chicago Daily Tribune*, August 3, 1919.

89. Amy Kaplan, "Manifest Domesticity," *American Literature* 70 (3) (1998), 581–585.

90. Laura Wexler, "Seeing Sentiment: Photography, Race, and the Innocent Eye," *Female Subjects in Black and White: Race, Psychoanalysis, Feminism*, ed. Elizabeth Abel, Barbara Christian, and Helene Moglen (Berkeley and Los Angeles: University of California Press, 1997), 166–167.

91. There are only slight differences between these two representations of Ms. Simmons and her namesake, but they are part of the same photo shoot. In the *Tribune* her smile is wider, and the baby's face and gaze are drawn downward toward the milk jug, whereas their portrait in the Commission Report captures her with a closed smile and the baby's eyes directly engaging the photographer. Notably, in the Commission Report, all of the photographed subjects are left unidentified and the occasion for their portraits is left unspecified.

92. Wexler, "Seeing Sentiment," 165–167.

CHAPTER 5

1. James Weldon Johnson, "The Truth About Haiti" *Crisis*, 20 (5) September 1920: 221.

2. Only the previous year Johnson had urged a congressional investigation into the race riots in 1919. His demands came on the heels of the violent melees in Washington and in Chicago. See Schneider, "*We Return Fighting*," 24–25.

3. The official records listed 3,000 insurgents killed by U.S. Marines, but records show a more accurate number is 11,500. The corvee was said to have ended by 1918, but in fact persisted in northern areas of the country. Mary Renda, *Taking Haiti: Military Occupation and the Culture of U.S. Imperialism 1915–1940* (Chapel Hill: University of North Carolina Press, 2001), 10.

4. W. E. B. Du Bois, Letter from Du Bois concerning the situation in Haiti and the actions of the U. S. government and recommending formation of a Haitian government. In *The Papers of W. E. B. Du Bois, Correspondence, 1887–1965* (Sandford, N.C.: Microfilming Corporation of America, 1980).

5. Ibid.

6. Black Americans like W. E. B. Du Bois, Anna Julia Cooper, Paul Robeson, DuBose Heyward, James Weldon Johnson, Zora Neale Hurston, Langston Hughes, Jacob Lawrence, Arna Bontemps, Rayford Logan, Josephine Baker, and Hubert Harrison were among the many black Americans whose work engaged Haiti during, and in the immediate aftermath of the U.S. occupation.

7. Paul Gilroy, *The Black Atlantic: Modernity and Double Consciousness* (Cambridge, Mass.: Harvard University Press, 1993), 220.

8. Paul Gilroy, "Living Memory: A Meeting with Toni Morrison," in *Small Acts: Thoughts on the Politics of Black Cultures* (London: Serpent's Tail, 1993), 178.

9. These ambitions also traded on state fears over the possibility that Germany and England might both become interested in the island following the conclusion of the world war. The occupation was conceived, then, as one solution to this perceived threat. See Du Bois, "Haiti," in *The Papers of W. E. B. Du Bois, Articles, 1887–1968*; James Weldon Johnson and Haiti," *Phylon* 32 (4) (1971), 399.

10. James Weldon Johnson, "Self-Determining Haiti," *The Collected Writings*, ed. William Andrews *(New York: Modern Library, [1920] 2004)*: 660.

11. David Levering Lewis, *W. E. B. Du Bois: Biography of a Race 1868–1919* (New York: Henry Holt, 1993), 522; Smith, *American Empire*, 197.

12. Robert H. Zieger, *America's Great War: World War I and the American Experience* (New York: Rowman and Littlefield, 2000), 157.

13. Smith, *American Empire*, 6.

14. Melville Herskovits, *Life in a Haitian Valley* (New York: Alfred A. Knopf, 1937), viii. Herskovits's *Life in a Haitian Valley* (1937) represents his corrective to the representational politics circumscribing the narratives and theses generated about the island. Herskovits spent three months in Haiti in 1934 collecting material for this book. See also, Ralph Thompson, "Books of the Times," *New York Times*, March 17, 1937.

15. Robeson went on to star in the film adaptation of the play in 1933, for which DuBose Heyward drafted the screenplay. Ten thousand people gathered at Lafayette Theater for the sold-out premiere of Welles's *Voodoo Macbeth* on April 14, 1936, featuring performances by Jack Carter, Canada Lee, and Edna Thomas. The stage productions traveled from New York City to Los Angeles, Hartford, Boston, Dallas, and Cincinnati.

16. Mary Renda argues that paternalism was a critical "element of U.S. foreign policy"; Renda, *Taking Haiti*, 15.

17. Johnson, "The Truth About Haiti," 224.

18. Ibid.

19. For additional reading see Plummer, "The Afro-American Response," 128.

20. Qtd. in Brenda Gayle Plummer, "The Afro-American Response to the Occupation of Haiti, 1915–1934," *Phylon* 43 (2) (1982), 127.

21. Qtd. in Plummer, "The Afro-American Response," 130.

22. W. E. B. Du Bois, "Race Intelligence," in *W. E. B. Du Bois: Writings*, edited by *Nathan Huggins*, (New York: Library of America, 1986), 1182–1183. Herskovits's anthropologic and sociological study, *The American Negro*, conducted during the 1920s on Blacks in public schools, higher education, in cities, and in rural communities countermanded these kinds of assessments. An extended version of this survey appeared in 1930 under the title, *The Anthropometry of the American Negro*. Melville Herskovits, *The Anthropometry of the American Negro* (New York: Columbia University Press, 1930).

23. See also, Robert Bennet Bean, "Some Racial Peculiarities of the Negro Brain," *American Journal of Anatomy* 5 (September) (1906): 353–432, and Marion J. Mayo, *The Mental Capacity of the American Negro* (New York: Science Press, 1913). Interlacing eugenic interests and the image of custodial care in his 1926 article for the *American Journal of Sociology*, Indiana University sociologist Ulysses Weatherly adjudicated the U.S. occupation on the island by likening Haitians to delinquents and defectives requiring restraint. See "Haiti: An Experiment in Pragmatism," *American Journal of Sociology* 32 (November) (1926), 353–354.

24. *Inquiry into the Occupation and Administration of Haiti and Santo Domingo: Hearings Before a Select Committee on Haiti and Santo Domingo*. U.S. Senate 67 Congress S. Res. 112 (1 and 2) (Washington, D.C.: U.S. Government Publishing Office, 1922), 517.

25. Smith, *American Empire*, 15–20.

26. John R. Hurst, "Haiti," *Crisis*, 17 (1) May 1920: 34.

27. Ibid.

28. Gruening, "Haiti Under American Occupation," *The Century* 103 (April) (1922): 837.

29. Johnson, "The Truth About Haiti," 229. Johnson reiterated these concerns in his four-part article series for *The Nation*. See Rayford Logan, "James Weldon Johnson and Haiti," *Phylon* 32 (4) (1971), 396–402; and Langston Hughes, "People Without Shoes," and "White Shadows in a Black Land," *The Collected Works of Langston Hughes*. Vol. 9, *Essays on Art, Race, Politics, and World Affairs*, ed. with an intro. by Christopher C. De Santis (Columbia: University of Missouri Press, 2002), 46–49; 51–53.

30. Hubert Harrison, "Help Wanted for Hayti," *When Africa Awakes* (New York: Porro Press, 1920), 105.

31. Certainly, not all black Americans were opposed to the occupation. For those who subscribed to the cultural narrative of disease, dissolution, and savagery attached to the island, the equally prevalent rhetoric of benign protector and rehabilitator that couched so much of the propaganda regarding the occupation was attractive. See Plummer, "The Afro-American Response," 125–143.

32. Hughes began his coverage on the war in 1937.

33. Langston Hughes, "Writers, Words and the World," *Collected Works*, Vol. 9, 198–199.

34. See also Hughes, "To Negro Writers," *Collected Works*, Vol. 9, 131–132.

35. Arnold Rampersad, *The Life of Langston Hughes*. Vol. II, *1941–1967, I Dream A World* (New York: Oxford University Press, 2002).

36. Hughes, "'Organ Grinder's Swing' Heard above Gunfire in Spain," *Collected Works of Langston Hughes*, Vol. 9, 168.

37. Hughes, "Writers, Words and the World," 198.

38. Ibid., emphasis in original.

39. Ibid. Fulgenico Batista Zaldivar's first coup, "The Sergeant's Revolt," in 1933, overthrew Gerardo Machado. By 1934, Batista had inserted Carlos Mendieta as president following the compelled resignation of interim president, Ramon Grau San Martin. By 1937, Hughes would cite Batista among the "semi-fascistic types of dictatorships" burdening the West Indies. "Hughes Bombed in Spain," *Collected Works*, Vol. 9, 159.

40. Nicole Waligora-Davis, "Jagged Words: Black Left, 1930s–1940s" in *Cambridge History of African American Literature*, ed. Maryemma Graham and Jerry Ward, 389–427 (Cambridge: Cambridge University Press, 2011), 390–391. Robet Zangrando records that of the twenty-one reported lynchings in 1930, only six led to indictments and less than a handful of the forty-nine defendants involved received convictions (107). Based on Arthur Raper's and the Southern Commission on the Study of Lynchings's investigations, NAACP secretary, Walter White argued before a Senate Judiciary Subcommittee in 1934 that at least thirteen of these twenty-one victims were innocent of any crime (White 10). Robert Zangrando, "The NAACP and a Federal Anti-lynching Bill, 1934–1940," in *Journal of Negro History* 50 (2) (1965), 106–117; Walter White, Testimony. Senate Judiciary Subcommittee, 73 Cong., 2 Sess., *Hearings* (S. 1978), (February 20–21, 1934), 9–37.

41. Arnold Rampersad, *The Life of Langston Hughes*. Vol. I, *1902–1941, I, Too, Sing America* (New York: Oxford University Press, 2002), 229. Hughes's biographer, Arnold Rampersad rightly suggests a correlation between Hughes's increasing socialist leanings and the aftermath of the Scottsboro case. Arnold Rampersad, *The Life of Langston Hughes*. Vol. II, *1941–1967, I Dream A World* (New York: Oxford University Press, 2002), 5. In the Scottsboro case, nine African American youths ages thirteen to nineteen were indicted for allegedly raping two white women on a train. Eight of these teenagers were sentenced to death in April 1931, one, a thirteen-year-old, was sentenced to life in prison.

42. Waligora-Davis, "Jagged Words," 395–396.

43. Mark Solomon, *The Cry Was Unity: Communists and African Americans, 1917–1936* (Jackson: University Press of Mississippi, 1998), 191–190. The American Communist Party's (CPUSA) involvement in the Scottsboro case reflected the Party's more recent emphasis on racial inequality as a national problem, and their acknowledgement of black self-determination as the crux upon

which a Communist-based anti-capitalist campaign might succeed. The West-Indian native and radical poet Claude McKay was instrumental in this turn of affairs. Speaking before the Fourth Congress of the Third Communist International in 1922, McKay critiqued Communists and Socialists for subscribing to the same racial prejudices impending labor solidarity, and urged a serious engagement with the "Negro Question" (McKay 1973: 91–95). From this Congress arose a "Negro Commission" and a proposal ("Resolutions on the Negro Question") squarely addressing the particularities of African American racial discrimination in the United States (Cooper 23). Taking center stage within CP policy by 1928, the "Negro problem" emerged as the pivot within a larger national problem and the key to producing a revolutionary social transformation in the United States. Their Black Belt Nation thesis argued that African Americans in the South were a nation within a nation, "subject," in William Maxwell's words "to special oppression but boasting a distinct, oppositional culture" (7). Claude McKay, "Speech to the Fourth Congress of the Third Communist International, Moscow," in *The Passion of Claude McKay: Selected Prose and Poetry 1912–1948*, edited and with an introduction by Wayne Cooper (New York: Schocken Books, 1973), 91–95; William Maxwell. *New Negro, Old Left: African American Writing and Communism Between the Wars* (New York: New York University Press, 1999).

44. FBI investigations and surveillance of Hughes begun in 1940 intensified with both this poem and his columns in the *Chicago Defender*. Rampersad, *Life of Langston Hughes*. Vol. II, 4, 92. Balking under the pressure of federal investigation and the accusations of the House of Representatives Special Committee on Un-American activities, Hughes began to refuse to participate and ask to be removed from rosters that the federal administration perceived as either sibling to, or a division of the Communist Party. To further demarcate this separation, he facetiously asserted his affiliation with the NAACP in one of his Jesse Simple columns for *The Chicago Defender* in the spring of 1945. Ibid., 98.

45. Rampersad, *Life of Langston Hughes*. Vol. II, 25

46. Langston Hughes, *I Wonder as I Wander*, intro. Arnold Rampersad (New York: Hill and Wang, 1956), 28.

47. Seabrooks, *Magic Island*, 48. Ironically, among the letters of introduction that Hughes traveled with to Haiti, was one from William Seabrook, whom he would accuse of exoticizing blacks years later. "I did not use the letters of introduction Walter White, William Seabrooks, Arthur Springarn and James Weldon Johnson had given me to the cultural and political elite." Hughes, *I Wonder as I Wander*, 15.

48. Hughes, "People Without Shoes," *Collected Works of Langston Hughes*. Vol. 9, 46–47.

49. Ibid., 47–48.

50. See Plummer, "Afro-American Response," 125–143.

51. See Langston Hughes's 1951 poem, "Harlem."

52. Hughes, "White Shadows in a Black Land," *Collected Works*, Vol. 9, 51–53.

53. James Baldwin, *Just Above My Head* (New York: Delta Trade Paperbacks, 1978), 185.

54. Hughes, "White Shadows in a Black Land," 51–52.

55. Ibid., 52.

56. Hereafter, *Troubled Island, Emperor of Haiti* will be referred to as *Emperor of Haiti* to distinguish the play from Hughes's opera, *Troubled Island*.

57. Hughes, *Collected Works*, Vol. II, 25, 152.

58. Leslie Catherine, "Editorial Notes," In *"Emperor of Haiti (Troubled Island),"* in *The Collected Works of Langston Hughes*. Vol. 5, *The Plays to 1942: "Mulatto" to "The Sun Do Move,"* ed.

with intro. by Leslie Catherine Sanders and Nancy Johnston (Columbia: University of Missouri Press, 2002), 278–332.

59. Ibid., 278–279. Rampersad, *Life of Langston Hughes*. Vol. II, 25.

60. Ibid., 279. Robeson was angered with the divergences between O'Neill's play and its screen adaptation. One year later (1934), he began working on *Black Majesty*, a film that was never produced, tracing the history of the island. The same year of Hughes's premiere, Robeson performed in C. L. R. James's theatrical piece, *Toussaint L'Ouverture. Writings, Speeches, Interviews 1918–1974*, ed. Philip S. Foner (Seaucus, N.J.: Citadel Press, 1978), 121–122, 30–31, 72.

61. Hughes, "White Shadows," *Collected Works*, Vol. 9, 52. Hughes, who admired Vandercooks's history on Christophe in *Black Majesty*, was captivated by the architectural triumph of Dessalines and Christophe's citadel, describing this monument and defensive stronghold for *Crisis* readers in 1932, and again in *Popo and Fifina*.

62. James Weldon Johnson, *Along this Way: The Autobiography of James Weldon Johnson* (New York: Da Capo Press [1933], 2000), 346.

63. Reflecting on Stokowski's promise to conduct and stage *Troubled Island*, Still remarked, "'It will be the biggest thing that has ever been done for the Negro culturally.'" Stokowski's investment in the opera reflected a desire in Still's words "not only to prove that Negroes can sing opera, but that Negroes can create it. Nothing like it has ever been done before, and nobody but Stokowski is big enough to do it." Cited in Rampersad, *Life of Langston Hughes*, Vol. II, 98.

64. Leslie Catherine, "Editorial Notes," in *Gospel Plays, Operas, and Later Dramatic Works*, in *The Collected Works of Langston Hughes*. Vol. 6, ed. with intro. Leslie Catherine (Columbia: University of Missouri Press, 2004), 15–51.

65. Rampersad, *Life of Langston Hughes*, Vol. II, 166. Still and Hughes's enthusiasm for the opera did not translate into the audience. Critics described the opera as "'a turgid, confused mishap,'" laying their most strident critiques on Still's music score (166).

66. Catherine, "Editorial Notes," in *Gospel Plays, Operas, and Later Dramatic Works*, 15–16.

67. Bill Mullen, *Popular Fronts: Chicago and African-American Cultural Politics, 1935–1946* (Urbana: University of Illinois Press, 1999), 3.

68. Ibid., 64. See Nicole A. Waligora-Davis, "Jagged Words: Black Left, 1930s–1940s," in *Cambridge History of African American Literature,* ed. by Maryemma Graham and Jerry Ward (Cambridge: Cambridge University Press, 2011), 389–427. Two years after he wrote *Emperor of Haiti*, Hughes returned to the figure of the slave and slave rebellion to engage contemporary racial and political economies and labor arrangements in *Don't You Want to Be Free? A Poetry Play: From Slavery Through the Blues to Now—and then some! With Singing, Music and Dancing* (1938). Premiering only months after his tenure in Spain ended, at the Harlem Suitcase theater he cofounded with Louise Thompson, *Don't You Want to Be Free?* served as a springboard for other "new radical black theater groups" across the nation. Rampersad, *I, Too, Sing America*, 359.

69. More than a century after the revolution, a representative of the British government rehearsed this "savage" history to Haiti's delegate during a meeting of the League of Nations. C. L. R. James, *The Black Jacobins: Toussaint L'Ouverture and the San Domingo Revolution* (New York: Vintage Press, 1963), 370.

70. Hughes's writings overlap with the indigenist literary movement in Haiti and with Senghor's Negritude in Paris. See Gilroy, *Black Atlantic*, 211. Arguably, Hughes's translation of Jacques Roumain's *Masters of the Dew*, helped to extend the reach of Haitian indigenism.

71. Saidiya Hartman, *Scenes of Subjection: Terror, Slavery, and Self-Making in Nineteenth-Century America* (New York: Oxford University Press, 1997), 3.

72. W. E. B. Du Bois, *Suppression of the African Slave-Trade* (New York: Library of America, [1896, 1946] 1986), 74.

73. See C. L. R. James, *The Black Jacobins: Toussaint L'Ouverture and the San Domingo Revolution* (New York: Vintage, 1963).

74. Hughes, *Emperor of Haiti*, 311

75. See James, *Black Jacobins*, 311.

76. James, *Black Jacobins*, 362.

77. That revenge and a request by the British government who bartered colonial French settlers' lives in exchange for military defense assistance and trade alliances with Haiti motivated Dessalines's ethnic cleansing, mattered little. James, *Black Jacobins*, 374.

78. Ibid.

79. William Wells Brown, *The Black Man, His Antecedents, His Genius, and His Achievements* (New York: Thomas Hamilton; Boston: R.F. Wallcut, 1863), 111.

80. Amy Wilentz, "Haiti's Man of the People Lost His Way," *The New York Times*, February 15, 2004.

81. Hughes, *Emperor of Haiti*, 295.

82. Ibid.

83. Ibid., 301–302.

84. Ibid., 302.

85. Ibid., emphasis in original.

86. Ibid., 320.

87. Ibid., 321.

88. Hughes, *Emperor of Haiti*, 302.

89. Ibid., 328.

90. Dessalines required Haitians to either serve in the military or work on plantations, the later part of his enforced agricultural labor program, *caporalisme agraire*. See Michel-Rolph Trouillot, *Haiti, State Against Nation: The Origins and Legacy of Duvalierism* (New York: Monthly Review Press, 1990).

91. Hughes, *Emperor of Haiti*, 317; emphasis in original.

92. Ibid., 305.

93. See Hughes, "Hughes Bombed Spain," *Collected Works*, Vol. 9, 159.

94. James Weldon Johnson, "Self Determining Haiti," in *The Collected Writings* (New York: Library of America, 2004), 667.

95. Quoted in Michel de Certeau, *The Writing of History*, trans. Tom Conley (New York: Columbia University Press, 1988), 11.

96. James, *Black Jacobins*, 296. Although James does not cite him in his text, this line is likely drawn from Carl von Clausewitz's 1832 text, *On War*.

97. Walter Benjamin, "Theses on the Philosophy of History," *Illuminations: Essays and Reflections*, ed. with intro. Hannah Arendt (New York: Schocken Books, 1968), 257.

98. De Certeau, *Writing History*, 48.

99. Hughes, "Hughes Finds Moors Being Used as Pawns by Fascists in Spain," *Collected Works*, Vol. 9, 160.

100. Hughes, "Negroes in Spain," *Collected Works*, Vol. 9, 156.

101. Ibid., 157.

102. Ibid., 164–165.

103. See Winston James, *Holding Aloft the Banner of Ethiopia: Caribbean Radicalism in Early Twentieth-Century America* (New York: Verso, 1998); William Scott, "Black Nationalism and the Italo-Ethiopian conflict 1934–1936," *Journal of Negro History* 63 (April 1978), 118–134; W. E. B. Du Bois, "Ethiopia: State Socialism Under an Emperor," in *The World and Africa: An Inquiry into the Part Which Africa has Played in World History* (New York: International Publishers, [1946] 1996), 268–269.

104. W. E. B. Du Bois, *Black Reconstruction in America: 1860–1880*, intro. David Levering Lewis (New York: Atheneum, [1935] 1992), 715.

105. Hughes, "Soldiers from Many Lands United in Spanish Fight," *Collected Works*, Vol. 9, 181.

106. Langston Hughes, *I Wonder as I Wander*, intro. Arnold Rampersad (New York: Hill and Wang, [1956] 1993), 399–400.

107. Hughes, "My America," *Collected Works*, Vol. 9, 239.

108. Giorgio Agamben, *Homo Sacer: Sovereign Power and Bare Life* (Stanford, Calif.: Stanford University Press, [1995] 1998), 130.

109. Richard Slotkin, *Lost Battalions: The Great War and the Crisis of American Nationality* (New York: Henry Holt, 2005), 451–455; Gilroy, *Black Atlantic*, 213–214.

110. De Certeau, *Writing of History*, 5.

111. James Baldwin, "Many Thousands Gone," in *James Baldwin: The Collected Essays*, edited by Toni Morrison (New York: Library of America, 1998), 33. By this I am referring to the ways in which the death of the black body frequently marks an invalidation of black life, precisely the ways in which this body does not matter, while concurrently (if even paradoxically) the mortality testified by the corpse proves the fiction underlying this presumption.

112. Of this Hughes writes, "They burned Mackandal for trying to be free, didn't they. They had no mercy on him. We'll show no mercy on them." Hughes, *Emperor of Haiti*, 284.

113. Ibid., 330–331; emphasis in original.

114. James, *Black Jacobins*, 301.

115. Hughes, *Emperor of Haiti*, 332.

116. Spillers, "Mama's Baby, Papa's Maybe," *Black, White, and in Color: Essays On American Literature and Culture* (Chicago: University of Chicago Press, 2003), 207, emphasis in original.

117. Gilroy, *Black Atlantic*, 198.

118. Du Bois, "Haiti," 4.

119. Baldwin, "The Price of the Ticket," in *Collected Essays*, 841.

120. Hughes, *Emperor of Haiti*, 297.

121. Cited in Rampersad, *Life of Langston Hughes*, 104.

122. Arguably, U.S. aid—occupation—in Haiti aggravated declining economic conditions even though it may have allowed for militarily necessary infrastructural improvements.

EPILOGUE: REQUIEM

1. "Act I," *When the Levees Broke: A Requiem in Four Acts*, DVD, directed by Spike Lee (Hollywood, Calif.: HBO Documentary Films and 40 Acres and a Mule, 2006).

2. Ibid.; Melissa Harris-Lacewell, "'Do You Know What It Means . . . ?' Mapping Emotion in the Aftermath of Katrina," in *Seeking Higher Ground: The Hurricane Katrina Crisis, Race, and Public Policy Reader*, ed. Manning Marable and Kristen Clarke, 153–171 (New York: Palgrave

Macmillan, 2008), 153; Ruth Berggren's and Tyler Curiel's essay for the *New England Journal of Medicine*, "After the Storm-Health Care Infrastructure in Post Katrina New Orleans," revealed that compared with January 2005, death rates in New Orleans in January 2006 were 25 percent higher. Cited in Michael Dawson, "After the Deluge: Publics and Publicity in Katrina's Wake," *Du Bois Review* 3 (1) (2006), 245.

3. Judith Shklar, *American Citizenship*, referenced in Dawson, "After the Deluge," 246.

4. W. E. B. Du Bois, *The Souls of Black Folk*, in *Du Bois: Writings*, edited by Nathan Huggins (New York: Modern Library, 1986), 368. The role of the veil as a symbol of black death and black mourning in *The Souls of Black Folk* intimates Du Bois's loss of his son from nasopharyngeal diphtheria after being unable to procure adequate medical care.

5. Melissa Harris-Lacewell, "Do you know what it means," 157, 164. Harris-Lacewell notes that "67% of whites reported that they had felt no impairment of life activities" (156–157).

6. Cited in Dawson, "After the Deluge," 240. A study conducted by Shanto Iyengar and Richard Morin mapping the impact of racial cues in the media on public responses to federal aid for hurricane victims produced similar results. Here too, willingness to support federal relief efforts was predicated on racial markers: "[R]esponses to Katrina were influenced by the mere inclusion of racial cues in news media coverage . . . this group awarded lower levels of hurricane assistance after reading about looting or after encountering an African-American family displaced by the hurricane" (Shanto Iyengar and Richard Morin, "Natural Disasters in Black and White: How Racial Cues Influenced Public Response to Hurricane Katrina," *Washington Post*, June 8, 2006). Likewise, a survey by the *Washington Post*, the Kaiser Family Foundation, and Harvard University of hurricane victims relocated to Houston revealed that sixty-one percent felt abandoned by the government whereas 68 percent expressed that race determined the rapidity of federal government's response (Bruce Alpert, "Racism Cost Lives, N.O. Evacuees Say; Bitter Exchanges Erupt as They Testify in D.C.," *Times-Picayune* [New Orleans], December 7, 2005).

7. See Barbara Ransby, "Katrina, Black Women, and the Deadly Discourse on Black Poverty in America," *Du Bois Review* 3 (1) (2006), 215–222. Reporting the findings of the Institute for Women's Policy Research, Ransby writes, "the percentage of women in poverty in New Orleans before the storm was considerably higher than in other parts of the country: more than half of the poor families of the city were headed by single mothers, and the median income for African American workers in New Orleans before the storm was a paltry $19,951 a year" (216).

8. "Hurricane Katrina Turns 'Refugee' Into Word of the Year," *Washington Post*, December 16, 2005. In a "Fresh Air" interview, on September 8, 2005, Geoffrey Nunberg studied the usage of the terms refugee versus evacuee, reporting that in Nexis wire service articles mentioning Katrina over the past week, articles containing "evacuee" outnumber those containing "refugee" by 56% to 44% (n=1522). But in contexts in which the words appear within 10 words of "poor" or "black," "refugee" is favored by 68% to 32% (n=85). And in contexts in which the words appear within ten words of "Astrodome," "refugee" is favored by 53% to 37% (n=461). Those disparities no doubt reflect the image of refugees as poor, bedraggled, and forlorn, and they suggest that there's a genuine basis for impression that the words tend to single out one group, even unwittingly. Cited in John R. Rickford, "Racism in Media Language and Law Enforcement's Officer's Actions After Hurricane." Contribution to panel on "Media, Culture and the Politics of Representation," for a course, "Confronting Katrina," at Stanford University, Stanford, Calif., 1–2.

9. 2000 U.S. Census Report; Michael Dawson et al. *2005 Racial Attitudes and the Katrina Disaster Study*, Center for the Study of Race Politics and Culture (University of Chicago, 2006), 1; Barbara Lee, "A Tale of Two Americas," *Mississippi Link*, September 22–28, 2005, A4.

10. Dana Hull, "What's In a Name?" *American Journalism Review* 27 (5) (2005), 23–36.

11. Dawson, "After the Deluge," 240.

12. Harris-Lacewell, "Do you know what it means," 5.

13. "Act 1" *When the Levees Broke.*

14. See David Cole, *Enemy Aliens: Double Standards and Constitutional Freedoms in the War on Terrorism* (New York: New Press, 2003).

15. See Joan Fitzpatrick, "Flight from Asylum: Trends Toward Temporary 'Refuge' and Local Responses to Forced Migrations," *Virginia Journal of International Law* 35 (13) (1994), 13–70; Jacqueline Bhabha, "European Harmonisation of Asylum Policy: A Flawed Process," *Virginia Journal of International Law* 25 (1994), 101–114; James C. Hathaway, "Harmonization for Whom? The Devaluation of Refugee Protection in the Era of European Economic Integration," *Cornell International Law Journal* 26 (1993), 719–735.

16. Anti-immigrationism refueled in the wake of the Mariel Cubans' Freedom Flotilla (1980) and by an economic recession led to the Haitian Interdiction program (1981–1991). The Interdiction Program detained more than 36,000 Haitians in Guantanamo Bay, refugees forced to await asylum in the face of an almost zero percent acceptance rate for Haitians. During its ten years, 24,000 Haitians were captured, and only twenty-eight were documented as having credible claims for asylum. The program repatriated thousands who feared for the lives, but were recognized by the United States as simply economic immigrants and therefore ineligible for asylum. See Janice Villiers, "Closed Borders, Closed Ports: The Plight of Haitians Seeking Political Asylum in the United States," *Brooklyn Law Review* 60 (3) (1990), 841–928.

17. Nicole A. Waligora-Davis. "The Ghetto: Illness and the Formation of the 'Suspect' in American Polity." *Forum for Modern Language Studies* 40 (2004), 182–203.

18. AP Newswire, August 20, 2005; AP Newswire, August 30, 2005.

19. "Katrina: The Lying Media," Editorial. *Baltimore Afro-American*, September 17–23, 2005.

20. Harris-Lacewell, "'Do You Know What It Means . . .?'"; Dawson, et al., *2005 Racial Attitudes and the Katrina Disaster Study*.

21. Dawson et al., *2005 Racial Attitudes and the Katrina Disaster Study*.

22. Dawson, "After the Deluge," 240.

23. Shoshana Felman, *The Juridical Unconscious: Trials and Traumas in the Twentieth Century* (Cambridge, Mass.: Harvard University Press, 2002).

24. "Suit Filed Over Katrina Bridge Blockade," Associated Press, January 4, 2006; "No Mercy at the Bridge," *Times-Picayune* (New Orleans), September 25, 2005.

25. Bill Torpy, "Hurricane Katrina: Cities Dread Influx of the Poor, Black," *Atlanta Journal-Constitution*, September 4, 2005.

26. See Michelle Krupa, "Jefferson to Help Gretna Defend Lawsuit; Cops Blocked Evacuees Fleeing Across Bridge," *Times-Picayune* (New Orleans), January 12, 2006; "Suit Filed Over Katrina Bridge Blockade," Associated Press, January 4, 2006; Richard Webster, "Gretna Mayor Cites Support for Post-Katrina Barricades," *Journal of Jefferson Parish*, September 22, 2006; "No Mercy at The Bridge," *Times-Picayune* (New Orleans), September 25, 2005.

27. "Lott Should Resign," Editorial. *The Nation*, December 20, 2002; Dan Glaister, "Abort All Black Babies and Cut Crime, says Republican" *Guardian*, October 1, 2005; Goldberg, "Deva-Stating Disasters," 85.

28. "Barbara Bush Calls Evacuees Better Off," *New York Times*, September 7, 2005.

29. Goldberg, "Deva-stating Disasters," 84.

30. See Dawson, "After the Deluge," emphasis in original.

31. Ibid.

32. A 1996 study published in *The New England Journal of Medicine* proved the raced inequities in medical care, reporting that "Blacks with heart disease were 55 percent less likely to receive sophisticated treatments such as bypass surgery or balloon angioplasty. Blacks with circulatory problems were 264 percent more likely to have a leg amputated. Black men with advanced prostate cancer were 145 percent more likely to be treated by having their testicles removed." "*The New England Journal of Medicine* Produces Flat-Out Proof of Racism in Medicare-Funded Medicine," *Journal of Blacks in Higher Education* 13 (Autumn) (1996), 39. See also Karla Holloway, "Accidental Communities: Race, Emergency Medicine, and the Problem of PolyHeme," *American Journal of Bioethics* 6 (3) (2006), 1–11.

33. Vernellia Randal, "Slavery, Segregation and Racism: Trusting the Health Care System Ain't Always Easy! An African American Perspective on Bioethics," *St. Louis University Public Law Review* 15 (1919) (1996), 1–43.

34. Witness the way in which legislated medical waivers for refugees seeking asylum have been suspended in the case of HIV-positive Haitians seeking entry into the United States. In addition, the "deliberate indifference" claims filed by HIV positive patients quarantined to AIDS wards in prisons speaks to the ways in which civil liberties are being stripped along racialized axes of disease. See Amy Fairchild and Eileen Tynan, "Policies of Containment: Immigration in the Era of AIDS," *American Journal of Public Health* 84 (12) (1994), 2016; *Congressional Record*, February 17, 1993 2861; *Sullivan v. County of Pierce*.

35. James Baldwin, *Evidence of Things Not Seen* (New York: Henry Holt, 1985), 31.

SELECTED BIBLIOGRAPHY

Abel, Elizabeth, Barbara Christian, and Helene Moglen, eds. *Female Subjects in Black and White: Race Psychoanalysis, Feminism.* Berkeley and Los Angeles: University of California Press, 1997.

Abbott, R. S. "The Test." *Chicago Defender,* April 28, 1917, editorial page.

Ahearne, Jeremy. *Michel de Certeau: Interpretation and Its Other.* Stanford, Calif.: Stanford University Press, 1995.

Alpert, Bruce. "Racism Cost Lives, N.O. Evacuees Say; Bitter Exchanges Erupt as They Testify in D.C." *Times-Picayune* (New Orleans), December 7, 2005.

Agamben, Giorgio. *Means Without End: Notes on Politics.* Translated by Vincenzo Binetti and Cesare Casarino. Minneapolis: University of Minnesota Press, 2000.

———. *Homo sacer: Sovereign Power and Bare Life.* Translated by Daniel Heller-Roazen. Stanford, Calif.: Stanford University Press, 1998.

———. *State of Exception.* Translated by Kevin Attell. Chicago: University of Chicago Press, 2005.

Anderson, Carol. *Eyes Off the Prize: The United Nations and the African American Struggle for Human Rights, 1944–1955.* Cambridge, UK: Cambridge University Press, 2003.

———. "The NAACP and Black Communists." In *Window on Freedom: Race, Civil Rights, and Foreign Affairs, 1945–1988,* edited by Brenda Gayle Plummer, 93–114. Chapel Hill: University of North Carolina Press, 2003.

Appadurai, Arjun. *Modernity at Large: Cultural Dimensions of Globalization.* Minneapolis: University of Minnesota Press, 1996.

Appiah, Kwame Anthony. "Cosmopolitan Patriots." In *Cosmopolitics: Thinking and Feeling Beyond the Nation,* edited by Pheng Cheah and Bruce Robbins, 91–114. Minneapolis: University of Minnesota Press, 1998.

———. "Ethics in a World of Strangers: W. E. B. Du Bois and the Spirit of Cosmopolitanism." *Berlin Journal* 11 (2005): 23–26.

——. *Cosmopolitanism: Ethics in a World of Strangers*. New York: Norton, 2006.

——. "The Uncompleted Argument: Du Bois and the Illusion of Race." "Race," Writing, and Difference. Special Issue, *Critical Inquiry* 12 (1) (1985): 21–37.

Aptheker, Herbet, ed. *The Correspondence of W.E.B. Du Bois. Vol.1 Selections 1877–1934*. Boston: University of Massachusetts Press, 1973.

Aptheker, Herbert. "Editorial Notation" for "Flashes from Transcaucasia." *In Against Racism. Unpublished Essays, Papers, Addresses, 1887–1961*, edited by Herbert Aptheker, 254–256. Amherst: University of Massachusetts Press, 1985.

Arendt, Hannah. *The Origins of Totalitarianism*. San Diego, Cal.: Harcourt, [1968] 1976.

Armstrong, Henry E. "The Sergeant of Marines Who Played at Being a King." *New York Times*, April 12, 1931.

Associated Press & Local Wire, "Suit Filed Over Katrina Bridge Blockade," January 4, 2006, http://www.lexis-nexis.com/.

Bachelard, Gaston. *The Poetics of Space: The Classic Look at How We Experience Intimate Places*. Translated by Maria Jolas. Boston: Beacon Press, 1958.

Baker, Houston, Jr. *Blues, Ideology, and Afro-American Literature: A Vernacular Theory*. Chicago: University of Chicago Press, 1984.

——. *Modernism and the Harlem Renaissance*. Chicago: University of Chicago Press, 1987.

——. *Workings of the Spirit: The Poetics of Afro-American Women's Writing*. Chicago: University of Chicago Press, 1991.

Balch, Emily, ed. *Occupied Haiti*. New York: Writers Publishing, 1927.

Baldwin, James. *Evidence of Things Not Seen*. New York: Henry Holt, 1985.

———. "Price of the Ticket." In *James Baldwin: Collected Essays*, edited by Toni Morrison, 830–842. New York: Library of America, 1998.

——. "Many Thousands Gone." In *Collected Essays*, edited by Toni Morrison, 19–34. New York: Library of America, 1998.

——. *Just Above My Head*. New York: Delta Trade Paperbacks, 1978.

Balibar, Etienne. "Is There a 'Neo-Racism'?" In *Race, Nation, Class: Ambiguous Identities*, edited by Etienne Balibar and Immanuel Wallerstein. Translated by Chris Turner, 17–28. New York: Verso, 1991.

Baltimore Afro-American, "Katrina: The Lying Media," September 17–23, 2005.

Barthes, Roland. *Camera Lucida: Reflections on Photography*. Translated by Richard Howard. New York: Hill and Wang, 1981.

Bean, Robert Bennet, "Some Racial Peculiarities of the Negro Brain," *American Journal of Anatomy* 5 (1906): 353–432.

Beavers, Herman. "Romancing the Body Politic: Du Bois's Propaganda of the Dark World." *Annals of the American Academy of Political and Social Science* 568 (2000): 250–264.

Bell, Howard H. "Introduction." In *Black Separatism and the Caribbean 1860* by James Theodore Holly and Dennis Harris, edited with an introduction by Howard H. Bell. Ann Arbor: University of Michigan Press, 1970.

Belnap, Jeffrey and Raul Fernandez, eds. *Jose Marti's "Our America": From National to Hemispheric Cultural Studies*. Durham, N.C.: Duke University Press, 1998.

Benhabib, Seyla. *The Rights of Others: Aliens, Residents, and Citizens*. Cambridge, UK: Cambridge University Press, 2004.

——. *Another Cosmopolitanism*. Edited by Robert Post. New York: Oxford University Press, 2008.

Benjamin, Walter. *One Way Street And Other Writings.* London: Verso, 1985.

———. *Illuminations: Essays and Reflections.* Edited with an introduction by Hannah Arendt. New York: Schocken Books, 1968.

———. *Reflections: Essays, Aphorisms, Autobiographical Writings.* Edited with an introduction by Peter Demetz. New York: Schocken Books, 1978.

———. "Theses on the Philosophy of History." In *Illuminations: Essays and Reflections,* edited with an introduction by Hannah Arendt, 253–264. New York: Schocken, 1968.

Berlant, Lauren. *The Queen of America Goes to Washington City: Essays on Sex and Citizenship.* Durham, N.C.: Duke University Press, 1997.

———. "Poor Eliza." *American Literature* 70 (September) (1998): 636–668.

Bertillon, Alphonse. *Signaletic Instructions: Including the Theory and Practice of Anthropometrical Identification.* Edited by R.W. McClaughry. Chicago: The Werner Co., [1893] 1896.

Best, Stephen. *The Fugitive's Properties: Law and the Poetics of Possession.* Chicago: University of Chicago, 2004.

Bhabha, Homi. *The Location of Culture.* New York: Routledge, 1994.

Bhabha, Jacqueline. *European Harmonisation of Asylum Policy: A Flawed Process.* 35 *Virginia Journal of International Law* 101 (Fall) (1994).

———. "Embodied Rights: Gender Persecution, State Sovereignty, and Refugees." *Public Culture* 9 (1996): 3–32.

Black, Edwin. *War Against the Weak: Eugenics and America's Campaign to Create a Master Race.* New York: Four Walls Eight Windows, 2003.

Blackburn, Robin. *The Overthrow of Colonial Slavery, 1776–1848.* London: Verso, 1988.

Blakely, Robert L. and Judith M. Harrington, eds. *Bones in the Basement: Postmortem Racism in Nineteenth-Century Medical Training.* Washington, D.C.: Smithsonian Institution Press, 1997.

Blassingame, John W. and John R. McKivigan, eds. *The Frederick Douglass Papers.* 5 vols. New Haven, Conn.: Yale University Press, 1992.

Bloomley, Nicholas K. *Law, Space, and the Geographies of Power.* New York: Guilford Press, 1994.

Bontemps, Arna and Langston Hughes. *Popo and Fifina.* Introduction and afterward by Arnold Rampersad. New York: Oxford University Press, 1932.

Boston Slave Riot, and Trial of Anthony Burns. Continuing the Report of the Faneuil Hall meeting; The Murder of Bachelder; Theodore Parker's Lesson for the Day; Speeches of Counsel on Both Sides, Corrected by Themselves; A Verbatim Report of Judge Loring's Decision; and Detailed Account of the Embarkation. Boston: Fetridge and Company, 1854.

Bourne, Randolph. *War and the Intellectuals: Essays by Randolph S. Bourne, 1915–1919.* New York: Harper and Row, 1964.

Boyle, Francis Anthony. *Foundations of World Order: The Legalist Approach to International Relations, 1898–1922.* Durham, N.C.: Duke University Press, 1999.

Boyd, Willis D. "James Redpath and American Negro Colonization in Haiti, 1860–1862." *The Americas* 12 (2) (1955): 169–182.

Brantlinger, Patrick. *Dark Vanishings: Discourse on the Extinction of Primitive Races, 1800–1930.* Ithaca, N.Y.: Cornell University Press, 2003.

Brawley, Benjamin. *A Social History of the American Negro: Being a History of the Negro Problem in the United States Including A History of the Study of the Republic of Liberia.* London: Collier Books [1921], 1970.

Brown, William Wells. *St. Domingo: Its Revolutions and its Patriots. A Lecture, Delivered Before the Metropolitan Athenaeum, London, May 16, and at St. Thomas' Church, Philadelphia, December 20, 1854*, with an introduction by M. Whiteman. Philadelphia: Rhistoric Publications, 1969.

Brief of Evidence The State v. *Rosa Lee Ingram, Wallace Ingram, Sammie Lee Ingram*, Supreme Court—Clerk of Court-Criminal Appeal Case, RG-SG-S 92–1–3; Georgia Archives.

Brown, Norma, ed. *A Black Diplomat in Haiti: the Diplomatic Correspondence of U.S. Minister Frederick Douglass from Haiti, 1889–1891.* Salisbury, N.C.: Documentary Publications, 1977.

Brown, Wendy. *States of Injury: Power and Freedom in Late Modernity.* Princeton, N.J.: Princeton University Press, 1995.

Buck-Morrs, Susan. *The Dialectics of Seeing: Walter Benjamin and the Arcades Project.* Cambridge, Mass.: MIT Press, 1989.

——. "Hegel and Haiti." *Critical Inquiry* 26 (4) (2000): 821–865.

Bullard, Robert D. and Beverly Wright, eds. *Race, Place and Environmental Justice After Hurricane Katrina: Struggles to Reclaim, Rebuild, and Revitalize New Orleans and the Gulf Coast.* Foreward by Marc H. Morial. Boulder, Colo.: Westview Press, 2009.

Burnett, Christina Duffy Burnett and Burke Marshall, *Foreign in a Domestic Sense: Puerto Rico, American Expansion, and the Constitution.* Durham, N.C.: Duke University Press, 2001.

Butler, Judith. *Subjects of Desire: Hegelian Reflections in Twentieth-Century France.* New York: Columbia University Press, 1987.

——. *Bodies that Matter: On the Discursive Limits of 'Sex.'* New York: Routledge, 1993.

——. *Excitable Speech: A Politic of the Performative.* New York: Routledge, 1997.

——. *The Psychic Life of Power: Theories in Subjection.* Stanford, Calif.: Stanford University Press, 1997.

——. *Precarious Life: The Powers of Mourning and Violence.* New York: Verso, 2004.

Byles, Joanna. "Psychoanalysis and War," Presentation at the Eighth Annual Conference of the Association for the Psychoanalysis of Culture and Society, University of Pennsylvania, October 25–27, 2002.

Carter, Dan T. *Scottsboro: A Tragedy of the American South.* New York: Oxford University Press, 1969.

Carter, Purvis M. *Congressional and Public Reaction to Wilson's Caribbean Policy, 1913–1917.* New York: Vantage Press, 1977.

Caruth, Cathy. *Unclaimed Experience: Trauma, Narrative, and History.* Baltimore, Md.: Johns Hopkins University Press, 1996.

——. "Violence and Time." *Assemblage* 20 (1993): 24–25.

Casey, Edward. *The Fate of Place: A Philosophical History.* Berkeley and Los Angeles: University of California Press, 1997.

Castiglia, Christopher and Russ Castronovo. "A 'Hive of Subtlety': Aesthetics and the End(s) of Cultural Studies." *American Literature* 76 (3) (2004): 423–435.

Catherine, Leslie. "Editorial Notes" for *Troubled Island: An Opera in Three Acts* In *The Collected Works of Langston Hughes,* Vol. 6, *Gospel Plays, Operas, and Later Dramatic Works,* edited with an introduction by Leslie Catherine, 15–16. Columbia: University of Missouri Press, 2004.

Chandler, Nahum D. "The Figure of W. E. B. Du Bois as a Problem for Thought." *New Centennial Review* 6 (3) (2006): 29–55.

———. "Between." *Assemblage* 20 (1993): 26–27.

———. "The Economy of Desedimentation: W. E. B. Du Bois and the Discourses of the Negro." *Callaloo* 19 (1) (1996): 78–93.

Chatterjee, Partha. *Nationalist Thought and the Colonial World: A Derivative Discourse?* Minneapolis: University of Minnesota Press, 1986.

Chaudhary, Zahid. "Phantasmagoric Aesthetics: Colonial Violence and the Management of Perception." *Cultural Critique* 59 (Winter) (2005): 63–119.

Chicago Daily Tribune. "Calls Copper Responsible for Rioting: Chief Garrity Strips the Star From D. L. Callahan," July 30, 1919.

———. "Downstate Troops Called to Aid Chicago: Local Militia Ready: Lowden Defers to Mayor," July 30, 1919.

———. "Five Regiments Begin Patrol of Riot Areas: Rushed to Trouble Zone in Trucks, Taxi Fleet, and on Foot," July 31, 1919.

———. "More Dead and Wounded in Chicago Race Riots," July 31, 1919.

———. "Negro Business Men Act to Curtail Lawlessness," July 30, 1919.

———. "Negroes Call on Mayor, Lowden, to Stop Riots; Visit City Hall; Blame the Police in Part for Race Clashes" July 31, 1919.

——— "Negroes Seek Safety Haven At Milwaukee: Hundreds Flee From Chicago to Escape Rioters," July 31, 1919.

———. "New Grand Jury To Get Evidence on Race Riots," July 30, 1919.

———. "Patrol Burned Homes to Foil New Terrorism: Troops Act on Hint of Revenge Raid on Black Belt," August 3, 1919.

———. "Priests to Aid Peace Efforts in Riot District: Chancellor Arranges Special Masses and Addresses," August 3, 1919.

———. "Race Riot Zone, Seen From Taxi, Ominous, Quiet: Olive Drab, Police Blue, Show Iron Hand Over All," July 29, 1919.

———. "Riot Refugees Flee to Police Fearful of Mob: Colored Citizens Jam Stations; Go Home in Closed Vans," July 30, 1919

———. "Torch Rioters Give Firemen Continuous Job: Alarms by Score During the Night: Stones Fly," July 31, 1919.

———. "Troops Armed, Ready to Act; No Order Given: Lowden Defers to the Mayor, Who Withholds Action," July 30, 1919.

———. "Two Killed, Fifty Hurt in Race Riots: Bathing Beach Fight Spreads To Black Belt: All Police Reserves Called to Guard South Side," July 28, 1919.

———. "Upset Plan to Put Negroes Back in Yards," August 3, 1919.

———. "3500 Troops Ready to Go Into Riot Zone: Daybreak May See Black Belt Under Military Rule," July 29, 1919.

Chicago Commission on Race Relations. *The Negro in Chicago: A Study of Race Relations and a Race Riot.* Chicago: University of Chicago Press, 1922.

Chicago Defender, "Millions Prepare to Leave the South Following Brutal Burning of Human," May 26, 1917.

Civil Rights Cases, 109 U.S. 33 S. Ct. (1883) WL 18.

Cohen, William. *At Freedom's Edge: Black Mobility and the Southern White Quest for Racial Control 1861–1915.* Baton Rouge: Louisiana State University Press, 1991.

Cole, David. *Enemy Aliens: Double Standards and Constitutional Freedoms in the War on Terrorism.* New York: New Press, 2003.

Coleman, Finnie D. *Sutton E. Griggs and the Struggle Against White Supremacy.* Knoxville: University of Tennessee Press, 2007.

The Constitution of the United States with Acts of Congress Relating to Slavery Embracing the Constitution, The Fugitive Slave Act of 1793. Division of Rare and Manuscript Collections, Carl A. Kroch Library, Cornell University, Ithaca, N.Y.

The Constitution of the United States with Acts of Congress Relating to Slavery Embracing the Constitution, The Fugitive Slave Act of 1793, the Missouri Compromise Act of 1820, The Fugitive Slave Law of 1850, and the Nebraska and Kansas Bill. Compiled by D.M. Dewey. Rochester: Arcade Hall, 1854. Division of Rare and Manuscript Collections, Carl A. Kroch Library, Cornell University, Ithaca, N.Y.

Cooper, Wayne. "Introduction," in *The Passion of Claude McKay: Selected Prose and Poetry 1912–1948,* edited and with an introduction by Wayne Cooper, 1–45. New York: Schocken Books, 1973.

Couch, W. T. "Publisher's Introduction." In *What the Negro Wants,* edited by Rayford Logan with a new introduction by Kenneth Robert Janken, ix–xxiii, Notre Dame, Ind.: University of Notre Dame Press, [1944] 2001.

Cox, Oliver. "Lynching and the Status Quo." *Journal of Negro Education* 14 (4) (1945): 577–588.

Craige, John H. *Black Bagdad.* New York: Minton, Balch & Company, 1933.

———. *Cannibal Cousins.* New York: Minton, Balch and Company, 1934.

Curtin, Philip D. *Imperialism.* New York: Harper and Row, 1971.

Danticat, Edwidge. *The Farming of Bones.* New York: Soho Press, 1998.

Davis, Thadious. *Games of Property: Law, Race, Gender, and Faulkner's "Go Down Moses."* Durham, N.C.: Duke University Press, 2003.

Dawson, Michael. "After the Deluge: Publics and Publicity in Katrina's Wake." *Du Bois Review,* 3 (1) (2006): 239–249.

Dawson, Michael et al. *2005 Racial Attitudes and the Katrina Disaster Study.* University of Chicago Center for the Study of Race Politics and Culture. Initial Report, 1–6, January 2006.

Dayan, Joan. *Haiti, History, and the Gods.* Berkeley and Los Angeles: University of California Press, 1995.

Delbanco, Andrew. *Melville: His World and Work.* New York: Knopf, 2005.

de Certeau, Michel. *The Writing of History.* Translated by Tom Conley. New York: Columbia University Press, 1988.

———. *The Practice of Everyday Life.* Translated by Steven Rendall. Berkeley and Los Angeles: University of California Press, 1984.

De Puech Parham, Althéa, ed. and trans. *My Odyssey: Experiences of a Young Refugee From Two Revolutions. By A Creole of Saint Domingue,* with an introduction by Selden Rodman. Baton Rouge: Louisiana State University Press, 1959.

Delaney, David. *Race, Place, and the Law: 1836–1948.* Austin: University of Texas Press, 1998.

———. "The Space that Race Makes." *Professional Geographer* 54 (1) (2002): 6–13.

Delgado, Richard. *The Coming Race War? And Other Apocalyptic Tales of America After Affirmative Action and Welfare.* Introduction by Andrew Hacker. New York: New York University Press, 1996.

Derrida, Jacques. *The Truth in Painting.* Translated by Geoff Bennington and Ian McLeod. Chicago: University of Chicago Press, 1987.

———. *Limited Inc.* Evanston, Ill.: Northwestern University Press, 1988.

——. *Resistances of Psychoanalysis.* Translated by Peggy Kamuf, Pascale-Anne Brault, and Michael Naas. Stanford, Calif.: Stanford University Press, 1998.

——. *Of Grammatology.* Translated by Gayatri Chakravorty Spivak. Baltimore, Md.: Johns Hopkins University Press, 1974.

——. *The Post Card: From Socrates to Freud and Beyond.* Translated by Alan Bass. Chicago: University of Chicago Press, 1987.

——. "Before the Law." In *Acts of Literature,* edited by Derek Attridge, 181–220. New York: Routledge, 1992.

——. "' . . . That Dangerous Supplement." In *Acts of Literature,* edited by Derek Attridge, 76–109. New York: Routledge, 1992.

——. "Force and Signification." *Writing and Difference.* Translated by Alan Bass, 3–30. Chicago: University of Chicago Press, 1978.

——. *On Cosmopolitanism and Forgiveness.* Translated by Mark Dooley and Michael Hughes. New York: Routledge, [2001] 2002.

"The Destinies of the South." *Southern Quarterly Review* 7 (13) (1853): 178–205.

Doane, Mary Ann. "Dark Continents: Epistemologies of Racial and Sexual Difference in Psychoanalysis and the Cinema." In *Femmes Fatales: Feminism, Film Theory, Psychoanalysis.* New York: Routledge, 1991: 209–248.

Douglass, Frederick. *Narrative of the Life of Frederick Douglass: An American Slave Written By Himself.* Edited by David Blight. Boston: Bedford Books, [1845] 1993.

——. *My Bondage and My Freedom.* Introduction by Philip S. Foner. New York: Dover, [1855], 1969.

——. *Life and Times of Frederick Douglass. Frederick Douglass Autobiographies.* Edited by Henry Louis Gates, Jr. New York: Library of America, [1881] 1994.

——. "Lecture on Haiti." *The Haitian pavilion dedication ceremonies delivered at the World's Fair in Jackson Park, Chicago, January 2d. 1883: By the Honorable Frederick Douglass.* Frederick Douglass Papers. Library of Congress, Manuscript Division.

——. "A Nation in the Midst of a Nation: An Address Delivered in New York, New York, on May 11, 1853." In *The Frederick Douglass Papers, 1847–1854,* Vol. 2, edited by John Blassingame, 423–440. New Haven, Conn.: Yale University Press, 1982.

Downes v. Bidwell 182 U.S. 244, 21 S.Ct. 770 (1901), WL 770.

Downes, Paul. "Melville's *Benito Cereno* and the Politics of Humanitarian Intervention." *South Atlantic Quarterly* 103 (2/3) (2004): 465–488.

Dred Scott v. Sandford. 163 U.S. 180. U.S. Sup. Court. 1895.

Du Bois, W. E. B. "The Afro American." In *The Papers of W.E.B. Du Bois, 1877–1963.* Sandford, N.C.: Microfilming Company, 1980.

——. "American Negro and the Darker World." In *W.E.B. Du Bois: Pamphlets and Leaflets,* edited by Herbert Aptheker, 329–353. Amherst: University of Massachusetts Press, 1986.

——. "The American Negro in Paris." *American Monthly Reviews* 22 (November) (1900): 575–577.

——. *An Appeal to the World; A Statement on the Denial of Human Rights to Minorities in the Case of citizens of Negro Descent in the United States of America and an Appeal to the United Nations for Redress.* New York: National Association for the Advancement of Colored People, 1947.

——. *Battle for Peace.* Introduction by Herbert Aptheker. Millwood, N.Y.: Kraus-Thomson, [1952] 1976.

————. "The Black Man in the Revolution of 1914–1918," *Crisis,* 17 (5) March 1919: 218–223.

————. *Black Reconstruction in America.* Introduction by David Levering Lewis. New York: Atheneum, [1935] 1992.

————. "Close Ranks," *Crisis,* 16 (3) July 1918: 111.

————. "Colonialism, Democracy, and Peace After the War (Summer 1944)." In *Against Racism: Unpublished Essays, Papers, Addresses, 1887–1961,* edited by Herbert Aptheker, 229–249. Amherst: University of Massachusetts Press, 1985.

————. "The Color Line Belts the World." In *W. E. B. Du Bois: A Reader,* edited by David Levering Lewis, 42–43. New York: Henry Holt, 1995.

————. *Color and Democracy: Colonies and Peace.* New York: Harcourt, Brace and Company, 1945.

————. *Dark Princess.* Introduction by Claudia Tate. Jackson: University Press of Mississippi, [1928] 1995.

————. *Darkwater: Voices From Within the Veil.* Mineola, N.Y.: Dover, [1920] 1999.

————. "Documents of the War Collected by W. E. B. Du Bois." *Crisis,* 14 (3) July 1917: 16–21.

————. *Dusk of Dawn.* in *W. E. B. Du Bois: Writings,* edited by Nathan Huggins, 549–802. New York: Library of America, 1986.

————. Editorial. "The Immortal Children." *Crisis* 12 (6) (1916): 267–268.

————. "Ethiopia: State Socialism Under an Emperor." In *The World and Africa: An Inquiry into the Part Which Africa has Played in World History,* 268–269. New York: International Publishers, [1946] 1996.

————. "An Essay toward a History of the Black Man in the Great War." In *W. E. B. Du Bois: Writings,* edited by Nathan Huggins, 879–922. New York: Library of America, 1986.

————. "Flashes from Transcaucasia." In *Against Racism: Unpublished Essays, Papers, Addresses, 1887–1961,* edited by Herbert Aptheker, 254–260. Amherst: University of Massachusetts Press, 1985.

———. "Georgia: Invisible Empire State," In *Writings by W. E. B. Du Bois in Non-Periodical Literature Edited by Others,* edited by Herbert Aptheker, 136–147. New York: Kraus-Thomson, 1982.

————. "Haiti." In *The Papers of W. E. B. Du Bois, 1887–1968.* Sandford, N.C.: Microfilming Corporation of America, 1980.

————. *The Health and Physique of the Negro American. Report of a Social Study Made Under the Direction of Atlanta University; Together with the Proceedings of the Eleventh Conference for the Study of the Negro Problems held at Atlanta University, on May the 29th, 1906.* New York: Arno Press/ *The New York Times,* [1906] 1968.

————. "Introduction." In *An Appeal to the World; A Statement on the Denial of Human Rights to Minorities in the Case of Citizens of Negro Descent in the United States of America and an Appeal to the United Nations for Redress,* 1–15. New York: National Association for the Advancement of Colored People, 1947.

————. "The Looking Glass," *Crisis,* 18 (3) July 1919: 144–148.

————. "Miscegenation." Manuscript. Manuscripts, Archives, and Rare Books Division, Schomburg Center for Research in Black Culture, The New York Public Library, New York, N.Y.

————. "My Evolving Program for Negro Freedom." In *What the Negro Wants,* edited by Rayford Logan. Introduction by Kenneth Robert Janken, 31–70. Notre Dame, Ind.: Notre Dame University Press, [1944] 2001.

————. "My Mission," *Crisis,* 18 (1) May 1919: 7–9.

————. *The Negro*. Afterword by Robert Gregg. Philadelphia: University of Pennsylvania Press, [1915] 2001.

————. "Negro Citizen." In *Writings by W. E. B. Du Bois in Non-Periodical Literature Edited by Others*, edited by Herbert Aptheker, 157–163. Millwood, N.Y.: Kraus-Thomson, 1982.

————. "The Negro Soldier in Service Abroad During the First World War." *Journal of Negro Education* 12 (3) (1943): 324–334.

————. "News from Pan-Africa." In *The Papers of W. E. B. Du Bois, 1887–1968*, 1389–1409. Sandford, N.C.: Microfilming Corporation of America, 1980.

————. "Our Success and Failure." *Crisis* 18 (3) July 1919: 127–131.

————. "The Pan-African Movement." In *W. E. B. Du Bois Speaks: Speeches and Addresses 1920–1963*, edited by Philip S. Foner, 181–199. New York: Pathfinder, 1970.

————. "A Petition to the Human Rights Commission of the Social and Economic Council of the United Nations; and to the General Assembly of the United Nations; and to the Several Delegations of the Member States of the United Nations." In *Against Racism: Unpublished Essays, Papers, Addresses, 1887–1961*, edited by Herbert Aptheker, 261–265. Amherst: University of Massachusetts Press, 1985.

————. "Prospect for a World Without Race Conflict." *American Journal of Sociology* 49 (5) (1944): 450–456.

————. "Race Intelligence," in *W. E. B. Du Bois: Writings*, edited by Nathan Huggins, 1181–1183. New York: Library of America, 1986.

————. "Race Relations in the United States: 1917–1918." In *Writings by W. E. B. Du Bois in Periodicals Edited by Others*. Vol. 4, 1945–1961, edited by Herbert Aptheker, 66–76. Millwood, N.Y.: Kraus-Thomson, 1982.

————. "Roosevelt." Manuscript. Manuscripts, Archives, and Rare Books Division, Schomburg Center for Research in Black Culture, New York Public Library, New York, N.Y.: 1–25.

————. *Souls of Black Folk*. In *W. E. B. Du Bois: Writings*, edited by Nathan Huggins, 357–548. New York: Library of America, [1903] 1986.

————. "Worlds of Color." In *Writings by W. E. B. Du Bois in Periodicals Edited by Others*. Vol. 2, 1910–1934, edited by Herbert Aptheker, 241–256. Millwood, N.Y.: Kraus-Thomson, 1982.

————. *Suppression of the African Slave-Trade*. New York: Library of America, [1896, 1946] 1986.

————. "Testimony on the United Nations Charter Before the Committee on Foreign Relations." In *The Papers of W. E. B. Du Bois, Correspondence, 1877–1965*. Sandford, N.C.: Microfilming Corporation of America, 1980.

————. *The World and Africa: An Inquiry into the Part Which Africa has Played in World History*. New York: International Publishers, [1946] 1996.

Dubois, Laurent. *Avengers of the New World. The Story of the Haitian Revolution*. Cambridge, Mass.: Belknap Press of Harvard University Press, 2004.

————. *A Colony of Citizens: Revolution and Slave Emancipation in the French Caribbean, 1787–1804*. Chapel Hill: University of North Carolina Press, 2004.

Dula, Annette and Sara Goering, eds. *"It Just Ain't Fair": The Ethics of Health Care for African Americans*. Westport, Conn.: Praeger, 1994.

Dunbar, Paul Laurence. "Is Higher Education for the Negro Hopeless." *The Paul Laurence Dunbar Reader*, edited by Jay Martin and Gossie H. Hudson, 45–47. New York: Dodd, Mead, 1975.

Duncan, James and David Ley, eds. *Place/Culture/Representation*. New York: Routledge, 1993.

Dyson, Michael Eric. *Come Hell or High Water: Hurricane Katrina and the Color of Disaster*. New York: Basic Books, 2005.

Eastland, Terry. *Ending Affirmative Action: The Case for Colorblind Justice*. New York: Basic Books, 1996.

Edwards, Brent Hayes. "The Uses of *Diaspora*," *Social Text* 66, 19 (1) (2001): 45–73.

———. *The Practice of Diaspora: Literature, Translation, and the Rise of Black Internationalism*. Cambridge, Mass.: Harvard University Press, 2003.

Ellis, Mark. *Race, War, and Surveillance: African Americans and the United States Government During World War I*. Bloomington: Indiana University Press, 2001.

Ellison, Ralph. *Invisible Man*. New York: Modern Library, 1994.

———. "Some Questions and Some Answers." In *The Collected Essays of Ralph Ellison*, edited by John F. Callahan, 291–301. New York: Modern Library, 1995.

———. "Harlem Is Nowhere." In *The Collected Essays of Ralph Ellison*, edited by John F. Callahan, 320–327. New York: Modern Library, 1995.

Ellsworth, Scott. *Death in a Promised Land: The Tulsa Race Riot of 1921*. Baton Rouge: Louisiana State University Press, 1982.

Fabre, Michel. *The Unfinished Quest of Richard Wright*. Translated by Isabel Barzun. New York: Morrow, 1973.

———. *The World of Richard Wright*. Jackson: University Press of Mississippi, 1985.

Fanon, Frantz. *Black Skin, White Masks*. Translated by Charles Lam Markmann. New York: Grove Press, 1967.

Fairchild, Amy L., and Eileen A Tynan. "Policies of Containment: Immigration in the Era of AIDS." *American Journal of Public Health* 84 (12) (1994): 2011–2022.

Faulkner, William. *Absalom, Absalom!* New York: Modern Library, [1936] 1993.

Fede, Andre. *People Without Rights: An Interpretation of the Fundamentals of the Law of Slavery in the U.S. South*. New York: Garland, 1992.

Fehrenbacher, Don E. *Slavery, Law, and Politics: The Dred Scott Case in Historical Perspective*. New York: Oxford University Press, 1981.

Felman, Shoshana. *The Juridical Unconscious: Trials and Traumas in the Twentieth Century*. Cambridge, Mass.: Harvard University Press, 2002.

Fleming, Robert. "Sutton E. Griggs: Militant Black Novelist." *Phylon* 34 (1) (1973): 73–77.

Fick, Carolyn. *The Making of Haiti: The Saint-Domingue Revolution from Below*. Knoxville: University of Tennessee Press, 1990.

Finkelman, Paul. *Dred Scott v. Sandford: A Brief History with Documents*. Boston: Bedford Books, 1997.

Finnemore, Martha. *National Interests in International Society*. Ithaca, N.Y.: Cornell University Press, 1996.

Fischer, Sibylle. *Modernity Disavowed: Haiti and the Cultures of Slavery in the Age of Revolution*. Durham, N.C.: Duke University Press, 2004.

Fisher, George. *The Jury's Rise as Lie Detector*. 107 YALE LAW JOURNAL 575 (December) (1997).

Fitzpatrick, Joan. *Flight from Asylum: Trends Toward Temporary "Refuge" and Local Responses to Forced Migrations*. 35 VIRGINIA JOURNAL OF INTERNATIONAL LAW 13 (Fall 1994).

Flint, Henry Martyn. *Life of Stephen A Douglas: To Which Are Added His Speeches and Reports*. Philadelphia: J. E. Potterr and Company, 1863.

Foner, Philip S., ed. *Paul Robeson Speaks: Writings, Speeches, Interviews 1918–1974.* Seacus, N.J.: Citadel Press, 1978.

Foucault, Michel. "Of Other Spaces." *Diacritics* 16 (Spring) (1986): 22–27.

———. *Discipline and Punish: the Birth of the Prison.* Translated by Alan Sheridan. New York: Vintage Books, 1977.

———. *Power/Knowldge: Selected Interviews & Other Writings 1972–1977.* Edited by Colin Gordon. New York: Pantheon Books, 1980.

———. *The Archaeology of Knowledge & the Discourse on Language.* Translated by A. M. Sheridan Smith. New York: Pantheon Books, 1972.

———. "Space, knowledge and power." *Michel Foucault Power: Essential Works of Foucault, 1954–1984.* Vol. 3, edited by James D. Faubion. Translated by Robert Hurley et al., 349–364. New York: New Press, 1994.

———. *Madness and Civilization: A History of Insanity in the Age of Reason.* Translated by Richard Howard. New York: Vintage Books, 1965.

———. *Ethics: Subjectivity and Truth: Essential Works of Foucault 1954–1984,* Vol. 1. Edited by Paul Rabinow. New York: New Press, 1994.

———. *The History of Sexuality: An Introduction.* Vol. 1. New York: Vintage 1990.

Fox-Genovese, Elizabeth. *Within the Plantation Household: Black and White Women of the South.* Chapel Hill: University of North Carolina Press, 1988.

Fox-Genovese, Elizabeth, and Eugene D. Genovese. *Fruits of Merchant Capital: Slavery and Bourgeois Property in the Rise and Expansion of Capitalism.* New York: Oxford University Press, 1983.

Franklin, H. Bruce. *The Wake of the Gods: Melville's Mythology.* Stanford, Calif.: Stanford University Press, 1963.

Fraser, Nancy. *Justice Interruptus: Critical Reflections on the "Postsocialist" Condition.* New York: Routledge, 1997.

Frederickson, George M. *The Black Image in the White Mind: The Debate on Afro-American Character and Destiny 1817–1914.* New York: Harper and Row, 1971.

Freud, Sigmund. *Beyond the Pleasure Principle.* Translated and edited by James Strachey. New York: Norton, 1961.

———. *Totem and Taboo.* New York: Norton, 1989.

———. "The Uncanny." Vol 17, *Standard Edition of the Complete Psychological Works of Sigmund Freud,* edited by James Strachey. London: Hogarth Press, 1955.

———. "Mourning and Melancholia." Vol. 14, *Standard Edition of the Complete Psychological Works of Sigmund Freud,* edited by James Strachey. London: Hogarth Press, 1957.

———. "Repression." Vol. 14, *Standard Edition of the Complete Psychological Works of Sigmund Freud,* edited by James Strachey. London: Hogarth Press, 1957.

———. "The Unconscious." Vol. 14, *Standard Edition of the Complete Psychological Works of Sigmund Freud,* edited by James Strachey. London: Hogarth Press, 1957.

———. *Group Psychology and the Analysis of the Ego.* Translated by James Strachey. New York: Norton, 1959.

———. "Thoughts For The Times On War and Death." Vol.14, *Standard Edition of the Complete Psychological Works of Sigmund Freud,* edited by James Strachey, 273–300. London: Hogarth Press, 1955.

———. "Why War?" Vol. 22, *Standard Edition of the Complete Psychological Works of Sigmund Freud,* edited by James Strachey. London: Hogarth Press, 1955.

————. *Civilization and Its Discontents.* Translated by James Strachey. New York: Norton, [1930] 1961.

Freeman, Clarke James. *A Discourse on Christian Politics, Delivered in William's Hall, Boston, on Whitsunday, June 4, 1854.* Boston: Crosby, Nichols, & Co., and Prentiss & Sawyer, 1854. Division of Rare and Manuscript Collections, Carl A. Kroch Library, Cornell University, Ithaca, N.Y.

Fugitive Slave Law (1793) 2nd Cong., 2 sess. 2, Ch. 7, 1793.

Fugitive Slave Law (1850) 31st Cong., 1 sess., Ch. 60, 1850.

Gaines, Jane. *The Absurdity of Property in the Person.* 10 YALE JOURNAL OF LAW AND THE HUMANITIES 537 (Summer) (1998).

————. *Fire and Desire: Mixed-Race Movies in the Silent Era.* Chicago: University of Chicago Press, 2001.

Geggus, David. *Slavery, War and Revolution.* Oxford: Oxford University Press, 1982.

————. *Haitian Revolutionary Studies.* Bloomington: Indiana University Press, 2002.

Geggus, David, ed. *Impact of the Haitian Revolution in the Atlantic World.* Columbia: University of South Carolina Press, 2001.

Gilman, Sander L. *Difference and Pathology: Stereotypes of Sexuality, Race, and Madness.* Ithaca, N.Y.: Cornell University Press, 1985.

————. *Freud, Race, and Gender.* Princeton, N.J.: Princeton University Press, 1993.

Gillman, Susan. *Blood Talk: American Race Melodrama and the Culture of the Occult.* Chicago: University of Chicago Press, 2003.

Gilmore, Ruth Wilson. "Fatal Couplings of Power and Difference." *Professional Geographer* 54 (1) (2002): 15–24.

Gilroy, Paul. *The Black Atlantic: Modernity and Double Consciousness.* Cambridge, Mass.: Harvard University Press, 1993.

————. *Against Race: Imagining Political Culture Beyond the Color Line.* Cambridge, Mass.: Belknap Press of Harvard University Press, 2000.

————. "Living Memory: A Meeting with Toni Morrison." In *Small Acts: Thoughts on the Politics of Black Cultures,* 175–182. London: Serpent's Tail, 1993.

Ginzberg, Ralph. *100 Years of Lynching.* Baltimore, Md.: Black Classic Press, 1962.

Glaister, Dan. "Abort All Black Babies and Cut Crime, Says Republican," *Guardian,* October 1, 2005.

Goldberg, David Theo. *The Racial State.* Malden, Mass.: Blackwell Publishers, 2002.

————. "The End(s) of Race." *Journal of Postcolonial Studies* 7 (2) (2004): 211–230.

————. "Deva-Stating Disasters: Race in the Shadow(s) of New Orleans." *Du Bois Review* 3 (1): 84–87.

————. *The Threat of Race: Reflections on Racial Neoliberalism.* New York: Wiley-Blackwell, 2008.

Goodell, William. *The American Slave Code in Theory and Practice: Its Distinctive Features Shown by Its Statutes, Judicial Decisions, and Illustrative Facts.* New York: Negro Universities Press, 1968.

Gorman, Deborah Ann. *Indefinite Detention: The Supreme Court's Inaction Prolongs the Wait of Detained Aliens.* 8 GEORGETOWN IMMIGRATION LAW JOURNAL 47 (Winter) (1994).

Greenhouse, Linda. "High Court Backs Policy of Halting Haitian Refugees," *New York Times* June 22, 1993: A1.

Griffin, Farah Jasmine. *"Who Set you Flowin'?" The African-American Migration Narrative*. New York: Oxford University Press, 1995.

Griggs, Sutton. *Imperium in Imperio*. Preface by A.J. Verdell and introduction by Cornell West. New York: Random House, 2004.

Grosz, Elizabeth. *Space, Time, and Perversion: Essays on the Politics of Bodies*. New York: Routledge, 1995.

Gruening, Ernest H. "Haiti Under American Occupation." *Century* 103 (April) (1922): 836–845.

Guinier, Lani. *The Tyranny of the Majority: Fundamental Fairness in Representative Democracy*. New York: Free Press, 1994

Haller, John S., Jr. "The Physician Versus the Negro: Medical and Anthropological Concepts of Race in the Late Nineteenth Century." *Bulletin of the History of Medicine* 66 (1992): 154–167.

Hardt, Michael and Antonio Negri. *Empire*. Cambridge, Mass.: Harvard University Press, 2001.

Harris, Cheryl. "Whiteness as Property." *Critical Race Theory: The Key Writings that Formed the Movement*, edited by Kimberle Crenshaw, Neil Gotanda, Garry Peller, and Kendall Thomas, 276–291. New York: New Press, 1995.

Harris-Lacewell, Melissa. "Do you know what it means . . . Mapping Emotion in the Aftermath of Katrina." In *Seeking Higher Ground: The Hurricane Katrina Crisis, Race, and Public Policy Reader*, edited by Manning Marable and Kristen Clarke, 153–172. New York: Palgrave Macmillan, 2008.

Harrison, Hubert. *When Africa Awakes*. New York: Porro Press, 1920.

Harcourt, Brace, and Howe to W. E. B. Du Bois "Re: publication of *Darkwater*." *The Papers of W.E.B. Du Bois, Correspondence, 1887–1932*. Sandford, N.C.: Microfilming Corporation of America, 1980.

Hartman, Saidiya. *Scenes of Subjection: Terror, Slavery, and Self-Making in Nineteenth-Century America*. New York: Oxford University Press, 1997.

Harvey, David. *The New Imperialism*. London: Oxford University Press, 2003.

Hathaway, James C. *The Law of Refugee Status*. Toronto: Butterworths, 1991.

———. Harmonization for Whom? The Devaluation of Refugee Protection in the Era of European Economic Integration. 26 *Cornell International Law Journal* 719 (1993).

Henderson, Mae G. "Borders, Boundaries and Frame(work)s." In *Borders, Boundaries, and Frames: Cultural Criticism and Cultural Studies*, edited with an introduction by Mae Henderson, 1–32. New York: Routledge, 1995.

Henriksen, Thomas H. *Clinton's Foreign Policy in Somalia, Bosnia, Haiti, and North Korea*. Stanford, Calif.: Stanford University Press, 1996.

Herskovits, Melville. *The American Negro: A Study in Racial Crossing*. Bloomington: Indiana University Press, 1928.

———. *The Anthropometry of the American Negro*. New York: Columbia University Press, 1930.

———. *Life in a Haitian Valley*. New York: Octagon Books, [1937] 1964.

Higginbotham, A. Leon, Jr. *In the Matter of Color: Race & The American Legal Process: The Colonial Period*. Oxford: Oxford University Press, 1978.

———. *Shades of Freedom: Racial Politics and Presumptions of the American Legal Process*. London: Oxford University Press, 1996.

———. The *"Law Only as an Enemy": The Legitimization of Racial Powerlessness through the Colonial and Antebellum Criminal Laws of Virginia*. 70 NORTH CAROLINA LAW REVIEW (April) (1992), WL 969.

Higginbotham, Leon, and Barabra K. Kopytoff. *Property First, Humanity Second: The Recognition of the Slave's Human Nature in Virginia Civil Law.* 50 OHIO STATE LAW JOURNAL (1989), WL 511.

Higginson, Thomas Wentworth. *Massachusetts in Mourning. A Sermon, Preached in Worcester, on Sunday, June 4, 1854 by Thomas Wentworth Higginson, Minister of the Worcester Free Church. Reprinted by Request, From the Worcester Daily Spy.* Boston: James Munroe and Company, 1854. Division of Rare and Manuscript Collections, Carl A. Kroch Library. Cornell University, Ithaca, N.Y.

Highet, Keith. Decision: *Sale v. Haitian Centers Council, Inc.* 88 AMERICAN JOURNAL INTERNATIONAL LAW 114 (1994).

Himes, Chester. *Plan B.* Edited with an introduction by Michel Fabre and Robert E. Skinner. Jackson: University Press of Mississippi, 1993.

Hoar, E. R. *Charge to the Grand Jury at the July Term of the Municipal Court in Boston, 1854.* Boston: Little, Brown, & Company, 1854. Division of Rare and Manuscript Collections, Carl A. Kroch Library, Cornell University, Ithaca, N.Y.

Hobbs et al v. Fogg 6 Watts 553 (PA. Sup. Ct.1837), WL 3128 (Pa.).

Holland, Sharon Patricia. *Raising the Dead: Readings of Death and (Black) Subjectivity.* Durham, N.C.: Duke University Press, 2000.

Holloway, Karla F. C. *Moorings & Metaphors: Figures of Culture and Gender in Black Women's Literature.* New Brunswick, N.J.: Rutgers University Press, 1992.

———. *Passed On: African American Mourning Stories.* Durham, N.C.: Duke University Press, 2002.

———. "Accidental Communities: Race, Emergency Medicine, and the Problem of PolyHeme." *American Journal of Bioethics* 6 (3) (2006): 1–11.

Holly, James T. "Thoughts on Haiti." *Anglo-African Magazine* 1 (August) (1859): 241–243.

Horne, Gerald. *Communist Front?: The Civil Rights Congress, 1946–1956.* Rutherford, N.J.: Fairleigh Dickinson University Press, 1988.

———. "Race from Power: U.S. Foreign Policy and the General Crisis of White Supremacy." In *Window On Freedom: Race, Civil Rights, and Foreign Affairs, 1945–1988,* edited by Brenda Gayle Plummer, 45–66. Chapel Hill: University of North Carolina Press, 2003.

Horsley-Meacham, Gloria. "The Monastic Slaver: Images and Meaning in 'Benito Cereno.'" *Critical Essays on Herman Melville's "Benito Cereno,"* edited by Robert E. Burkholder, 94–98. New York: G. K. Hall, 1992.

Hughes, Langston. "Air Raid: Barcelona." In *The Collected Poems of Langston Hughes,* edited by Arnold Rampersad and David Roessel, 207–209. New York: Vintage Books, 1994.

———. "August 19th . . . A Poem for Clarence Norris." In *The Collected Poems of Langston Hughes,* edited by Arnold Rampersad and David Roessel, 168. New York: Vintage Books, 1994.

———. "Brown America in Jail: Kilby." In *Good Morning Revolution: Uncollected Writings of Social Protest by Langston Hughes,* edited by Faith Berry, 51. Westport, Conn.: Lawrence Hill, 1973.

———. "Concerning 'Goodbye, Christ.'" In *Good Morning Revolution: Uncollected Writings of Social Protest by Langston Hughes,* edited by Faith Berry, 133–135. Westport, Conn.: Lawrence Hill, 1973.

———. *"Don't You Want to Be Free?"* In *The Collected Works of Langston Hughes.* Vol. 5, *The Plays to 1942: "Mulatto" to "The Sun Do Move,"* edited with an introduction by Leslie Catherine Sanders and Nancy Johnston, 538–573. Columbia: University of Missouri Press, 2002.

———. "Emperor of Haiti (Troubled Island)." In *The Collected Works of Langston Hughes*. Vol. 5, *The Plays to 1942: "Mulatto" to "The Sun Do Move,"* edited with an introduction by Leslie Catherine Sanders and Nancy Johnston, 278–332. Columbia: University of Missouri Press, 2002.

———. "Hughes Bombed in Spain." In *The Collected Works of Langston Hughes*. Vol. 9, *Essays on Art, Race, Politics, and World Affairs,* edited with an introduction by Christopher C. De Santis, 158–161. Columbia: University of Missouri Press, 2002.

———. *I Wonder as I Wander.* Introduction by Arnold Rampersad. New York: Hill and Wang, 1956.

———. "Milt Herndon Died Trying to Rescue Wounded Pal." In *The Collected Works of Langston Hughes*. Vol. 9, *Essays on Art, Race, Politics, and World Affairs,* edited with an introduction by Christopher C. De Santis, 181–185. Columbia: University of Missouri Press, 2002.

———. "My America." In *The Collected Works of Langston Hughes*. Vol. 9, *Essays on Art, Race, Politics, and World Affairs,* edited with an introduction by Christopher C. De Santis, 232–239. Columbia: University of Missouri Press, 2002.

———. "Negroes in Spain." *The Collected Works of Langston Hughes*. Vol. 9, *Essays on Art, Race, Politics, and World Affairs,* edited with an introduction by Christopher C. De Santis, 157–158. Columbia: University of Missouri Press, 2002.

———. "'Organ Grinder's Swing' Heard above Gunfire in Spain." In *The Collected Works of Langston Hughes*. Vol. 9, *Essays on Art, Race, Politics, and World Affairs,* edited with an introduction by Christopher C. De Santis, 165–169. Columbia: University of Missouri Press, 2002.

———. "People Without Shoes." In *The Collected Works of Langston Hughes*. Vol. 9, *Essays on Art, Race, Politics, and World Affairs,* edited with an introduction by Christopher C. De Santis, 46–49. Columbia: University of Missouri Press, 2002.

———. "Refugee in America." *Saturday Evening Post,* February 6, 1943.

———. "Scottsboro Limited: A One-Act Play." *The Collected Works of Langston Hughes.* Vol. 5, *The Plays to 1942: "Mulatto" to "The Sun Do Move,"* edited with an introduction by Leslie Catherine Sanders and Nancy Johnston, 116–129. Columbia: University of Missouri Press, 2002.

———. "Soldiers from Many Lands United in Spanish Fight." In *The Collected Works of Langston Hughes*. Vol. 9, *Essays on Art, Race, Politics, and World Affairs,* edited with an introduction by Christopher C. De Santis, 178–181. Columbia: University of Missouri Press, 2002.

———. "Song of the Refugee Road." In *The Collected Works of Langston Hughes*. Vol. 3, *The Poems: 1951–1967,* edited with an introduction by Arnold Rampersad, 265. Columbia: University of Missouri Press, 2001.

———. "Southern Gentlemen, White Prostitutes, Mill-Owners, and Negroes." In *Good Morning Revolution: Uncollected Writings of Social Protest by Langston Hughes,* edited by Faith Berry, 49. Westport, Conn.: Lawrence Hill, 1973.

———. "Swords over Asia." In *The Collected Works of Langston Hughes*. Vol. 9, *Essays on Art, Race, Politics, and World Affairs,* edited with an introduction by Christopher C. De Santis, 102–105. Columbia: University of Missouri Press, 2002.

———. "To Negro Writers." In *The Collected Works of Langston Hughes*. Vol. 9, *Essays on Art, Race, Politics, and World Affairs,* edited with an introduction by Christopher C. De Santis. 131–132. Columbia: University of Missouri Press, 2002.

———. "Troubled Island." In *The Collected Works of Langston Hughes*. Vol. 6, *The Gospel Plays, Operas, and Later Dramatic Works,* edited with an introduction Leslie Catherine, 15–51. Columbia: University of Missouri Press, 2004.

——. "White Shadows in a Black Land." In *The Collected Works of Langston Hughes.* Vol. 9, *Essays on Art, Race, Politics, and World Affairs,* edited with an introduction by Christopher C. De Santis, 51–53. Columbia: University of Missouri Press, 2002.

——. "Writers, Words and the World." In *The Collected Works of Langston Hughes.* Vol. 9, *Essays on Art, Race, Politics, and World Affairs,* edited with an introduction by Christopher C. De Santis, 198–199. Columbia: University of Missouri Press, 2002.

Hull, Dana. "What's In a Name?" *American Journalism Review* 27 (5) (2005): 23–36.

Hunter, Tera W. *To 'Joy My Freedom: Southern Black Women's Lives and Labors After The Civil War.* Cambridge, Mass.: Harvard University Press, 1997.

Hurst, John. "Haiti." *Crisis,* 17 (1) May 1920: 29–34.

Hurston, Zora Neale. *Tell My Horse: Voodoo and Life in Haiti and Jamaica.* New York: Harper and Row, [1938] 1990.

Hyde, Alan. *Bodies of Law.* Princeton, N.J.: Princeton University Press, 1997.

Informer, "Negroes To the Philippines," 6 (9) (1903): 3.

Ingram v. State, 204 GA. 164, 48 S.E. 2d 891 (1948).

Inquiry Into the Occupation and Administration of Haiti and Santo Domingo. Hearings Before a Select Committee on Haiti and Santo Domingo. U.S. Senate 67 Congress S. Res. 112. v. 1 & 2. Washington, D.C.: U.S. Government Publishing Office, 1922.

Iyengar, Shanto and Richard Morin. "Natural Disasters in Black and White: How Racial Cues Influenced Public Response to Hurricane Katrina." *Washington Post,* June 8, 2006.

James, C. L. R. *The Black Jacobins: Toussaint L'Ouverture and the San Domingo Revolution.* New York: Vintage, 1963.

James, Winston. *Holding Aloft the Banner of Ethiopia: Caribbean Radicalism in Early Twentieth-Century America.* New York: Verso, 1998

Jameson, Fredric. *The Political Unconscious: Narrative as a Socially Symbolic Act.* Ithaca, N.Y.: Cornell University Press, 1981.

——. *Archaeologies of the Future: The Desire Called Utopia and Other Science Fictions.* New York: Verso, 2005.

Janken, Robert. "Introduction." In *What the Negro Wants,* edited by Rayford Logan, vii–xxx. Notre Dame, Ind.: University of Notre Dame Press, [1944] 2001.

Jefferson, Thomas. *Notes on the State of Virgina.* Edited by Frank Shuffelton. New York: Penguin Books, 1999.

Johnson, James Weldon. *Along this Way: The Autobiography of James Weldon Johnson.* Introduction by Sondra Kathryn Wilson. New York: Da Capo Press, [1933] 2000.

——. "The Truth About Haiti," *Crisis,* 20 (5) September 1920: 217–224.

——. "Self Determining Haiti," *Collected Writings,* edited by William Andrews, 660–687. New York: Library of America, 2004.

Johnston, Harry. "Haiti, the Home of the Twin Republics," *National Geographic* 38 (December) (1920): 483–496.

Johnson, Samuel. *The Crisis in Freedom. Sermon Preached at the Free Church in Lynn.* Division of Rare and Manuscript Collections, Carl A. Kroch Library, Cornell University, Ithaca, N.Y.

Jones, J. Richardson. "'Please Get me Out!' My Children Need Me, Doomed Mother Cries" *Pittsburgh Courier,* February 21, 1948.

Jones, Thomas. *A Human Rights Tragedy: The Cuban and Haitian Refugee Crises Revisited.* 9 GEORGETOWN IMMIGRATION LAW JOURNAL 479 (Summer) (1995).

Kairys, David, ed., *The Politics of Law: A Progressive Critique*. New York: Basic Books, 1982.

Kaplan, Amy and Donald E. Pease, eds. *Cultures of United States Imperialism*. Durham, N.C.: Duke University Press, 1993.

Kaplan, Amy. *The Anarchy of Empire in the Making of U.S. Culture*. Cambridge, Mass.: Harvard University Press, 2002.

———. "Manifest Domesticity." *American Literature* 70 (3) (1998): 581–605.

Kant, Immanuel. *Perpetual Peace and Other Essays*. Translated by Ted Humphrey. New York: Hackett Publishing, 1983.

Katz, Cindi. "The Terrors of Hypervigilance: Globalization, Security and the Compromised Spaces of Contemporary Childhood," Public Lecture. Cornell University. Ithaca, N.Y., October 24, 2003.

Keith, Michael and Steve Pile, eds. *Place and the Politics of Identity*. New York: Routledge, 1993.

Kelley, Robin D. G. "'But a Local Phase of a World Problem': Black History's Global Vision, 1883–1950." *Journal of American History* 86 (3) (1999): 1045–1077.

———. *Race Rebels: Culture, Politics, and the Black Working Class*. New York: Free Press, 1996.

Kelly, Nancy. *Gender-Related Persecution: Assessing the Asylum Claims of Women*. 26 CORNELL INTERNATIONAL LAW JOURNAL 625 (1993).

Kenney, John A., "Health Problems of the Negroes." Special Issue, "The Public Health Movement," *Annals of the American Academy of Political and Social Science* 37 (2) (1911): 110–120.

Kernodle, Tammy L. "Arias, Communists, and Conspiracies: The History of Still's 'Troubled Island.'" *Musical Quarterly* 83 (4) (1999): 487–508.

Khanna, Ranjanna. *Dark Continents: Psychoanalysis and Colonialism*. Durham, N.C.: Duke University Press, 2003.

———. "Asylum." 41 TEXAS INTERNATIONAL LAW JOURNAL 471 (2006).

———. "Indignity." *positions* 16 (1) (2008): 39–77.

———. "Disposability." *differences* 20 (1) (2009): 181–198.

Kidder, Rebecca. *Administrative Discretion Gone Awry: The Reintroduction of the Public Charge Exclusion for HIV-Positive Refugees and Asylees*. 106 YALE LAW JOURNAL 389 (1996).

Kiple, Kenneth F. *Another Dimension to the Black Diaspora: Diet, Disease, and Racism*. Cambridge: Cambridge University Press, 1981.

Kondracke, Morton. "Bush's Plan Ignores 500,000 Displaced Children." *Roll Call*, September 19, 2005.

Kornweibel, Theodore, Jr. *"Seeing Red": Federal Campaigns Against Black Militancy, 1919–1925*. Bloomington: Indiana University Press, 1998.

———. *"Investigate Everything": Federal Efforts to Compel Black Loyalty During World War I*. Bloomington: Indiana University Press, 2002.

Kraut, Alan M. *Silent Travelers: Germs, Genes, and the "Immigrant Menace."* New York: Basic Books, 1994.

Kristeva, Julia. *Desire in Language: A Semiotic Approach to Literature and Art*. New York: Columbia University Press, 1980.

———. *Powers of Horror: An Essay on Abjection*. New York: Columbia University Press, 1982.

Krupa, Michelle, "Jefferson to Help Gretna Defend Lawsuit; Cops Blocked Evacuees Fleeing Across Bridge." *Times-Picayune* (New Orleans), January 12, 2006.

Kutler, Stanley I., ed. *The Dred Scot Decision: Law or Politics?* Boston: Houghton Mifflin, 1967.

Laguerre, Michael S. *The Military and Society in Haiti.* Knoxville: University of Tennessee Press, 1993.

Largey, Michael. "'Ouanga!': An African-American Opera About Haiti." *Lenox Avenue* 2 (1996): 35–54.

Lee, Barbara, "A Tale of Two Americas." *Mississippi Link,* September 22–28, 2005.

Lee, Maurice S. "Melville's Subversive Political Philosophy: 'Benito Cereno' and the Fate of Speech." *American Literature* 72 (3) (2000): 495–519.

Lee, Spike, dir. *When the Levees Broke: A Requiem in Four Acts.* DVD. Hollywood, Calif.: HBO Documentary Films and 40 Acres and a Mule, 2006.

Lefebvre, Henri. *The Production of Space.* Oxford: Blackwell, 1992.

Leslie, Joshua and Sterling Stuckey. "The Death of Benito Cereno: A Reading of Herman Melville on Slavery: The Revolt on Board the *Tyral." Journal of Negro History* 67 (4) (1982): 287–301.

Lewis, David Levering. *W. E. B. DuBois: Biography of a Race 1868–1919.* New York: Henry Holt, 1993.

———. *W. E. B.: The Fight for Equality and the American Century, 1919–1963.* New York: Owl Books, 2000.

Leyburn, James G. *The Haitian People.* New Haven, Conn.: Yale University Press, 1941.

Linebaugh, Peter and Marcus Rediker. *The Many-Headed Hydra: Sailors, Slaves, Commoners, and the Hidden History of the Revolutionary Atlantic.* New York: Beacon, 2000.

Litwack, Leon. *Trouble in Mind: Black Southerners in the Age of Jim Crow.* New York: Vintage, 1998.

Loederer, Richard A. *Voodoo Fire in Haiti.* New York: Literary Guild, 1935.

Logan, Rayford W. "The International Status of the Negro." *Journal of Negro History* 18 (1) (1933): 33–38.

———. "James Weldon Johnson and Haiti." *Phylon* 32 (4) (1971): 396–402.

Logan, Rayford W., ed. *What the Negro Wants.* Notre Dame, Ind.: University of Notre Dame Press, [1944] 2001

"The Looking Glass," *Crisis* July 1919: 144–149.

Love, David A. "Human Rights Abuses in Our Own Back Yard." *Wire Services,* October 15, 1998.

Macmillan, Margaret. *Paris 1919.* New York: Random House, 2003.

Maltz, Earl M. *Civil Rights, the Constitution, and Congress, 1863–1869.* Lawrence: University Press of Kansas, 1990.

Marable, Manning. *W. E. B. DuBois: Black Radical Democrat.* Boston: Twayne, 1986.

Marcuse, Herbert. *Eros and Civilization: A Philosophical Inquiry into Freud.* Boston: Beacon Press, 1955.

Marti, Jose. *Our America: Writings on Latin American and the Struggle for Cuban Independence.* Edited by Philip Foner. New York: Monthly Review Press, 1977.

Martin, Charles. *Race, Gender, and Southern Justice: The Rosa Lee Ingram Case.* 29 *American Journal of Legal History* 251 (1985).

Massey, David and Nancy Denton. *American Apartheid: Segregation and the Making of the Underclass.* Cambridge, Mass.: Harvard University Press, 1998.

Maxwell, William. *New Negro, Old Left: African-American Writing and Communism Between the Wars.* New York: Columbia University Press, 1999.

Mayo, Marion J. *The Mental Capacity of the American Negro.* New York: Science Press, 1913.

Melville, Herman. "Benito Cereno." *Billy Budd and Other Stories,* edited and introduction by Frederick Busch, 159–258. New York: Penguin Books, [1855] 1986.

Michaelsen, Scott. "Between Japanese American Internment and the USA PATRIOT Act: The Borderlands and the Permanent State of Racial Exception." *Aztlan* 30 (2) (2005): 87–111.

Michelman, Frank. "Parsing 'A Right to Have Rights.'" *Constellations* 3 (2) (1996): 200–208.

McClintock, Ann. *Imperial Leather: Race, Gender and Sexuality in the Colonial Contest*. New York: Routledge, 1995.

McDowell, Deborah and Arnold Rampersad. *Slavery and the Literary Imagination*. Baltimore, Md.: Johns Hopkins University Press, 1989.

McLaurin, Melton, ed. *Celia, A Slave*. New York: Avon Books, 1991.

McKay, Claude. "If We Must Die." *Complete Poems*, edited by William J. Maxwell, 177–178. Urbana: University of Illinois Press, 2004.

———. "Outcast," *Complete Poems,* edited by William J. Maxwell, 173–174. Urbana: University of Illinois Press, 2004.

———. "Speech to the Fourth Congress of the Third Communist International, Moscow." *The Passion of Claude McKay: Selected Prose and Poetry 1912–1948*, edited by Wayne Cooper, 91–95. New York: Schocken Books, 1973.

Mignolo, Walter. "The Many Faces of Cosmo-polis: Border Thinking and Critical Cosmopolitanism." *Public Culture* 12 (3) (2000): 721–748.

Mills, Nicolaus, ed. *Arguing Immigration*. New York: Simon and Schuster, 1994.

Mitchell, Michele. *Righteous Propagation: African Americans and the Politics of Racial Destiny After Reconstruction*. Chapel Hill: University of North Carolina Press, 2004.

Mitchell, W. J. T. *Picture Theory: Essays on Verbal and Visual Representation*. Chicago: University of Chicago Press, 1994.

Montage, Ludwell Lee. *Haiti and the United States 1714–1938*. Durham, N.C.: Duke University Press, 1940.

Montejano, David. "On the Question of Inclusion." In *Chicano Politics and Society in the Late Twentieth Century*, edited by David Montejano, xi–xxvi. Austin: University of Texas Press, 1999.

———. "On the Future of Anglo-Mexican Relations in the United States." *Chicano Politics and Society in the Late Twentieth Century*, edited by David Montejano, 234–258. Austin: University of Texas Press, 1999.

Morris, Thomas. *Southern Slavery and the Law: 1619–1860*. Chapel Hill: University of North Carolina Press, 1996.

Morrison, Toni. *Playing in the Dark: Whiteness and the Literary Imagination*. New York: Vintage, 1993.

———. *Paradise*. New York: Alfred A. Knopf, 1998.

Moses, Wilson Jeremiah, ed. *Liberian Dreams: Back-to-Africa Narratives from the 1850s*. University Park: Pennsylvania State University Press, 1998.

———. "Literary Garveyism: The Novels of Reverend Sutton E. Griggs." *Phylon* 40 (3) (1979): 203–216.

Mullen, Bill V. "Du Bois, *Dark Princess,* and the Afro-Asian International." *positions* 11 (1) (2003): 218–239.

———. *Popular Fronts: Chicago and African-American Cultural Politics, 1935–1946*. Urbana: University of Illinois Press, 1999.

Munro, Dana G. "The American Withdrawal from Haiti, 1929–1934." *Hispanic American Historical Review* 49 (1) (1969): 1–26.

————. *Intervention and Dollar Diplomacy in the Caribbean 1900–1921*. Princeton, N.J.: Princeton University Press, 1964.

Naficy, Hamid, ed. *Home, Exile, Homeland: Film, Media, and the Politics of Place*. New York: Routledge, 1999.

Naison, Mark. *Communists in Harlem During the Depression*. Urbana: University of Illinois Press, 1983.

The Nation. "The Haiti Commission's Report." 130 (3379) (April 9, 1930): 433–435.

————. "Lott Should Resign." Editorial, December 20, 2002.

National Geographic. "Haiti and Its Regeneration by the United States," December 1920: 497–511.

Nelson, Dana. *National Manhood: Capitalist Citizenship and the Imagined Fraternity of White Men*. Durham, N.C.: Duke University Press, 1998.

Neuman, Gerald. *Surveying Law and Borders: Anomalous Zones*. STANFORD LAW REVIEW 48 (1996) WL *1197.

"The New England Journal of Medicine Produces Flat-Out Proof of Racism in Medicare-Funded Medicine." *Journal of Blacks in Higher Education* 13 (Autumn) (1996): 39.

New York Amsterdam News. Editorial, December 29, 1934.

New York Times. "Anti-War Pledge Accepted by Haiti," December 27, 1937.

————. "Barbara Bush Calls Evacuees Better Off," September 7, 2005.

————. "Conditions in Haiti Called Satisfactory. Senator Pomerene Says Charges Against Our Troops Appear to be Exaggerated," December 22, 1921.

————. "In Furious Race Riots in Chicago Negroes are Victims, Policemen Among Wounded in Clash Spreading to State Street," July 29, 1919.

————. "For Martial Law in Haiti. General Cole Asserts It is the Only Way to Rule There," November 15, 1921.

————. "Haitian Incidents Stir U.S. Concern," November 7, 1937.

————. "Navy Court Clears Marines in Haiti. Finds Only Two Unjustifiable Homicides and Asserts Guilty in Each Were Disciplined," December 19, 1920.

————. "Negroes in Clash With Chicago Mob," August 1, 1919.

————. "Of Haitian Treaty: It Will, It is Believed, Solve Caribbean Problem and Prevent Complications," August 27, 1915.

————. "Order Prevails in Chicago," August 4, 1919.

————. "Roosevelt Praises Dominican Stand: Thanks President Trujillo for Accepting Pact Procedure in Dispute with Haiti," December 21, 1937.

————. "Says Natives Ate Marine. Witness Tells Senators of Cannibalism Among Haitian Bandits," November 17, 1921.

————. "Street Battles At Night: Five Negroes are Killed in One Fight—Rioting Subsides at Midnight," July 29, 1919.

————. "Tells of Outrages By Haitian Bandits: Colonial Hooker of the Gendarmie Says that 2,000 Peaceful Haitians Have Been Killer. Marine Answers Charges. Hearing In Island Ends and Admiral Mayo Announces It will Be Resumed in Washington," December 1, 1920.

————. "Text of the Communist Party's Platform for the Presidential Election," August 7, 1948.

————. "Troopers Restore Order in Chicago," August 3, 1919.

————. "28 Dead, 500 Hurt In Three-Day Race Riots in Chicago," July 30, 1919.

————. "2,000 Slain in Haiti, Major Turner Says. That Number Killed in Action in Six Years, Marine Officer Tells Committee. Forced to Work On Roads. Witness Heard of Order to 'Bump off the Cacos'"—Denies Prisoners Were Killed," October 27, 1921.

———. "6,000 Troops Called Out in Chicago To Check New Riots; Negroes Fire At Soldiers, Attack Passing Trains . . . Five More on Death Toll: Two Shot and Killed During Day: Three Succumb to Wounds," July 31, 1919.

O'Neill, Eugene. *The Emperor Jones*. New York: Appleton-Century-Crofts, 1921.

Osterhout, Major G. H., Jr., "A Little Known Marvel of the Western Hemisphere: Christophe's Citadel, a Monument to the Tyranny and Genius of Haiti's King of Slaves." *National Geographic* 38 (December) (1920): 469–482.

Ott, Thomas. *The Haitian Revolution: 1789–1804*. Knoxville: University of Tennessee Press, 1973.

Painter, Nell. *Exodusters: Black Migration to Kansas after Reconstruction*. New York: Alfred E. Knopf, 1977.

Parker, Hershel. *Herman Melville A Biography*. Vol. 1, *1819–1851*. Baltimore, Md.: Johns Hopkins University Press, 2002.

———. *Herman Melville A Biography*. Vol. 2, *1851–1891*. Baltimore, Md.: Johns Hopkins University Press, 2002.

Parker, Theodore. *The Trial of Theodore Parker for the "Misdemeanor" of a Speech in Faneuil Hall Against Kidnapping Before the Circuit Court of the United States at Boston, April 3, 1855 with the Defense by Theodore Parker Minister of the Twenty-Eighth Congregational Society in Boston*. Boston, 1865. Division of Rare and Manuscript Collections, Carl A. Kroch Library, Cornell University, Ithaca, N.Y.

Patterson, Orlando. *Slavery and Social Death: A Comparative Study*. Cambridge, Mass.: Harvard University Press, 1982.

Phillips, Wendell Esq. *Argument of Wendell Phillips, Esq. Against the Repeal of the Personal Liberty Law, Before the Committee of the Legislature, Tuesday, January 29, 1861*. Boston: R.F. Wallcut, 1861. Division of Rare and Manuscript Collections, Carl A. Kroch Library, Cornell University, Ithaca, N.Y.

Pittsburgh Courier, "'He Tried to Go with Me'" March 20, 1948.

——— "Doomed Georgia Widow Has Never Been Out of State," April 3, 1948.

———,"Judge Silent on Ingram Plea: Takes Case Under Advisement; Jury Erred, Court Told," April 3, 1948.

———, "Mrs. Rosa Lee Ingram Tells Her Own Story," July 10, 1948.

Plessy v. Ferguson 163 U.S., 537. U.S. S.Ct. (1896), WL 1138.

Plummer, Brenda Gayle. "The Afro-American Response to the Occupation of Haiti, 1915–1934." *Phylon* 43 (2) (1982): 125–143.

———. *Haiti and the Great Powers: 1902–1915*. Baton Rouge: Louisiana State University Press, 1988.

———. *Haiti and the United States: The Psychological Moment*. Athens: University of Georgia Press, 1992.

Pomerance, Michla. "The United States and Self-Determination: Perspectives on the Wilsonian Conception." 70 AMERICAN JOURNAL OF INTERNATIONAL LAW 1 (January) (1976).

Prigg v. Pennsylvania 41 U.S. 539, 16 Pet. 539, 10 L.Ed. 1060

Proceedings of the U.S. Senate, on the Fugitive Slave Bill, the Abolition of the Slave Trade in the District of Columbia, and the Imprisonment of Free Colored Seamen. Division of Rare and Manuscript Collections, Carl A. Kroch Library, Cornell University, Ithaca, N.Y.

Rampersad, Arnold. *The Life of Langston Hughes*, Vol. 1, *1902–1941, I, Too, Sing America*. New York: Oxford University Press, 2002.

————. *The Life of Langston Hughes*. Vol. 2, *1941–1967, I Dream A World*. New York: Oxford University Press, 2002.

Randall, Vernellia. *Slavery, Segregation and Racism: Trusting the Health Care System Ain't Always Easy! An African American Perspective on Bioethics*. 15 ST. LOUIS UNIVERSITY PUBLIC LAW REVIEW 191 (1996).

Ransby, Barbara "Katrina, Black Women, and the Deadly Discourse on Black Poverty in America." *Du Bois Review* 3 (1) (2006): 215–222.

Raspberry, William. "Human Rights Abuses, Not Abroad, but at Home." *Washington Post,* October 12, 1998.

Redpath, James, ed. *A Guide to Hayti. Boston: Haytian Bureau of Emigration*. Boston: 1861. Division of Rare Book and Manuscript Collections, Carl A. Kroch Library, Cornell University, Ithaca, N.Y.

Refugee Act of 1980 Pub. L. No. 96–212, 94 Stat. 102 (1980)

Reid, John D. and Everett S. Lee, "A Review of the W. E. B. Du Bois Conference on Black Health." *Phylon* 38 (4) (1977): 341–351.

Reimers, David M. *Unwelcome Strangers: American Identity and the Turn Against Immigration*. New York: Columbia University Press, 1998.

Renda, Mary A. *Taking Haiti: Military Occupation and the Culture of U.S. Imperialism 1915–1940*. Chapel Hill: University of North Carolina Press, 2001.

Resek, Carl, ed. *War and the Intellectuals: Essays by Randolph S. Bourne, 1915–1919*. New York: Harper Torchbooks, 1964.

Review of *The Negro in Chicago. A Study of Race Relations and a Race Riot* by the Chicago Commission on Race Relations. *Annals of the American Academy of Political and Social Science* 110 (November) (1923): 227.

Review of *The Negro in Chicago. A Study of Race Relations and a Race Riot* by the Chicago Commission on Race Relations. *Journal of Negro History* 8 (1) (1923): 112–114.

"Review. Troubled Opera." *Time*, April 4, 1949: 71.

Robertson-Lorant, Laurie. *Melville: A Biography*. New York: Clarkson Potter, 1996.

Robeson, Paul. *Here I Stand*. New York: Beacon Press, [1958] 1988.

Robinson, Cedric. *Black Marxism: The Making of the Black Radical Tradition*. Chapel Hill: University of North Carolina Press, 2000.

Rogin, Michael. "Mutiny and Slave Revolt." In *Melville's Short Novels*, edited by Dan McCall, 317–329. New York: Norton, 2002.

————. "'The Sword Became a Flashing Vision' D.W. Griffith's *Birth of a Nation*." In *Ronald Reagan, the Movie, and Other Episodes in Political Demonology*, 190–35. Berkeley and Los Angeles: University of California Press, 1987.

————. "The Two Declarations of American Independence." In *Race and Representation*, edited by Robert Post and Michael Rogin, 73–96. New York: Zone Books, 1998.

Rowley, Hazel. *Richard Wright: The Life and Times*. New York: Henry Holt, 2001.

Rudwick, Elliott M. "W. E. B. Du Bois and the Universal Races Congress of 1911." *Phylon Quarterly* 20 (4) (1959): 372–378.

Sabin, Robert. "Troubled Island." Review. *Musical America* 69 (April 4) (1949): 5, 32.

Said, Edward. "Reflections on Exile." In *Reflections on Exile and Other Essays*, 173–186. Cambridge, Mass.: Harvard University Press, 2000.

Saldivar, Jose David. *Border Matters: Remapping American Cultural Studies*. Berkeley and Los Angeles: University of California Press, 1997.

Sanborn, Geoffrey. *The Sign of the Cannibal: Melville and the Making of a Postcolonial Reader.* Durham, N.C.: Duke University, 1998.

Sandberg, Carl. *The Chicago Race Riots: July 1919.* New York: Harcourt, Brace & World, 1919.

Saunders, Prince. *A Memoir Presented to the American Convention for Promoting the Abolition of Slavery, and Improving the condition of the African Race, December 11, 1818. Containing Some Remarks Upon the Civil Dissentions of the hitherto Afflicted People of Hayti, as the Inhabitants of that Island may be Connected with Plans for the Emmigration of Free Persons of colour as may Be Disposed to Remove to It, In Case Its Reunion, Pacification and Independence should be Established. Together with Some Account of the Origin and Progress of the Efforts for Effecting the Abolition of Slavery in Pennsylvania and its Neighbourhood, and Throughout the World.* Philadelphia: Dennis Heartt, 1818. Division of Rare and Manuscript Collections, Carl A. Kroch Library, Cornell University, Ithaca, N.Y.

Schleifer, Nancy. *Territorial Asylum in the Americas: Practical Considerations for Relocation.* 12 *Lawyer of the Americas* 359 (Spring) (1980).

Schneider, Mark Robert. *"We Return Fighting": The Civil Rights Movement in the Jazz Age.* Boston: Northeastern University Press, 2002.

Schuyler, George. *Black Empire.* Edited and afterword by Robert A. Hill and R. Kent Rasmussen, with a foreword by John A. Williams. Boston, Mass.: Northeastern University Press and The Regents of the University of California, [1936, 1937], 1991.

Scott, David. *Conscripts of Modernity: The Tragedy of Colonial Enlightenment.* Durham, N.C.: Duke University Press, 2004.

Scott, Emmett Jay. *Scott's Official History of the America Negro in the World War.* Chicago: Homewood Press, 1919. Division of Rare and Manuscript Collections, Carl A. Kroch Library, Cornell University, Ithaca, N.Y.

Scott, William. "Black Nationalism and the Italo-Ethiopian Conflict 1934–1936." *Journal of Negro History* 63 (April) (1978): 118–134.

Seabrook, William B. "Introduction." In *The White King of La Gonave* by Faustin Wirkus and Taney Dudley. New York, Doubleday, Doran, 1932.

———. *The Magic Island.* London: George G. Harrap, 1929.

Seraille, William. "Afro-American Emigration to Haiti during the American Civil War." *The Americas* 35 (2) (1978): 185–200.

Shacochis, Bob. *The Immaculate Invasion.* New York: Viking, 1999.

Shelby, Tommie. "Cosmopolitanism, Blackness, and Utopia: A Conversation with Paul Gilroy." *Transition* 98 (2008): 116–135.

Silencing a People: The Destruction of Civil Society in Haiti. New York: Human Rights Watch, 1993.

Silverman, Kaja. *Threshold of the Visible World.* New York: Routledge, 1996.

Singh, Nikhil Pal. *Black is a Country: Race and the Unfinished Struggle for Democracy.* Cambridge, Mass.: Harvard University Press, 2005.

Skrentny, John David. "The Effect of the Cold War on African-American Civil Rights: America and the World Audience, 1945–1968. *Theory and Society* 27 (2) (1998): 237–285.

Slaughter-House Cases, 83 U.S. 36 (1872), WL 15386 (U.S. La.)

Slotkin, Richard. *Lost Battalions: The Great War and the Crisis of American Nationality.* New York: Henry Holt, 2005.

Smethurst, James. "The Adventures of a Social Poet: Langston Hughes From the Popular Front to Black Power." In *A Historical Guide to Langston Hughes,* edited by Steven C. Tracy, 141–168. New York: Oxford University Press, 2004.

Smith, Douglass. *Citizenship and the Fourteenth Amendment.* 34 SAN DIEGO LAW REVIEW (May–June) (1997) WL 681.

Smith, James McCune. *A Lecture on the Haytien Revolutions; with a Sketch of the Character of Toussaint L'Ouverture. Delivered at the Styuvestant Institute (For the Benefit of the Colored Orphan Asylum).* New York: Daniel Fanshaw, 1841. Division of Rare and Manuscript Collections, Carl A. Kroch Library, Cornell University, Ithaca, N.Y.

Smith, Neil. *American Empire: Roosevelt's Geographer and the Prelude to Globalization.* Berkeley and Los Angeles: University of California Press, 2003.

Smith, Shawn Michelle. *Photography on the Color Line: W. E. B. Du Bois, Race, and Visual Culture.* Durham, N.C.: Duke University Press, 2004.

Snead, James. *White Screens Black Images,* edited by Colin McCabe and Cornell West. New York: Routledge, 1994.

Solomon, Mark. *The Cry Was Unity: Communists and African Americans, 1917–1936.* Jackson: University Press of Mississippi, 1998.

Sontag, Susan. *Illness as Metaphor and AIDS and Its Metaphors.* New York: Anchor Books, [1977] 1988.

———. *Regarding the Pain of Others.* New York: Picador, 2003.

South End Press Collective, ed. *What Lies Beneath: Katrina, Race, And the State of the Nation.* Afterword by Joy James. Cambridge, Mass.: South End Press, 2007.

"Spanish and Cuban Views on Annexation." *De Bows Review* 18 (3) (1855): 305–311.

Spear, Allan H. *Black Chicago: The Making of a Negro Ghetto 1890–1920.* Chicago: University of Chicago Press, 1967.

Spillers, Hortense J. "Who Cuts the Border? Some Readings on 'America.'" *Comparative American Identities: Race, Sex, and Nationality in the Modern Text,* edited with an introduction by Hortense J. Spillers, 1–25. New York: Routledge, 1991.

———. "Mama's Baby/Papa's Maybe." In *Black, White, and in Color: Essays on American Literature and Culture,* 203–229. Chicago: University of Chicago Press, 2003.

———. "Changing the Letter: The Yokes, The Jokes of Discourse, Or, Mrs. Stowe, Mr. Reed." In *Slavery and the Literary Imagination,* edited by Deborah McDowell and Arnold Rampersad, 25–61. Baltimore, Md.: Johns Hopkins University Press, 1989.

———. "'The Permanent Obliquity of an In(pha)llibly Straight': In the Time of the Daughters and the Fathers." *Changing Our Own Words: Essay on Criticism, Theory, and Writing by Black Women,* edited by Cheryl A. Wall, 127–149. New Brunswick, N.J.: Rutgers University Press, 1989.

———. "'All the Things You Could Be By Now, If Sigmund Freud's Wife Was Your Mother': Psychoanalysis and Race." *Female Subjects in Black and White: Race, Psychoanalysis, Feminism,* edited by Elizabeth Abel, Barbara Christian, and Helene Moglen, 135–158. Berkeley and Los Angeles: University of California Press, 1997.

Springarn, Arthur B. "The Health and Morals of Colored Troops," *Crisis,* August 1918.

St. Clair, Drake and Horace Cayton. *Black Metropolis: A Study of Negro Life in a Northern City.* Chicago, Ill.: University of Chicago Press [1945] 1993.

Stannard, Ray, ed., *Public Papers of Woodrow Wilson v. 1&2.* New York: Harper and Brothers, 1926.

Stephens, Michelle. *Black Empire: The Masculine Global Imaginary of Caribbean Intellectuals in the United States, 1914–1962.* Durham, N.C.: Duke University Press, 2005.

Stephenson, Gilbert Thomas. *Race Distinctions in American Law.* New York: Negro Universities Press, [1910] 1969.

Stevens, Charles Emery. *Anthony Burns: A History.* New York: Arno Press, 1969.

Still, Judith Anne and Lisa M. Headlee, eds., *Just Tell the Story: Troubled Island.* Flagstaff, Ariz.: Master-Player Library, 2006.

Stoddard, T. Lothrup. *The Rising Tide of Color Against White Supremacy.* New York: Charles Scribner's Sons, 1920.

Stoler, Ann Laura. *Carnal Knowledge and Imperial Power: Race and the Intimate in Colonial Rule.* Berkeley and Los Angeles: University of California Press, 2002.

———. "Intimidations of Empire: Predicaments of the Tactile and Unseen." In *Haunted by Empire: Geographies of Intimacy in North American Empire,* edited by Ann Stoler, 1–22. Durham, N.C.: Duke University Press, 2006.

———. *Race and the Education of Desire: Foucault's History of Sexuality and the Colonial Order of Things.* Durham, N.C.: Duke University Press, 1995.

———. "Tense and Tender Ties: The Politics of Comparison in North American History and (Post) Colonial Studies." In *Haunted by Empire: Geographies of Intimacy in North American Empire,* edited by Ann Stoler, 23–70. Durham, N.C.: Duke University Press, 2006.

Stone, James W. *Trial of Thomas Sims, on an Issue of Personal Liberty on the Claim of James Potter, of Georgia, Against Him, as an Alleged Fugitive From Service. Arguments of Robert Rantoul, Jr. And Charles G. Loring, with the Decision of George T. Curtis. Boston, April 7–11, 1851.* Boston: Wm. S. Damrell & Co., 1851. Division of Rare Book and Manuscript Collections, Carl A. Kroch Library, Cornell University, Ithaca, N.Y.

Stuckey, Sterling. *African Culture and Melville's Art: The Creative Process in Benito Cereno and Moby-Dick.* New York: Oxford University Press, 2009.

Suggs, Henry Lewis. "The Response of the African American Press to the United States Occupation of Haiti, 1915–1934." *Journal of Negro History* 73 (1/4) (1988): 33–45.

Sundquist, Eric. "'Benito Cereno' and New World Slavery." In *Reconstructing American Literary History,* edited by Sacvan Bercovitch, 93–122. Cambridge, Mass.: Harvard University Press, 1986.

———. *To Wake the Nations: Race in the Making of American Literature.* Cambridge, Mass.: Harvard University Press, 1993.

Taft, Edna. *A Puritan in Voodoo-Land.* Philadelphia: Penn Publishing, 1938.

Thompson, Richard Ford. *The Race Card: How Bluffing About Bias Makes Race Relations Worse.* New York: Picador, 2008.

Thoby-Marcelin, Philippe. *Canape-Vert.* New York: Farrar and Rinehart, 1944.

Thoby-Marcelin, Philippe and Pierre Marcelin. *The Beast of the Haitian Hills.* New York: Rinehart, 1946.

Tidwell, John Edgar and Cheryl R. Rager, eds. *Montage of a Dream: The Art and Life of Langston Hughes.* Foreword by Arnold Rampersad. Columbia: University of Missouri Press, 2007.

Time Magazine. "Books," April 6, 1931.

Times-Picayune (New Orleans). "No Mercy at the Bridge," September 25, 2005.

Tobing Rony, Fatimah. *The Third Eye: Race, Cinema, and Ethnographic Spectacle.* Durham, N.C.: Duke University Press, 1996.

Torpy, Bill. "Hurricane Katrina: Cities Dread Influx of the Poor, Black." *Atlanta Journal-Constitution,* September 4, 2005.

Trotter, Joe William, Jr. *The Great Migration in Historical Perspective: New Dimensions of Race, Class, and Gender.* Bloomington: Indiana University Press, 1991.

Trouillot, Michel-Roph. *Haiti, State Against Nation: The Origins and Legacy of Duvalierism*. New York: Monthly Review Press, 1990.

Troutt, David Dante, ed. *After the Storm: Black Intellectuals Explore the Meaning of Hurricane Katrina*. New York: New Press, 2007.

Tuttle, William M., Jr. *Race Riot: Chicago in the Red Summer of 1919*. Urbana: University of Illinois Press, 1996.

Urban, C. Stanley. "The Ideology of Southern Imperialism: New Orleans and the Caribbean, 1845–1860." *Louisiana Historical Quarterly* 39 (1) (1956): 48–73.

Vandercook, John W. *Black Majesty: The Life of Christophe King of Haiti*. New York: Harper and Brothers, 1928.

VanLandingham, Mark. "'Divided' Images Can Warp City's Recovery." *Times-Picayune* (New Orleans), April 17, 2006.

Villiers, Janice D. *Closed Borders, Closed Ports: The Plight of Haitians Seeking Political Asylum in the United States*. 60 BROOKLYN LAW REVIEW 841 (1990).

Von Eschen, Penny M. *Race Against Empire: Black Americans and Anticolonialism, 1937–1957*. Ithaca, N.Y.: Cornell University Press, 1997.

Wald, Alan M. *Trinity of Passion: The Literary Left and the Antifascist Crusade*. Chapel Hill: University of North Carolina Press, 2006.

Waligora-Davis, Nicole. "The Ghetto: Illness and the Formation of the 'Suspect' in American Polity." *Forum for Modern Language Studies* 40 (2004): 182–203.

———. "Jagged Words: Black Left, 1930s–1940s." In *Cambridge History of African American Literature*, edited by Maryemma Graham and Jerry Ward, 389–427. Cambridge: Cambridge University Press, 2011.

———. "W. E. B. Du Bois and the Fourth Dimension." *New Centennial Review* 6 (3) (2006): 57–90.

———. "'Riotous Discontent': Ellison's 'Birth of a Nation.'" *Modern Fiction Studies* 50 (2) (2004): 385–410.

Walker, David and Peter Hinks. *David Walker's Appeal*. Edited by Peter Hinks. University Park, Penn.: Penn State University Press, [1829] 2000.

Walker, Samuel R. "Cuba and the South." *De Bow's Review* 17 (5) (1854): 519–525.

Wallace, Maurice. *Constructing the Black Masculine: Identity and Ideality in African American Men's Literature and Culture*. Durham, N.C.: Duke University Press, 2002.

Wallace, Robert K. "Fugitive Justice: Douglass, Shaw, Melville." In *Frederick Douglass and Herman Melville: Essays in Relation*, edited Robert S. Levine and Samuel Otter, 39–68. Chapel Hill: University of North Carolina Press, 2008.

Wallerstein, Immanuel. "The Construction of Peoplehood: Racism, Nationalism, Ethnicity." London: Verso 1991: 71–85.

"Wards of the United States." *National Geographic* 30 (August) (1916): 143–177.

Washington, Charles. "Ingrams Have Spent Eight Months in Jail," *Pittsburgh Courier,* June 26, 1948.

Washington Post. "Georgia Jury Assailed as 'Hog Wild'" March 26, 1948.

———, "Hurricane Katrina Turns 'Refugee' Into Word of the Year," December 16, 2005.

Weatherly, Ulysses G. "The First Universal Races Congress." *American Journal of Sociology* 17 (3) (1911): 315–328.

———. "Haiti: An Experiment in Pragmatism." *American Journal of Sociology* 32 (3) (1926): 353–366.

Webb, Constance. *Richard Wright: A Biography.* New York: Putnam, 1968.

Webster, Richard. "Gretna Mayor Cites Support for Post-Katrina Barricades." *Journal of Jefferson Parish,* September 22, 2006.

Weed, Helena Hill. "Fresh Hope for Haiti." *The Nation,* March 19, (1930): 342–344.

———. "Hope for Haiti." *The Nation,* April 9, 1930: 413.

———. "Victory in Haiti." *The Nation,* March 26, 1930: 378–380.

Weiner, Mark S. *Americans Without Law: The Racial Boundaries of Citizenship.* New York: New York University Press, 2006.

Wells, Ida B. *Crusade for Justice. The Autobiography of Ida B. Wells,* edited by Alfreda M. Duster. Chicago: University of Chicago Press, 1970.

———. *The Reason Why the Colored American is not in the World's Columbian Exposition: The Afro-American's Contribution to Columbian Literature,* edited by Robert W. Rydell. Urbana: University of Illinois Press, [1893] 1999.

———. *Southern Horrors and Other Writings: The Anti-Lynching Campaign of Ida B. Wells, 1892–1900,* edited with an introduction by Jacqueline Jones Royster. New York: Bedford St. Martins, 1997.

Weston, Rubin Francis. *Racism in U.S. Imperialism: The Influence of Racial Assumptions on American Foreign Policy, 1893–1946.* Columbia: University of South Carolina Press, 1972.

Wexler, Laura. "Seeing Sentiment: Photography, Race, and the Innocent Eye." In *Female Subjects in Black and White: Race, Psychoanalysis, Feminism,* edited by Elizabeth Abel, Barbara Christian, and Helene Moglen, 159–186. Berkeley and Los Angeles: University of California Press, 1997.

"When Pride Becomes a Virtue," *Crisis,* 17 (5) (March 1919): 216–217.

White, Walter. *Rope and Faggot.* New York: Arno Press, [1929] 1969.

———. Testimony. U.S. Senate Judiciary Subcommittee, 73 Cong., 2 Sess., *Hearings* (S. 1978), (February 20–21, 1934): 9–37.

Wilentz, Amy. "Haiti's Man of the People Lost His Way," *New York Times,* February 15, 2004.

Williams, Linda. *Playing the Race Card: Melodramas of Black and White From Uncle Tom to O. J. Simpson.* Princeton, N.J.: Princeton University Press, 2001.

Williams, Patricia J. *The Alchemy of Race and Rights: Diary of a Law Professor.* Cambridge, Mass: Harvard University Press, 1991.

———. *Seeing A Color-Blind Future: The Paradox of Race.* New York: Noonday Press, 1997.

Willis, Deborah. "The Sociologist's Eye: W. E. B. Du Bois and the Paris Exposition." In *A Small Nation of People: W. E. B. Du Bois and African American Portraits of Progress,* with essays by David Levering Lewis and Deborah Willis. New York: Amistad Press, 2003: 51–78.

Wiegman, Robyn. *American Anatomies: Theorizing Race and Gender.* Durham, N.C.: Duke University Press, 1995.

Wirkus, Faustin E. "If America Intervenes in Haiti." *Liberty,* February 5, 1938.

Wirkus, Faustin E. and Taney Dudley. *The White King of La Gonave,* with an introduction by William B. Seabrook. New York: Doubleday, Doran, 1932.

Woodson, Carter G. "Fifty Years of Negro Citizenship as Qualified by the United States Supreme Court." *Journal of Negro History* 6 (1) (1921): 1–53.

Wright, Richard. *Black Boy.* Introduction by Jerry Ward. New York: Harper Perennial, [1944] 1993.

———. *Native Son.* Introduction by Arnold Rampersad. New York: Harper Perennial, [1940] 1996.

———. "I Choose Exile." In Richard Wright Papers. Yale Collection of American Literature, Beinecke Rare Book and Manuscript Library, Yale University, New Haven, Conn. Undated manuscript.

———. *White Man, Listen!* New York: Doubleday, 1957.

———. *Eight Men.* Introduction by Paul Gilroy. New York: Harper Perennial, [1946, 1961] 1996.

Young, Iris. *Inclusion and Democracy.* New York: Oxford University Press, 2000.

Zangrando, Robert L. "The NAACP and a Federal Antilynching Bill, 1934–1940." *Journal of Negro History* 50 (2) (1965): 106–117.

Zieger, Robert H. *America's Great War: World War I and the American Experience.* New York: Rowman & Littlefield, 2000.

8 U.S.C. §§1252–1434 (1998) (Supp. covering 1971–1997).

8 U.S.C. §§1–1251 (1998). (Supp. covering 1971–1997).

INDEX